Double
FANTASY

The Eclectic
Volumes 1 & 2
1999-2001

Lincoln MacVeagh

David Garcia III

T.E. MacVeagh

A.H. Seidel

Tower House Books
New York

A note from the editor:

Before taking *The Eclectic* to the copy shop each month, I used to read the proofs over and over until I was certain they were perfect. They never were, and as soon as I started stapling the pages together, I'd see obvious groaners that I'd missed only the day before.

Putting this compilation together, my first thought was to fix all the mistakes, but it turned out to be harder than expected because I couldn't leave well enough alone. When I looked for typos, I continually found myself wanting to re-write whole pages. That seemed like a very bad idea, not to mention a great deal of work.

In the end I have kept everything as it was originally published. There's a lot to shake your head at, but there's plenty left to like.

Lincoln MacVeagh

Double
FANTASY

The Eclectic
Volumes 1 & 2
1999-2001

TOWER HOUSE BOOKS
4304 Newtown Road, New York 11103

ISBN: 978-0-9858948-2-5

www.towerhousebooks.com

Printed in the United States of America
1   3   5   7   9   10   8   6   4   2

The
ECLECTIC

February 1999   Volume 1 Number 1   Free

CONTENTS

Quotations

"I can't understand these chaps who go round American universities explaining how they write poems: it's like going round explaining how you sleep with your wife. Of course, they'd do that too if their agents could fix it." Phillip Larkin in *Required Writing*.

"Tradition forbade the strangling of virgins; so, when little girls had been condemned to die in this way, the executioners began by violating them." The reign of Tiberius as described by Seutonius in *The Twelve Caesars*.

"The hardest thing was watching the Persian Gulf War. I knew that if any American died it would be my fault [for not being President] *"* Gary Hart defines hubris in *The New Yorker*, April 19th, 1993.

"I had not learnt that when you go to a party it is your business to do your best to add to its success." Somerset Maugham in *A Vagrant Mood*.

A Decent Bloke

Phillip Larkin wasn't as bad as they say

Lincoln MacVeagh

The first I ever heard about Larkin was after he died when his collected letters were published. I was living in England at the time and the Sunday papers were filled with articles about him. Most of the commentary was unkind. Larkin was described as a bigot, a misogynist, or at best, just a plain old curmudgeon.

Nonetheless, I liked him. Larkin came across as a funny and interesting man, and what sealed it for me was a line quoted from a thank you note Larkin wrote to his friend Robert Conquest. Larkin was thanking him for a dirty magazine full of women dressed up as naughty schoolgirls. "*Dear Bob,*" said the letter, "*Yes, I got the pictures — whacko.*" Who could resist?

Phillip Larkin was born in Coventry, England in 1922. He had a sister ten years older than himself, and his parents were solid members of the middle class. His father was a severe and gloomy man, a respectable English bureaucrat who also happened to be a great admirer of Germany and German politics. Larkin's mother appears to have been a rather sad and pathetic woman.

Larkin once described his boyhood as a period of constant boredom, interrupted only occasionally by brief

Yes I got the pictures — whacko!

moments of terror. I don't think he was a happy child. He hated being at home; he hated being at school only a little less; and he stammered terribly: "*I mean stammered to the point of handing over little slips of paper at the railway station saying 'third-class return to Brighton' instead of trying to get it out.*"

Fortunately, boys grow up and as Larkin got older his misery lessened. For a long time he thought he hated everybody. Eventually he realized it was only children he didn't like. He learned how to make friends. Along the way he also picked up a passion for American jazz music, so by the time he went off to Oxford he was pretty well versed in the elements of cool.

One of Larkin's best friends at university was Kingsley Amis, the novelist who wrote *Lucky Jim.* This is how Amis remembered their first meeting: "*He had a biggish nose, a fresh complexion and a head of rather nice light-brown hair that was already, though he was only eighteen, showing signs of recession. As soon as he opened his mouth he revealed himself as afflicted with a painful stammer that sometimes hindered communication. Nothing else did. After the initial awkwardness, his manner proved to be friendly, informal, even rather noisy, and loaded with imitations of public-school men."*

Larkin graduated from Oxford in 1943. World War II was still raging and like everyone else, Larkin assumed he would have to join the army. He was not keen on it. At Oxford he had been inspired with an intense devotion to art and literature. More than anything else Larkin wanted to be a novelist and he couldn't see how getting killed in France would help him write many books. Fortunately, he was rejected by the army on account of his poor eyesight and instead of going in to the trenches he went out to look for a job. He ended up as a librarian in a tiny town called Wellington, in the middle of nowhere.

Larkin jokingly described his first job as *"handing out tripey novels to morons"* but one gets the feeling that he was quite at home in Wellington. At least he was out of his parents' house, and being a fastidious man, he was well suited to library work. In fact, Larkin remained a librarian for the rest of his life. When he died in 1985 he was sixty three and he had been head librarian at the University of Hull for all of the last thirty years.

Larkin's literary career began while he was still in Wellington. During his three years there he stole enough time (at night and on Sundays, since Larkin worked six days a week) to finish two novels. The first of these, *Jill*, is a story about a sensitive but graceless boy named John Kemp who goes off to Oxford and is constantly abused by his richer, hipper roommate. Kemp makes the mistake of falling in love with a girl who is socially above him and for a while he even convinces himself that she might love him back. In the end, however, he's brought crashing down to earth. Larkin's second novel, *A Girl In Winter*, is about a young French woman working in England during the War. She is surrounded by not very nice people, bad things happen, and she winds up feeling bitter.

Both books are engaging and easy to read (especially *Jill*) and they earned their author a short burst of applause from various critics. The applause went to Larkin's head and for a moment he allowed himself to dream of becoming a famous writer. He dreamed of a house on the Cote D'Azur, of breezing off five hundred words a day, and of spending the rest of his time with booze and pretty women and Lord Howdidoo begging for an advance peek at his next masterpiece.

It didn't pan out like that. The rights to *A Girl In Winter* paid Larkin the equivalent of a week's wages at the library. *Jill* paid even less. He was still only twenty four. He did some quick arithmetic and he decided to find another library job. He never wrote novels again.

Years later, Larkin explained his change of course by saying simply that *"his knack for fiction dried up."* The truth is probably more complicated. Kingsley Amis once suggested that it was likely *"a matter of that underrated agency in human affairs, fear of failure."* Then again, Amis made a big name for himself and a fair amount of money with the very first book he published, and he seems to have forgotten about Larkin what people with money often forget about people without money. That is, they have to work for a living. Whether you're a banker in Manhattan or a librarian in the north of England, work takes up a lot of time and energy. Writing fiction takes up time and energy, too. And the trouble is, it's very hard to do both things at once. Larkin put in three years of desperate effort as a novelist and then he was faced with a choice. Either he could give up the rest of his life to fiction and its uncertain rewards, or else he could content himself with being a librarian and have time left over for the world beyond books.

Larkin chose to be a librarian and it's not surprising. As passionate as Larkin was about his favorite authors, he had no

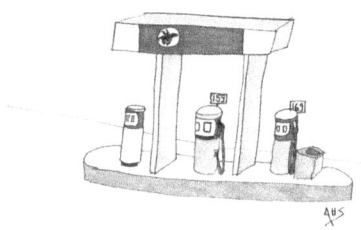

romantic notions about the importance of books. He was not a believer in art for art's sake. Or to put it in Larkin's own words when he was a rebellious university student: *"When will these sodding loudmouthed cunting shitstuffed pisswashed sons of poxed-up bitches learn that there is something greater than <u>literature</u>?"*

Like Chekhov, Larkin believed that the essential facts of man's life were work, cabbage soup and fights with the wife. He was suspicious of all things out of the ordinary. *"I am getting to the stage,"* he wrote in an early letter, *"where I HATE anybody who does anything UNUSUAL at ALL, whether it's make a lot of MONEY or dress in silly CLOTHES or read books in foreign WORDS... BECAUSE THEY ARE USUALLY SUCH SODDING NASTY PEOPLE THAT I KNOW IT IS 1000-1 THAT THEY ARE SHOWING OFF..."* Larkin preferred routine and after he gave up on novels, his routine was finally fixed. It was only then that he turned seriously to writing poetry.

Over the next three decades Larkin published six slim volumes of poetry. With each collection his reputation grew, but despite his popularity Larkin's routine remained unchanged. It was a very simple one. He woke up, went to work and went home. At night he sometimes worked on a poem. Sometimes he wrote letters or articles for the newspapers. Often he would just drink gin and listen to jazz. Then he would go to bed and get ready to do it all again. There must have been things bubbling under the surface, but on the outside, Larkin's life was incredibly dull. When Larkin's sixtieth birthday party was announced one of his friends protested that a celebration was inappropriate. *"Apparently Phillip is sixty,"* the friend said, *"But when was he anything else? Like Lady Dumbleton he has been sixty for the last twenty five years."*

Given Larkin's notorious stodginess, it is quite remarkable that he became as well known as he did. The best explanation for it is that he wrote very good poems. Like El Greco's paintings, Larkin's best poems (*"Self's The Man"*, *"This Be The Verse"*, *"Vers de Société"*, etc.) are distinctively his own. In part, this distinctiveness was a reaction against the literary theorists. Larkin hated the theorists. He thought abstract art was twaddle and so he made a conscious effort to write poems that scream out at you "It's me!" Larkin was emphasizing the point that poetry is written by ordinary people, but his distinctiveness was more that just a literary argument. The reason he is so good at making us believe that there's a real person behind his poetry is because there is a real person behind it. When Larkin screamed "It's me!" he meant it.

The voice in Larkin's poetry is clear-eyed, sensitive and remarkably free of self-deception. These qualities are not easy to fake, and from all that I have read I gather that Larkin himself possessed them too. So I am puzzled by what seems to have become the accepted wisdom about Larkin: that he wrote nice poems but deep down was a horrid little man.

Almost all the contemporary criticism contains at least one section in which the critic takes pains to say that yes, Larkin was a bad seed but we shouldn't let the poet's personal failings interfere with our appreciation of his work. I object to this sort of song and dance for a number of reasons (for one thing, it's old hat), but in Larkin's case my principal objection is that it's neither fair nor accurate. Larkin was a decent man.

Ever since the publication of Andrew Motion's captious biography, Larkin has been accused of three great sins: misanthropy in general, and racism and misogyny in particular. Against the charge of misanthropy there is little to be said. Larkin was not born with a smiley face printed on his soul, but he was invariably kind to both friends and strangers and there's nothing more that one can ask.

There's not much to say about Larkin's racism either. It's true. Privately, Larkin was a racist. It is possible to make excuses. One could point out that Larkin grew up in the thirties when the question of race in English society hardly existed; one could point out that Larkin never tried to express his views on race publicly; one could even argue that Larkin's racism is irrelevant – in 800 pages of his collected letters he talks about race only a handful of times. No matter what, we can't help but be shocked when we read the fiftyish Larkin write in a letter: *"(we don't go to test matches now, too many fucking niggers about.)"* That's an ugly line, but ugly as it is, I don't think it defines Larkin's character.

The third and most common accusa-tion made against Larkin is that he was a misogynist. I do not know why crit-ics insist on calling Larkin a misogynist. Maybe it's because he collected pornog-raphy, or maybe it's because he never married. Neither of these arguments cut ice. Pornography isn't so awful as people pretend, and if Larkin never got married it was not because he hated the idea of waking up next to a WOMAN. He hated the idea of waking up next to SOMEONE ELSE. He couldn't even stand the thought of having a cat.

The real reason Larkin is so often called a misogynist is probably because he never managed to work out his sex life in a way satisfactory to English majors. Larkin had, I think, five affairs in his life-time. The first of these started when he was in Wellington with an enthusiastic young girl to whom Larkin referred as *"the school captain."* It was two years of bicycle rides and chit-chat before they finally slept together and then the affair petered out. A few years later there was a short fling with the wife of a colleague in Belfast. The rest of Larkin's affairs were long running emotional attach-ments with women who were primar-ily his friends. Unfortunately, Larkin's two most important friends knew about each other. His love life was not so active that he had to go hopping from bed to

Still Life

bed, but it got messy anyway. For fifteen years Larkin was unable to decide which woman he liked best and each time the matter came close to being finally settled, he got cold feet and jumped ship. For Larkin, being asked to pick between two lovers was like being asked to pick between two books you haven't read.

Larkin seems to have viewed women as a puzzle. For a long time they were a puzzle about which he knew absolutely nothing. When he was twenty three Larkin wrote to a friend, *"...the only advance I ever made to a woman was producing of such scorching embarrassment that the wound is still rawly open. That was over 2 yrs. ago and if I forget it in 10 I shall be agreeably surprised."* To the modern reader this may sound like an over-reaction, but the idea that boys and girls are essentially the same cereal, just in different boxes, is a relatively new one. Until Larkin went to Oxford he didn't know any girls other than his sister, so it's no wonder he was shy around them. *"I'm afraid of them chiefly,"* he said in a letter, *"They send me rigid with fear."*

Later in life, Larkin's feelings changed somewhat, but the basic mystery remained. At one point, Kingsley Amis published a novel filled with nasty remarks about the opposite sex and he wrote to Larkin asking for comment. Larkin's response was this: *"I don't think I've seen enough of women to feel fed up with them to that extent: anyway, I work with about sixty of them and I just treat them like men, well, more or less."* To my ear, this doesn't sound like misogyny. It sounds like honesty.

Larkin was not a woman hater, nor more generally speaking, was he a bad man. Of course, he had his faults but in the main he was a man who faced life bravely and with a sense of humor. It is a mistake to think that Larkin's personality diminishes his work. Larkin's personality – grumpy, honest, insightful and funny – is exactly what makes him worth reading.

Reviews

The Autobiography Of An Ex-Colored Man

by James Weldon Johnson

Dover Thrift Editions, 1995 (reprint)

When I was in college the English department never offered courses in Dostoevsky and if you wanted to read Proust you had to cross your fingers and hope there was something on offer at the Romance Languages building. Academics are territorial and they like to divide books up into neat little categories. It doesn't make much sense. A good book is a good book no matter where the author was born or what language he spoke. As far as I'm concerned the greatest English prose stylist of the last hundred and fifty years was probably Tolstoy's translator.

All writers suffer from this sort of pigeonholing, but I suspect black writers suffer more than most. Being black, their subject matter is often deemed exotic; their books get shunted off to the Afro-American Studies Department and we never hear from them again. This is a pity because writers like James Weldon Johnson are worth twenty Nathaniel Wests. *The Autobiography Of An Ex-Colored Man* is so cleanly written that its short one hundred pages read like twenty five.

The Autobiography... brings to life a man of mixed race at the turn of the century. Early on he is shocked when a schoolteacher tells him he is colored. The rest of the book traces his intellectual and emotional development as he moves back and forth between two very different Americas.

The set-up of Johnson's novel (it's a novel despite the title – Johnson was a brown skinned man who could not have passed) provides plenty of room to comment on race relations circa 1900 and much of the commentary is surprisingly, perhaps depressingly, up-to-date. For example: *"I noticed that among this class of colored men* [pool sharks and hustlers] *the word 'nigger' was used in about the same sense as the word 'fellow', and sometimes as a term of almost endearment; but I soon learned that its use was positively prohibited to white men."*

However, the book is a much more than an essay on race. It is about a man searching for himself in a world where he has no easy place. Richard Wright took on a similar theme in his novel *The Outsider.* So did James Baldwin in *Giovanni's Room.* But it would be monstrous to pretend that the crisis of identity is a singularly "black" experience. It is a universal experience and as such, *The Autobiography Of An Ex-Colored Man* deserves a wider audience than it has received thus far.

First published in 1912, *The Autobiography...* has been re-issued by Dover Thrift Editions. With a retail price of $1, it's a bargain.

Coming Of Age In Mississippi
by Anne Moody
Mass Market Paperback, 1997 (reprint)

It is often said that everyone has at least one book in them. I'm not sure what is meant by this, but if it is meant that everyone has one *good* book, then certainly it's not true. No matter how interesting one's life, it is damnably difficult to make other people want to read about it. Anne Moody is the exception.

Coming Of Age In Mississippi is the story of a dark-skinned black girl born poor in 1946. Living under Jim Crow, she grows up to be an intelligent, ambitious, and very angry young woman. *"I was fifteen years old,"* she writes, *"When I began to hate people."* She is not posing.

Eventually Moody's indignation draws her in to the Civil Rights Movement. She was one of three demonstrators at the famous Jackson, Mississippi, Woolworth's lunch counter sit-in and

the last section of her book describes her work as a campaigner for the NAACP.

Looking back on the sixties today, it is easy to think that the victory of the Civil Rights Movement was somehow inevitable. After all, how could justice not triumph? Anne Moody reminds us that justice had not triumphed her whole life long and that the fight for Civil Rights was an enormous struggle, the outcome of which remained ever in doubt. *Coming Of Age In Mississippi* is not a particularly happy book, but it is a good one.

Naked

by David Sedaris

Little Brown & Company, 1997

David Sedaris' lastest collection of essays, *Naked*, is a wonderful book and one of the most interesting things about it is that it is so much better than his previous book *Barrel Fever*. *Barrel Fever* was brilliant at times, but it was spotty. You had to read through the slow bits. In *Naked* there are no slow bits.

In short, David Sedaris has improved and this is a curious thing. It is not unusual for writers to get better as they go along but just how it happens remains an enigma. It is notoriously impossible to teach someone how to write, and yet somehow David Sedaris has learned. How can you learn something that cannot be taught?

Socrates answered this question by saying that we are all infinitely wise to begin with, but then we forget stuff. Socrates argued that when we learn something new what we are really doing is remembering something we already knew. No doubt there is a grain of truth to this but it is hardly a complete explanation. However much David Sedaris has remembered in the last few years, I bet he put in a lot of hard work too. In *Naked* he tells marvelous stories and writes as if he's completely at ease. No one achieves that without sweating for it.

Nietzsche In Traffic

T.E. MacVeagh

"Cheerfulness, the good conscience, the joyful deed, confidence in the future – all of them depend in the case of the individual as of a nation, on the existence of a line dividing the bright and discernable from the unilluminable and dark; on one's being just as able to forget at the right time as to remember at the right time; on a powerful instinct for sensing when it is necessary to feel historically and when unhistorically."

Nietzsche, <u>Untimely Meditations</u> II, I

I came across this quote the other day and realized that Neitzsche was just repeating the rule of driving in traffic: "When I swerve suddenly into someone else's lane, it is because I am not sure where I am going, because I did not have enough sleep last night, and because I just had a fight with my friend. When you do it, you are a dangerous idiot."

Not only are we all familiar with this rule, but I suspect that we do not lose much sleep over the inconsistency, the unjustness with which we attack the character and morals of total strangers for acts which we regularly commit ourselves. When we curse at the person in front of us for failing to signal a turn moments after we (quite understandably) signaled right to turn left, we are happily "forgetting at the right time." And it is easy enough to see how such "forgetting" is what makes driving bearable. How tedious it would be to have to forgive every tourist admiring the sights or every lunatic cab driver their numerous trespasses. And how chilling the very idea of getting in the car if we truly felt that each missed traffic light, each inelegant merge, each sudden brake

was proof of our own ethical weakness.

This is the point, I think, that "literary philosophers" like Nietzsche, Thoreau and Montaigne make over and over again against the philosophers of the grand system like Kant and Hegel. Life is too big and complex a thing to be reduced to anything like rules of morality. Moral rules have an important but limited rule to play within the broader tapestry of life. There is a time and a place to be concerned with morality, and a time and a place not to be. Perhaps driving in traffic is a trivial example, but there are many others. The value of forgetting, of acting unhistorically, is vital in political life. One example that springs to mind is FDR's decision (if decision it was) not to warn the navy of Japan's imminent attack on Pearl Harbor. It did not matter whether permitting the attack was "moral"; FDR realized it was not a time for fine distinctions. The U.S. had to enter the war, and there was no better way to get the country involved.

Now, systematic philosophers do not roll over at this point. They argue that if entry into the war was an overriding good, then it should be captured by a more complicated system of moral calculus, one that determines when you may sanction the deaths of hundreds to prevent the deaths of thousands. But this response inevitably fails to keep pace with the criticism, because the diversity and complexity of human experience and imagination easily muddies the original purpose, beauty and strength of the systematic morality. Instead of "Thou Shalt Not Lie" we get "On Tuesdays, unless it is raining and thou hast a slight temperature, thou shalt not lie." No, it is far better to keep our morality simple and admit that it just does not always apply.

But Nietzsche and his sympathizers always leave one feeling somewhat empty. Even if we accept that it is important "to know when to remember and when to forget", the prettily chosen examples all tend to show when to forget. What about the other side of the equation? When should we remember? When is morality important? If morality is of limited value (rather than no value), shouldn't there be some other sort of "übercode" for determining when morality applies and when it does not, when we must act historically and when not. Otherwise, how can we know FDR was right that "morality did not apply" to his decision. What if I think he was wrong? What if the schoolyard bully doesn't think morality applies to his decision to kick me in the head? If there is such a code, isn't it really this that people mean by "morality"? It is, after all, "the way we determine how we should act." And if there is not such a code, aren't we forced to admit that all of our opinions are equally unfounded aesthetic feelings. Why bother thinking, philosophizing or moralizing at all? Relativity engulfs all distinctions.

These are not easy questions, and there is no doubt that Neitzsche paid too little attention to them. I think his answer is that knowing when to act historically is a matter of aesthetics, of taste, but this does not mean there are no right answers. It just means that it is as complicated and "holistic" an activity as trying to judge beauty (and who says beauty is a relative matter – no one has asked me to sing for them recently but I'm sure Celine Dion cannot say the

same thing). Nietzsche's style hovers oddly between philosophy and literature, because I suspect, he really thought he should be writing literature. The real answer to the most difficult questions are to be found in the sensitivity of literature and not the rationalism of philosophy.

AHS

A healthy dose of Neitzsche leads us away from reading Kant and Hegel and towards Tolstoy and Doestoevsky. Novels have several hundred pages to explore the growth and development of a single person or a single event. They have time to build up from the solid, undisputed details of everyday life a fair defense or critique of an act or decision. The correct answer to any question "How can I know whether such-and-such an act is permissible" is: "Could it be justified in a novel?" "If you read a life history of the person committing the act, would you forgive him or would you not?"

Richard Wright's *Native Son* is a great novel because it assumes the challenge of showing us when to remember and when to forget with stunning directness. It shows us that a sullen teenager can murder a girl, saw her limbs off and stuff her in a furnace, and still be morally blameless. This is not because he acted morally but because his acts occurred within a social (and personal) context where morality was not relevant. When Bigger kills Beth, we sense that Bigger may have entered a moral arena and failed but the qualms are minor. At the trial, the rooting interest is for release.

Only by taking the time to live in Bigger's shoes, do we learn to judge his actions. The understanding we reach is not formulaic (waiting to be decoded by a future Deep Blue of moral decision-making), rather it has the nature of revelation, of direct awareness or when and where morality matters.

People can learn to understand each other, or at least, understand the nature of their disagreements. But it requires that we engage each other in the way that an author engages the lives of his characters. Exhaustively, obsessively, sensitively—throw in your adjective of choice. There are no shortcuts.

Reminiscence

Mr. Bohm's Azaleas

Lincoln MacVeagh

Eugene Bohm was a Manhattan socialite who went to Ecuador on business as a young man in 1949 and never quite managed to leave. When I met him he was the headmaster of the Colegio Americano de Quito. He had been at the job for ten years and he'd been trying to leave for the last three. He stayed on only because there was no one to take his place. The contentious Ecuadorians were incapable of agreeing on his successor.

In his seventies, Eugene walked with a cane during the day and with the help of a manservant when he went out at night. Except at school and at dinner parties, Eugene and his manservant were inseparable. The manservant's name was Lenin and he was a middle-aged Ecuadorian man who dressed well and always maintained, in public at least, a dignified and stony silence. I never figured out their relationship. Some people whispered that Eugene and his manservant were lovers, but I don't know if that was true.

Eugene was an odd looking man. He had skinny, gimpy legs and a distended stomach that stuck out to one side as if there were a balloon in his shirt. He wore brightly colored ties. He had a big head, a bulbous nose and very white cheeks splotched with pink. He looked a little like a string puppet. Eugene was wonderfully cultivated and he spoke fluent Spanish and German, both of which he pronounced with a French accent. He also knew how to get along in Ecuador. He did not strain himself unduly at the Colegio, and he did not expect those who worked under him to strain themselves

either. He was a popular headmaster.

Eugene was good company. He was dry and worldly, and he told funny stories. If he had any failing it was that he was a snob and he would sometimes adopt an overly formal manner with people he did not know. But there was always a sense of humor underneath. I remember him taking one woman aside — a young teacher from Arkansas whom he had offended with a comment about the uncultured South — and asking her forgiveness by explaining that he was too rich to be nice and too old to be taken seriously.

Like many seventy year olds, Mr. Bohm was prone to telling the same stories again and again. But in Eugene's case, many of the stories were worth it. There is one in particular that I remember. I heard him tell it twice. It was his answer to the question of Ecuadorian witch doctors and native Indian beliefs.

In his late twenties, Eugene married into one of Quito's wealthiest and most prominent German families. He and his wife had three boys and while the children were growing up the couple remained in the city. After the youngest son was sent off to boarding school in New England, Eugene and his wife moved out to live on their finca in the country.

The finca was a vast estate that had previously belonged to Mrs. Bohm's parents, but although magnificent, it was in need of sprucing up. Work began immediately. With the help of his wife's money, Eugene had the inside of the house gutted and refurbished in high style, and when the last bathroom was finally finished, Eugene started landscaping the grounds.

The main house was built on a hill and there was a large double staircase leading up from the driveway to the front door. The little incline between the staircases was ugly and barren and Eugene did not like it. He decided to have the slope between the staircases terraced and planted with long rows of azaleas. He wanted a bright rush of color to greet the eye when you looked up at the house.

Eugene gave instructions to the gardener and soon the slope was cut into steps and a great mass of young flowers were brought in and planted. It looked very pretty.

One week later all of the azaleas were dead. Eugene scratched his head and told the gardener to try again. More azaleas were brought in and the flowers were re-planted, but in a short time these flowers also died. They went from healthy blooming green to stale dry brown in less time than it takes Monday to become Friday. Eugene suspected sabotage.

He questioned everyone in his household and at last one of the parlor maids told him the truth. Jorge, the gardener, was methodically poisoning the plants at night.

Puzzled, Eugene went to talk to Jorge. "You've been killing my azaleas," he said, "You've been poisoning them at night, haven't you?"

"Yes, patron, I cannot lie."

AHS

"But why?"

"I had to poison them," said Jorge, "It's for your safety."

"I don't understand," said Eugene.

"Because, patron, you cannot keep this flower near the house. It is bad. The azalea brings death. You must not plant her."

Eugene was impressed by the old gardener's honesty and good will, and he respected the man's superstition. Nonetheless, he did not want to be governed by it.

"Of course, you are right," Eugene said tactfully, "Azaleas can be very dangerous. For Ecuadorians. But you see, I am an American and my wife is half German. For foreigners the forces are different. For us, the azalea brings luck. It is only the gardenia that must be kept away from the house."

Jorge looked suspicious, but he allowed himself to be convinced. He agreed to plant the azaleas once more and he agreed not to poison them on account of the patron being a gringo. Two months later, Eugene's flowers were in glorious bloom and the little slope between the staircases was awash in pinks and whites and yellows.

Two months after that, Eugene's wife died. It was sudden and mysterious and the doctor could not pinpoint the cause of her death. He wrote it down as heart failure, but many of the locals did not find this explanation convincing. They blamed Eugene and his azaleas.

The first time I heard Eugene tell this story I was shocked. I didn't know how to react. The whole dinner table went silent and we all tried to put on sad faces. I knit my brow and stared down at my soup. But when I finally looked up again I was surprised to find Eugene throwing me a devilish wink.

"And for years afterwards," he announced with a loud laugh, "It was actually rumored that I murdered my wife!"

Games

Sir Laffalot

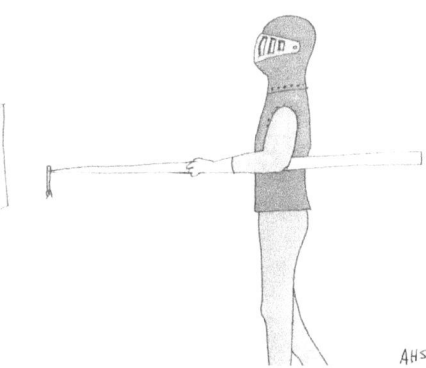

There comes a time in every man's education when Duck-Duck-Goose loses its luster and he realizes that Tic-Tac-Toe usually results in a stalemate. This is the time when most people stop playing games and turn instead to the lifelong diversions of alcohol and the opposite sex. Sir Laffalot tips his hat to both booze and girls, but he often finds the conversation wanting. In short, he would rather play Charades than hear another person gush "Grey is the new black!"

To fill the void, Sir Laffalot presents his column on games. This month's game is *Rhyme Or Reason*. It is a word game in which players must come up with words that either rhyme with, or are reasonably related to previous words.

Sir Laffalot once played *Rhyme Or Reason* with a group of ESL students. The word was "Frog" and the turn passed to Chen, a Taiwanese boy. Without a moment's hesitation, Chen said "Floor". Sir Laffalot had to stop the game and explain that "Frog" and "Floor" are not reasonably related.

"I know," Chen protested, "But they rhyme! Flah! Frah! Flah! Frah!"

Rhyme Or Reason: How To Play
1) Player 1 starts with any word of five letters or less. He then begins counting to seven out loud.
2) Player 2 must now come up with another word of five letters or less that either rhymes with, or is reasonably related to the previous word. Player 2 then starts counting and the turn passes to Player 3.
3) Play is continuous until someone (a) fails to think of a rhyming or related word within seven seconds (b) repeats a word already used (c) uses a word of more than five letters. Whoever stops play receives a "P" (as in "P-I-G"). That player then restarts the game with a new word.
4) When a player spells "P-I-G" he is out and the game continues without him until there is only one player left.

Notes:
a) "Reasonably related" is loosely defined. Generally speaking, antonyms, synonyms and common word phrases are acceptable. In the event of a dispute the game should be momentarily suspended and the question decided by a group vote.
b) No word can be repeated throughout the *entire* game.

A Typical Game:
1st Player: "Boat"
2nd Player: "Ship"
3rd Player: "Barge"
1st Player: "Large"
2nd Player: "Big"
3rd Player: "Fig"
1st Player: "Tree"
2nd Player: "Maple"
3rd Player: "Syrup"
1st Player: "..."

Quick, can you think of a word, five letters or less, that rhymes with or is related to "syrup"?

Sir Laffalot says: TOODALOO!!

Kitty Goes Krazy

David Garcia III

Recently I fell prey to another marathon visitation by my friend-who-must-be-Zeke, fresh from Oregon and a vasectomy, despite his Jehovah Witness vow never to have sex before marriage.

Zeke said that his friend Spanky was sexually harassed by a 60 year old executive last week and now is trying to get a settlement. Everyone needs a little Spanky at the end of a hard day, I joked, but it didn't go over well.

Laura (aka Grendel's mother) is still in residence, until I can find a mobile liposuction unit that will remove 120 pounds of unwanted fat from my apartment floor. Her first night, Laura tried to flush a feminine product down my toilet, woke me with a monologue about it, but didn't want me to get up because I would find out what she did. She ended up plunging it herself while giving me a running commentary. Time: 3:30 am.

Then it was Saturday morning and I was in a very deep sleep. Suddenly, Kitty lost all reason and tried to murder me. I had seen flashes of rage from her before, but nothing had prepared me for this. I was yelling "Kitty, what's wrong?" as she hissed and snarled like a mad beast and cut my back and scalp with her claws. I threw a blanket over her but she continued her seizure. I was bleeding when I took a quick look out the window. Another snarling cat had climbed up the five flights of the fire escape and was crouched against the screen. Kitty got loose from under the blanket and chased me into the bathroom. Laura screamed and Zeke managed to blockade the bloodlusting monster (Kitty, not Laura) into the backroom as I scooted out the door to buy much needed Band-Aids. By the time I got back, le petite feline was all cozy again and wanting to be fed.

My only guess is that it had been so long since Kitty had seen another cat that she got freaked out by primal instincts. The other possibility is of course that this was her big chance to mate and she was taking it out on me for (a) closing the window, or (b) not telling her that I am not a cat and that other cats exist. On the downside, my Mom said, "one more time and you have to put it down." However, the upside is that, like Spiderman, I now have uncanny feline powers with which to combat evil. Now I really must go.

The
ECLECTIC

March 1999   Volume 1 Number 2   Free

CONTENTS

Quotations

"Possibly blue movies shown in the classroom by a teacher with a pointer are what is really needed." Mary McCarthy remembers the inadequacy of her high school's sexual education in *How I Grew.*

"No woman whose appearance depended on safety pins can ever have felt really comfortable." Aldous Huxley on the fashions of Ancient Rome in *Comfort.*

"I coveted popularity with a covetousness that was almost mean. It seemed to me that there would be an Elysium in the intimacy of those very boys whom I was bound to hate because they hated me. Something of the disgrace of my school days has clung to me all through life." Anthony Trollope in *An Autobiography.*

"It isn't writing at all — it's typing." Truman Capote critiques Jack Kerouac and the Beat Generation on the televison show *Open End,* 1959.

The Eclectic is owned and published by Linoleum Palace, Inc., 43-05 31st Ave., #2, Astoria, NY 11103. Copyright ©
1999 by Lincoln MacVeagh. All rights reserved. Unsolicited submissions will not be considered or returned.

Two-Headed Calf

The Life of Truman Capote Briefly Told

Lincoln MacVeagh

Question: What do Kurt Vonnegut, Charlie Chaplin, Pearl Bailey and Ronald Reagan have in common? Answer: They were all friends of Truman Capote's. For twenty years Truman Capote was A-list in the little black book of every rich and famous person west of Moscow and east of Los Angeles. Jackie Kennedy invited him into her bedroom while she dressed for dinner at the White House; Marilyn Monroe cried on his shirtsleeve; and when Andy Warhol first arrived in New York he used to stand for hours outside Truman's apartment waiting for a chance to shake the great man's hand. Truman was king.

A mind as wicked as Egypt.

"*I could have had any woman in the world,*" he boasted, "*from Garbo to Deitrich.*" As it happened Truman didn't like girls in that way, but his collection of male conquests was almost equally impressive.

Of John Garfield: "*He was one of the nicest people I've ever known. My mother saw him just once and tried to get him into bed with her.*"

Of Errol Flynn: "*What I can't stand is he treats me like a girl... he's like all those others who can't face up to the fact they're with a man with balls as hairy as their own*

and so they have to pretend this man they're with is really some baby doll in disguise.*"

Of Albert Camus: "*He was a homely little thing, but attractive, with sensitive eyes and a compassionate face. He was my editor at Gallimard, and he took me to dinner. One thing led to another, and one afternoon he came to my room and we just went to bed. It was as simple as that. I don't think he was homosexual in any way. But that was the period when I looked my best.*"

It's impossible to know how much of what Truman said is true, but there can be no doubt that as a young man he was one of the most charming and exotic creatures ever to drink a martini.

Truman often described his own popularity as that of a two-headed calf at the state fair. He was a glorious freak of nature, a novelty that no one could resist. At the age of twenty-five, he was an acclaimed novelist, unsullied by formal education ("*I can add but I can't subtract*"), and he was the first openly gay celebrity the 20th century had ever seen. He stood five foot three in his loafers and he had soft blonde hair, pretty blue eyes and permanently limp wrists. His voice was high and squeaky. He lisped. But he was bursting with enthusiasm and people everywhere were enchanted.

On Truman's first trip to Paris, Andre Gide was so taken he gave him a sapphire ring. Jean Cocteau doted on him. Only Collette was above the excitement and pronounced sniffily that she'd never heard of Truman Capote. Cocteau then told her that Truman *"looked like a ten year old and had a mind as wicked as Egypt."* Collette invited Capote to tea.

Truman Capote was born Truman Streckfus Persons in New Orleans on September 30th, 1924. His parents never lived together and two years after marrying they divorced. Truman's father was a southern shyster. Joe Persons was a convincing salesman but an unreliable man. He fought a brief child custody battle for his son, but he had to abandon it when he was sent to prison for forging checks.

Truman's mother, Lillie Mae, was a small town Alabama girl. She is said to have been extremely beautiful. Every picture I have ever seen of her makes her look plain, but perhaps she had charisma. Certainly she had ambition. She also knew how difficult it would be to find a second husband with Truman running in her wake. Lillie Mae spent two years dragging him around the South with her, locking him in hotel rooms when she went out for the night with her boyfriends, then she gave him up. Lillie Mae left Truman to live with his aunts in Alabama. She changed her name to Nina and headed for Manhattan.

Five years later Nina met Joe Capote, a rich mild-mannered Cuban who worked on Wall Street. They lived together for a year while Capote waited to divorce his first wife and a week after the divorce came through Nina and Joe were married. Only then did Nina send for her son. Truman was nine.

Nina's second marriage was happier than her first but not by much. Joe Capote was a playboy and his wife resented it. Both of them drank and when they drank, they fought. During one fight Nina grabbed Joe's testicles so hard he had to run off to the hospital in his bathrobe. The melodrama was never-ending and finally Nina killed herself. Truman's mother overdosed on barbiturates at the age of forty eight and one year after that Truman's stepfather, Joe Capote, was convicted of embezzlement and sentenced to twelve months in Sing Sing prison.

By that time, however, Truman was long gone. When his mother died, Truman was already living in Italy with Jack Dunphy, the man who would be his lover-turned-companion for the next thirty years. He had won two O'Henry awards for his short stories; his first novel *"Other Voices Other Rooms"* was a success; and he was about to start work on his second Broadway production. Truman was a celebrity, and as one friend put it, *"his name now turned up in the papers as frequently as the Duke of Windsor's."*

Somehow Truman had managed to escape his miserable youth intact. His adult life was not quite so bad. Speaking glibly, it can be divided into four phases: the Literary, the Hollywood, the Jet Set, and the Desperate. At least the literary phase must be regarded as a success.

As long as he could remember, Truman wanted to write. He started when he was five and he was published even before he left Alabama. At the age of eight he wrote a story called *"Mrs. Busybody"* that was printed in the *Mobile Register*. (It was a story about Harper Lee's mother. Harper Lee, who later wrote To *Kill A Mockingbird*, was Truman's best friend in childhood. Her mother was an eccentric and slightly deranged. She twice tried to drown Harper in the bathtub.)

Still nursing ambition, Truman dropped out of high school at seventeen to become an odd-jobs man at the *The New Yorker*. He was rejected for military service in World War II on psychological grounds (*"I've been turned down for everything, including the WACs."*) and meanwhile he worked like a dog, cultivating every writer and editor in Manhattan.

Truman was an instant hit, and not least because he wrote great stories. Excitement built up around him and when *"Other Voices Other Rooms"* was published it sold well. He had his first serious love affair with a tweedy professor from Smith College and at the same time he became friends with Carson McCullers, Lillian Hellman and almost everyone else who had made a name for themselves in publishing. Truman seemed to have found a place for himself.

But he was unable to rest content. Truman grew bored of the literary world. It was too small to contain him. He was tired of its donnish ways and its weird assortment of neurotics. Writers are not generally glamorous

people and Truman wanted glamour. After one too many evenings spent listening to Carson McCullers complain about the progress of her latest novel, Capote called it quits.

In 1954 he wrote *Beat The Devil*, a screenplay starring Humphrey Bogart, and thus began the second phase of Truman's adulthood. He was off and running with the movie stars. Gertrude Stein and Alice B. Toklas were replaced in Truman's affections by Liz Taylor and Montgomery Clift. John Malcolm Brinnan, a poet friend of Truman's, described a dinner with him in 1955 as follows: *"After a meal at The Colony, we went on to The Blue Angel. In both places he took the attentions of people who came to our table with an unruffled air of noblesse oblige. Someone told him his movie was 'mad, mad fun.' Someone reported what C.C. said to Boo-boo in the ladies room at Bergdorf..."*

Naturally, the writers felt jilted but Truman didn't seem to care, and blithely he went on to conquer Holly-

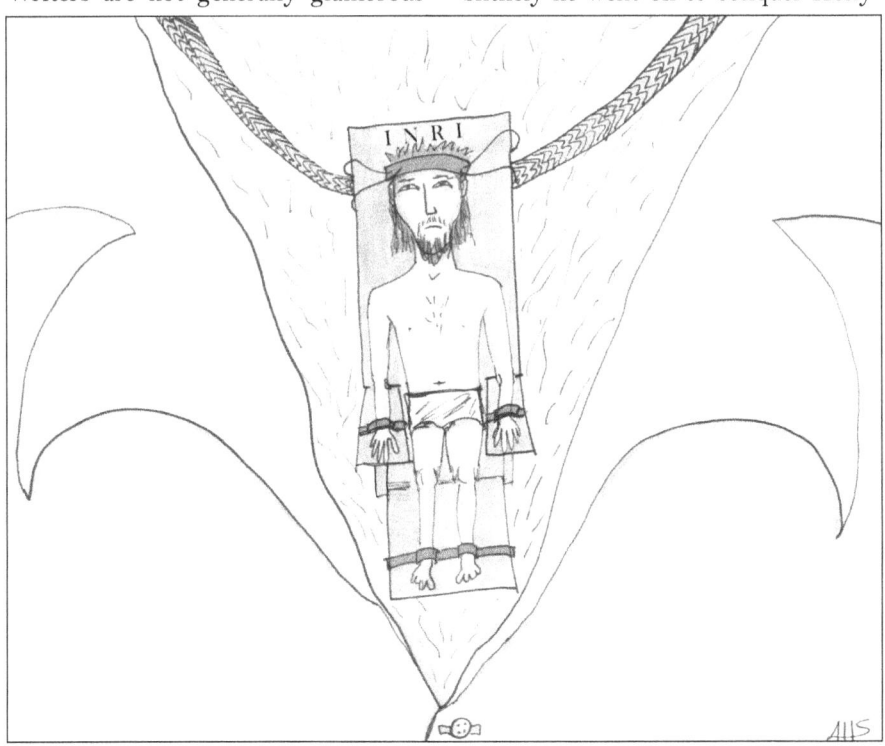

wood. Having done so, however, Truman found there was one last social mountain left to climb.

In 1955 there were probably only a few hundred households the world over where Hollywood stars were not considered suitable dinner guests. These were the households of the establishment's super-rich, the strange collection of tycoons and heiresses that made up the jet set. At some point in the 1950's, Truman discovered the existence of this café society and from then on he could not rest until he had become part of it.

When Odysseus sailed past the land of the Sirens he covered his ears. Truman was braver than that and he took his boat to shore. He went as an explorer. Truman was not a snob and he was not a social climber. He was at first only curious: *"I simply had to know what it was like."* Brinnan reports Truman saying. *"Years and years I'd wondered: What if you woke up in the morning, so rich you were famous for it, being rich. What if you had your orange juice, read your paper, finished your coffee, all the while knowing that if there was anything to buy you could buy it, any place to go you could go there today. Would you make life into a game? Manipulate people like chil-*

dren? What would absolutely limitless means do to your appetites?"

It did not take Truman long to find out what he wanted to know: *"..that there's nothing much to find out. The rich are as bored with themselves as you are, as I am – children, without the imagination of children."* But by then it was already too late. Truman had fallen in love with the scent of money and he could not tear himself away from it. His romance with the jet set lasted two decades. Then, all at once, Truman's fancy friends dropped him and thus began the last phase of Capote's life, the desperate phase.

Capote's collapse can be traced to any number of things. The six years he spent writing *In Cold Blood* took a lot out of him. *In Cold Blood* is a true-crime story about a multiple murder in a small Kansas town, and from the time the two killers were arrested in 1961 until the time of their hanging in 1966, Truman played the difficult role of mentor and friend to both of them. This role was made all the more difficult because of Truman's obvious self-interest as a reporter and the nagging sense that he was using the killers unfairly. The mental strain was enormous, but perhaps Truman could have weathered it had

he not relied on pills and booze to help him through. Capote slowly turned into a grapefruit-and-vodka for breakfast man and the constant drinking sapped his mental strength. So when the final blow came, Truman had nothing left to fall back on.

The final blow for Truman was café society's rejection of him. It was prompted by the publication of three of his stories in *Esquire* magazine. For a long time, even before he began work on *In Cold Blood*, Capote had in mind to write a novel called *Answered Prayers*. It was to be a book about the establishment rich that he had come to know. By 1975, Capote had published nothing significant in almost ten years, he had talked about *Answered Prayers* so much that his pride obligated him to publish parts of it. He gave *Esquire* three stories, ostensibly chapters from the novel, and these stories were full of gossip about Truman's rich friends. The stories are funny and interesting, but to the people whom the characters were modeled after, they were incredibly mean. When Kurt Vonnegut was asked for his reaction he said: *"It's fine, but it's amazing that he would claw those people the way he did."*

Perhaps Truman was right to claw them. Rich people are often fatuous. But these rich people were Truman's friends, and as soon as *Esquire* hit the presses they dropped him like a stone. One woman even killed herself. Anne Woodward committed suicide upon discovering that Capote's story "La Cote Basque" repeated rumors of her having murdered her husband.

Before *Esquire* ran the stories from *Answered Prayers*, Truman was an unhappy man with social cachet. Afterwards, he lost his cachet and the last nine years of Capote's life reads like a torturously slow move from frying pan to fire. He begged his old friends to take him back and they refused; he found a new lover and the lover left him so he paid two goons to fire bomb the lover's car and they succeeded; he took to peeing down the back stairs of his apartment because he could never find the bathroom.

In 1980 Capote published a beautiful collection of short pieces called *Music For Chameleons*, and in 1984 he was dead. Like his mother, he overdosed on barbiturates. He was sixty years old and he died without friends. All that were left were courtesans and hangers on. It's not easy being a two-headed calf.

Reviews

The Story of My Experiments With Truth

by Mohandas K. Ghandi

Dover Thrift Editions, 1995 (reprint)

Men are egotistical. We all like to think of ourselves as Apollo driving the chariot that pulls the Sun behind it. Most of us eventually figure out that the Sun rises and sets of its own accord. Not Mohandas K. Gandhi. Simply put, Gandhi was the most self-important man ever to go barefoot.

Gandhi's autobiography, *The Story of My Experiments With Truth* is an astonishing book. One reads it with greedy interest. It is honest and entertaining; it is well and plainly written; it gives clear insight into events which effected hundreds of millions of people. It is also the self-portrait of a monstrous man. If Gandhi was a saint, he was a very cold and calculating one.

As a child, Gandhi tells us, he experimented with befriending a naughty boy, an *evildoer* as he puts it. He reasons that he will have a happy effect on his friend. The bad boy, Gandhi hopes, will learn from the good. It doesn't work out and little-boy Gandhi draws the moral: *"...I had calculated wrongly. A reformer cannot afford to have close intimacy with him whom he seeks to reform... I am of the opinion that all exclusive intimacies are to be avoided; for man takes in vice far more readily than virtue. And he who would be friends with God must remain alone..."*

Gandhi was married at thirteen. For a few years he wallowed in unspeakable debauchery (i.e., he had sex with his wife) and then he went off to University in England. By the time he got back to India, his life's determination was fixed. He would be perfect. He had already given up meat. Now he must fret over whether it is sinful to drink milk. Finally in 1906, after a great struggle of conscience, he takes the vow of "brahmacharya", the vow of chastity: *"I had not*

shared my thoughts with my wife until then, but only consulted her at the time of taking the vow. She had no objection."

Having thus cleansed himself, Gandhi went on to lead one of the great rebellions of the 20th century, but unlike many political memoirs, *"The Story of My Experiments…"* never bogs down in historical detail. Gandhi keeps his book personal and for that reason it is always fascinating.

In the following passage Gandhi describes a serious illness that befell his wife in middle age. It's important to note that by this time Gandhi had put his wife on a highly restricted diet consisting mainly of fruit, and that Gandhi's own constitution had been seriously weakened by malnutrition:

"So when all my remedies failed, I entreated her to give up salt and pulses [lentils and chickpeas]. *She would not agree, however much I pleaded with her. At last she challenged me, saying that even I could not give up these two articles if I was advised to do so. I was pained and equally, delighted – delighted in that I got an opportunity to shower my love on her. I said to her: 'You are mistaken. If I was ailing and the doctor advised me to give up these or any other articles, I should unhesitatingly do so. But there! Without any medical advice, I give up salt and pulses for one year, whether you do so or not.'*

She was rudely shocked and exclaimed in deep sorrow: 'Pray forgive me. Knowing you I should not have provoked you. I promise to abstain from these things, but for heaven's sake take back your vow. This is too hard on me.'

'It is very good for you to forego these articles. I have not the slightest doubt that you will be all the better without them. As for me, I cannot retract a vow seriously taken. And it is sure to benefit me, for all restraint, whatever prompts it, is wholesome for men…

I would like to count this incident as an instance of Satyagraha [standing firm for Truth], *and it is one of the sweetest recollections of my life."*

Gandhi was a very strange man. His autobiography is riveting.

Are Republicans Evil?

T.E. MacVeagh

I do not think that I am a wild-eyed radical. Most of my friends and I would describe ourselves as moderate liberals who grew up with the conviction that the New Deal and the Warren Court were beacons of justice and rationality. We are dismayed at the attack that even moderate Republicans seem willing to launch on our most cherished ideals. A typical Republican platform: promote school prayer; outlaw abortion; dismantle gun control; get rid of the exclusionary rule; replace progressive taxation with a flat tax; abolish affirmative action, welfare, Medicaid, and key environmental regulations. What are Republicans aiming at? A Christian theocracy, in which people of deviant beliefs are squashed? An oligopoly run by the very wealthy? The question that seems to come up every time my friends and I discuss the political scene is this: Are republicans evil?

Before delving into the question, let us deal with two collateral issues. First, I know that a more radical political position suggests that the whole Republican/Democratic power structure is evil, and that voters from either party serve to uphold a corrupt system. It is a delicate position to argue that the small distinction between Republican and Democrat, which a radical political thinker will consider scarcely visible, makes the difference between good and evil. Second, some people might say that it is impossible to distinguish between the moral worth of Republican and Democratic politicians. Trent Lott might be evil, but he cannot be more corrupt than Ted Kennedy, Dick Gephardt or Bill Clinton. After all, the argument runs, politicians on the national scene are all whores, willing to say anything to gain and keep power. Sometimes such deep cynicism seems unavoidable, so to pursue the argument in the face of it, let us not consider the politicians themselves, but the ordinary citizens who vote for them.

The whole issue is trickier now. It is not holy warriors like Pat Robertson we are characterizing as evil, but our family and friends who vote Republican. The idea begins to seem preposterous. And yet . . . why do ordinary Republicans vote for candidates who support the appalling political program outlined above?

You begin to get suspicious when you notice that the people you know who vote Republicans include a large predominance of rich, white men (and women who can afford to fly to Europe if they need an abortion). And you notice that all the policies your Republican friends support, in the name of fiscal responsibility, social order and other familiar justifications, seem to inure to their benefit. Getting rid of welfare and affirmative action does not hurt them. And Republican fiscal policies only serve to decrease their taxes and increase the value of their corporate stock.

The other point that inflames the

suspicion of a liberal democrat is the readiness of the Republican voter, even if just a "fiscal conservative" who considers himself socially liberal, to jump into bed with the radical right. If we are in a holy war with Pat Robertson, what should be our attitude towards the collaborators who forward his ends? George Pataki may not himself long for a theocratic dictatorship, but can we treat him as a friend when he is helping the cause of those that do? Von Hindenberg was not Hitler, but neither was he a force for good.

Of course, Republican voters argue that they are not being selfish when they support tax breaks. Sure the policies of the Republican party make them better off, but they are also good for the country as a whole. Tax cuts *et alia* serve the poor, black and white, male and female, as well as the rich. Indeed, misty-eyed do-gooders who want to extend welfare, affirmative action, etc. end up hurting the very people that they intend to help. Welfare breeds welfare cheats and a culture of dependence. It's a dog-eat-dog world, and a political program which ignores that fact is doomed to failure. As for cooperation with Pat Robertson, it is certainly less dangerous than an alliance with the radical left. Robertson's Christianity, beside being more in harmony with American tradition, is also more compatible with a free society than Dworkian feminism, Greenpeace Environmentalism, or Marxist economics, each of which Democrats seem to consider a legitimate part of the political debate.

For the moment, let's put aside the issue of cooperation with radical groups, and consider the basic point of the moderate Republican defense. If I may paraphrase, the Republicans are saying to Democrats: if you think we are evil, we think you are idiots, bound for hell on a road paved with good intentions. It's a tough world out

there, and liberal Democrats are being impossibly naive if they think their "everybody-lets-love-each-other" policies will do anything but bankrupt the social coffers.

Now, this kind of answer should give us a clue as to why we liberal democrats find it so hard not to attribute evil motives to Republicans. Republicans have an essentially dark view of humanity. In their view humans are greedy, self-interested individuals who do not respond to the good of the community, but to carrots (tax-breaks) and sticks (three-strikes-and-you're-out) which affect their self-interest directly. What a liberal Democrat hears when a Republican says that welfare mothers cheat; that if you raise taxes people won't pay them; that murderers are irreparably twisted and need to be killed is that the Republican who speaks can himself imagine cheating on welfare and taxes, or murdering someone out of sheer brutality.

And this is fair enough. Certainly we look at the people around us to help us form our judgments of human nature, but in the end we rely most profoundly on our understanding of our own character. If someone says something like

"Prejudice is part of human nature," he may be right, but you can bet it is part of his nature.

So are Republicans evil? Well, maybe, maybe not. They may also be right. Perhaps liberal Democrats simply have a stupidly naive view of human nature. Worse, if Republicans are right, the Democrats are self-deluded fools who are unable to see their own faults and longings objectively.

Before dismissing this Republican response, liberal democrats should do well to think about their reaction to Marxists. Marxists, the Democrats often argue, have noble goals, but a hopelessly romantic idea of humanity which ends up making everyone worse off. The point is, we all lie somewhere along a continuum, thinking people to our left are deluded romantics, people to our right are fascist tyrants. Are we confident enough in our personal view of humanity, in our own self-understanding, to accuse Republicans of being evil on the basis of a different view of humanity? Are we so sure that we occupy a privileged place on this continuum?

But just because it would be arrogant to call Republicans evil, does not mean we should not do it. For years, Republicans have been lambasting Democratic domestic policies as dangerous and deluded and Democratic foreign policy as next to treasonous in its passivity. The only good comeback liberals have at their disposal is that Republicans are heartless villains. Lately, we have heard a lot of concern expressed about the "level of political debate", with suggestions that people should show more

respect for each other in talking about the issues. Calling your political opponents "evil" surely qualifies as dragging down the political debate. But politics is a dirty, rough and tumble business. Polite requests to "Please, let's talk about issues" don't really get you anywhere. Over the last twenty years, Republicans have not shied away from equating the word "liberal" with the word "traitor".

Maybe the Republicans are right about human nature. But if you don't think so and you care about Democratic values, ideals and policies, it may be strategically necessary to brand Republicans as evil. Evil, racist, misogynist oligopolists who are engaged in a campaign to reduce every last working and middle class person to wage slavery and impose a rigid cultural hegemony on a diverse nation. In other words, tar the moderate Republicans with every crime of the radical right, the way Republicans have tarred Democrats with the crimes of the far left. If every Democrat is a closet Stalinist, then every Republican is a closet Nazi.

Only as one says these dreadful things, one should retain a sense of proportion, if only for one's own sanity. Liberals cannot know that they have chosen the right place on the continuum; the moderate Republicans may turn out to be on the side of the saints after all. And consider one further nagging doubt: If liberals fight Republican fire with fire will it alienate Republican party moderates and drive them into closer ties with the radical right?

Reminiscence

Mr. Taylor Reads
La Prensa Libre

Lincoln MacVeagh

Zachary Taylor is a Costa Rican of American descent. He is long since retired and his wife says he has a bad heart. He owns a plot of land in a suburb of San Jose and on this land he has built a compound of five bungalows, all varying in size but none larger than the living room of a fancy house on the Long Island Sound. Zachary and his wife live in one of the bungalows and the rest are rented out to gringos at slightly inflated prices.

Mr. Taylor is part of Costa Rica's middle class. He has two daughters living in New Jersey. His father made a good living as the manager of a banana plantation back in the days when United Fruit ran the country as a more or less sovereign power. Thanks to his father's job Zachary received a good education and he grew up to become a communications engineer. Thirty years ago, he helped set up Costa Rica's first ever telephone network.

I know all this about Zachary Taylor because he used to be my landlord. He was nice man but he liked to talk and each month when I paid my rent I got an earful. Mr. Taylor watched the world through his kitchen window and if by chance he missed you coming, his dog would start barking like mad so there wasn't much you could do. I never managed to get out in less than fifteen minutes and one day early on I made the foolish mistake of asking to borrow yesterday's newspaper.

"Which paper do you want? *La Nacion* (The Nation) or *La Prensa Libre* (The Free Press)?" Mr. Taylor had a devious grin on his face. Since I was only interested in the movie listings I didn't much care which paper he gave me and I asked for *La Nacion.* *La Nacion* is a conservative paper; it is the paper of the middle class; and I assumed that it was the only paper Mr. Taylor had on hand. I was wrong.

"Hah!" he burst out, "I read *La Prensa Libre!* Surprised?"

In fact, I was somewhat surprised. *La Prensa Libre* was the leftist paper read by trade union officials and coconut sellers in the park.

"Yes, indeed, I haven't read *La Nacion* for decades," Zachary went on, "And I can tell you a very interesting story about that. You see, many years ago I worked as a communications expert in Honduras. The Honduran President was under pressure from the Marxists and it was practically a revolution. There was a horde of foreign journalists in Tegucigalpa covering the uprising and every day the reporters wanted to send their stories out on the wires. But the Hondurans didn't have the expertise to handle the volume, so I was called in. Why me? I had been active in politics for years and my name was known. Besides, I was a Costa Rican and the Honduran President trusted me. As soon as I got to Tegucigalpa they put me in charge of the newsroom, and since there was only one newsroom in the entire country, everyone had to go through me.

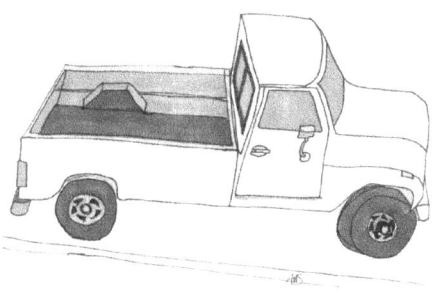

"Now, I tell you I don't judge a man by his ideology. It's respect that counts. If you respect me, I'll respect you. That's just how I am. But I never liked the Marxists. I've fought against them all over Central America and I could never pass up a chance to ruffle their feathers.

"So when I was in the newsroom these was this one fellow, a Chilean, who wrote for a Marxist paper in Santiago and all of his stories were critical of the Honduran President, praising the rebels who were causing all the trouble. I didn't like what he stood for and I always put him and his friends at the end of the waiting list. He'd file a report on Monday morning but I wouldn't send it out until Wednesday, see? In those days everything was happening so fast that a three day old story was almost worthless. The Chilean used to get really angry but I'd just smile and tell him that there was a big backlog of stories filed before his.

"Finally after about two weeks of this, the Chilean journalist invited me to dinner and I went. He got right down to business. He said he knew I was holding up his reports and he asked me to stop. He started talking about freedom of speech and freedom of the press. He told me he didn't want any special favors, he just wanted me to send out the wires according to first come, first served. What can you do when a man asks you for something like that? When he puts it so straightforward? Anyway, I agreed to do what he wanted and then we started talking about other things.

"It turned out that this guy had worked in Costa Rica for a few years and I asked him which paper he liked the most. You know what he said? He said *La Prensa Libre*. This Chilean was an educated man and that night he taught me something about newspapers. He said *La Prensa Libre* was the best paper because it's written by real journalists, right here in Costa Rica. They write their stories at night and they see them in print the next morning. Whereas, *La Nacion* it's a mishmash. It's stuff they buy from the press services. For all you know *La Nacion* could have been written four days ago in London or New York. It's not real reporting. That's what this Chilean taught me and that's why I read *La Prensa Libre*. Understand?"

I nodded my head in a vague sort of way. I had been edging my way towards the front door for some time and I was now slowly backing out of it. Zachary had followed me step for step. He was still right in front of me. He looked me deep in the eye.

"Ever since then," he went on, "Every time someone asks me which newspaper I read I always tell them *La Prensa Libre*. I tell them about this Chilean fellow and how he taught me to tell a good paper from a bad one. I tell this to all my friends about the importance of working journalists, about originality, about not relying on the press services. And you know something?"

At the height of his emotion, Mr. Taylor stopped speaking for a moment. He looked down at the floor. He looked over at the dog licking itself on the lawn. He looked at me fiddling with my watchstrap. Suddenly his whole face relaxed and his voice lost its intensity.

"I tell all my friends this. And you know something?"

"Yes?" I said hesitantly. He put a hand on my shoulder and started to chuckle as if at some private joke.

"You know something?," he said, "No one gives a damn and for the life of me I can't figure out why they should!"

Mr. Taylor wished me good morning and that afternoon I went to see *Wayne's World* at the three o'clock show.

Sir Laffalot

Sir Laffalot was young once too, and as a child he was often asked to play "Truth or Dare." He didn't like it. The trouble is the dares. It's impossible to find good ones. I dare you to stomp on Matron's flower bed! I dare you to curse at the janitor! Where's the fun in that? The only dares that weren't either dangerous or mean usually involved taking your clothes off in public. Sir Laffalot would rather not.

There are better truth games that do not require getting undressed. This week's game is "I Lie." The great philosopher Soren Kierkagaard used to play a version of this game on his nights out in Copenhagen. The rules are simple.

I Lie: How To Play

1) Everyone thinks of three interesting or peculiar facts about themselves. Two of these "facts" must be true. The third is false.
2) A volunteer agrees to go first. He bravely announces his three "facts" to the group.
3) Play then goes around in a circle with everyone else trying to pick out the lie.
4) When all have made their guesses, the real lie is revealed.
5) There is no scoring but the fun is in trying to make people guess incorrectly.

Sir Laffalot has played "I Lie" with all sorts of people but by far his best moment came at a party of stuffed shirts in London. All the guests at the party were very much aware of their good breeding, except one poor fellow named David who hailed from the suburbs of Liverpool. David was studying pschology at University and he came to the party as the boyfriend of a dumpy little heiress who knew everybody. David knew nobody and Sir Laffalot could tell right away that he felt like a fish out of water. Throughout most of the evening David looked bored, but he cheered up visibly when the rules of "I Lie" were explained to him.

After everyone thought up their three "facts", the dumpy heiress volunteered to go first. "My father went to Oxford with the Prime Minister," she said, "I once lost £1,000 playing roullette. I failed French when I was nine." Sir Laffalot bet on the £1,000 but he was wrong. It turned out the heiress had a Belgian nanny and she'd spoken French fluently since infancy.

David went next and he wasted no time. "Number one: I have masturbated in a train." The room fell silent. "Number two: I have masturbated in a plane." Jaws dropped. "Number three: I have masturbated in an automobile." Uncontrollable nervous laughter.

David : 1 – Stuffed Shirts : 0. He was the hit of the party. The bit about the train, that was false.

Sir Laffalot says: **HAPPY DAYS!!**

The high life

The Beast Within

David Garcia III

I hit bottom. It could happen to anybody.

It's the day before payday. Stumble home, go through pockets, not even enough change for cat food. I remember I have a bunch of change somewhere, and I mean silver not just pennies. But where? I dismantle my entire closet. One quarter in a back pack lining! Despair. Feel faint. Where is oasis of change?

I recall the events of the last week. The $750 dentist copayment, the money lent to my brother, the glamorous cab rides to work. I spent my last $15 on top-of-the-line roach traps. I sacrificed my budget to deluxe motels of entomologic doom.

The traps claim that after the poison is ingested the roaches will have the good manners to take the elephant graveyard approach and go off to die someplace private. Those in the know scoff at this assertion. In reality, the substance causes its victims to lose their minds. That's when you get those big, stoned roaches brazenly approaching you across tabletops as you try to read the new Proust biography, and attempting to violate the sanctity of the toothbrush area as you are trying to prepare for the day. But I digress.

Falling to my knees from lack of nutrients, I chance to spy an overlooked cardboard box under the shelves next to the IBM Selectric. Like a kid at Christmas, I slide the book out from under. Something is wrong but I can't pinpoint what. I open the top of the box and take out an old glove, under which is a layer of receipts and ticket stubs (I seem to have attended far too many Ethan Hawke vehicles. Why? Why?). I remove the receipts and to my delight, my eyes shine with the glints of a bevy of bounty. But why does it seem to... *move?*

To my horror I realize it is crawling with multitudes of hairy ugly chittering winged creatures – yes, cockroaches. A nest.

I stagger backwards in shock, murmuring "you filthy vermin..." as they dance amongst my horde of quarters, nickels and dimes. My hand keeps spasmodically reaching toward the box, then pulls away.

I have to think fast as my energy ebbs with each passing moment. I put the box inside a bigger box. Okay. Next, I decide to take the box out into the hallway, praying that the Swedish couple (who practically live in the hall brushing their dog) will not be there. Coast is clear but it's obvious dumping a mound of change and scurrying creatures onto the floor will bring out unamused neighbors, who seeing the spectacle, will in turn have me evicted, ultimately leading to a triumph of the roaches (*aka* the forces of evil). Stealthily I make my way to the roof.

In the moonlight, I dump out the change and let the wee demons scatter (prey not upon my pantlegs). I pluck lunar kissed doubloons from the pile – over seven dollars worth. Too hungry to weep, I am off to the bodega for sustenance.

After my frugal repast, I begin the inner process of healing the nights damage. I move on, deciding to get very into reggae and to cover my walls with tinfoil in homage to Andy Warhol's Factory. Kitty gives me an understanding look that says, "Listen, you did what you had to do and it's over. Forgive. Forget. Now, pony up with the Friskie's Buffet or I will be forced to maul you with my claws."

**FOR SUBSCRIPTIONS
TURN TO PAGE 7.**

The
ECLECTIC

| April 1999 | Volume 1 Number 3 | Free |

CONTENTS

Quotations

"Did you ever admire an empty headed writer for his or her mastery of the language? No." Kurt Vonnegut in *Palm Sunday.*

"It is difficult to appreciate the poets when your shoe is pinching." Henri de Montherlant in *The Girls.*

"Men are OK from thirty to forty-five; if they're careful they can stay about the same. After that it's an increasing struggle because of jowl and neck lines, even if the waist can be restrained." Alan Clark bemoans the loss of his good looks in *Mrs. Thatcher's Minister.*

"A terrible, terrible thing. She started coming out into the street and telling people the truth about themselves." A small town woman slips into madness in Moritz Thomsen's *Living Poor.*

Books

Failure Artist

The Courage and Sadness of Moritz Thomsen
Lincoln MacVeagh

In 1964 Moritz Thomsen joined the Peace Corps and was sent to Ecuador. Moritz had a terrible time learning Spanish, but he was nothing if not determined and slowly he picked up the language by sheer force of will. He noticed that the Ecuadorians liked fancy phrases and whenever he was introduced to someone he was greeted with the formal phrase, "A sus ordenes," at your service. *"...I began to reply with a few gracious comments of my own. 'A su servicio,'*

Moritz Thomsen: a su servicio.

I would say, smiling brightly and shaking my new friend's hand. 'A su servicio,' at your service. Someone drew me aside one day and pointed out very discreetly that if I were saying anything at all, I was only making a toast, 'Here's to your bathroom.'" Moritz was always the butt of his own jokes.

Thomsen was born in 1915. He was the grandson of a Danish peasant who left home at the age of twelve because his family could no longer afford to feed him. He went to sea. At twenty five Moritz's grandfather married and came to America. He worked as a day-laborer in Maine and as a meat-packer in Chicago; he tried homesteading in Nebraska. Nothing paid. Then some-thing miraculous happened. He moved his family to Seattle, went in to business and became one of the richest men in America. In the early 1900's he bought the entire peninsula of Acapulco thinking to build a railroad, and in 1927 he sold one of his companies to Nabisco for $12 million. Moritz's grandfather even survived the stock market crash with a small fortune in tact. In 1932 one of the Seattle newspapers ran a picture of him with the caption, "Losses twenty-two million; still smiling."

Like other successful men of his age, Moritz's grandfather was a tyrant, but he was a stylish and talented one. Moritz's father, in contrast, was just a bully. Charley Thomsen, heir to a vast and complicated business empire, was a callow and self-important man. We can forgive many of the failings of someone born to great expectations who has not the personality to live up to them, but Moritz's father was worse than weak. He was touched by evil.

Late in life, Moritz wrote to his mother asking if she remembered any good qualities in his father, her ex-husband. *"Well,"* she wrote back, *"he had beautiful blue eyes."* Beyond that she could only remember a story her sister-in-law had told her: *"In Seattle when he was fifteen, sixteen, he wired two cats together by their tails and hung them over a clothes line, then he sat there on the back steps and watched them tear each other to pieces."*

Moritz's parents were married for five years. During the separation Charley Thomsen paid his friends in the Seattle police to spy on his wife's house, collecting bogus evidence of adultery, and after the divorce Charley kept the children. The family moved into an enormous mansion, which Moritz's father had built and christened Wildcliffe, and which Moritz and his sister mockingly referred to as *Ye Wildee Cliffee.*

Wildcliffe was Charley Thomsen's dream house, but even he was unhappy there. He was especially unhappy one day in 1931 when the dog Missy broke into the hen house and killed all the hens. Moritz watched what happened afterwards from his window. *"The hen house was hidden by the trees but after a time my father appeared, walking backward and dragging the dog by her hind feet. When she tried to nip or lick his hands he clubbed her flat. Near a barbed wire fence he took a short loose roll of wire and twisted one end of it around the dog's head; then he wrapped her body to the fence so that she stood upright but immobilized. He disappeared but returned immediately with the bodies of a dozen dead chickens, and he strung these around the dog's neck, a necklace of dead birds, all the time yelling and kicking at the howling dog... My father went to the barn finally; the dog, fastened to the fence as though she had been nailed there, did not move or cry until my father appeared with the shotgun, and the dog covered with mud, feathers, blood, and her own shit, began to howl. And my father, wanting to kill her slowly, I suppose, steadily cursing, stood ten yards or so away and fired three times into the shuddering carcass."*

Moritz was sixteen when his father killed Missy and he detested his father ever since. Family was the first great disaster of his life. The second was World War II.

Moritz was drafted in 1940, shortly after graduating from Columbia. He spent a while on permanent KP duty and a few months guarding an army base water tower in California. After Pearl Harbor he volunteered to become a pilot. He failed his pilot training and became a bombardier instead.

"Does the fudge brownie come in low fat?"

The bombardier is the person on a bombing crew who actually aims and drops the bombs, and by 1943 Moritz was stationed at an airfield in England. He flew twenty-seven missions over Europe. It was the general rule that 50% of the airmen died before finishing their term of active duty and during the next eighteen months Moritz watched roughly half of his friends die. Many of the others went insane. Moritz describes the disintegration of his neighbor Lieutenant Hall as typical. Hall was about to be made squadron commander and as a result he was moved into a better cottage: *"That night in his new cottage he dreamed a dream. Those in the upstairs rooms awoke to hear him yelling, 'Bail out, bail out, bail out' – and the crashing of broken glass. He burst out of the second-story window, bounced off the roof of a little downstairs room where the enlisted soldiers shined shoes, and still shouting, still asleep, landed on the cement entranceway with a grotesquely broken leg."* Hall was dismissed with an LMF. Lack of Moral Fiber.

Meanwhile, in the wartime press the American bomber crews were praised as heroes. Moritz was a reliable bombardier but he was never able to see the glory in it. Flying combat missions was a matter of soul shattering terror and it was more or less useless to boot. The bombs he dropped were more likely to fall on German cabbages than German bridges. Targeting was not an exact science and for many bombardiers like Moritz the war ended not in victory but in shame. On D-Day, while the infantry stormed the beaches, the airforce got lost in cloud cover. Whole squadrons dropped their payloads on the advancing allied troops and when the truth came out it was an embarrassment to be seen around London in an airforce uniform.

The war left Moritz empty. Then he went home to visit father and discovered that all of his former possessions had been sold or thrown away. In their place

Moritz found only a gold starred banner tucked away in a kitchen drawer: *"A gold star in your window was a real feather in your cap; it announced to the public that your son (or your brother, husband, uncle – you name it) was dead."* Moritz gave up. He lost interest in humanity and determined to spend the rest of his days in seclusion.

For the next twenty years Moritz farmed a small ranch in northern California. He raised pigs and each year he lost a little more money. By 1964 it cost him 18 cents a pound to get a hog to market and the selling price was 12 cents a pound. He went bankrupt. His assets totaled $23. Desperate and too proud to appeal to his wealthy father for money, Moritz applied for the Peace Corps. He was accepted and sent to a far away place called Ecuador: *"Spewed out of that deadening rural life, screaming with rage and self-pity, as bloody and battered as a new-born child, I was given another chance at a brand new kind of life."* Moritz was forty-eight.

At the same time that he became a Peace Corps volunteer, Moritz also became a writer. He had always wanted to write and now he got the idea of sending articles about the Peace Corps to the *San Francisco Sunday Chronicle.* Before leaving for Ecuador, Moritz presented the idea to an editor named Stanleigh Arnold. Arnold politely told him the paper wasn't interested: *"The rest of the story simply doesn't make sense. I went* into Peace Corps training, started writing about it, and sent the articles to Stan – who published them."

The result was the basis of Moritz's first book, *Living Poor: A Peace Corps Chronicle.* It is an engrossing book and in plain language it describes a world which most literate people have never seen nor even imagined. *Living Poor* does not read like a series of newspaper articles strung together. It reads like a well-plotted novel and it tells the story of four years that Moritz spent living in the desperately poor coastal town of Rio Verde, in the black populated province of Esmeraldas. Rio Verde was a brutal place where some men died quickly in drunken brawls; others died slowly of starvation; and everyone greeted death with more relief than fear: *"...on the beach I watched a Policia Rural beating a man with the flat of his machete as he drove him along the sand where the sea had wet it; the man while drunk had raped a nine-month-old baby and was being taken to die... There are things that cannot be atoned for, and as the machete came down again and again upon the man's body there was a look on his face that I can only say was joyful. How he longed, how he yearned to die."*

Despite the misery, something in Moritz responded to Rio Verde with singing heart, and although all of his bright-eyed Peace Corps ventures failed miserably to help the town, his time there was not wasted. Moritz left Rio Verde with something he had never had before. A friend. The man's name was Ramon Prado and he was the first human being Moritz ever loved and the first human being who ever loved him back:

"'I think you're a good man; let's be brothers,' Ramon Prado, the young fisherman, said to me as we sat eating oranges and talking by candlelight on a night of profound darkness, and it was said so naturally, so sweetly, that for a second the room actually blazed with light.

'Yes,' I said, extremely moved, 'let's be brothers.'"

In Rio Verde Moritz helped Ramon crawl out of poverty and in return Ramon taught Moritz joy. When Moritz left the Peace Corps the two of them joined forces. For $4,000 they bought a vast tract of land in the jungle and set about trying to farm it. Moritz was in the jungle for ten years and the record of his life there is contained in his brilliant memoir *The Farm On The River Of Emeralds.* It is Moritz's best book but it is also deeply tragic. If Rio Verde was brutal, the jungle was more so, and the struggle for survival took its toll. The friendship between Moritz and Ramon fell apart over bitter disputes about money and power, and Moritz was eventually forced off the farm. It was the third great disaster of Moritz's life. He was past sixty and his health was failing. He retired to the city of Guayaquil and started work on his last two books, *The Saddest Pleasure* and *My Two Wars.*

In 1990 I was living Quito and I had the chance to meet Moritz. A neighbor of mine who was also his close friend gave me his address and asked me to deliver a tin full of chocolate chip cookies to him. I was pleased to do it. Moritz was something of a legend in Ecuador. During his time in the Peace Corps he had played a small political role in the country and among the poor blacks in Esmeraldas province he was still remembered for his courage and honesty. He was also well known among Quito's literati. He had by then published his first two books, both to excellent reviews, and he was preparing to publish his third. In short, he was Ecuador's most famous writer. In my imagination I pictured him as a stern intellectual figure, sitting in a leather chair, surrounded by bookcases.

Wandering around Gauyaquil, looking for his apartment, I was surprised to discover that Moritz lived two flights above a seedy Chinese restaurant in the middle of a busy commercial street. I climbed the stairs and knocked on his door. There was no answer. I knocked again and minutes later Moritz appeared. He said he had difficulty walking; he apologized for the delay and invited me in. I hesitated momentarily. I was shocked by Moritz's physical appearance and even more shocked by the squalor of his surroundings. Here was an old man with sunken cheeks, ragged clothes and no teeth, who lived in a small two room apartment the walls of which were cracked and stained brown with mildew. All around were scattered piles of rotting papers and worm-eaten books. The door to his bedroom was open and when I peeked in I saw nothing but a single twin bed and a mosquito netting that hung from the ceiling.

Moritz was a poor man. Somehow it never occurred to me that a gringo in Ecuador could be poor and it took me some time to recover from my embarrassment. Surely Moritz had seen enough boys like me to know exactly what I was thinking but he did not hold it against me. We started talking and I soon forgot that his shirt had no buttons and his kitchen had no fridge. Moritz was funny, interesting, kind and thoughtful. One knew at once that he was admirable. I wanted to be like him and secretly I wondered if it were possible to do so without being quite *that* poor.

I visited Moritz three times over the next few days and little by little he told me pieces of his history. The last time I saw him he told me about the day he went bankrupt in California and he hinted at the terrible unhappiness that accompanied the failure of his pig farm. I was surprised to hear him speak of unhappiness. I insisted that, in the end, he must be pleased to have gone broke, to have been forced into the Peace Corps, to have come to Ecuador. He had learned so much about himself and others since leaving the States; I could not believe that he would give that knowledge up for anything in the world.

I do not remember Moritz's exact words but he said something to the effect: *"Shit, if I had my choice I would still prefer to be a successful hog farmer. To hell with wisdom and suffering."*

Moritz Thomsen died of cholera in 1991. He was buried in a cemetery near the slums, and five people attended the funeral. One of them was a doctor who later billed him for the three hours she spent at the ceremony. Only Moritz could have appreciated the joke.

Reviews

The Autobiography of Jawaharlal Nehru

by Jawaharlal Nehru

Oxford University Press, 1990 (reprint)

Last month I reviewed Gandhi's auto-biography. This month it is Nehru's turn. Jawaharlal Nehru was India's *other* politician. A generation younger than Gandhi, Nehru came to prominence in the Congress Party during the late 1920's and over the next two decades he spent more than eight years in jail as a political prisoner. In 1947 India was granted independence and Nehru was elected the country's first Prime Minister. He governed until his death in 1964 and was succeeded in power first by his daughter Indira and later by his grandson Rajiv (both of whom, confoundingly enough, had the last name Gandhi — no relation).

Nehru's autobiography, originally published in 1936 under the title *Toward Freedom*, tells the story of his early life. He was born in 1889 the only son of a prominent lawyer. His youth was easy and pleasant and at sixteen he was sent to England for his education. Nehru was 23 when he returned to India as a qualified barrister and already the pattern of his life seemed set. He was to marry and follow his father into practice, and in twenty years time he was to send his own son off to England for an education. Fair enough, but Nehru couldn't do it. He found the law excruciatingly dull. He pursued it listlessly and was no good. His interest drifted toward politics.

In 1916 Nehru met Gandhi and fell in with the non-violence movement. While others pushed for the modest goal of Dominion status, Nehru argued the need for full independence. He became very popular very quickly and soon he was besieged by supporters everywhere he went. Songs were written about him

The People Downstairs

Hello! I see you're almost all moved in. Great job painting the place.

Thanks!

MOM

and on holy days large crowds of well-wishers gathered outside his house. Nehru viewed his new found adulation with remarkable coolness. *"I took to the crowd, and the crowd took to me, and yet I never lost myself in it; always felt apart from it… I could not get rid of the idea that their affection was meant not for me as I was, but for some fanciful image of me that they had formed."*

Nehru's modesty seems genuine. While he became a hero to the masses he was teased for it at home. *"The high-sounding and pompous words and titles that were often used for all those prominent in the national movement, were picked out by my wife and sisters and others and bandied about irreverently. I was addressed as* Bharat Bhushan – *"Jewel of India"*, Tyagamurti – *"O Embodiment of Sacrifice"; this light hearted treatment soothed me, and the tension of those solemn public gatherings, where I had to remain on my best behavior, gradually relaxed. Even my little daughter joined in the game. Only my mother insisted on taking me seriously, and she never wholly approved of any sarcasm or raillery at the expense of her darling boy."*

Throughout his book, Nehru demonstrates a quiet personal charm that is in marked contrast to the hard egotism of his political mentor. Nehru admired Gandhi tremendously but there was also something about Gandhi's rigidity that outraged Nehru's sense of decency: *"There was something unknown about him, which, in spite of the closest association for fourteen years, I could not understand at all and filled me with apprehension."* And as to Gandhi's abhorrence of sex, *"Personally I find this attitude unnatural and shocking, and if he is right, then I am a criminal on the verge of imbecility and nervous prostration."*

Nehru's autobiography is often insightful and rarely dull. It is not as gripping as Gandhi's book, but then Gandhi had the advantage of being inspired by an insane fanaticism. Simple human decency rarely makes for such good copy.

Commentary

Apple Tort

T.E. MacVeagh

Adam, Eve, and their Progeny v. GOD, the Omnipotent Creator of Heaven and Earth

Traditionally, Adam and Eve have accepted blame for eating the Apple from the Tree of Knowledge, and the consequences visited upon them because of the incident have been considered just. But modern tort theory allows another reading of the biblical tale; one which suggests that the apple tree was an attractive nuisance; that God's placement of the tree was negligent; that God was in breach of the duty of care owed to his guests; and that God owes tort damages to the estates of Adam and Eve. To explore these questions, we granted certiorari.

Facts

Sometime shortly after creation, and after the creation of the first woman, the plaintiff Eve was persuaded by the Serpent, a third party whose relationship to the Defendant has not been properly established, to eat an apple from the Tree of Knowledge in the Garden of Eden, a residence owned and maintained by the Defendant. Shortly thereafter Adam also ate of the apple. As a direct result of eating this apple, plaintiffs alleged and have adequately shown damages of permanent discomfort during labor and birth, effecting both themselves and their descendants; a lowered standard of living requiring plaintiff Adam and his descendants to work full time; and loss of domicile.

They also claim pain and suffering damages equal to the total value of mankind's anguish computed since the beginning of time. Plaintiffs sue for injunctive relief, seeking salvation.

Warrant of Habitability

The plaintiffs present two theories of liability. First, plaintiffs claim that the home provided by the Defendant violated an implied promise of habitability. They claim that the presence of the Tree of Knowledge in the Garden of Eden rendered the premises unfit for human habitability. Defendant counters that He warned plaintiffs of the defect before they took residence in the Defendant's property. We find that the Defendant's express warning was sufficient to overcome any normally implied warranty. The plaintiffs argue that due to a shortage of housing there is a disparity of bargaining power between plaintiffs and Defendant, such that the Defendant-landlord possessed an unconscionable advantage over the plaintiff-tenants. Upon this ground, it is said, any waiver of a warranty of fitness should be voided as contrary to public policy. O'Callaghan v. Waller Beckwith Realty Co., 155 N.E.2d 545 (1958).

The plaintiffs, however, are estopped from utilizing such an argument by reason of their own actions: plaintiffs made no show that they were concerned about the presence of the Tree of Knowledge, that they tried to negotiate with the Defendant about its modification or elimination, or that they made an effort to find an alternative residence. Besides, we agree with the Supreme Court of Illinois that, "judicial determinations of public policy cannot readily take account of sporadic and transitory circumstances [like housing shortages]. They should rather, we think, rest upon a durable moral basis." O'Callaghan v. Waller Beckwith Realty Co., 155 N.E.2d 545 (1958).

Duty Owed A Createe

The plaintiffs' second theory of liability suggests that as guests in the Defendant's residence, they were owed a duty of care such that the Defendant maintain the property in reasonably safe condition so that invitees would not be unnecessarily exposed to danger. This includes a duty to warn if the possessor is unable to maintain the property in reasonably safe condition. Basso v. Miller 352 N.E.2d 868 (1976). The Defendant argues that at the time of construction it was technologically impossible to create a worldly paradise without the presence of a Tree of Knowledge, and that therefore his warning to the plaintiffs was sufficient to satisfy his duty to his invitees.

Deferring to the Defendant's unique expertise in the field, the plaintiffs do not suggest that the Tree of Knowledge was an avoidable defect. Rather they argue that the duty of the Defendant goes beyond that of owner to invitee: the relationship rather is one of creator to createe, and a standard of strict liability should adhere. A mere warning, therefore, was not enough to excuse the Defendant of liability.

The question as to the duty a creator owes to a createe is one of first impression for this court. While Defendant suggests an analogy to the duty between parent and child, we agree with the plaintiffs that the comparison is not perfectly apt. Plaintiffs have argued that one reason parents may not always be held accountable for the harm done to their children is that their act of bringing children into the world is often the result of strong biological urges rather than conscious decision. The Defendant's act of creation, by contrast, is reported to be an entirely voluntary act. Plaintiffs suggest, therefore, an analogy to the strict liability that a manufacturer bears for its products. This analogy also is not precisely on point in that the liability of a manufacturer generally extends to injury suffered by third parties rather than by the products themselves. However, we have the unusual situation in this case that the products are the third party. As always, the obligation of this court is to the spirit of the rules rather than their letter. Accordingly we find

that a regime of strict liability should govern the relationship between creator and createe. As Defendant admits to being creator, His liability has been adequately shown.

Remedy

Remedy is also a matter of dispute. There was some indication at the trial that the pain and suffering of mankind was an inappropriate measure of injury. The Defendant suggested that an offset be allowed for the value placed on human dignity, free will, and intelligence. But we agree with the plaintiffs that these are of little worth compared to the loss of eternal life and happiness. It seems therefore that to the extent that eating the apple has kept mankind from gaining heaven in the afterlife, some remedy must be made available. As monetary damages are insufficient to compensate the loss of eternal happiness, we grant an injunction: the Defendant must open the gates of heaven to all of those that have been denied entrance.

Some controversy has arisen over whether or not the ordered relief has already been granted. Some years after the apple incident, while the case was still in the pre-trial stage, one Jesus Christ, apparently an agent of the Defendant, came to the plaintiffs and "died for the sins of mankind." The effect of this action is unclear, though some testimony suggested that it would have the required effect, offering salvation to humanity. However, the question of how far this offer of salvation extends remains unanswered. We remand the case to the trial court for further hearings on the meaning of Christ's message with instructions to dismiss the plaintiffs' suit if it turns out that the remedy we have ordered has already been extended in private negotiations. If Christ's death fails to provide the ordered relief, the court is instructed to order injunctions against the Defendant supplementing the relief as necessary to conform with this opinion.

It is so ordered.

Reminiscence

Dooley's Boat

Lincoln MacVeagh

At the age of fifty-two Pat Dooley was still a handsome man. He was six foot five, strong and vital. He had thick auburn hair and he kept a bushy mustache of the same color. He looked like Paul Bunyon.

Dooley was a fisherman. In 1991 he left his Seattle home to buy a second-hand boat in New Orleans. He got a good price at auction and after just three weeks he was ready for the trip home. He headed out into the Gulf, then down through the Panama Canal, and soon he was working his way back up the Mexican coast.

At the port city of Salinas, Dooley went ashore to re-fuel. His timing was unlucky. He arrived in Salinas the day before the Mexican President was scheduled to speak at a conference there and the local authorities were on high alert.

Two hundred meters from the dock Dooley was met by a Mexican Coast Guard vessel. The belligerence of the officials surprised him. Maybe they suspected Dooley was hauling marijuana and they thought a big bust would impress the President. In any case, they boarded Dooley's boat and started yelling questions at him.

Dooley spoke no Spanish and a terrible confusion arose. More officials were called over and the boat was searched. No drugs were found, but the search did turn up three shotguns and two high-powered rifles. In English, Dooley tried to explain. He said he used the guns to kill tuna and swordfish once they got hooked; he said the firearms were all legally purchased in the United States; he offered to show the officials his permits.

The Mexicans were not interested. In all likelihood they were just looking for a bribe and they talked up the guns so as to make Dooley understand that the bribe would have to be substantial. But Dooley was not accustomed to paying bribes and moreover, he was not conscious of any wrongdoing. He lost his temper and after a brief scuffle he was arrested.

For the next forty-eight hours Dooley was kept without food and interrogated under gun-point. He thought he was going to die. Finally he agreed to sign a confession that said he was an international terrorist helping to train Mexican insurgents. Dooley was sent off to prison and the next day his confession was amended to include a charge of attempted assassination against the Mexican President. This made sense since the President almost never goes to Salinas and the coincidence was too striking to overlook.

Dooley was sent to an open air prison some 100 kilometers inland. To an American it seemed a very unusual prison. It had both a distinct political culture and a well-defined class structure. The prison was run by a democratically elected President, and he and his lieutenants formed the upper classes. The lower class was made up of inmates who did not have enough money to buy their own food. These prisoners had to work for the President cleaning toilets in exchange for two meals a day at the prison restaurant.

Everything revolved around money. If your were poor you slept on cement; if you had a little money you could buy a hammock; and if you had lots to spend (and if you were committed to staying) you could buy blocks and mortar with which to build a small house. Whatever you needed from the outside, you could arrange to buy it for a small commission and there were even a number of prostitutes available. The prostitutes, however, were expensive, old and hideously ugly.

While it was possible to buy pretty much anything, Dooley quickly realized that having means didn't make prison life much more pleasant. It was impossible to keep money on you. Anyone who was thought to have more than the next man was so badgered by requests for loans that he soon went broke. And if he was resolute and didn't give his money away he was robbed.

Except for robbery, the prison was not a violent place. There were no guns and not many knives and at six foot five Dooley towered over everyone, so nobody bothered him. But even the smallest inmates were free from fear. There was a law against fighting. If two people were caught fighting the President had them thrown into special detention cells. Only the President had keys to these cells and he was allowed to keep inmates locked up as long as he wanted.

The big drawback of prison life was the food. Dooley could not get used to the cockroaches and flies that infested everything he ate and he was continually subject to the pains of amoebas and dysentery. Beyond that, Dooley's worst trouble was anxiety. Since he was never sentenced, nor even tried, Dooley had no idea how long he would be stuck in jail. Each passing week seemed like a decade and after the first month Dooley started thinking about escape.

In the old days you could arrange an escape simply by paying off the guards. But then the Governor passed a decree saying that prison guards had to serve out the sentence of any escapees and that option was more or less

closed off. Still it wasn't an impossible job. Dooley figured it would be easy to scramble onto the roof of the mess hall, and after that you just had to figure out a way to survive the thirty foot drop over the fence. As for slipping past the guards, you had to wait for a violent thunderstorm at night. The guards were all superstitious and they left their posts whenever lightning got too close.

Fortunately, Dooley never had to try escaping. He was a member of his local Rotary Club in Seattle and it happened that the Rotary Club was planning a big convention in Mexico City that year. Thanks to intense lobbying by some of his friends, the Rotary Club threatened to cancel the convention if Dooley was not set free. Suddenly the government in Salinas was willing to negotiate. After three months in prison Dooley paid a $5,000 fine to cover the cost of his arrest and he was released into the care of the U.S. Consul.

I was living with the Consul at the time and I spent the next two weeks showing Dooley around. He was a very nice man. He was remarkably free of bitterness and he had no inclination to make long speeches about the injustices he had suffered. He was mostly interested in flirting with the middle aged women in town and getting his boat back. He was too sick to have much success with either endeavor. Dooley had lost 55 lbs. in prison and his skin had turned a horrible yellow color. We took him to a doctor and found out he had hepatitis. The next day he flew home. It took him years to get his boat back.

Games

Sir Laffalot

Most people know Sir Laffalot as a fearless warrior, slow to anger but deadly when roused. It's true. But he has a sensitive side too and when he's not out slaying dragons he likes nothing better than to cuddle up with a romantic novel. He's even tried writing one himself.

The Darkness of the Duke's Back Passage is Sir Laffalot's first offering and like every good novel it strives to combine four central themes: religion, society, sex and mystery. Sir Laffalot starts with a bang and his opening sentence is near perfect: *"My God!" said the Duchess, "I'm pregnant! Whodunit?"* It goes downhill from there.

Sir Laffalot should stick to playing *Ex Libris*. This month's game is very similar to the well-known *Dictionary*, but instead of inventing fake dictionary definitions, players of *Ex Libris* re-write the first sentence of a novel.

Ex Libris: How To Play

1) Everyone is given a pen and a piece of paper. A player is chosen to lead the round and the leader selects a book from the bookcase: Willa Cather's *My Antonia*, for example.
2) Over the next few minutes everyone writes a fake opening sentence for *My Antonia*. Meanwhile, the leader copies out the real first sentence.
3) When everyone is finished writing, the leader collects all papers and jumbles them up. Being careful not to let the others see which paper he is reading from, the leader reads all the different opening sentences back to the assembled group.
4) Play then goes around in a circle with everyone trying to guess the proper first sentence.
5) When all players have made their guesses the correct answer is revealed.
6) Whoever has managed to trick the most people with his fake first sentence becomes the leader of the next round and a new book is chosen.

So, which of the following is the real first sentence of *My Antonia*?

a) Long after the first settlers crossed the plains, long after the first homesteaders built their farms, there were still young men travelling across the West, desperately searching for a small piece of land to call their own.
b) Billy Hunter looked up and asked for a drink.
c) The great Sir Laffalot™ buried his sword deep into the evil Duke's heart and Antonia swooned.
d) Antonia, my Antonia, was not a girl that everyone could have loved.
e) Last summer, in a season of intense heat, Jim Burden and I happened to be crossing Iowa on the same train.

Sir Laffalot says: **TOODALOO!!**

(The answer is e.)

The high life

TV Luv

David Garcia III

I dropped by my friend Neil's house the other night, and we ended up watching *2001* on TV. The place looked very neat, and I noticed that he had made a shrine to his girlfriend (who recently broke things off) on the mantle. There was a school picture of her in third grade, and lots of little colored rocks and shells. We opened some beers, and he got in bed, motioning me to sit in the chair as he turned on the television. The next thing he did was reach over to the nightstand, where a small doll monkey was perched, and he turned its head so that it could see the TV screen. I let this pass. It occurs to me that I now have three friends with monkey dolls. I think it was something the g-friend left behind.

After the movie he started flipping channels around. We saw:

An interview with Cher. On second thought, it might have been an interview with someone playing Cher in a TV movie. Cher no longer has flesh, only features. If she ever retires, Easter Island is the place.

A few moments of a Barbra Striesand vehicle, *Nuts,* in which she plays a wildly successful mid-life prostitute with sanity issues.

A snippet of a VH-1 program with one of the sisters from Heart discussing her notoriously overweight sibling. She says, "Well, the truth is that the whole thing was kind of the opposite of what people think. She thought she looked okay, but no one else did."

On Baywatch, an impossibly gorgeous girl lifeguard cries in a shower scene. She has lost a swimmer that very day. I want to say to her, "Forget him, move on with your life. He was only a guest star, not a series regular. Why don't you go look in the mirror – that can't help but cheer you up."

We flip to another program, apparently from the would-be Olympian ski instructor's genre. Two guys on the slopes are staring at a haughty beauty. She approaches them, shakes her raven tresses, and puts on sunglasses to talk to them. The guys, not the sunglasses. I kind of recognize this actress. I think her name is Finola or something. She is always cast as an aristocratic dancer, a soap opera vixen, or the snobbish unfaithful wife of a rich man. She's never in remotely good movies, and I think she's been doing the exact same thing for about 15 years. I find it oddly sad that she hasn't moved on to more prestige projects, or more varied rolls, or even to a fulfilling life outside of film. I know this is silly. She probably has a great life, and tons of money from steady work as a lowbrow-highbrow babe.

She saunters off majestically, and the men eye her lithe, cheetah hindquarters and comment:

"Dude. She was checkin' you out, TJ."

"Forget it, Dude. Her earrings are bigger than my balls."

**FOR SUBSCRIPTIONS
TURN TO PAGE 7.**

The
ECLECTIC

May 1999	Volume 1 Number 4	Free

CONTENTS

Quotations

"Do you know how one says never in camp slang? 'Morgen früh,' tomorrow morning." Primo Levi in *Life In Auschwitz*.

"Every young woman is sitting on her fortune, if she only knew it." What Dorothy Parker learned from a prostitute's lecture in *The Constant Reader*.

"It is the dirtiest, filthiest, lousiest, most obscene piece of writing that I have ever seen in print... But it comes from a Negro and you cannot expect any better from a person of this type." Democrat Thomas Bilbo of Mississippi denounces Richard Wright's autobiography Black Boy on the floor of the U.S. Senate, from *The Congressional Record, 1945*.

"I once asked a colored waiter who seemed specially hearty and friendly in his work, why he smiled all the time. 'I am not smiling,' he answered, 'I am just showing my teeth.'" Richard Wright in *Conversations With Richard Wright*.

The Eclectic is owned and published by Linoleum Palace, Inc., 43-05 31st Ave., #2, Astoria, NY 11103. Copyright © 1999 by Lincoln MacVeagh. All rights reserved. Unsolicited submissions will not be considered or returned.

Past Sixty-Third And Stoney Island

Richard Wright Leaves Home

Lincoln MacVeagh

The first time Richard Wright applied for permanent work at the post office in Chicago he was turned down because, after a lifetime of malnutrition, he did not pass the minimum 125lb weight requirement. He gorged himself to fatten up. In 1937 he re-applied and was offered a job. *"When a Negro in Chicago gets a job in the post-office that's about as high as he can get. So he tells his friends he's at Sixty-third and Stoney Island –* the southern boundary of the Black Belt, the hurdle into the white man's world."* It would have meant $2,000 a year and a place in the upper echelon of black society, but Wright turned it down. He didn't want to live on Sixty-third and Stoney Island. He moved to New York to write instead: *"I thought I ought to give myself a chance and that's what I did."*

Less than ten years later Wright had proved himself beyond a shadow of a doubt. His first collection of stories *Uncle Tom's Children* (1937) was followed by *Native Son* (1940), *12 Million Black Voices* (1941), *Black Boy* (1945) and *American Hunger* (not published until 1977). Few authors this century have had such a run and Wright's work was not only good but also massively

I have stopped practicing the '-isms.'

popular. *Native Son* was the first book by a black author to be chosen as a Book-of-the-Month Club selection and it sold 215,000 copies within three weeks. *Black Boy* sold more than 500,000 copies in its first six months. Before Wright broke with the Communist Party, even the Soviets were eager to read him. Marking a sure sign of his importance, both literary and political, the USSR printed 75,000 copies of *Uncle Tom's Children* in Russian.

During the same period that Wright became famous, he also became a husband and a father. Actually, he became a husband twice, but the first one doesn't count. Wright proposed to Dhima Meadman because he was afraid that Ellen Poplar, the woman he was in love with, would refuse to marry a black man. In fact, Ellen would have taken him if he were green and it came as a nasty surprise when she got back from a long vacation and Richard told her he was engaged. Fortunately, Wright's marriage to Dhima only lasted a year and Ellen was still around when he got divorced. Richard and Ellen were married immediately and shortly afterwards Wright witnessed the birth of

his first daughter, Julia.

For a moment it seemed that Wright had all a man could ask for. He had a good income, an international reputation and a loving family. But when Wright looked about him, he still felt trapped on Sixty-third and Stoney Island.

In the early 40's Wright read a newspaper story about a black family that owned a home in Brooklyn but always dressed as servants in their own house to avoid antagonizing their white neighbors. Wright thought that by proving himself intellectually he could escape that sort of nonsense, but he was wrong. It didn't matter how many books he'd written, when Wright wanted to buy a house in Greenwich Village he had to set up the bogus "Richelieu Realty Co." and have his lawyer act as intermediary so as not to give away his race.

Wright had a thick skin. He was accustomed to the venom of both the Communists, who considered him a traitor, and of the right wing who hated him for ever having been a Red in the first place; he was used to being vilified by segregationist whites and he was not surprised when black church leaders denounced *Native Son* for using the angry and violent character of Bigger Thomas to portray black youth. These attacks were largely political and Wright had learned to ignore them. But what he could not ignore were the constant restrictions placed upon his personal life because of his color. It galled him that he had to travel 100 blocks up to Harlem to get a haircut and it infuriated him that he could not walk down the street with Ellen, who was white, without being insulted. Wright yearned to escape and in 1945 he put a deposit down on an isolated farmhouse in Vermont. The deal was called off at the last minute when the seller found out Wright was colored. It was one indignity too many.

"When the war is over and if I am lucky," he wrote to a friend, *"I want to leave the hatreds of race and the pressures of the United States behind and go live in a foreign land where the currency is cheap…"*

For Wright, however, nothing was easy. The U.S. government was afraid of his opinions and was reluctant to let him leave the country. Wright had to enlist the help of Levi-Strauss and Gertrude Stein to get the French authorities to give him an official invitation, and only after a prolonged struggle with the State Department (which twice "lost" his invitation) was he granted a passport.

Wright finally got to Paris in 1946 and from the moment he set foot on French soil he was enchanted. It is no wonder. Whereas in the United States Wright was seen as a dangerous political figure, in France he was treated as a literary celebrity. Despite the trouble of constant social obligations, he enjoyed it. More importantly, he was amazed by the perfect freedom of movement and association the Parisians allowed him. In an interview given after his return to New York, Wright said: *"I did not encounter one iota of racial feeling in*

France. Not a bit of it. As an American Negro I was naturally sensitive to their attitude. But a Negro is not a Negro in Paris. He's just another Frenchman. Their definition of a Frenchman is cultural, not biological. The French just have no attitude toward Negroes because they don't seem to be aware of any necessity to treat them any differently from anyone else."

For Wright life in France was a revelation and it made his re-adjustment to American difficult. In New York he was immediately re-introduced to the ugly problem of being black. His Italian neighbors in Greenwich Village muttered "nigger" under their breath as he walked by; the local shopkeepers called him "boy"; certain restaurants were once again off limits; and on one occasion, while eating with a white woman, he was served salted coffee (apparently a popular trick played on blacks at the time).

To most Americans, both white and black, such occurrences were so commonplace as to be beneath notice, but to Wright, who had seen a better way to live, they were intolerable. More-over, he did not want to expose his daughters to the trauma of racism and already the five-year-old Julia had been barred from using a department store rest room because of her color. After just a few months in the States, Wright decided to take his family back to Paris. In 1947 they went to France to settle permanently. The decision was widely criticized and Wright was accused of walking out on the struggle for civil rights, but he didn't much care. He'd had enough salted coffee.

The first direct result of Wright's moving to Paris was the filming of *Native Son.* The book had earlier been adapted for the stage (Orson Welles directed it on Broadway in 1941) and the play had made money, but Wright had never received a serious proposal for producing a movie version. Holly-wood had shown interest in *Native Son,* but in its own way. When Metro-Gold-wyn-Mayer offered to buy the rights they insisted on changing all the black characters to white ones. Then an independent producer named Joseph Fields wrote Wright's agent with an even

"The doctor says in six months we'll be ready for the real thing!"

better idea: *"Bigger Thomas, recast as a member of a white ethnic minority, would be one of four character types – a Negro, and Italian, and Jew and a Pole – applying for the same job. The Negro and the Jew, voluntarily withdrawing in favor of the neediest candidate, the one who had a family to feed, would realize at the end of the film that they, too, could have benefited from solidarity, as could anyone who did not enjoy equality."*

In France it seemed possible to make *Native Son* without bastardizing the book and when Wright was approached by the director Jacques Chenal, he threw all his energy behind the project. He not only wrote the script but, at the insistence of Chenal, he also agreed to act the lead role of Bigger. (He had to lose thirty pounds to do it, and in the movie stills he looks rather silly, but apparently he was okay.) Despite Wright's effort, the film was plagued by production problems.

Responding to American pressure, the French would not let Chenal begin shooting in Paris and Italy was also off-limits for similar reasons. At the same time, no well known actors were willing to appear in the film. *Native Son* was shot in Argentina with a cast of largely amateurs but Wright remained proud of the film at least up until its release in the States. By then the censor boards had so drastically cut the movie that much of it made no sense. For example, in the movie's climactic courtroom scene, censors objected to the politically charged speech of the defense and forced the soundtrack to be removed. *"As you know,"* Wright wrote his agent, *"the trial is shown with arms waving and mouths moving but nothing is heard."*

The film version of *Native Son* was a modest failure, both commercially and critically, and in the end so was everything else Wright worked on in France. Over the last nine years of his life Wright pushed himself hard, publishing three novels, five books of essays and travel writing, and countless short pieces, but nothing he wrote lived up to his earlier successes. Of the novels, *The Outsider* (1953) was the best, but its story did not support its length of 600 pages and it didn't sell well. *Savage Holiday* (1954) and *The Long Dream* (1960) had other faults and they sold not at all.

Naturally these failures disappointed Wright, but it would be wrong to make too much of them or to imagine his years in France as entirely bleak and unhappy. Wright was content in Europe. He traveled frequently; he became a citizen of the world; and he did not regret it: *"Paris has given me everything I hoped for – and even more."*

Still he was not without anguish. In 1959 Wright wrote to a friend: *"I am alone. I belong to no gang or clique or party or organization. If I'm attacked there is nobody to come to my aid or defense."* It was a sentiment that Wright often voiced toward the end of his life, and critics in the American press were quick to suggest that his exile had made him paranoid. It was not true. Wright was cautious because he had reason to be. (Files obtained under the Freedom of Information Act in the 1970's show that Wright had lived under FBI surveillance at least since 1942 when he was investigated for possible sedition charges, and the CIA kept track of Wright's activities in Paris using a number of paid informers). And if Wright felt alone, it's because he was alone.

Richard Wright was a humanist and a man of reason at a time when both racial hatred and the Cold War insisted on dividing men into separate camps. Black or White. Communist or Anti-Communist. Wright refused to be nailed down. *"I am a human being before being an American,"* he said in 1960, *"I am a human being before being a Negro."* Four months later Wright died of a sudden heart attack.

HA HA

Nick Bienstock

Top research scientists are performing a secret study to determine the origins of human nature. Why are some people eternal pessimists, while others can look on the sunny side of life despite the worst circumstances? To address this question, an elaborate controlled experiment is set up.

The scientists identify two identical twin boys raised in identical circumstances. One is a terrible lil' pessimist and the other is an unrepentant lil' optimist.

The scientists take the lil' pessimist and lower him by a rope to the center of a specially constructed room. The room is filled with everything that a little boy could want – candy, television, movies, computer games, trains, etc.. The scientists drop the boy in and watch through a one-way mirror. The lil' pessimist doesn't budge. He stands motionless in the center of the room. After four hours they pull him up and interview him.

"Why, lil' pessimist, did you just stand there in the room? Why didn't you play with the toys?"

"Well," he replies, "Nobody said I could play with them – and I didn't want to get into trouble. Besides, there were lots of sharp edges. Who knows, I could have hurt myself."

The scientists carefully note his comments.

They then lower the lil' optimist into an identical room, but this room is full of horse shit – up to his chest. The lil' optimist immediately begins to dance around the room, laughing and throwing the manure right and left with cries of joy.

The scientists can't believe what they are seeing and after watching for 15 minutes they pull him up, hose him off and interview him.

"Why, lil' optimist, were you so happy? You were dropped into a room full of shit up to your chest! But you were running around laughing and enjoying yourself. What were you thinking?"

"Well," says the lil' optimist, "With all that poop, I figured there must be a pony in there somewhere!"

~~~~~~~~~

PARDON ME, MR. GIULIANI!
[City street sign at 65th and Madison]

UNNECESSARY NOISE PROHIBITED

Reviews

Book of the Eskimos
by Peter Freuchen

(out of print)

Peter Freuchen first went to the Arctic in 1906 on board a Danish expedition ship. In 1910 he returned to Greenland to start a trading post on the western coast, just 900 miles south of the North Pole. Freuchen named his trading post Thule and for the next eleven years he lived amongst a remarkable tribe of people known as the Polar Eskimos. *Book of the Eskimos*, first published in 1961, is part social anthropology, part existential test case, and a good deal of Ripley's *Believe It Or Not!*

Consider the Eskimo delicacy *griviak*. In Summer the blubbery skin of a seal is stuffed with small birds and buried beneath a pile of rocks. Months pass and slowly the seal fat seeps into the birds, curing their meat. Now it is Winter and time for a feast. The *griviak* is dug up and brought inside. On the first day of the feast the little birds are still frozen. *"You get feathers and bones in your mouth, of course, but you just spit them out. Frozen meat always has an enticing taste, and as it dissolves in your mouth, you get the full aroma of the raw fermented bird... If you happen to come across a fully developed egg inside a bird, it tastes like a dream."* On the second day the birds have thawed out and their flavor changes. *"The breast is eaten by biting down on each side of the bone, and the bone can then be thrown away. This bares the innards and you can enjoy the various parts one by one. The blood clot around the heart has coagulated and glues the teeth together, the liver and the gall bladder have a spicy taste, while the bitter aroma of the intestines reminds one of a lager beer."* Ughh!

Beyond the nasty food and the remarkable sexual openness (Freuchen was pleasantly surprised when, setting

The People Downstairs

Introducing the people downstairs!

I wish I was dead!

Give me my CD back!

MRS BAGGALECCIO

DARCY

out on a long sled journey, one of his new friends lent him his wife for the trip), *Book of the Eskimos* describes a culture of strange philosophical depth developed in the face of an insanely brutal struggle to survive.

The English essayist Thomas De Quincy once remarked that the reason he did not often weep was because his thoughts descended *"a thousand fathoms too deep for tears."* But if De Quincy's knowledge was too deep for tears, think of the smiling young Eskimo woman Itusarssuk. Freuchen tells us that Itusarssuk was renowned for her love of children: *"She loved children because once, during a hunger period, she had to kill four of her own to spare them from the death of starvation. The oldest daughter was then so old that she could already sew mittens… This daughter had understood that it was hopeless to try to subsist, for there were no men at the place who could supply them with meat. She had seen that 'life was heavier than death' and had helped the mother hang*

three younger children, whereupon she had placed the string around her own neck so that the mother could pull it and fasten it to a hook… Itusarssuk was highly respected because of her deed."

Freuchen has a number of such fascinating stories and he tells them all with a good sense of humor and an easy, natural manner. Freuchen himself comes off as intelligent, adventurous and just slightly goofy. In the beginning of the book he talks about the eagerness with which he awaits a visit from his Danish girlfriend Michella. She has promised to spend three months with him, but when Michella's boat finally arrives there is no girlfriend on board, only *"one of those clumsy letters it is as embarrassing to write as to receive."* Freuchen is devastated, but it's hard not to side with Michella. What sort of nut expects his girlfriend to follow him to the Arctic Circle?

Book of the Eskimos is out of print in English but copies are still available at most libraries.

Commentary

Kosovo

T.E. MacVeagh

Kosovo is complicated. My general sympathies are pro-intervention. Milosovic and Serbia were committing great atrocities against a defenseless population and they had to be stopped. (Although the decision to bomb may have precipitated events, I do not believe that the bombing changed the essential nature of what was about to happen.) Somewhere behind my pro-intervention inclinations, I suppose I am committing myself to a general rule about how we should behave in situations like this. The rule would be something like: don't let people commit atrocities.

Although this rule sounds fairly inoffensive, it's awfully simplistic. The rule may be fine to determine our ideal, but in the real world you have to get soldiers to shoot at people to make it work. So there is no simple choice between "preventing an atrocity" and not preventing an atrocity. Also there is no way to prevent an atrocity easily. You have to put real live people at risk of death to have any hope of success. You may cause the deaths of these people and still fail to prevent the atrocity. And, in the end, your action to prevent an atrocity may inadvertently cause a greater atrocity.

These pesky questions quickly force us into a more nuanced position. Are you willing to act to prevent an atrocity if you have no chance of succeeding? Are you willing to act if you have a low chance of succeeding and you are likely to hurt yourself in the process? Are you willing to act if more of your people must die in the prevention than would have died in the atrocity? Are you willing to act if, as a result, a bigger atrocity occurs later?

To govern our practice, the rule has to be modified somewhat: don't let people commit atrocities when (i) it is in your power to prevent them; (ii) the necessary measures to prevent the atrocity will not cause you more suffering than you are trying to prevent; and (iii) your action will not give rise to a more awful situation down the road.

This more nuanced rule makes it possible to explain seemingly contradictory feelings about Kosovo, Chechnya, Tibet, Rwanda, East Timor, and other trouble spots. We couldn't intervene in Chechnya or Tibet because we could not risk a full-scale war between the U.S. and Russia or China. We could not intervene effectively in Rwanda because, perhaps, the killing happened too quickly and on too local a level. We could not intervene in East Timor because the level of atrocity did not justify the force that would be necessary to prevent it. Et cetera. If these distinctions sound somehow false and self-serving, it is not really the fault of the distinctions themselves. Given our rule above, they are perfectly sound if they are true. The trouble is distinguishing truth from convenience, distinguishing genuinely moral choices from merely self-interested ones.

Arguments are hard to resolve in this area because we have to figure out what "would have happened" in complex counter-factual situations. Could World War II have been averted if Chamberlain had opposed Hitler at Munich or if the Treaty of Versailles had been less punitive? These questions are worth discussing, but it is hard to know how to go about making a useful evaluation of the answers. We tend to rely on a few articles of faith, some received paradigms of historical causality and perhaps some random, floating prejudices.

In order to support U.S. intervention in Kosovo, we have to believe that we can stop the atrocity, that we can do so without significant casualties and that we will not destabilize the region in doing so. All of these are difficult arguments. Opposing the Serb military may well be necessary to stop future atrocities (in Montenegro, Macedonia, Bulgaria and Albania) as well as current ones, and if so it substantially strengthens the argument for intervention. But if you ask me to give evidence of how big an atrocity we may prevent, how much risk U.S. troops face, or how

destabilizing our intervention might be, of course, I am hard-pressed to provide specifics. Moreover, if we take our cues more from received historical paradigms and less from random floating prejudices, I have to admit that pro-intervention sympathies face at least one fairly overwhelming counterargument. Kosovo is recognized to be part of Serbia. Intervening to prevent Serbian atrocities in Kosovo is intervening in a sovereign nation's internal policies.

Now one might say that Serbia's particular set of internal policies is not worthy of much respect. But sovereignty, the rule that a nation may behave as it likes as regards its own nationals and within its own borders, has been the basis of our international legal system at least since Hobbes. And whatever theoretical respect you believe international law is worthy of, the rule of sovereignty can be understood as the summation of a vast practical experience with "what would happen" if you try to interfere with policies being executed within national borders.

"Aren't you ready yet?"

It is hard to stop nations doing what they want in their own territory. You're likely to suffer big set-backs. And you tend to destabilize things, both because all the other nations worry about when you might decide to interfere with their affairs, and because some other nation may use your example to invade or bully some neighbor with a less just cause.

Like the exclusionary rule in domestic courts, sovereignty is a hard rule to love. It seems to trump substantive morality and justice with procedural fussiness. Letting an ethnic majority persecute a minority because from some accident of history they live in one nation is as unsatisfactory as leaving a triple murderer at large because the proof of his crime was gathered without a warrant. And in both cases, we have revisionists busily questioning the value of the rules.

Those challenging the value of sovereignty as a guiding rule point out that sovereignty assumes problems are local. The rise of the global economy and environmental awareness challenges this assumption (Austria has reason to be unhappy if Germany builds unsafe nuclear plants on its border). More significantly, advocates of human rights, often relying on the appalling example of the Holocaust, challenge the assumption that the sanctity of nationhood outweighs opposition to intervention in any purely national atrocity. And now, in the wake of the demise of the Soviet Union as a polarizing force, some would argue the United States and the West finally have the overwhelming force to succeed in such interventions.

It may be that the revisionists will eventually rewrite our paradigms. But I admit that I still feel the world is too dangerous a place to give up the hard-won lessons embodied in the rule of sovereignty without further evidence. And reflection on the rule forces me to reconsider my pro-intervention stance. I remain unsure how we should act.

"It's the biggest Sport Utility Vehicle on the market."

Reminiscence

Selling Stories

Lincoln MacVeagh

In Madrid there is an old man who sits on the sidewalk of *La Gran Via* selling poems for 100 pesetas each. He is rude to his customers and his poems are bad but there is something romantic about selling poems on the street. Two summers ago, in New York, I tried it myself.

I cannot write poems so I sold stories instead. I bought a pegboard and painted it pink; I made a big sign saying "$1 Stories"; and on a Tuesday morning I set up shop outside the Metropolitan Museum.

Immediately I regretted my decision. No one was remotely interested in my stories. I smiled at an Asian hipster girl and she turned away in horror. A middle-aged woman with a miniature dog stopped in front of my pegboard on her way to the park.

"What is this?" she demanded.

"I'm selling stories."

"Yeah, I'll bet."

Standing next me was a roly-poly Hispanic man selling watercolor cityscapes (the same pictures one sees all over Manhattan; they are garish with a dark blue matting and they come from a distributorship in Queens). After half an hour he stepped over to chat.

"Stories," he said, "That's interesting. Sell many?"

"It's my first day."

"I figured. Let me tell you, one dollar, that's a joke. I sell my pictures for $25. If I sell five pictures I have a good day. You, you sell a story for a dollar, you need to sell a hundred stories. How you gonna do that? My advice is go home and fix your sign. It should say $5 for a story. You can go broke out here."

At ten o'clock the woman with the miniature dog passed by again. She looked angry.

"Okay, okay!" she said, "I'll buy a story. What are they about?"

I launched into a long plot description but she cut me off.

"<u>ONE</u> sentence."

"Sure," I said, "This one is about a man obsessed with sex; this one is about a fortune teller; this one is about a woman who hates her husband..."

"I'll take the last one." She handed me a dollar and walked off.

After the ice broke, I did fairly well. I sold twenty three stories before two o'clock. The buyers were tourists and rich housewives from the Upper East Side. Hating the husband was by far my most popular plot.

After a week outside the Met, I went down to Wall Street for the afternoon rush hour. I placed myself in front a blocked subway entrance on Broadway, across from the Church, and the first story I sold was to a young Caribbean boy passing out strip-joint flyers on the corner. He called me "Story Man" and he bought the story about a man obsessed with sex.

"Story Man!" he said the next day, "That was crazy!"

My first repeat customer was a man named David who worked in a typing pool at the Bank of New York. He wore a white, short-sleeved shirt and his plain red tie had a large inkstain on it.

"I'll buy a story," he said.

"Which one?"

"Whichever one you like best, I'm not fussy. Say, do you ever use the public toilets?"

"Not really."

"Well you shouldn't. They're awful! You should see them. Hideous! They're so dirty. And such nasty people. They're a disgrace to the City. You sure you never use the public toilets?"

I told David I was from out of town.

"You're a nice boy," he said, "I'll see you tomorrow." David bought a different story every day that week and he never mentioned the toilets again.

Whereas at the Met I was surrounded by people selling paintings and photographs, on Wall Street the merchants sold fruit, neckties and children's books. There was also a man named Yusef who sold newspapers to the commuters. Yusef was curious about the stories I sold and he bought one. When there was a lull in the street traffic he asked me where I was from. Yusef was from Nepal. He was newly arrived in New York and he liked to talk about his homeland.

To make conversation I asked Yusef the name of a famous Nepalese writer. Unfortunately, I forget the writer's name, but Yusef gave me a very detailed account of one of his stories. It was about a man who runs into an old woman friend. She suggests having lunch. The man has no money but he dares not admit it. The woman chooses a fancy restaurant and the man's heart sinks. He recommends the cheapest dishes. She selects the most expensive. She keeps ordering more and more food. When finally the bill comes, the man is

too gallant to refuse payment and while the woman calmly finishes her coffee he runs outside to pawn his bicycle. Then he has to pawn his clothes. The man is left completely broke and in the end he gets thrown in jail for being a pauper.

"It's very funny," said Yusef.

I agreed, but I had heard it before. Strangely enough, the story Yusef outlined had exactly the same plot as a story by Somerset Maugham titled *The Luncheon*. I have been curious ever since to know whether Maugham stole his plot from the Nepalese writer, or whether the Nepalese writer, knowing that few people in Nepal read English, stole his plot from Maugham.

After five days on Wall Street, Yusef felt comfortable enough to ask me a favor. He needed to get to the bank before it closed and he wanted me to watch his stack of papers. It was not a big deal. Most people who want to buy a paper don't care whether or not there is someone selling them. Yusef had left a pile of coins out and I watched six people in a row put their money down and make change all by themselves. The seventh man, however, didn't get it. He was a bulldogish man in a three piece suit and he stood in front of the stack of newspapers waiting to be served. Eventually I stepped over to help him.

"Thank you," he said gruffly, "Give me the *New York Post.*" He gave me a dollar and I handed him the *Post.* He waited impatiently for his change, but I didn't know how much change to give him. Having never bought the *Post* I didn't know how much it costs. I snatched the paper out of his hand and took a look at the top right hand corner. I had to squint to see the price.

"You don't know how much the paper costs?" The man was incredulous.

I gave him back his sixty cents change and he walked away muttering to himself. "A paper boy who doesn't know how much the paper costs! No wonder this city is going to pot!"

Games

Sir Laffalot

When Arthur pulled the sword out of the stone the whole kingdom went nuts. No one stopped to ask about the clever chap who put it there in the first place.

Sir Laffalot accepts that many of his accomplishments will go unheralded, but today he feels compelled to let you in on a secret. Sir Laffalot is a brilliant linguist.

His talent first became evident many years ago while playing a travel game with his mother. *The Alphabet Game* is a game for children on long car rides and Sir Laffalot enjoys it tremendously.

The Alphabet Game: How To Play
1) The object of the game is to find all the letters of the alphabet, in order, by examining road signs, billboards, license plates, etc..
2) Someone says "Start!" and everyone begins looking for an "A" printed outside the car.
3) When you find a letter, repeat it along with the word in which you spotted it. For example, "A – Florida" or "B – Buick." Two people cannot use the same letter from the same road sign.
4) After finding a letter, move on to look for the next letter in the alphabet.
5) The first person to find a "Z" wins.

Sir Laffalot was a whiz at *The Alphabet Game* and he has since gone on to greater linguistic challenges. The highest test for the linguist is the writing of palindromes and Sir Laffalot is a master of the art. His method is surprisingly simple: just think of sentences that read the same backwards as forwards. Wow!

Sir Laffalot can express almost any-thing as a palindrome and to prove it he offers a number of examples. Below are six sentences that Sir Laffalot has re-written as palindromes. Can you keep up with him?

Example 1: "Watch out Mrs. Karennina, the train's coming!"
Sir Laffalot: "Anna!"
Example 2: "Look Mr. Van Gogh, you've painted his left eye the wrong color."
Sir Laffalot: "Bad dab."
Example 3: "I started introducing myself as Rodney after I met my wife Dora."
Sir Laffalot: "A Rod was I ere I saw Dora."
Example 4: "The poet's rhyme scheme is trite and predictable."
Sir Laffalot: "A-B-B-A"
Example 5: "If you're asking me whether I looked at your diary Robert, the answer is yes."
Sir Laffalot: "Bob did I peep? I did Bob."
Example 6: "Out of clay, the Almighty fashioned the first man and called him Adam. Then He made the first woman and called her Eve. Eve loved Adam."
Sir Laffalot: "God pots Mom, Dad. Dad Mom's top dog."

Sir Laffalot says: TOODADOOT!!

The high life

Steve The Loser

David Garcia III

Of all the people I converse with on a daily basis, Anthony O. was the one I talked to most. He was a researcher for a large medical advertising firm and one of my biggest clients. Things were going swimmingly for him up until a few years ago, when he got promoted. What actually happened was that his company downsized all the other researchers, and left him in charge of everything. He was given an impressive title, and (I assume) a largish salary, and in exchange, he was asked to take on all the work of everyone that got fired. He managed this by "outsourcing" to people like me and he began to call every day. Anthony, who was in his late thirties at the time of his promotion, became a slave to the mania of his job. He was always paging me over the PA, calling me in a panic, leaving anxious voicemails, and sending terrified faxes and e-mails. Then he had a stroke. He recovered after a few months, and got right back on the treadmill, probably because he needed the job. For a week or two he was a changed man, calmer, and more laid back, but soon the workload got to him, and with the added stress of health worries, he was worse than ever. The other day he died, at his desk, from a heart attack. As I write this, I am still in a state of disbelief.

I met Steve the Loser at a Neil Young concert the night of the day that Anthony O. passed away. He was with my friend Pete, who bestows nicknames (Weasel, Jimmy Landlord, Freak Boy) on all his friends. Steve the Loser's father left the family to become a hairy Italian transsexual.

His brother just got out of jail sporting a colostomy bag. Steve the Loser is 30 and lives at his Mom's house, in a tiny room that he pays $700 for. He can't move out because he has two large dogs, inherited from a previous girlfriend, and he works painting boxes at a medical supply company. Every morning, he wakes up early to "smoke a bowl" of pot, walk his dogs and go to work. He spends the day getting high (his supervisors look the other way) and painting boxes. "Ah me and my drugs," he says, "I'll push a broom if I have to."

At the concert he is wearing big sloppy pants and a T-shirt with Bugs Bunny characters on it. "I support no band," he says. He is overweight, walks with a swaying lope, and has a sweet, gentle face. His body looks soft like a veal raised in captivity. Between songs, I find myself probing The Loser for an underlying depression but I find none. He does not yearn for the corridors of power. Steve The Loser is content to sweep those corridors. I don't call him by his nickname, but he doesn't seem to mind when the others do.

After every song, Steve the Loser lets out an incredible concert yell, the best I've ever heard. It's a primal whoop, which cuts through everything with freedom and violent joy. Neil Young plays *After the Goldrush* and everyone goes crazy. Steve the Loser whoops over and over, until I seriously think my eardrum is being damaged. A corporate type behind us tries to scream also, but it is pathetic in contrast to the powerful Loser.

There will always be pot, and funny TV shows like the Simpsons. Anthony O. was downsized to death. It's something to think about: Steve the Loser is happy and you're not.

**FOR SUBSCRIPTIONS
TURN TO PAGE 7.**

The
ECLECTIC

| June 1999 | Volume 1 Number 5 | Free |

CONTENTS

Quotations

"A Spartan seeing a man taking up a collection for the gods, said that he did not think much of gods who were poorer than himself." Plutarch in *The Moralia.*

"If falsehood, like truth, had only one face we would be in better shape. For we would take as certain the opposite of what the liar said. But the reverse of truth has a hundred thousand shapes and a limitless field." Montaigne in *Of prompt or slow speech.*

"Sir, I am not saying that you could live in friendship with a man from whom you differ as to some point; I am only saying that I could do it." Dr. Johnson wins his argument in Boswell's *Life Of Johnson.*

"There was never, I believe, a creature of our kind with less vanity than I." Jean Jacques Rousseau falls on his own sword in *The Confessions.*

Julia's Secret

Lincoln MacVeagh

This is a story about Julia Billegudd (pronounced "Bill Good") who was, for a time, the girlfriend of my friend David Harbright. I knew David in Costa Rica. The year I taught sixth grade math at the Country Day School, David taught seventh grade biology in the classroom next to mine. He was more or less my only friend. The rest of the faculty was cuckoo. They were all thumbs-up, let's-make-the-best-of-it types. In my first week at school fully six of them expressed their good feeling by winking at me from across a room. Go get 'em kid.

David, on the other hand, was thoughtful and subdued. He was an intense little man and it would never occur to him to pat someone on the back. When I first met him I thought he was much too serious for me. He was five foot six inches tall, skinny and muscular; he had short black hair and bright blue eyes; and he worked like he was serving a penance. During the week he got to school at five thirty every morning, and each Friday afternoon he took a long bus ride down to the Pacific Coast where he spent the whole weekend in the jungle, collecting information for a book he was writing about Costa Rican trees.

David was incredibly devoted to trees. I once asked him what he would do with himself if he didn't have to work for a living and he answered without hesitation that he'd spend all his time thinking about trees. When he showed me the manuscript of his book, it was already four hundred pages long and he said it was only half finished.

David was a difficult person to get to know. We didn't talk much in the beginning, but as time passed he became more relaxed around me and we started to become friends. I would like to think it was my own great charm that brought David out of his shell but I don't think that was the case. David relaxed because he found a girlfriend. He didn't tell me about her directly, but one Saturday, when David was meant to be in the jungle, I spied him holding hands with someone in the park.

The woman was Julia Billegudd, the same woman I mentioned earlier. Julia was a second grade teacher at Country Day. I didn't know her well, but I did meet her briefly at one of our enforced faculty get-togethers in the cafeteria.

I remembered her because when she introduced herself, her last name rang a bell. I went to college with a boy name Phillip Billegudd from New York and I asked her if she was related. She said she wasn't, and that was the end of it. Shortly afterwards we were interrupted by Mr. Phelps, the history teacher, who was yearning to get a Civil War

anecdote off his chest.

Apart from her last name, all I knew about David's new girlfriend was the gossip I picked up in the faculty lounge. The accepted wisdom at Country Day was that Julia was a cold fish and she was said to be rude and stand-offish. I heard a lot of nasty remarks about the way she dressed and, to be honest, some of them were justified. Julia could have been pretty if she tried but she made no effort whatsoever. She let her hair hang down on her face like a sullen teenager and she chose the most hideous slacks and blouse combinations imaginable.

Even so, you can't dislike someone for wearing ugly trousers and I suspect the real reason most people had it in for Julia was because she kept to herself so much. No one knew what she did with herself after school and unlike the rest of us, myself included, she never attended any of the dreary parties given by the various faculty members on Saturday nights.

So that was the girl David had matched up with. As soon as I saw them in the park together I was dying

to know more, but David was not someone I dared question about personal matters. Nonetheless, I guessed from David's manner that the romance was still on, and one day he made it official. I was sitting in his classroom after school when he came out with the news.

"I don't know if you know, but I've been seeing Julia Billegudd."

Not wanting to seem like a busybody, I told David I knew nothing about it and I asked him how it was going. He said Julia was a nice person. He said he liked her a great deal and he told me that it angered him to hear what others at the school said about her. There was a long pause in the conversation and then David coughed into his hand. Without looking up he said:

"I want to ask you something. It's not a big deal but I don't know what to make of it. I've been seeing Julia for a while now and I think we're pretty close but there's something I can't figure out. She never wants to see me on Thursday night. She's always busy. She says it's something private but she won't tell me what it is. If I ask her out to dinner

on a Thursday she won't come, but she won't say why either. She doesn't make excuses. She just says she won't tell me until she knows me better. It's sort of driving me crazy, but I can't decide whether it's any of my business."

I am always nervous about giving advice with regards to amoré, but David was clearly looking for some, so I simply told him that everyone has quirks and not to worry. I pointed out that David himself, with his mad love of trees, was not the most ordinary man and I said that two months isn't much time to know a person well. I told him to trust his feelings.

Of course I was talking out my ear, but David liked Julia so why not reassure him? It didn't much matter what she did on Thursday nights unless she turned out to be an axe murderer, and neither of us thought she was that.

Whatever I said, it must have been the right thing because the following weekend, on a Friday night (though I didn't make a point of it), David and Julia asked me to dinner at her apartment. I was flattered by the invitation. I wanted to know both of them better and I was especially interested to see how Julia lived. It turned out she lived very modestly, and her apartment was a dingy, third floor walk-up at least two or three cuts below what most of us could afford. Her apartment was across from the big cemetery downtown so it was quite noisy with all the street traffic. It was also small and dark and I gathered from the looks of the place that Julia lived entirely on her salary.

The Country Day School did not pay well. As a first year teacher I earned $600 a month; others with more seniority got as much as $900; but many of the teachers needed extra money to get by. Often the women had rich husbands who supported them, or else, like myself, they took money from savings in the States. Few of the Americans lived solely on their monthly check, but

Julia appeared to be one of them. She didn't even have a television.

The sitting room where we ate contained nothing but a rectangular table and four wooden chairs, and the only homey touch in the apartment was provided by a little brick fireplace built into the wall. It was a cold night and Julia had laid a nice fire. She served chicken, with rice and beans and all three of us drank a good deal of the local puro mixed with Coca-Cola. I'm afraid to say I got quite drunk, but neither of them held it against me.

Julia was a different person at home than she was at school and it was obvious why David liked her. She wasn't at all the mouse I expected her to be. She had strong opinions and a sense of humor and she had a wonderful rapport with David. They didn't pet each other and play kissy-kissy, but I often caught them exchanging affectionate glances. We played cards until one in the morning and when I left, David stayed behind. It was perfectly natural that he would.

After that night, David and Julia seemed to make up their minds about me and I was accepted as a mutual friend of the couple. I didn't see them frequently, but we got together for dinner once a fortnight or so, and the more I saw of Julia, the more I liked her. She was a sophisticated woman, every bit David's intellectual equal, and it was lovely to see how happy he was in her company. Naturally, I was still curious about the Thursday night business, but David stopped talking about it and I assumed it had resolved itself. I didn't think of it again until the end of March.

At Country Day we got our paychecks every other Tuesday and the trick was to get to the bank as soon as possible because later in the week the waits were horrendous. I remember it was the middle of the day on a Thursday and I still hadn't cashed my check,

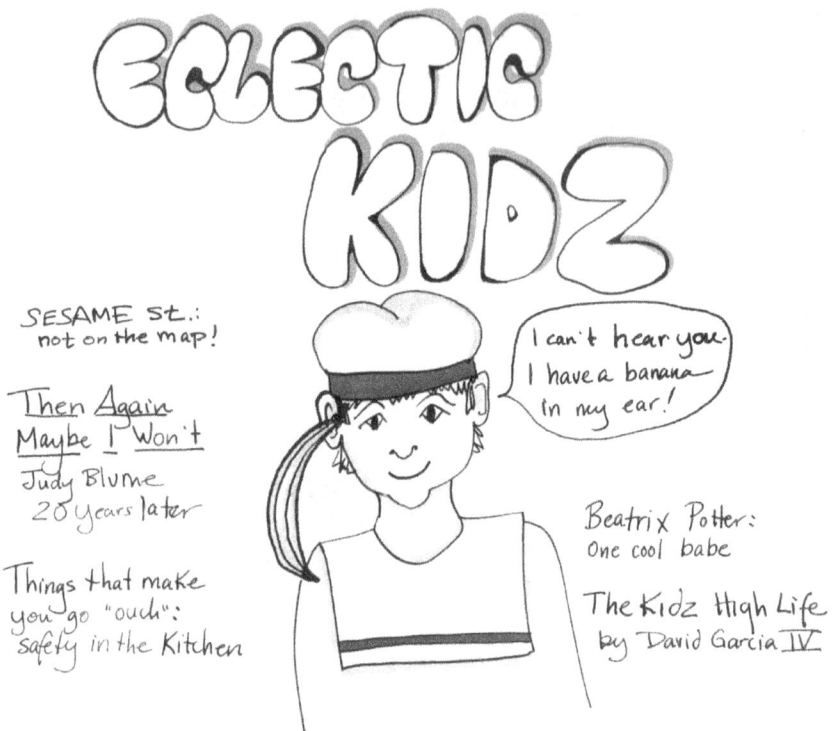

ECLECTIC KIDZ

SESAME St.:
not on the map!

Then Again
Maybe I Won't
Judy Blume
20 years later

Things that make
you go "ouch":
safety in the Kitchen

I can't hear you.
I have a banana
in my ear!

Beatrix Potter:
One cool babe

The Kidz High Life
by David Garcia IV

when thanks to a special sports event, my sixth period class was cancelled. If I jumped in a taxi and raced to the bank I could get back to school before seventh period and avoid the long line at the teller's window that night. It was frowned upon for teachers to leave during school hours, but no one would miss me.

At two o'clock in the afternoon the bank was almost empty and I took my place at the end of a short line. I was nervous about the time and I was watching the clock above the entrance, when I saw a woman walk in wearing a long black dress, dark glasses and a big, floppy sun hat. I stared at her for a moment and thought I caught a look of recognition on her face. She turned her head away and rushed past the line of people to talk to one of the bank managers. As soon as he saw her, the bank manager got up from his desk and scooted off to a back room, out of sight. A few minutes later he returned

with a large, brown paper package. He handed it to the woman and she put it in a shoulder bag and hurried out.

Though I couldn't be certain, I could have sworn the woman was Julia and I couldn't stop thinking about her on my way back to school. I never said anything to David, however, because I didn't have the chance. It was coming up on the Easter holidays and I was preparing for a trip back to New York.

I suppose everyone knows the feeling of having just learned a brand new word and then seeing that same word show up everywhere one looks. It was a little like that with Julia. I was still thinking about our run in at the bank, when I got back to New York and discovered something else peculiar about her.

You will remember that I went to college with a boy named Phillip Billegudd. Well, the night I landed in New York a friend of mine took me to a party at Phillip's. Phillip was a notorious playboy and his parties were not to be missed. He was fantastically wealthy and the story I heard was that his parents were both killed in a car crash while he was still in boarding school. The father was said to have been a big Swedish industrialist and when Phillip was a college freshman he was rumored to be worth more than $90 million. I don't know if that figure was accurate but in any case, Phillip lived in a three-story penthouse on Broadway with its own indoor swimming pool, and he spared no expense entertaining.

There were hundreds of people at the party but at one point I ran into Phillip and he asked me what I was doing. I said I was teaching school in Costa Rica and to make conversation I told him I'd met a woman in San Jose who shared his last name. I asked Phillip if there was any relation, and to my great surprise he said that Julia was his sister. Phillip didn't look pleased about it. Without prompting he said that they were on difficult terms and I didn't want to press. I changed the subject and we talked about the stock market instead. Could there possibly be *two* Julia Billegudds in San Jose?

I was burning to find out more and when I went back to Costa Rica two weeks later the great question on my mind was whether I should try talking to David. If I were a better man I might have kept mute, but I'm terrible with secrets and shortly after I returned, David invited me out for a drink. For the record, I'd like to say that he brought it up first.

"Do you remember," he said, "A few months ago when I told you that weird thing about Julia and how she's always busy on Thursday nights? She still won't tell me what she does and it's really starting to bother me. Sometimes I think I'm in love with her but then this thing gets in the way and I feel all twisted around. I don't know what she's doing and I don't know why she

won't tell me. What is she afraid of? Does she think I won't love her if I find out? She always says it's nothing. She says it's totally unimportant and that I shouldn't get worked up. But if that's the case why doesn't she just tell me?"

Without saying anything in particular, I asked David what he knew about Julia's family. He said that her parents were dead and that she had a brother in New York whom she wasn't close to. I asked him if Julia's family had money and he told me they were poor as church mice.

I know I should have kept my mouth shut but David was grasping at straws, so I told him what I knew. I told him about the strange woman at the bank and I told him about Phillip being

Julia's brother. The moment the words left my mouth I started feeling guilty. I waited anxiously for David's response but I couldn't tell if he was listening.

Over the next few days David appeared very tense at school and on the following Friday he didn't come to work at all. As the weeks passed he grew increasingly taciturn. David stopped talking to me about Julia and soon he stopped talking altogether. I hardly saw him. He went back to his trees and he began spending weekends in the jungle again. I guessed that David and Julia had split up and since I never even ran into Julia, I suspected she was avoiding me. I found it quite upsetting to lose my only two friends at the school and I blamed my own loose tongue.

Initially I signed a two year contract with Country Day. However, I did not enjoy teaching and I was bad at it, and together the administration and I decided that I would not return for a second year. July would be my last month in San Jose. I was happy to be leaving but I was still sad about the coldness of my friendship with David. I wanted us part on good terms but I had not spoken to him much since the night we got drunk together and I worried that in some way he held me responsible for the end of his affair with Julia.

Three days before I left, I swallowed my nerves and asked David to have dinner with me. To my relief he accepted gladly, and to get the awkwardness over with as quickly as possible, I started apologizing even before we said hello. I must have sounded a fool because I hardly knew what I was apologizing for, but David saved me from my embarrassment. He said he was not the least bit angry with me. He hadn't been avoiding me; he'd been avoiding everyone; he said he'd been wrapped up in his own thoughts. I asked him how his book of trees was going. Finally I got up the courage to ask what had happened between him and Julia and this is what he told me:

He said that despite loving Julia, he had been tortured by the mystery of

The People Downstairs

the Thursday nights. He would bug her about it for a while and then he would give up. But it always stayed lodged in the back of his mind that she was hiding something, and while I was away over Easter, the trouble erupted.

One night David told Julia that he couldn't go on seeing her unless he found out what she did on Thursday nights. She told him to let it go. She said it didn't matter because they loved each other and she asked him to trust her. David said he did trust her but he stood firm. He said he needed to know or else he would leave her, and in the end the fear of losing him persuaded Julia to give in. She set a date for a Thursday night and promised to tell him her secret.

Throughout the next week David was in a frenzy. That was the week that David and I got drunk together, but nothing I said made any impression on him. He was too completely focused on his own ideas about what Julia would tell him. He had a vague hope that she spent Thursday nights nursing a crazy

uncle whom she was embarrassed to talk about; then he thought perhaps she was a drug addict who smoked heroin once a week; at last he convinced himself that Julia kept a lover on the side. None of it seemed possible but David had to steel himself to any eventuality. He loved Julia and he intended to continue loving her.

After many sleepless nights, David arrived at Julia's apartment at seven o'clock on Thursday evening and she welcomed him with a smile. Both of them were very nervous and they talked with difficulty. Julia said she thought it best to get right down to business. She asked David to sit down and disappeared into the bedroom. It was a hot night and David was surprised to see a fire burning in the fireplace.

A moment later Julia came back holding a package wrapped in brown paper. She put it on David's lap and asked him to open it. David was amazed to find that inside were thick wads of $100 bills. Julia said it was $60,000 worth.

David asked her where she got the money, and Julia calmly explained that the money had belonged to her father. It was her inheritance, or more precisely it was twice the weekly income generated by her inheritance. David asked what she was going to do with it. Without saying a word, Julia took the money from his lap and slowly, stack by stack, she placed $60,000 in the fire. David was dumbfounded. Why did she do it?

Julia she said that she burned part of her inheritance every Thursday night because money was a great evil in the world. She said that money caused suffering, jealousy and pain and that it was at the root of injustice and war. She said she burned the money to rid the world of one small portion of its sin.

David still did not understand. If she hated money so much, why didn't she give it away? Julia answered that money was a curse and that to give it away was merely to curse others. Then David asked her why she had to destroy the money so methodically. Why not burn it all, once and for all? Julia said she did not believe in making decisions rashly and she drew an analogy to the search for truth. One cannot, she said, search for truth only once.

There was a long silence during which neither David nor Julia dared look at each other. At last Julia asked David if he would still be her lover and against his will, David began to cry. Julia cried too. Five minutes later David left the apartment and he never went back.

Three months later, when David told me the story, he was still confused and upset. Deep inside him, he did not know what he should have done. But he did not ask me for any advice and if he had, I don't know what I would have told him.

All I can say is that I've been thinking about Julia Billegudd ever since.

Reviews

The Autobiography of Bertrand Russell 1872-1914

by Bertrand Russell

Bantam Books, 1968 (out of print)

The trouble with many intelligent and opinionated men is that they have a hard time keeping it to themselves. Like children who have learned to tie their shoelaces, they can't rest easy until everyone else has acknowledged how clever they are. Bertrand Russell was both extremely bright and extremely outspoken; in later life he was hated throughout England for his pacifist campaign against World War I; but it is impossible to read his autobiography and come away thinking of him as a know-it-all. When he was just a boy, he went to lunch with his maternal grandmother, Lady Stanley: *"I remember telling her that I had grown 2 1/2 inches in the last seven months, and at that rate I should grow 4 2/7 inches in a year. 'Don't you know,' she said, 'that you should never talk about any fractions except halves and quarters? – it is pedantic!'"*

It was hardly fair of Lady Stanley to come down so fiercely, but Russell seems to have learned his lesson, and as a result his autobiography is a delightfully human book, entirely devoid of pomposity. As an undergraduate student, Russell says he made a vow never to suppose that lecturing did any good, and he has kept his vow. For example, when Russell writes about his first extra-marital affair, he does not start off with a long argument in favor of free-love (which he believed in). Instead he begins with two simple memories of visiting his lover's house as a child. *"The first of these memories was of a children's party at which I first tasted ice-cream. I thought it was an ordinary pudding and took a large spoonful.*

The shock caused me to burst into tears, to the dismay of the elders, who could not make out what had happened. The other experience was even more unpleasant. In getting out of a carriage at her door, I fell on the paving-stones, hurting my penis. After this I had to sit twice a day in a hot bath and sponge it carefully."

Bertrand Russell, author of *Principia Mathematica*, was born in 1872. Both of his parents were dead before he was five and he was sent to live with his father's mother. Lady Russell was a quintessentially Victorian woman. Politically liberal but emotionally tight-fisted, she disliked wine, abhorred tobacco and hated sex: *"She ate only the plainest food, breakfasted at eight, and until she reached the age of eighty, never say in a comfortable chair until after tea."* She was not the sort to pamper a boy and she believed that children benefited from deprivation. God made life unpleasant for a reason and when, at the age of six, Bertrand confessed to her that he wished his parents were alive, *"...she proceeded to tell me that it was very fortunate for me that they had died."* It is no wonder that Bertrand grew up with a strong sense of guilt.

Russell stayed with his grandmother until he was sixteen, at which time he was sent to an Army crammer school in preparation for university. He was desperately unhappy there. Shocked by the frivolity of his school mates, he was teased mercilessly, and his teenage diary was filled with thoughts of doing himself in: *"I used to go across the fields to New Southgate, and I used to go there alone to watch the sunset and contemplate suicide. I did not, however, commit suicide because I wished to know more of mathematics."*

Saved by mathematics, Russell ended up at Cambridge where he flourished. Still it was a long time before he was able to shed the morbidity that his grandmother had instilled in him. Of Cambridge, Russell writes: *"My first experience of the place was in December 1889 when I was examined for entrance scholarships. I stayed in rooms in the New Court, and I was too shy to enquire the way to the lavatory, so that I walked every morning to the station before the examination began."*

Such shyness can destroy men, but Russell eventually awoke to the discovery that not all pleasure need be sin, nor all self-confidence hubris. He was greatly helped along by a new set of friends and Russell was especially struck by the charisma of the famous socialist Beatrice Webb. Beatrice was the first woman Russell ever met who was not only worthy and good, but also lively and immodest: *"I asked her whether in her youth she had ever had any feeling of shyness. 'Oh no,' she said, 'If I ever felt inclined to be timid as I was going into a room full of people, I would say to myself, "You're the cleverest member of one of the cleverest families in the cleverest class of the cleverest nation in the world, why should you be frightened?"'"*

By the time Russell reached his twenties, he was a man of independent mind and strong enough to marry against the wishes of his family. He chose an old-money Philadelphia Quaker named Alys Pearsall Smith. Lady Russell, oblivious to American social distinctions, disliked Alys intensely and never got past thinking of her as a gold-digger. Worst of all, Lady Russell was incapable of hiding her feelings. In the following letter, she writes to thank Alys for sending some photographs and her remarks are so blithely cruel as to be almost comic: *"Dearest Alys: We are delighted with the Bertie photo – It is perfect, such a natural, not a photographic smile. As for you, we don't like you, and I hope Bertie doesn't, neither pose, nor dusky face, nor white humpy tippet..."*

Despite the problems of family, Russell and Alys remained happily married for almost ten years. Then Russell fell out of love. and it is here, just before the outbreak of World War I, that this installment of his autobiography ends. The Bantam edition, covering only the first thirty years of the life, is no longer in print, but the complete text is still available from Routledge Books. Altogether, the thing runs to 800 pages. That may seem like a long slog, but if Russell is as good at describing his maturity as he is at describing his youth, I imagine it goes quite quickly. Russell writes with charm, honesty and intelligence. He was an appealing man.

HA HA!

Nick Bienstock

Four doctors are out duck hunting – an internist, a psychiatrist, a surgeon and a coroner. They are sitting in the duck blind with their decoys set in the water, blowing their duck calls and waiting for the first duck to come in. The doctors have agreed that they will take turns, with the internist to shoot first.

All of a sudden, a bird comes flying toward them out of the rising sun. The internist jumps up and aims his shotgun at the bird, but does not fire. "What happened?" they ask the internist. "Well," he says, "I'm not sure it was a duck."

Next, it is the psychiatrist's turn. Sure enough, another bird appears out of the rising sun, flying low. The psychiatrist lines up his shot, but he too does not fire. "What happened? You had a perfect shot," they ask. "Well," says the psychiatrist, "I thought it was a duck, but I was not sure that it knew that it was a duck!" "Ahh..." they say.

Next it is the surgeon's turn. A bird appears out of the rising sun, the surgeon lines up his shot and BANG - shoots it out of the air. The surgeon turns to the coroner and says, "Go see if that's a duck."

To Bury Reading

T.E. MacVeagh

We, the literate elite, hold reading as a cherished talisman which insures our entrance into the hallowed halls of the intelligensia and through which our many intellectual sins are forgiven.

We explain to incredulous office mates that we read in the evening rather than watch TV. We do not miss a chance to point out that we have *not* seen the latest movie, but we *have* read the book on which it was based. We scoff at computers in the class room; teach children how to read, we say, and they can teach themselves how to use computers. We shudder at the gaucheness of those who believe that a bookstore is incomplete without a café. And, as we luxuriate in those very cafés, we curse the fate that has not allowed us to read the latest biography of Napoleon or Daniel Pinkerton's book on linguistics. It is sad when minds such as ours go to waste.

It is true that many of us have been known, in moments of weakness, to read novels that do not require such heavy lifting. Some of us enjoy a good thriller, a science fiction, a fantasy. Some of us make repeated journeys back to the small villages and grand Ducal estates of rural England to pursue the remarkable number of murderers that inhabit those places. Some of us even enjoy ourselves with tales of beautiful and desirable damsels being saved from the awful clutches of the Wrong Man by tall, dark, handsome and hopefully very rich Mr. Rights. We recognize that we do not deserve as much credit for our thirteenth Agatha Christie novel as we do for *The Sound and the Fury*, but we comfort ourselves with the thought that reading junk is still better than TV, better than movies, better than computer games. Reading junk is a near cousin of serious reading. And serious reading is one of the high callings of life, an unalloyed good.

What we tend to forget is that the family resemblance goes both ways. I have begun to realize that reading Faulkner has more in common with reading Ludlum, and thus more in common with Star Trek marathons, than we care to realize. Opening *Absalom, Absalom* may be a difficult experience, but most good novels gather momentum at a certain point. Somewhere in the middle we stop reading them for the dry experience of self-improvement, and we start reading them to shut out the slings and arrows of outrageous reality. During the morning commute, we are eager to open our books by Joyce or Tolstoy, Hardy or Bukowski; we race back not to educate ourselves, not to think, but simply to lose ourselves in the streets of Dublin or the Battlefields of Russia, in pastoral England or underground LA.

The effect is not limited to fiction. Subjects as abstruse as Quinian philosophy can be read more for escape than anything else. Eventually, the mere mention of Gavagais can leave a sense of warm, fuzziness in the soul. A screed against the "concept of meaning" becomes familiar and calming. And you return to the strange, clinical, bloodless world of Quine's radical translators as a shelter from the storm. Even the brutal concentration camp genre can provide a comfortable home away from home by the time you have read three or four. Read a few books by Solznenitsyn, Levi and Wiesel, and you feel a certain pleasant nostalgia when the protagonist once again finds himself jostling around the chow line, clutching a piece of black bread, and working out where to stand to get the thickest bowl of soup.

You see, reading is not thinking, although this is hard to remember. And it is all too easy to use reading like music, TV, or any other sensory stimulus: as a way to avoid thinking rather than as a way to inspire it.

I have nothing against avoiding thinking. God knows it is necessary at times. But when we admire ourselves for our reading habits, we often tend to confuse reading and thinking. They are not the same; they are often in conflict. We are so awash in books and maga-

zines and newspapers, that we can turn into mere intellectual tourists. Another sojourn to Vonnegut's weird America, through Somerset Maugham's post-Victorian London, around Achebe's matter-of-fact Africa. We really need not pause to think at all.

Have you ever sat in a subway train cursing yourself because you forgot your book and hardly knew what to do with yourself for the six station stops you have to endure? You sit crowded by people, sweaty and real, of all shapes and sizes, laughing and scowling, care-worn and weather beaten or doe-eyed and innocent, and all you want is to open your book and escape. You sit surrounded by real stories which you can weave for yourself, but you yearn for someone else to do the work. As readers, we are like gourmets who have eaten at the best restaurants in the world but cannot cook. When we are given the raw materials of our meals, meat and onions, ginger root and potatoes still showing the dirt in which they were grown, we have no idea what to do with them.

When you finish your next book, think about this: go on a three month reading fast. See if you can entertain and amuse yourself without reading for a little while. When you next are trying to figure out how far away Jupiter is, don't look it up in a book, but try to come up with a way to figure it out for yourself. A false answer that has a little reason behind it may be worth more than a true answer supported by nothing but reading. Consider the questions that no reading can ever resolve: does a successful democracy need a capitalist economic structure? Has the concept of God been a beneficial influence on mankind? Has Christianity?

Reading is not thinking. Reading is fabulous. Thinking is better.

Games

Sir Laffalot

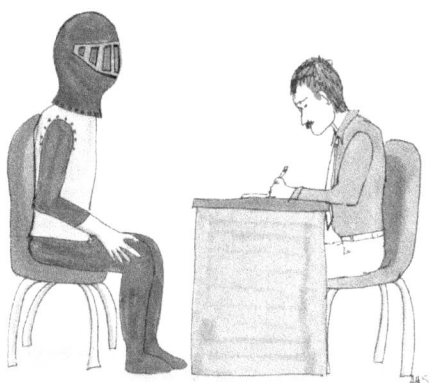

Sir Laffalot's been out of work. He went down to unemployent last week and they quizzed him about his last job. Who could forget Agincourt? Unfortunately, Sir Laffalot's memory of the great battle is tinged with bitterness. He had a winning pep-talk all planned out, but at the last minute Henry V nicked into his tent and stole his index cards. Sir Laffalot was still looking round for his notes when the King gave the speech himself:

"And gentlemen in England, now a-bed, / Shall think themselves accurs'd they were not here; / And hold their manhoods cheap whiles any speaks / That fought with us upon Saint Crispin's day."

Pure Sir Laffalot that is, but the man at unemployment didn't seem to care. He looked at Sir Laffalot blankly and asked about his professional qualifications. Sir Laffalot said he'd killed a thousand Frenchmen in a single day and they whisked him off to the Career Counseling Center for worker re-training.

The CCC was a classy place. No jeans, no see-through clothing, and no house dresses allowed. First Sir Laffalot got a lecture about modern interview techniques – don't chew gum and bathe beforehand – then they put him in a room with fifteen other hard luck cases and everyone was asked to introduce themselves. One lady broke down crying before she could get a word out. "My name is Julia," she sobbed, "I just got divorced and for the last twenty five years I've been a homemaker." Sir Laffalot's heart began to melt, but it hardened right up again when he announced that he was a Knight-At-Arms and the two hispanic boys in the back started to giggle.

The worst part of the CCC was the waiting and it was four hours before Sir Laffalot got an appointment with his career advisor. Fortunately, Sir Laffalot had brought along his friendly steward to keep him company. Sir Laffalot's steward is a clever young thing and to pass the time she taught him a new game. *The People Game* is best played by close friends who share the same circle of acquantances.

The People Game: How To Play

1) One player thinks of a mutual friend. (It is optional to reveal the person's sex.)
2) The other player then asks questions trying to figure who it is. All questions must take the form: If this person were a car what sort of car would he be? If this person were a cocktail what sort of cocktail would he be? Etc..
3) Questioning continues until the identity of the mutual friend is guessed or until the player asking the questions gives up.
4) After the mystery friend is revealed, both players cheerfully review the quality of the answers given.

Sir Laffalot says: TOODALOO!!

The high life

The Santa of Sebec

David Garcia III

First, you have to imagine a snapshot of me and my cousin Paul as toddlers on the beach. He's a toymaker now in Sebec Maine, with a wife, two kids and a snowmobile. We see each other when he comes to New York and we have a good time. Back then, however, he was my favorite person in the world, and I remember guiltily thinking that I loved him more than my parents and my brother, maybe even God.

This period lasted until we were both around eight, when his parents divorced. He was all set to stay with his mother, but in the courtroom his sister announced that she wanted to be with her Father instead. Paul wanted to stay with his sister, and the two of them went off to Maine.

Nine years later, Paul was back living with his Mom nearby my hometown, but we hardly knew each other. While I was playing "kick the can", he was in the fields with his buds, who passed teen time by beating the crap out of each other. When we saw each other at Christmas, I couldn't help wondering what this coarse, dull-eyed person had done with "my Paul". Later, I learned that he was drunk and on drugs most of the time. I went off to college, and he went back to Maine and got a job driving a truck. He would routinely drive through places like the Lincoln Tunnel drunk and stoned out of his mind on coke.

He moved on to logging, and a factory job, where he had an accident. He did something to his back, and that Christmas he showed me a box that fed electrical impulses to his spine to keep the pain under control. He was spiking his egg nog, and talking about a big workman's compensation check that he had just received. What I didn't know was that he had already made plans to use his injury money to buy a place in the woods where he would go drink himself to death. Before long he was in a boat stocked with guns and liquor on the way to a hunting cabin he had bought with a friend.

Before they got there, the friend wanted to check in with the only other resident of the area, a former Priest. The Priest said that years earlier he was a teacher at a Catholic School. One day he jumped on his motorcycle and drove away without a word. He left his life and his faith behind and became a recluse. Paul remembered one of his own teachers disappearing in the same way and they had one of those "small world" moments where they realized that the Priest had taught at Paul's school. The Priest asked Paul's last name and when he heard it he suddenly rushed back into his house to get something. Minutes later, the Priest came running out with a piece of paper in his hand. He said, "When I ran off on my bike, I only took one thing with me." He showed Paul the page of composition paper. On it, in wide pencil scrawl, a child had copied out a section from the Bible. "Read the last line," said the Priest. The child had made an error in his last sentence, which read:

"....and Jesus wacked off. by Paul Stiffler."

Of course, it was supposed to be "walked off" and everyone laughed, but something about it was like a ghost story to Paul. He never made it to the cabin in the woods. Instead he headed back to his Mom, and into rehab, where he found God and apologized to his girlfriend. On the website of his toy company, he is referred to as "The Santa of Sebec".

**FOR SUBSCRIPTIONS
TURN TO PAGE 7.**

The
ECLECTIC

August 1999   Volume 1 Number 6   Free

Little Known Effects of the Y2K Bug

Chicken is King

Sports turns into ballet

Madonna is cool again

World Peace

CONTENTS

Quotations

"Every man is working out his destiny in his own way and nobody can be of help except by being kind, generous and patient." Henry Miller in *Tropic of Capricorn*.

"LSD, yeah the big parade — everybody's doin' it now. Take LSD, then you are a poet, an intellectual. What a sick mob." Charles Bukowski in his collected letters, *Screams From The Balcony*.

"I was never any good in sports. I was always terrified if a tennis ball came over the fence and landed near me, because I could never get it over the fence." Physicist Richard Feynman remembers his childhood in *Surely You're Joking Mr. Feynman*.

"We have been seeing a lot of Maurice Chevalier. Not a bad chap, but rather a ham. I can't ever really like actors, can you?" P.G. Wodehouse in *Yours, Plum: The Letters of P.G. Wodehouse*.

Sweet Lamb

The Innocence of P.G. Wodehouse

Lincoln MacVeagh

Pelham Grenville Wodehouse, rhymes with "Good House" and known as Plum (say Pelham quickly), lived 93 years. He wrote 96 books, hundreds of short stories and countless song lyrics. His worst novels are readable and his best, of which there are at least fifteen, are unmatched. Wodehouse wrote farce. He made people laugh. He had no message.

Plum Wodehouse was born in 1881 with the soul of a dove. His father was a British civil servant in Hong Kong, as normal as rice pudding, and his mother was a genial, dull witted aristocrat who sent all of her children back to England for their education as soon as her eldest son turned six. Plum was two but he didn't seem to mind. *"Looking back I can see that I was just passed from hand to hand. It was an odd life with no home to go to, but I have always accepted everything that happens to me philosophically and I can't remember ever being unhappy in those days."*

A dreamy, reticent and well-behaved boy, Plum bounced around from guardian to guardian until landing at Dulwich College, a second-tier public school with an intelligent headmaster and beautiful grounds. Wodehouse fell in love with it instantly and remained devoted to Dulwich for the rest of his life. Long after he

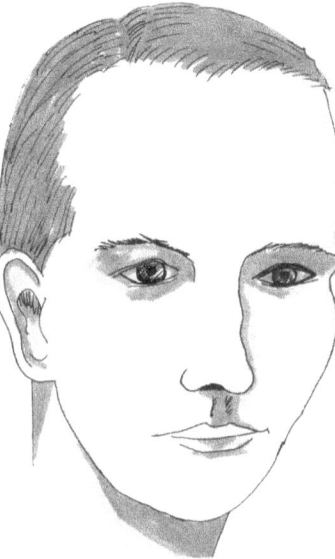

"I haven't any violent feeling about anything."

became famous, he was still sending fan mail to the captain of the school's Rugby XV.

As a student at Dulwich, Wodehouse was a good athlete and a good scholar, and he was popular despite his shyness. His VI form master's report gives a taste of his personality:

"He has the most distorted ideas about wit and humour; he draws all over his books and examination papers in the most distressing way and writes foolish rhymes in other people's books. Notwithstanding, he has a genuine interest in literature and can often talk with much enthusiasm and good sense about it. He does some things astonishingly well at times and writes good Latin verses.

He is a very useful boy in the school and in the VI form, and one is obliged to like him in spite of his vagaries."

After school, Wodehouse would have liked to go on to university, but his father, then retired and living on a pension pegged to the Indian rupee, could not afford it. Instead Plum was sent to work at a bank. He lived in a miserable bed-sit in King's Road and spent his spare time writing freelance stories and light verse for the pulp magazines. On weekends he went back to Dulwich to watch the boys play sport. It was a gray life and Wodehouse didn't like it, but after three years of freelancing he was offered a permanent job writing comic commentary for the *Globe* newspaper and he leapt at it. Wodehouse quit the bank in 1902 and in the same year he published his first novel, *The Pothunters.* He was a professional writer ever after.

By his own choosing, Wodehouse led a narrow existence. Although he traveled to New York and Paris, he rarely saw past his study window. Of Hollywood he said, *"The great advantage of this place is that it is so loathsome the moment you get outside the garden that there is no temptation to do anything but sit at home and work."*

The true love of Plum's life was writing and even romance had to be cut short for it. In 1914 Wodehouse met an English widow named Ethel Rowley and exactly one week later he asked her to marry him. Ethel accepted graciously but their marriage was one of cordiality and tender affection rather than passion. Plum's pet name for his wife was "The Bank Manager." Otherwise he called her Mummie. The couple shared houses, friends and checking accounts, but never a bedroom. One senses that Wodehouse

liked it that way.

Plum was a man of very simple tastes. He liked books, Pekingese dogs, pipe tobacco and Dulwich Rugby. He liked little else besides. For money he wanted a pound in his pocket but he was blissfully ignorant of larger sums, and he had no notion of worldliness. He was extremely awkward in society and despite having every opportunity to make fancy friends he was never comfortable doing so. The following excerpts are taken from his letters and describe typical Wodehouse celebrity encounters:

"I have reluctantly come to the conclusion that I must have one of those meaningless faces which makes no impression whatever on the beholder. This was – I think – the seventh time I had been introduced to Churchill, and I could see that I came upon him as a complete surprise once more."

"I like [H.G.] Wells. An odd bird, though. The first time I met him we had barely finished the initial pip-pippings when he said, apropos of nothing, 'My father was a professional cricketer.' If there's a good answer to that, you tell me. I thought of saying, 'Mine had a white moustache,' but finally

settled for 'Oh, ah,' and we went on to talk of other things."

"I remember coming away from a cricket match at Lord's one evening and seeing Somerset Maugham walking towards me. I thought, 'O Lord, we shall stop and say 'Hullo', and have nothing more whatever to say to each other. And I bet he's thinking just the same.' We both of us went down side-streets simultaneously."

Wodehouse was no good as a public figure. He did not tell jokes or funny stories, and in company he was large and smiling but generally silent. Nevertheless, the success of his novels made him extremely popular. He was a perennial best seller both in England and America and his books even sold well in Japan. I can't imagine how one translates Wodehouse into Japanese (*"Odd's boddikins, Jeeves,"* I said, *"I am in rare filth this a.m. Talk about exulting in my youth!"*), but it was done.

In the early thirties the critic Hillaire Belloc called Wodehouse the best writer of English alive and a great many people agreed with him. In 1939 Oxford University thumbed its nose at the highbrows by offering Wodehouse an honorary degree. It would be no exaggeration to say that Plum was beloved. To readers throughout the world he represented everything that was endearing about England.

And then something shocking happened.

One evening in 1941, in the midst of Germany's bombing campaign, millions of people tuned their radios to the BBC and listened to the program *Postscript.* It began: *"I have come to tell you tonight of the story of a rich man trying to make his last and greatest sale – that of his own country. It is a sombre story of self-respect, honour and decency being pawned to the Nazis for the price of a soft bed in a luxury hotel."*

The speech was ordered by England's Minister of Information; it was delivered by a heart thumping patriotic journalist who called himself Cassandra; and the rich man accused of selling his soul to the Nazis was none other than P.G. Wodehouse.

Cassandra's attack was prompted by a series of five radio talks which Wodehouse recorded in Berlin and which were broadcast to America over German radio. Wodehouse wrote and delivered the talks himself and the specific accusation made against him was that he had done so in exchange for money. This was plainly false, but the broader and more damaging accusation was unspoken. It was that Wodehouse was a Nazi sympathizer. Why else would he have agreed to perform on German radio?

The answer to this questions turns out to be almost tragically sad. Not because it reveals Wodehouse to have been a fascist at heart, but rather because it is horrible to think of such a good and honest man being so unfairly done in.

In 1939 Plum and his wife were living in the south of France. They had been there for seven years and despite rumblings in the east neither of them felt it necessary to leave. Few people thought war was imminent and certainly no one believed that it would come quickly. Nonetheless, it did come quickly. The Germans overran France in the blink of an eye, and Plum and his wife were caught stranded. In July of 1940 Wodehouse was arrested by the German army and interned.

Wodehouse kept a diary of his camp life and in many ways it was just what one would expect. He was packed into dark trains; he fretted about the soles of his shoes; and he developed a sharp eye for a slice of bread. *"August 18. People*

are starting to experiment with foods — man gathering berries on bank, probably poisonous."

Wodehouse was afforded no special treatment in camp. He had to fight for his biscuits like everyone else and he lost more than thirty pounds during his imprisonment. But beyond the obsession with food, there is something remarkable that comes through in his camp diary. Plum enjoyed himself. Wodehouse finished a full novel in prison and he played cricket for the first time in 27 years with a ball made out of twine. Camp reminded him of Dulwich, and many of the deprivations he suffered were overwhelmed by the long forgotten joy of camaraderie. *"November 14, 1940. I must make a note of this day as one of the absolutely flawless ones of my life."*

German policy was to release prisoners when they reached the age of sixty and Wodehouse was let go three weeks shy of his sixtieth birthday. He was sent to Berlin but he was still far from free. He could not leave the country and it was extremely difficult for him to communicate with the outside world.

Furthermore, having lived a year in isolation he had no idea how quickly the war had progressed. Nor had he any sense of what Nazism stood for. When a German friend proposed he make a series of radio addresses about his camp experiences, Wodehouse saw no harm in it. He wanted to tell his friends that he was alright, and more than that, he thought he was being quite clever: *"It seemed to me, when I wrote it [the radio addresses], that I was doing something mildly courageous and praiseworthy in showing that it was possible, even though in prison camp, to keep one's end-up and not belly-ache."*

Wodehouse's decision to broadcast from Berlin was the innocent mistake of a political naïf. The talks were not pro-Nazi; they were merely anecdotes taken from his camp diary; but their effect on Plum's reputation was devastating.

After Cassandra's BBC appearance, the rage against Wodehouse spread throughout Britain. Many of his friends came to his defense but many others did not. A.A. Milne used the opportunity to get off a sneering letter to the *Times* describing Wodehouse as a draft-dodger, tax evader and general all-around stink: *"I remember,"* wrote Milne, *"that he told me once he wished he had a son, and he added characteristically (and quite sincerely) 'but he would have to be born at the age of 15, when he was just getting into his House eleven.' You see the advantage of that. Bringing up a son throws considerable responsibility on a man; but by the time the boy is 15 one has shifted the responsibility to the housemaster, without forfeiting any reflected glory that may be about."* The fever of the moment was such that no one bothered to point out that Milne was quoting from Wodehouse's novel *Psmith in the City.*

Living in Berlin, there was little Plum could do to defend himself and the furor surrounding him did not die easily. Towards the end of the war Wodehouse and his wife were allowed to settle in Paris, but in 1946 he was re-arrested as an enemy of the French people. *"My arrest by the French came as a complete surprise. I have it from what is usually called a 'well-informed source' that an English woman was dining with the Prefect of Police, and said to him, 'Why don't you arrest P.G. Wodehouse?' He thought it a splendid idea…"*

After three months Wodehouse was released by the French, but meanwhile opposition politicians in London began using his name to score points off the government, and Wodehouse's lawyer advised him not to return to England for fear of facing prosecution for treason. Such a prosecution was unlikely, but Wodehouse did not want to risk it and having nowhere else to turn Plum and Ethel moved to New York.

Wodehouse never again returned to England and he never got to see another Dulwich rugby match. It would be easy to imagine him living out his dotage full of bitter seethings against the injustice of the world, but once established in Long Island, Wodehouse went about his work just as cheerfully as he had always done.

Plum was incapable of malice and perhaps the strongest proof of this is an extraordinary letter he wrote to Evelyn Waugh in 1961:

"I'm a bit concerned about this TV appearance of yours on July 15. I've just had a letter from Guy Bolton, who said that somebody had told him that you were going to make an attack on Cassandra of the Mirror. And the embarrassing thing (to me) is that for several years past he and I have been great friends. I had a very amiable letter from him one day when he was over here and we lunched together and got on fine. He sent me that Mirror book with a charming inscription, and since then we have been on first name and Christmas card terms. So I am hoping you will see your way to make your talk not so personal as you had planned. Is that possible?"

Never was there a man so innocent as P.G. Wodehouse. He died in 1973.

Reviews

Bridget Jones's Diary
by Helen Fielding
Viking, 1996

*B*ridget Jones's Diary is full of slang, brand names and mid-nineties zeitgeist. It helps to know that a *Silk Cut* is a cigarette, that *Edinburgh* is not so much a city as an arts festival, and that *Blind Date* starring Cilla Black is England's uncannily popular version of *The Dating Game.* The book is so distinctly hip that twenty years from now it may be unreadable. For the time being, however, it's extremely funny.

Helen Fielding's recent novel began life as a weekly newspaper column and the worry about novels which start out as weekly columns is that they tend to be disjointed. Few authors are good enough to get away with a loosely connected series of comic vignettes, no matter how delightful, and the dirty truth is that *picaresque* is usually just another way of saying don't bother. It is not enough simply to write well. Novels need plots to keep a reader's attention.

Fortunately, Helen Fielding knows all this, and despite its newspaper origins, *Bridget Jones's Diary* is a well-constructed book. It has a beginning and a middle, and it leaves no loose ends. Checkhov's rule was that the you mustn't hang a gun on the wall in Act 1 unless you intend to fire it in Act 4, and Fielding has played by his rules. She doesn't waste time introducing quirky bit-players who fade into nothingness ten pages down the road and she doesn't go chasing all over London for jokes. Instead she focuses her attention on a small group of central characters; she keeps them around long enough for us to get to know them; and she gets her laughs out of believable reactions to believable situations.

To say that *Bridget Jones's Diary* is a well-plotted book is not the same as to say that it deals with earth shattering events. Jane Austen's novels were well-plotted too, and she never got beyond girl-meets-boy. Helen Fielding writes in a similar vein and there's nothing wrong with that. A good comedy of manners is worth a thousand dull treatises on Truth, Death and Art. But whereas Austen rarely gets taken to task for not making Elizabeth Bennett march with the suffragettes, there has been a good deal of hand wringing in the press about Bridget Jones's inadequacy as a role model for the modern woman.

Bridget likes to headline each of her diary entries with her weight, alcohol intake, cigarette consumption and calorie count: *"124 lbs. (heavy internal weight completely vanished – mystery), alcohol units 1 (v.g.), cigarettes 9 (v.g.) calories 1800 (g.)."* As a result she has been condemned for being empty-headed, self-absorbed and borderline anorexic. Worse still she is boy crazy and she seems incapable of envisioning happiness without a strong man at her side to calm her fragile nerves. In short, Bridget is a disgrace to the sisterhood and some critics have argued that her diary is nothing but a tragic commentary on the state of feminism today.

Such criticism is silly. One might just as well argue that Bertie Wooster is a tragic character because he is so tragically dim. But leaving that aside, I disagree with the notion that Bridget Jones is a bad woman. Certainly she is flighty and weight-obsessed, but she is also smart, observant and has a lively sense of humor. Moreover, despite a hectic schedule, she has the self-discipline to sit down each night and write entertaining entries in her diary. How many people, male or female, can do that?

Bridget Jones's Diary is an admirable book.

Commentary

Tribalism

T.E. MacVeagh

The next challenge to democracy, now that communism has disappeared as a viable option, is tribalism. Tribalism is the notion that governmental and political units should be organized along the grounds of ethnic, religious or other recognizable identity traits.

The history of democracy is about more than expanding suffrage; it is about dividing "us" from "them" in ever broader terms. It is the history of the expansion of the definition of personhood, in which the line separating "barbarian" from "Greek" has constantly been pushed outward. Tribalism challenges the notion that a truly broadly-inclusive democracy is desirable or even possible.

The challenge is multi-faceted. On an intellectual level, tribalism denies there is any such thing as personhood or individual identity detached from the culture into which one is born. On a spiritual level, it argues that those elements which are most meaningful and most sacred in human life are the local and the traditional. And on a political level, to simplify, tribalism insists that it is better to be governed by a bad man who looks like you and eats the same thing as you do for breakfast, than a good one who does not.

The "rise" of tribalism is often noted internationally. In Yugoslavia and Africa, we have seen horrifying examples of national politics being overwhelmed by tribal schisms. Less drastically, commentators often note how ethnic groups like the Flemish, the Scottish, the Bavarians and the Milanese embrace the European Union as much to escape the yoke of perceived oppression within the nation-state as to enjoy the fruits of a global economy. And any study of the Islamic world or French politics include descriptions of how these societies are fighting to cling to their distinct traditions in the face of globalization.

Tribalism is also a phenomenon of the United States. On the left, the "identity politics" espoused on university campuses claims that oppressed groups (most often African Americans, gays and women) should act in the interests of their group rather than society at large. On the right, the militia movement should be seen at some level as a call for tribalism. Although the movement is fairly inarticulate, its message is pretty clearly that the federal government is too big and too diverse. Its members want to define their bonds of loyalty on a smaller, more manageable scale. The Christian Coalition offers a more articulate version of the same impulse, arguing more or less expressly that loyalty is owed to one's co-religionist before one's nation, and that divergent religious beliefs should be treated as a threat.

It is probably misleading to talk of the "rise" of tribalism. It is more accurate to say that the explicit articulation of the values of tribalism is a result of their decline in importance. I live in Boston, where as recently as fifty years ago an Irish candidate automatically won the Irish vote. Who needed to espouse identity politics back then? It was assumed. The cause of tribalism only has to be defended now because it is eroding more and more quickly in the face of economic and cultural globalization.

The spread of American pop culture is only part of the story. Politics, science, morality and even aesthetics have been globalized as well. The immigration of Asians, Africans and Arabs into Europe during the last fifty years has transformed previously insular nations into multicultural societies. Suddenly every country must try to follow the United States' difficult (and unfinished) road towards becoming a melting pot (or gorgeous mosaic, if you prefer a tribal-leaning metaphor). Meanwhile, scientists and moral philosophers argue that we have to care as much about distant rain forests and their inhabitants as about our neighbors and their backyards. Mavens of taste raise their eyebrows if we do not know the difference between northern and southern Indian cuisine, or have never seen Balinese dance.

But the fact that its decline is what has made tribalism an issue does not presage its inevitable defeat, or that it will die quietly. Although I do not support tribalism's political goals, the intellectual and cultural defense of the need for tribal identity is convincing. Humans need more than simple equality or naked justice to thrive. Before we are ready to establish a society, we have to establish ourselves. And to do that, we need to feel special. We need to belong. We need a sense of tribe. The problem is that "belonging" is a relative term. In order for us to feel that we belong, someone else has to belong less.

Just two days ago a friend told me a story which illustrated the point nicely. After six years of dealing with the INS trying to get her father naturalized, and meeting with polite disinterest at every turn, she lost her temper and began to yell at one of the agents. As she yelled, her Irish burr became obvious, and was overheard by one of the security guards. He introduced himself, explaining that he was also Irish. And he helped get her

in touch with a more senior INS representative who finally got her the forms she needed to finalize her application. Is this a heart-warming story or not? What about the Mexicans or Vietnamese who remained in the INS waiting room because they had no Irish burr?

While it may be difficult to defend special treatment, one cannot help feeling that the person who does not understand the joy of an end-around the INS procedures is missing something vital, perhaps a sense of humor. And surely the security guard has the right to bestow his own help as he sees fit. It would be a grey world if such acts of kindness were prescribed. Can there really be a requirement that we bestow largesse and generosity equally or even "fairly"? If you legislate that people treat everyone equally, people will protect themselves by treating everyone equally badly.

This is not to say that the universalist impulse of democratic morality is not compelling. But democracy cannot afford to wash its hand of tribalism entirely. Rather, it must learn from its competitor and co-opt the tribal impulse, as previously it learned from communism and built socialist structures and welfare states within democratic societies. What we need, perhaps, is not a theory of justice, but a theory of injustice. We need to carve out a sphere in which equality and justice can be ignored and discarded. We need a sphere in which tribal hatreds and unreasonable prejudices can be set free.

In the United States, one strategy which has seemed to give play to and

contain the tribal impulse at the same time is to emphasize the family structure over and against racial, religious or ethnic identities. Society can afford people to act with special benevolence to immediate family members because the unit is so small that it is not a threat to their broader democratic commitments. Family traditions and history, weddings and Thanksgiving dinners, can provide those intense and sacred personal moments without engulfing society in divisive schisms. It is more socially acceptable and less socially disruptive, to like your brother better than other men, than to like Italian men better than other men.

In its official and unofficial iconography, the United States has made the family into a sacred institution. This has served the values of a democratic melting pot by causing new immigrants to cease viewing themselves primarily as Polish or Irish within an Anglo culture, but rather as Lewbowskis or Murphys within the United States.

However, the same characteristic that makes the family unthreatening to democracy makes it a fragile institution. It is small. And if parents divorce or children run away or siblings don't like each other, one's tribal impulses have no outlet. Perhaps it is not surprising that the groups who have been particular

proponents of identity politics all have issues with the family: blacks because of the stress placed on family relationships by racism and poverty, women because of the traditional connection between the family and patriarchy, and gays because of the general unavailability of the family structure. It is not clear that the family is a robust enough institution to deflect the political challenge of tribalism.

Another possibility is that the creation of faux-tribal structures may provide a sense of kinship without defining the relationship of "belonging" in a destructive manner. In my English grade-school, everyone was divided into one of four houses: Nelson, Wellington, Marlborough and Drake. Siblings were placed together, but otherwise the teachers made an obvious effort to divide the jocks, the brains and the loons equally. Many school activities were organized along house lines and I remember feeling a surprisingly close tie to my fellow Nelsonites. So much so, that one could forget other easily-ridiculed characteristics: "Tommy might be fat, but he'll help Nelson in the pie eating contest"; "Larry might be dumb, but he's Nelson's biggest cheerleader." Cutting across the usual schoolboy divisions, the kinship bonds within these houses actually broadened rather than restricted our definitions of who could be included as "one of us".

Of course a society cannot place each of its citizens into artificial houses, but perhaps it can build more faux-tribal relationships, so that eventually we each become such a mish-mash of tribal and traditional commitments that we share some kinship bond with every person we encounter. We share a race, or an income, a sports team or a college, a gender or a religion, a chat group or a health plan. Our life is full enough of the dance of belonging and excluding, that we do not feel the need to belong to or exclude from our political structure. Our politics, rather, is democratic.

Smurf

Lincoln MacVeagh

Kim, the bitchy bartender, was a sexy blonde girl who worked most shifts alongside her twin sister Stacey. They worked in short black shorts so that when they bent over you could see their panties and they were very good at selling drinks and making tips.

Both of the twins were extremely rude but I liked them anyway. Especially Stacey. Stacey was the gentler of the two and she was nice to me. After I'd been at Uno's a couple of months, she found out from one of the managers that I'd gone to Harvard and she became quite flirtatious.

"Listen," she once said in passing, "If you need a girlfriend for the rest of the Summer, let me know."

I couldn't tell if she was joking, but in any case my face turned red and my mouth dried up, and when Kim saw me blushing she started laughing her head off.

Like many restaurants in New York City, the Uno's at South Street Seaport was essentially a segregated work place. The wait staff was white; the kitchen was black and latino; and there was an obvious racial tension between the two. I remember being puzzled the first time I heard bitchy Kim refer to Jones Beach as "Chicken Bone Beach". It took me a while to figure out what she meant: that Jones Beach was a place for black people.

Kim was a funny girl. I remember one slow afternoon waiting in the kitchen for a pizza. The kitchen was empty except for me and Dexter, one of the line-cooks. Dexter was tall and skinny, and he had a dark black skin that made him look African. He also had a reputation as a ladies man and later he caused a small stir when he started dating one of the white waitresses. Dexter and I were talking about the weather when we heard the shriek of Kim's voice coming around the corner:

"What's that racket? Who's making that noise? Boom, boom, boom! I can hardly hear myself think. It's like a whole tribe of Africans whacking away at their drums!"

Kim rushed towards us looking hysterical, then she suddenly pulled up short at the order window and became calm again.

"Oh Dex," she said as if waking from a dream, "It's just you." Dexter smiled and didn't miss a beat.

"That wasn't drumming you heard. That was the sound of me banging your idiot sister."

"Yeah, yeah," said Kim admitting defeat, "Well, quit banging my sister and get me an order of buffalo wings."

While there was always a slight tension between the kitchen and the wait staff, the worst aspect of race relations at Uno's had to do with the customers. I have worked at a number of different restaurants and the complaint is always the same: black people, it is said, don't tip well.

At Uno's there was a code name for black customers. They were called *smurfs*. If anyone was asked point blank, they'd say that *smurf* just meant a customer who left less than 15 percent. In theory, Europeans could be *smurfs* too. In practice, the racial connotation of *smurf* was no secret and everyone knew what it meant.

It was commonplace to hear waiters talking about *smurf* drinks (cognac and coke) and *smurf* pizzas (the *Sea Delico* came with cheese, shrimp and fake crab meat), and when a table left a bad tip waiters used to say, "I got *smurfed*." I once heard an angry waitress say to Rodney, a black host, that he'd been *smurfing* her all night and that he'd better stop. Rodney ignored her with equanimity. Later he told me that he'd seated her only white trash and minorities for the rest of the shift. So it went.

At Uno's, the racial problem came to a climax with the arrival of Steve. Steve was an ass. He was the boyfriend of one of the assistant managers and because his girlfriend made up the schedules he always got the best shifts, despite being an incompetent. Steve was a chubby frat boy. He wore Ray-Ban sunglasses when he worked on the sun deck and he was constantly throwing his hair back and running his fingers through his part. He had a cloying personality. He made a big effort to be in-the-know and one of the ways he expressed his coolness was by complaining loudest about *smurfs*.

A good waiter earns his tips; bad waiters deserve to get stiffed. Steve was the worst waiter imaginable, but that thought never occurred to him. Every time someone left him a dollar on a fifteen dollar check he'd throw his head in the air and announce to the world, "Fucking *smurfs*."

One Saturday night I was working next to Steve on the deck. We were extremely busy and Steve was hopelessly overwhelmed. Rather than ask the manager for help, Steve solved his problems by focusing his attention only on his three white tables. It was probably unconscious, but after a while two hispanic girls in his section figured out what was going on and they were furious.

One of the girls stormed up to the front of the restaurant to talk to Rodney, the host. Rodney walked her back to her table saying, "Some people are assholes, but we want your business." Then Rodney called over Alice, the manager on duty. Alice pulled Steve off the deck and asked for an explanation. Completely flustered, Steve started attacking Rodney and the two girls. He said the only complaint against him was that he was white. Rodney lost his temper and there was a loud shouting match before Alice managed to cool things down. The two hispanic girls were re-seated in a different section of the restaurant and given dinner on the house.

The next day when I went to work, Alice called everyone together before the shift and gave a speech about not saying *smurf* anymore, and about how you might get fired if you did. Later in the week Uno's hired three new waitresses, all of them black, and after that I rarely heard the word *smurf* again.

"Come in. Sit down. Make yourself comfortable."

Games

Sir Laffalot

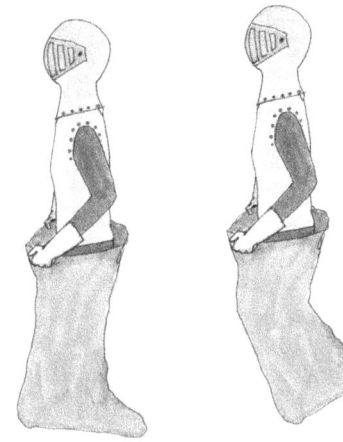

Sir Laffalot was born for the stage. Play on McDuff! He has a pleasant face, a nice singing voice and an easy sense of movement. Unfortunately, others have been slow to recognize his talent and he has long been forced to toil in the shadows. Slings and arrows. Actors have an unenviable fate.

Sir Laffalot's last big audition was for a singing waiter job at a Hungarian restaurant in Tribeca. The manager described it as dinner theater. First come the appetizers, then sketch comedy and show tunes until the main course is ready.

It was the last day of auditions and only two other hopefuls showed up. The first was a woman with a gypsy theme who wore beads and a long flowy dress. She sang "Age of Aquarius" from *Hair* and accompanied herself with a tambourine. Very engaging, but the manager said it wasn't what he was looking for.

The second fellow showed off a long résumé of summer stock productions and announced that he had just come off a three week run in Albany playing Jesus in *Jesus Christ Superstar*. He put a look of pathos on his face and boomed out an extended version of the musical's title song so loud that the glasses on the tables rattled.

Sir Laffalot was secretly pleased when Jesus' voice cracked on one of the high notes. The contest was still wide open.

When Sir Laffalot's turn came, he gave a soulful rendition of the George Gershwin classic "Summertime." The manager was obviously impressed and asked for an encore, something a little more upbeat. Unprepared, Sir Laffalot's mind went blank. All he could think of was the fight song for the British Grenadiers and he launched right in: "*Some talk of Alexander / And some of Hercules / Of Hector and Lysander / And such great names as these...*"

Sir Laffalot was still working through the first verse when the manager waved his hand in the air and asked him to stop. Too stiff. The manager told him to go home and work on extending his dramatic range. He suggested playing *In The Manner Of The Word*, a charades-like game in which players act out the meaning of different adverbs.

In The Manner Of The Word: How to Play.

1) One person leaves the room while the others jointly decide on an adverb (e.g. quickly, lazily, happily).
2) The outside player then comes back and asks everyone else to perform different actions in the manner of the chosen word. Get dressed in the manner of the word; drink tea in the manner of the word; propose marriage in the manner of the word, etc..
3) Once everyone has been given a chance to act out the adverb, the guesser has three tries to come up with the correct word. Cheers follow.

Confidently, Sir laffalot says:
TOODALOO!!

The high life

Wedding Bells

David Garcia III

In line at a wedding reception on Martha's Vineyard, I begin conversing with a guy who turns out to be Bobby, hairdresser to the bride for the last decade in D.C. "I'm doing the entire wedding party," he tells me. I also learn in short order that he owns his own Salon, two apartments, and a nearby summer house which is getting new floors installed. Bobby is doing well.

The sun has set, and lights have came on outside to help guide us past the couples playing one last game of croquet. The clouds are periwinkle and custard.

I compliment Bobby on the bride's hair, which in truth looks identical to how it looked at twelve. He points out another bridesmaid whom he has favored with a pixie cut. "Just like Liv Tyler," he says. I tell him that I saw Liv Tyler recently, bopping along the street in a sundress, singing Aerosmith, and looking truly beautiful, even without the long hair. "I take that as a compliment," says Bobby, "You don't know how long it took me to convince her to cut it short."

I am a childhood friend of the bride and Bobby is her hairdresser. Jokingly I say, "So, I have all the old dirt and you have all the new." Slightly less jokey he answers, "Let's get martinis and trade."

We quickly establish that we both know about the cake jumping, the tumultuous years with Mike Bellanger, and about the brother's suicide: "She came in for a trim one day, I took one look at her face, and I knew something was wrong. I said – you're coming in the back with me."

In the midst of our fun, I have second thoughts about gossiping about my friend on her special day. I resolve to get up and mingle, but find myself – as if hypnotized – telling Bobby about Mr. Perfect. A story I had almost forgotten, as it happened two years (and almost two fiancée's) back.

At the time Mindy was going steady with a guy who was so blindingly perfect that they wrote about him in the paper. I'm not kidding. She showed me an article once and it was about nothing so much as how he was handsome and worked with troubled kids. His marital suitability was *news*. True, he was emotionally distant at times, but Mindy decided to treat that as an added bonus.

Things were going great. They made plans for a getaway to a secluded cabin with another couple to watch the Superbowl. They got there on Saturday and did some skiing and all feasted on Mexican food. The Superbowl was the next day, and Mindy told herself, "He's going to pop the question tonight." She could feel it in the air, and it was all she could think about as they washed the dishes and made chit-chat with the other couple over drinks. Then the time came when they said goodnight and headed off to bed. She got into her nightgown, he stripped down to long underwear, and they got under the covers. The light went off, and he said to her, "You are not the one."

She didn't see it coming at all, like the stomach punch that killed Houdini. It was the middle of the night, she was half drunk, and she had to go back out in the snow and drive hundreds of miles home – ringless. Two weeks later Mr. Perfect died in a tragic tobogganing accident.

"Oh my God," says Bobby, "I never heard about that... but I think I did his hair."

"He had great hair."

TO SUBSCRIBE TO THE ECLECTIC TURN TO PAGE 7.

The
ECLECTIC

September 1999   Volume 1 Number 7   Free

CONTENTS

Quotations

"Polar exploration is at once the cleanest and most isolated way of having a bad time that has yet been devised." Apsley Cherry-Garrard describes life in the Antarctic in *The Worst Journey In The World.*

"I have lived some thirty-odd years on the planet, and I have yet to hear the first syllable of valuable or even earnest advice from my seniors." Henry David Thoreau writes in his journals.

"The Socialist who finds his children playing with tin soldiers is usually upset, but he is never able to think of a substitute for the tin soldiers; tin pacifists somehow won't do." George Orwell ponders the succcess of Hitler's militarism in *Collected Essays, Volume 2.*

"You will let him play with his thingummy, won't you?" Orwell interviews a nanny to look after his infant son in *Orwell Remembered.*

The Eclectic is owned and published by Linoleum Palace, Inc., 43-05 31st Ave., #2, Astoria, NY 11103. Copyright ©
1999 by Lincoln MacVeagh. All rights reserved. Unsolicited submissions will not be considered or returned.

A Man Not A Saint

George Orwell's Life

Lincoln MacVeagh

"I'm George Orwell."

A brief word on pseudonyms. In 1945 the English journalist Eric Blair went to Paris to report on post-war Europe. Earnest Hemingway was also in Paris at the time and Blair wanted to meet him. He tracked down Hemingway's hotel, knocked on his door and introduced himself. Hemingway was busy packing and made no reaction. Blair stood in the doorway.

"Well, what the fucking hell do you want?" boomed Hemingway.

"I'm George Orwell," said Blair apologetically.

"Why the fucking hell didn't you say so? Have a drink."

Pseudonyms make for confusion. To his friends, the author of *Animal Farm* was known as Eric Blair; to everyone else he is known as George Orwell; and when writing about him it's hard to know which name to use. I have settled on Orwell.

George Orwell was born in 1903 in India. His father was a docile, conservative man who worked as civil servant overseeing the production of opium and later came out of retirement at the age of sixty to serve as a subaltern in World War I. Orwell's mother was a lively French woman, eighteen years younger than her husband, who was once described as *"very kind to anyone poorer than herself, but if you had tuppence more, God help you."* Actually she seems to have been nicer than that.

Mrs. Blair left India for England the year after her son was born and Orwell grew up in Henley with his mother and two sisters. He was a sickly child and not naturally light-hearted. Mrs. Blair's diary records her son's recovery from an early illness saying, *"Baby much better. Calling things 'beastly'!!"*

Orwell's family was not rich but they were determined to push him along and at age eight George was sent away to St. Cyprian's, a private boarding school with the weird Latin motto: "**Forsan et haec olem meminesse juvabit.**" ("Perhaps one day even these things will be pleasant to remember.") For Orwell the motto proved false and in an essay about St. Cyprian's titled "Such, Such Were The Joys" he tells of getting beaten for bed-wetting and being scorned by the headmistress for not having money. A number of Orwell's fellow old boys were offended by this portrait of St. Cyprian's and one of them published his own essay in defense of the school. But if there was an argument, Orwell surely won. Even St. Cyprian's apologist starts out by saying that some of his schoolboy scars remain: *"Among them I should put*

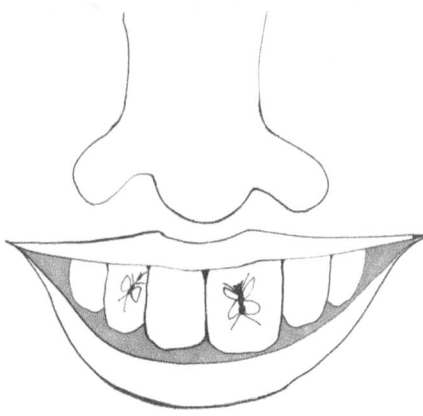

the cold pewter bowls of porridge with the thick slimy lumps, into which I was actually sick one day and made to stand at a side table and eat it up..."

After five years at St. Cyprian's Orwell won a scholarship to Eton, a school much more to his taste. Eton was unusual in that it allowed its students broad freedom to do as they wished: Orwell read widely, studied little and liked to think of himself as a rebel. One classmate remembered him always complaining about the degrading custom of tipping one's hat to the masters. Orwell was well served by Eton, but he was always near the bottom of his class and he left with no chance at a university scholarship. Following in his father's footsteps, he decided to join the British Empire instead.

Orwell was twenty when he went off to Burma as a police officer, and just two years later he was the sole head of a force governing 200,000 people. It was a large responsibility for a man his age: *"In Moulmein in Lower Burma, I was hated by large numbers of people – the only time in my life that I have been important enough for this to happen to me."* As a conscientious police officer Orwell had to quell disturbances and see to it that convicts were punished; as a white man he drank whiskey on the porch and was dressed by his manservant. In all outward appearance Orwell was a typical servant of the British Raj; in secret he detested colonial life.

Burma was Orwell's introduction to the concept of the Big Lie. In Burma, the Big Lie was this: that the British Empire was a benevolent force, bringing civilization and decency to grateful natives who were incapable of ruling themselves. The vast bulk of the English people believed it and Orwell himself believed it until experience disillusioned him. Seen from up close, the Empire looked like nothing but an exercise in power, a racket run for the benefit of the British. Orwell was shocked and the anger he felt at having been so massively deceived never quite left him.

Orwell resigned his Burma commission five years into his service. He returned to England without an anchor and distrustful of convention: *"Failure seemed to me to be the only virtue. Every suspicion of self-advancement, even to 'succeed' in life to the extent of earning a few hundreds a year, seemed to me spiritually ugly, a species of bullying."*

Orwell was determined to write, but he had not yet found his subject and for the time being he wasn't much good. To many of his acquaintances his literary ambitions simply made him a figure of fun. One such acquaintance was a lively woman poet named Ruth Pitter who told a BBC interviewer: *"And do you know, he wrote so badly. He had to teach himself writing, he was like a cow with a musket; it was a sheer grind... And we lent him an old oil stove and he started to write a story about two girls fine girls who lent a writer an oil stove! Oh dear, how we cruel girls laughed."*

In 1929 Orwell began his experiments with poverty. Dressing up in shoddy clothes, he would leave his parents' comfortable house in Southwald and go join the tramps on the streets of London. Given Orwell's background it was inevitable that he would sometimes come off badly as a tramp. Even some of his closest friends felt that he was shamming, and according to his sister, when Orwell started tramping he was still flicking his cigarette ashes on the floor at home, like a colonial sahib waiting for the maid to sweep them up. Ruth Pitter and her friends still thought Orwell absurd: *"He came to change into his rags at our workshop once or twice. He looked daggers at me as if to say laugh if you dare! But we did laugh a lot."*

Clever people sniggered, and meanwhile Orwell discovered a whole world that other people had refused to see. Somehow he learned to write about it in beautifully clear prose and the result was *Down And Out In Paris And London*, an almost true-to-life account of his years on the bum. Because of the book's subject matter, *Down and Out...* was rejected a number of times before finding a publisher, and when it did come out Orwell used a pseudonym to avoid embarrassing his parents. He chose the name "George Orwell" for its distinctive Englishness, and since he also considered calling himself "H. Lewis Allways" I think he chose well.

Down And Out... made no money, but it gave Orwell encouragement and he started to build a reputation as a novelist and essayist. He was still a long way from supporting himself as a writer and he made his living variously as a tutor, a teacher, a bookshop salesman and as the proprietor of small country grocery. One of the boys Orwell tutored gives us a good snapshot of him at the time: *"He had a slow disarming sort of smile which made us feel that he was interested in us, yet amused by us in a detached, impersonal sort of way... He never condescended; he never preached; he never intruded... I can only remember him getting indignant on one occasion when he told us how he thrashed a boy whom he caught blowing up a frog with a bicycle pump."* Orwell took the boys on long walks, discussed books with them and, incredibly, taught them how to make bombs.

Orwell seems to have enjoyed being a tutor, but as a schoolteacher and as a bookseller he was unhappy. His favorite job was running his grocery. He made a little store out of the front room of his cottage in Wallington and he sold bacon to housewives and sweets to the neighborhood children. If nothing else, he said, it was better than selling books: *"In a grocer's shop people come in to buy something, in a bookshop they come in to make a nuisance of themselves."*

When Orwell opened his shop he was already married to Eileen O'Shaughnessy and one can hardly imagine a luckier match for him. Eileen was game, attractive and intelligent, and she saw enough of Orwell's charm and merit not to be scared off by his quirks. Orwell was not easy to live with and weaker natures might have trembled when on the day of the wedding Orwell's mother and sister took Eileen upstairs to tell her how sorry they were for her. Eileen laughed it off. Her marriage to Orwell was not perfect (Orwell had at least two affairs and Eileen likely had one of her own) but it was extremely solid. Orwell admired his wife and she repaid him with patience and devotion.

Over the course of the next ten years, Eileen followed Orwell to Spain when he went to fight the fascists in the Civil War and it was her cunning that saved him from imprisonment by the Communists; she also stayed by him in London during the blitz and

accommodated herself to his energetic preparations for the coming German invasion (*"I can put up with bombs on the mantelpiece, but I will not have a machine gun under the bed"*); and lastly, she acquiesced when Orwell set his heart on the adoption of a baby boy. Then in 1946, at the age of 43, Eileen died during a routine surgery on her ovaries.

Orwell was horribly shaken by Eileen's death and in the year following he made desperate proposals of marriage to at least three different women. To Anne Popham he talked of his son Richard's need for a mother and of his own terrible loneliness. More morbidly, he tried to sell Anne on his weak health: *"What I am really asking you is whether you would like to be the widow of a literary man."* Clearly, Orwell was not at his best; Anne rejected his offer and so did everyone else.

Nonetheless Orwell picked himself up, and instead of a wife he found a marvelous nanny to look after Richard. Her name was Susan Watson and her account of her interview is amusing. Orwell watched her give Richard a bath and asked her if she was a good cook. Susan said no and Orwell said it didn't matter. Then he took her out to a restaurant: *"George said he had to leave me for a minute, would I order two drinks. Then he went to stand behind a pillar. I ordered the drinks and as soon as the waiter brought them, he emerged. Later he told me that he considered waiters to be very good judges of character, so because I had been served quickly, I earned the waiter's seal of approval."*

Sick of city life and needing peace, Orwell now moved his new household to a remote island off the Scottish coast and started writing *1984*. Orwell worked feverishly while in Scotland but one likes to think he was happy there. He was a country lover in the middle of the wilderness and thanks to the success of *Animal Farm*, he was free from money worries for the first time in his life. The only drawback was his health. His lungs were severely damaged by tuberculosis, bronchitis, and an outrageous number of cigarettes. After surviving just two winters he was forced back to London for medical treatment. In hospital he married his second wife Sonia Brownell (one of the more mercenary women to whom he had proposed a few years earlier) in a curious bedside ceremony, and three months later he was dead.

Orwell died at 46 and towards the

end of his life he frequently expressed the wish that no one should write his biography. He said that he himself was the only person who could tell his life properly. He added that he would never write an autobiography because, "*in an autobiography you had to tell the whole truth.*" The implication, of course, is that the truth would sting, and one gets the impression of a man with lots of dirty linen in his closet. It is a false impression. If anything, he was more like a well behaved schoolboy who trumpets his few misdeeds to impress his friends. The writer Anthony Powell tells a story of running into Orwell at a cocktail party. Orwell pulled Powell aside and asked darkly, "*Have you ever had a woman in the park?*" Orwell waited two beats and answered his own question saying, "*I have. I was forced to. Nowhere else to go.*"

For who-knows-why Orwell liked to see himself as a man with a past. However, making love to a girlfriend on the common hardly counts as a skeleton in the closet and one looks in vain for any truly discreditable episodes in his life. Orwell's worst failing was self-absorption, but his bedrock quality was decency. Of course, there are other reasons why he may not have wanted a biography written. For one thing, Orwell would have found it offensive to have his hard thought opinions dismissed as the by-product of some chance experience. For another, he probably disliked the way biography tends to freeze warm life on paper and present it as cold fact. Personally, I suspect he was just nervous of looking ridiculous.

It's not hard to make Orwell look silly. Orwell was a man of violent enthusiasms: it is funny when he raves about his favorite Greek restaurant and one his friends who had eaten there says: "*the wartime Moussaka looked like a dog's vomit.*" He was also a strange mixture of working class sympathies and upper class instincts, and again it is funny when we catch the champion of social justice solemnly chiding his wife for having put a pot of marmalade directly on the table: marmalade, he insisted, must always be decanted into a jam dish before serving. Finally, Orwell was a man of strong ideas and like all such men he was often wrong: one rumor has it that during World War II he kept an extensive diary in which he predicted each day what was going to happen in the next few days, but the diary was never published because none of his predictions came out.

The point is, I suppose, that Orwell wasn't perfect. We shouldn't make a fuss about it. Orwell didn't want to be a saint. He wanted to be a flesh and blood human being and in this he succeeded admirably. Read his books and you hear the voice of an honest man on every page.

Reviews

The Moon's A Balloon

by David Niven

Out of print

When the powers that be finally get around to making a list of all the people who are funnier, more gracious and better looking than you and I, the actor David Niven is sure to be near the top. Halfway through *The Moon's A Balloon* Niven is planning his first trip to New York City when he realizes that he hasn't enough money to pay for it. Suddenly he remembers having once danced with a pretty young American girl named Barbara Hutton. With fingers crossed he cables Barbara about his pending arrival. She is so excited to see him again that she gives him the Hutton family suite at the Hotel Pierre and has her friends buy him dinner every night for a month. It is tempting to gnash one's teeth in the face of such good fortune, but Niven is so charming and guileless that one can't help but be pleased by his success.

The Moon's A Balloon is Niven's memoir and it is immensely fun to read. Niven writes especially well about his childhood and the first two hundred pages run by like water. At the age of fourteen he is an enormously sympathetic character. Pudgy and lonely, Niven passes through a variety of boarding schools and detentions centers, and while his mother and stepfather struggle to keep a place in the upper classes, Niven's own best friend is Nessie, a cockney whore. In one of the book's most charming scenes, Niven has finally landed at a school he likes and Nessie insists on meeting the headmaster. *"Don't look a bit like a schoolmaster, dew yer dear?"* says Nessie. The headmaster is a perfect gentleman and after chatting amiably

for ten minutes, he takes his leave telling Nessie, *"David is very lucky to have such a charming visitor."* (More gnashing of teeth.)

By the time Nessie marries a rich American, Niven has become an Army officer stationed in Malta and although there are lots of colonel's wives to keep him entertained Niven finds that army life doesn't suit him. After four years he runs away to the U.S.. He tries to make a living as a liquor salesman in New York but eventually he is drawn out to California and into acting.

Niven's book fades somewhat once he gets to Hollywood. It remains lively and readable but it feels less genuine. On page 12, Niven writes of his father's death, *"I am afraid that my father's death meant little or nothing to me at the time..."* On page 228, he writes of the director Irving Thalberg's death, *"It was a staggering loss."*

When Niven talks about movie people he often sounds like a guest discussing his hosts (*"Marlene, the most glamorous of all, was also one of the kindest"*), and after a while one gets slightly weary of all the famous people he knows and how wonderful they are. I suspect it was Niven's publisher who insisted on all the star encounters. Niven himself seems almost embarrassed by his name dropping and in the introduction he apologizes, saying it was hard to avoid. He also argues that having met famous people, *"...it makes little sense to talk about the butler if Chairman Mao is sitting down to dinner."*

I'm pretty sure that last line was stolen from Somerset Maugham and when I first read it, it made a great deal of sense, but I'm no longer convinced. Nessie the cockney whore is one of the liveliest characters I've met in years and I'd gladly read a full book about her. From what Niven tells us about Marlene Dietrich, she barely merits two paragraphs in *Variety.*

Commentary

Creationism and the Limits of Debate

T.E. MacVeagh

One argument that creationism should be taught in schools goes something like this. Evolution is a "theory" the truth about which we are not sure. As it is just one possible theory, then it is a disservice to our children not to expose them to alternative theories. One ready alternative is offered by creationist science. And the mere fact that the weight of the evidence supports evolution is not reason enough to refuse to expose students to less popular theories.

This faux-rational argument relies on two premises: that there is some uncertainty to the theory of evolution and that there is some plausibility to creationism as an alternative theory. No one suggests that children be taught alternatives to the "theory" that George Washington was the first president of the United States. Nor do they suggest that children be taught as an alternative to evolution that human intelligence is the result of our brains having been designed by an alien civilization.

But from a scientific perspective, there is no uncertainty that the broad strokes of evolutionary theory are right. And there is no more plausibility to creationism than to bizarre theories about alien civilizations. Without reviewing the evidence, it is fairly clear that if the supporter of creationism accepts scientific standards of what counts as evidence, their cause is a losing proposition.

This is the point where a creationist shifts the argument, maintaining that traditional scientific notions of what counts as "evidence" are biased: mainstream science is not open to any explanations which rely on God. This is true. God explains too much for science. Scientists would soon stop looking for answers if they could invoke God as an explanation every time they ran into difficulty. Science, as creationists well understand, is what you do when you look for an explanation other than God.

The real question, then, is not whether creationism is sound science, but whether we should teach science in schools at all, or at least whether we should teach it to the exclusion of non-scientific ways of understanding the world, such as religion. It is a philosophical debate over the nature of what is "rational". When creationists present their supposed evidence in favor of creationism, scientists argue (correctly) that such evidence is not scientifically relevant. The creationists respond (also correctly) that the rejection of their evidence by the scientific community is based on a definition of rationality in which it is axiomatic that arguments based on faith must be rejected. Of course such an axiom makes it difficult to prove that God created man, but creationists reject the axiom. To support the claim that evolution is a superior theory to creationism, creationists say, scientists must first show that the scientific definition of rationality is superior to their religious one.

And this is the point at which people generally throw up their hands. These kinds of discussions about philosophy never seem to go anywhere. We would need some meta-framework in which everyone agreed about what counted as rational argument to even engage in debate. Otherwise, no matter how far you go, the evolutionist is going to say that faith based arguments have to be rejected. And the creationist is going to say that arguments based on faith are legitimate. It seems as if the decision to adopt a scientific world view is just as much a matter of "faith" as the decision to adopt a Christian world view. Reasoned argument would appear to have reached the limit of its ability to resolve disputes.

Where does that leave us in the debate between the evolutionists and the creationists or, as we can now characterize it, between the scientists and the theists? Each side claims victory within the rules of rational argument it accepts, but knows that the other side, safe within its alternative framework, remains unconvinced. Each side suspects that the only real resolution will be at the ballot box (or through less pleasant strong-arm tactics). Philosophical debates will not help; all they can really do is beat each other into submission. Rationality, like history, is defined by the victors.

The notion that philosophical debate is useless has infiltrated deep into our culture. But it is surely wrong. Philosophical debate is hard and slow. It reaches impasses which seem unbridgeable. And it may not be able to resolve every difference. But still philosophical debate can and does produce results. It narrows the differences between people, it forces reconsideration of entrenched beliefs, it even compels agreement. I know I have changed my mind on issues quite dear to me in the face of the implacable logic of others. And in the face of my own arguments, I have seen others converted. Even more often, I have seen wild, violent disagreements over morality reduced to genteel differences of interpretation.

These results are hard to notice because they rarely occur in the heat of debate. We do not surrender our ideas while surrounded by a hostile audience. We wait until we find a safe corner and can examine our wounds without fear of their bursting open again. Sometimes (not always) we realize that it was not lack of inspiration which prevented us from avoiding a particular barb, but an actual weakness in our position. We dare, tentatively and slightly afraid, to consider an alternative view, feeling inadequate for not having come to it first. It may still take weeks or years to accept the new position. But the groundwork has been laid.

The reason philosophical debate is possible is because our notions of "rationality" and "faith" which we often describe as fundamental are in fact quite low in the hierarchy of our beliefs. "Experimentation is the basis of knowledge" and "Justice requires democracy" are in fact much less central to our lives and outlook than, "You should look both ways when you cross the street" or "My father is admirable". For all of our disagreements about things like the nature of evidence and the existence of God, the people against whom we enter into philosophical debate are like us in the huge mass of beliefs which lie below the surface of those debates. It is recognition of this which makes us so angry at the fact that they insist on disagreeing with us in the first place.

Certainly the debate between science and theism seems particularly resistant to useful conclusion. There are so many fronts that it is difficult for all of the various attacks, defenses and counterattacks to be deployed in the course of one argument, or even one series of arguments. So that when we retreat to lick our wounds, we do not accept defeat. Rather, we realize that one of our defenses was not deployed, and we convince ourselves that our opponent has no counter for that one. As a result, the slow process by which philosophical argument changes minds extends to generations. Many are understandably unwilling to continue to engage in the disturbing, exhausting thrust and

parry of philosophical debate for such a period.

Further, both science and religion make claims about their superiority to more humble and instinctual observations and reasons. We get confused about whether we might not rather give up our common sense understanding that, for example, snow melts in the sun, than the grand claims of science or religion. But in fact, most of us cannot maintain the fiction that our decisions about epistemological or metaphysical issues are more important than our daily lives. And an argument which shows us a contradiction between those daily certainties and our grand theories casts a shadow over our epistemology rather than our desire for a hearty breakfast.

The general wisdom that the debate between evolutionists and creationists reaches an impasse is false. It is perfectly possible to debate the merits of creationist and evolutionist standards of rationality. This debate takes place not in some rarified meta-framework which floats above competing definitions of rationality, but in shared sub-frameworks which lurk under these definitions. The history of the debate shows a series of stunning losses for the creationist view of rationality. Not, as creationists would have you believe, because scientists are systematically oppressing theist beliefs, but because careful, painstaking philosophical debate has convinced theists that their metaphysics clashes with their acceptance of their commonplace beliefs.

I have not done the work here to show that creationism is wrong. But that work could be done if we had the time and the patience. A belief in creationism can be shown to be incompatible with the belief that you should look both ways when you cross the street and that snow melts in the sun. And despite the sense that philosophical debate is useless, such arguments do slowly win out.

Reminiscence

¡Apuntaté!

Lincoln MacVeagh

In 1989 I went to Mexico and I ended up living in a small town half an hour outside the city of Oaxaca. Having always thought of Mexico as the most developed of the Latin countries I was surprised to discover that large portions of the country, especially in the South, have remained largely outside the influence of the central government and untouched by modern culture. Tonya, my landlord's maid, was the first Mexican I ever met who spoke worse Spanish than I did. Her mother, who stayed with us one month, spoke no Spanish at all. Tonya and her mother came from a remote area in the mountains and their town, like Asterix's village in Gaul, was more or less its own sovereign state. On Tonya's mountainside everyone spoke a dialect of the Indian language Xapoteca. How do say goodnight in Xapoteca? *Hastashayana.*

The town of Huayapam, where I lived, was not a truly autonomous Indian town, but nor was it a fully incorporated part of the Mexican federation. Inhabitants still performed a yearly work duty – a holdover from earlier forms of communal taxation wherein each property owner had to spend two or three days laboring on some public work such as cutting brush back from the power lines or building new irrigation canals – and in many respects the town itself still represented the highest legal authority. At one time Huayapam was troubled by illegal squatters who were setting up shanties next to the reservoir. The town appealed to the state for help but the state refused to get involved saying that since it was town land, it was a town problem. So one night Huayapam assembled a band of men to torch the squatters out. You could see the flames burning from the highway three kilometers away, but no inquiries were ever made by the state.

The backwardness of the South has always been a cause of both concern and embarrassment to the industrial North and attempts are constantly being made to bring the Indians under the same tent as everyone else. During the time I lived in Mexico the central government was engaged in a massive voter registration campaign. A horde of young civil servants was sent out to the countryside to knock on doors and sign up the populous. *¡Apuntaté!* was the slogan and it could be seen all over: on TV, on billboards, and painted on the side of every government agency.

Despite the best intentions, the campaign was often thwarted by the ingrained prejudices of the people it was trying to reach. Most Indians have little contact with people in shirts and ties except for the Mormons and they don't like Mormons. They are not keen on government officials either. In the small towns of southern Mexico there are elaborate forms of local taxation – besides his work duty, my landlord paid a church tax, a light pole tax and a fiesta tax – and all of these taxes are collected separately by well-dressed men going from door to door. Since many people are behind on one payment or another, they have a tendency to stay away from officials.

The registration campaign passed through Huayapam twice while I was at home. The first man was very eager and bossy. He pressed me to sign up in spite of my blonde hair and American accent, and when I refused he gave me the sense that I wasn't doing my part. Then he pointed to the corrugated metal shack next door to my house and asked me where my neighbor was. I told him Señora Mercedes was at the market and he left in a huff.

Three months later a follow-up man came. The second man was sharp enough to recognize that I was not a potential voter and he cut straight to question of Señora Mercedes. Mercedes was not at home. She had spotted the official walking up our path and had quickly scrambled through her fence into the field in back of my house. I had watched her run away and when the official asked me where she was, I told him she was hiding behind the lime trees. Mercedes heard me say this and poked her head around a tree trunk. The official caught her eye and beckoned her to come out, but Mercedes ducked back behind the lime trees and wouldn't budge. I was enlisted to coax her out.

Mercedes was furious at me for giving her away but after a few minutes of hissed whispering behind the trees she agreed to talk. The resulting conversation was quite fruitless. Mercedes first insisted that all her taxes were paid up – which they weren't – while the official tried to explain that he wasn't a tax collector at all. Then the official gave a short speech on voter registration and Mercedes answered that she could take no action on such important business until her husband – she wasn't married – returned from work. In the end Mercedes started complaining about the bus service into town and the official gave up. He handed her a blank form and asked her to take it to the town clerk as soon as possible.

The next morning I was sitting outside in my chair when Mercedes came over to get water at our tap. Having filled her bucket she stopped to chat and gave me a banana for my breakfast. She complimented me on the zucchini in my garden and then she talked aimlessly for a while about various people in the town whom she disliked. Just before she left she took the blank voter registration form out of her pocket and handed it to me. She said she didn't need it anymore; she said that the government official had told her to give to me when she was done.

¡Apuntaté!

"Curveball, fastball, slider... Does it really matter in the end?"

Games

Sir Laffalot

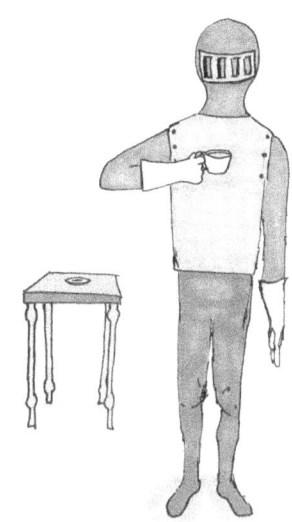

Password: How to Play.

Sir Laffalot was in the Queen's carriage last week and as it rumbled past CVS one of the ladies-in-waiting asked him to pop out and run a personal errand for her. Sir Laffalot agreed, but he is not accustomed to buying feminine protection and he was embarrassed to discover that it comes in an attention-getting, bright blue package. It felt like a hot potato when he picked it off the shelf.

There was an enormous line at the check-out and while an old woman at the front haggled over her coupons, Sir Laffalot got the sense that people were staring. To make matters worse, when he finally got up to the register he discovered he'd picked up a box that wouldn't ring through the scanner.

The check-out girl was a creature with no delicatesse. She simply waved the box high over her head and repeated 'Price Check!' over the intercom three times. When this led to nothing she took a few steps to her left and screamed down one of the side aisles to a stock boy in the back:

"Billie! How much for the tampax?"

"The kind you push in?" shouted Billie, "Or the kind you hammer in?"

"Not thumb tacks, you idiot! Tampax!"

Sir Laffalot returned to the royal carriage a bundle of nerves and to settle him down the Queen invited him back to the palace for tea. Unfortunately her majesty insists on pouring milk first, so it was not until Prince Edward suggested a rousing game of *Password* that Sir Laffalot's mood lifted. *Password* is a word association game for four players and Sir Laffalot and Fergie beat Edward and the Queen hands down.

1) The object of the game is to get your partner to guess a secret word using one word clues.

2) Divide into two teams of two. If there is a fifth player, he can be the master of ceremonies.

3) One player from each team is chosen as the clue-giver and together they decide on a secret word. The word can be picked from a book or magazine, or if there is a master of ceremonies he can assign it.

4) Play starts with one of the clue-givers giving his partner a clue. *One word only!*

5) If the partner fails to guess the secret word, the turn passes to the other team. Another clue is given and play goes back and forth between the teams until the secret word is discovered.

6) A team gets one point each time the secret word is guessed correctly, then the clue-givers become the guessers and vice-versa. A new secret word is chosen and the game starts over. Play best out of five. It's so darn fun!

Sir Laffalot says: TOODALOO!!

The high life

Vicky

David Garcia III

L ife was sweet for Vicky. Still young, she already had it all. The spacious condo on the Upper West Side, the Central Park View, the super-successful Doctor Husband. Not to mention her own career going full blast, the curtains, the bric-a-brac, the twins. Her figure had snapped back quickly after their birth. It was a matter of discipline.

I worked with Vicky and we were all a little in awe. Perhaps it was the briskness, the sheen; the outfits just a little kickier than the rest of us could afford. The air of rarity she exuded, swooping down the corridor as if on her own personal current. It was fun to watch, but hard to work with.

One Saturday Vicky stood at the summit, surveying the world she had created. Doctor Husband was out of town at a conference, the twins were visiting Grandma, and she finally had a moment to herself. Time to relax with some Calgon Bouquet and have an International Coffee Moment. After her bath, with a towel wrapped around her head turban style, she decided to drink her coffee on the balcony. As soon as she opened the door though, she saw it. It was thick and gloppy and disgusting. Pigeon droppings everywhere.

How horrible to find herself scrubbing, the fragrance of her Coconut Milk Bath Beads mixing with the odor of those filthy birds. These creatures had been mysteriously absent when the Real Estate Agent showed them the place. Why, she asked herself, is there always one drawback to the perfect apartment? This was Vicky's world they were violating, and she had to take action.

She had heard rumors that there was a product out there for just such a problem. Something semi-illegal, like fireworks or valium. She spent most of the day making calls, but she finally found a place that would sell it to her. She rushed to the store, wanting to wrap this up before the Husband returned. He would be proud of her initiative. The way she preserved their seamless world.

The man had told her "just one coat", but he didn't know these birds. They were real City pigeons, and they seemed to prefer her balcony to all the others. So Vicky painted five coats on the railing, and then one extra for good measure. Then she went shopping for beauty products. She had earned it.

Sunday came, and the twins and Husband returned. She cooked a marvelous dinner, which she planned to serve on the balcony. Dramatically, she opened the curtains to reveal the pristine surfaces, unsullied for once by the usual stains. Her husband had to rush to cover the children's eyes.

They could only stare in shock at the neat row of pigeon feet all along the railing. Maybe two dozen pairs. Apparently the pigeons had been cemented to the rail, and they had tried so hard to get away that they pulled their feet right off. Or perhaps they had to peck them off. Vicky closed the curtains in horror, and they decided to go out to dinner. It took a few days of negotiations, but an under-the-table payment persuaded the Super to clean up the mess quietly.

Unfortunately, Vicky's balcony can be seen from several of the neighbor's windows, and they reported her to the ASPCA. I was walking back to my desk from the coffee room when the commotion broke out. Three policemen came to the office, handcuffed Vicky, tearing one of her outfits, and dragged her out under protest. They made an example of her, and she was penalized with one of the largest fines in the history of cases of this kind.

The
ECLECTIC

October 1999   Volume 1 Number 8   Free

CONTENTS

Quotations

"As I know more of mankind, I expect less of them, and am ready now to call a man a good man upon easier terms than I was formerly." Dr. Johnson is mellowed by age in *Everybody's Boswell*.

"When you are eleven years old and you want to live your own life – which is perfectly natural: there's no time to lose – you lie continually and to everyone; it is the only defense, or almost." Henri de Montherlant in *The Boys*.

"...the human being is psychologically so infuriatingly complex that you can never explain his thoughts, actions, or character by trotting out a single superficial cause." Leonard Woolf from the third volume of his autobiography, *Beginning Again*.

"Clarissa came up, with her perfect manners, like a real hostess, and wanted to introduce him to someone – spoke as if they had never met, which enraged him." Virginia Woolf captures perfectly the relation between two former lovers in *Mrs. Dalloway*.

To Rise Above

Virginia Woolf's Achievemen

Lincoln MacVeagh

"Never think yourself singular, never think your own case much harder than other people's."

At the age of fifty-nine Virginia Woolf stuffed rocks in her pockets and walked into the river Ouse. Her body was not recovered until three weeks later. Virginia killed herself in 1941 and ever since then academics have been clamoring to tell us who she really was. The body of literature surrounding Woolf's life and work is so vast that one could never hope to read it all, but one need only dip one's foot in to realize that a large part of it is devoted to lurid questions about her sexuality and mental health. Was she a lesbian? Was she raped by her half-brother? Was she insane? I confess that I too am interested in these questions, but it turns out that they are very slippery, and the people who claim to have answered them definitively are all lying.

For some reason a great number of Woolf's biographers (with the notable exception of her nephew Quentin Bell) come to their subject with a battle axe in hand. They have a point to prove and their books are full of half-truths and intentional distortions. Reading them is like being led through a field of statistics by a politician: the Governor proudly points out that income tax rates have fallen but fails to tell you that sales taxes have trebled.

To give one example, Roger Poole has written a book of *"enormous influence"* (Mr. Poole's words) in which he stoutly rejects the idea that Virginia was ever mentally ill. He makes much of Virginia's troubles and of the incompetence of her doctors and he argues that she was *"not so much 'ill' as anguished."* It is a small point and there may be some merit in it, but it does not go very far to explaining why, during her breakdowns, Virginia would sometimes talk to herself non-stop for three days on end. Needless to say, Professor Poole makes no mention of such incidents.

In another popular Woolf book, Louise DeSalvo takes on the mystery of Virginia's sexuality and discovers that she grew up in a hothouse of incest and lust. There is a grain of truth here; Virginia probably was molested by her half-brother George Duckworth; but DeSalvo is not interested in grains of truth. She will not rest until Virginia has been brutally raped. What's more, she discovers that Virginia's father was probably sexually abusive; that her cousin was probably a serial rapist; and that Virginia and her sister Vanessa had a long running sexual affair dating back to their nursery days. DeSalvo's method is to pick excerpts from Virginia's enormous collection of letters, and she finds that the sisters formed "*a close conspiracy*" and a "*private nucleus*". Virginia even wrote of meeting Vanessa in "*the dark land under the nursery table, where a continuous romance seemed to go forward*". If this sort of thing amounts to lesbian sex, then innocence is dead.

Read enough of these Virginia Woolf biographies and one finally comes to realize that the questions of her sexuality and mental health are not only unanswerable, but irrelevant. Virginia Woolf's life was infinitely broader than such a narrow focus would suggest. Her interest was the universal, not the personal. She refused to be tied down to private complaints, and it was her constant struggle to rise above that gives both the diamond clarity to her essays and the weird ethereal quality to her fiction. Time and again Virginia argued that it was one's moral duty to seek the widest possible truth, and in *A Letter To A Young Poet* her advice was this: "*Never think yourself singular, never think your own case much harder than other people's.*"

Virginia Stephen was born into a complicated household. Her father was a widower who already had one child; her mother was a widow with three; and following their marriage Leslie and Julia Stephen quickly produced four more babies: Vanessa, Thoby, Virginia and Adrian. The family lived altogether in a large Victorian house at 22 Hyde Park Gate, and along with seven maidservants and a constant stream of visitors, it was a lively place.

The job of ordering the chaos fell to Virginia's mother and she seems to have been good at it. Julia Stephen was an intelligent and big hearted woman who bore her burdens with fortitude. Among these burdens was her husband. Leslie Stephen was a free-thinking literary man who was known to the outside world for his calm temper and sense of proportion. At home he was much more of a mixed bag. Liberal minded enough

to give Virginia free access to his library, Leslie could nonetheless be dictatorial. He had a passion for being obeyed and the worst side of his character is revealed in his neglect of his first daughter, Laura. Leslie said that Laura was backward, but she could not have been retarded in the usual sense, because she was reading *Robinson Crusoe* and studying German at the age of fourteen, and it's possible that Laura was simply recalcitrant. To Leslie that amounted to the same thing. By the time the family was established to Hyde Park Gate, Laura had been put in isolation, rather like Rochester's mother in *Jane Eyre*. The other Stephen children knew of Laura's existence but she was rarely seen or spoken of.

Eventually Laura went truly crazy and was sent to an asylum, but somehow her tragedy does not seem to have much affected the younger Stephen children. Virginia and her siblings adored each other and they amused themselves with books, cricket and the occasional play produced for the servants. "*DENIZENS OF THE KITCHEN,*" reads one of their advertisements, "*COME IN YOUR THOUSANDS!!*"

Virginia grew up in an intellectual atmosphere, and at the age of nine she began writing the *Hyde Park Gate News*, a newsletter about household events, which was published more or less weekly for the next four years. It was a good rag. Speaking of the arrival of a spinster cousin who had just returned from a visit to her married sister, Virginia wrote: "*We hope that no pangs of jealousy crossed her mind when she saw he sister so comfortably settled with a husband when she herself is searching the wide world in quest of matrimony. But we are wandering from our point like so many old people. She came on Monday and is still at Hyde Park Gate.*"

The sharp tongue came naturally to Virginia. So did the rebel's spirit, and at an early age she guessed that the world treated her sex unfairly. It seemed to her monstrous that Thoby would get sent off to a proper school while she and Vanessa were stuck in the nursery with needlepoint and music lessons. Virginia hated her music lessons and when she discovered that her teacher was devoutly religious, she hated them even more. Answering a question about the meaning of Christmas, Virginia replied that it was to celebrate the crucifixion. She then started laughing so hard that she had to be sent out of the room.

The last issue of the *Hyde Park Gate News* was published in April, 1985 and the date is significant because a month later Julia Stephen died and the family fell apart. Virginia had her first, short, nervous breakdown with symptoms of a racing pulse and a horrible fear of going outside, and thus began what she later referred to as her *"Greek slave period"*. The horror of the next several years was multiform. Virginia's father, always prone to self-pity, now turned into a grotesque in need of constant attention. Stella Duckworth, Virginia's half-sister, took over the household management but then she too died, and Hyde Park Gate became a place of unshakeable gloom. Leslie leaned heavily on the good will of his remaining daughters, and to make matters worse, both Vanessa and Virginia were surrounded by a horde of misery maids determined to cheer them up: *"They are good people I know but it would be a mercy if they could keep their virtues and their affections and all the rest of it to themselves."*

With her father incapacitated, Virginia's life was further complicated by George Duckworth's decision to make himself the man of the house. Extremely handsome, Virginia's half-brother was a dim-witted snob. But he knew that Virginia was pretty and from a good family, and he insisted on giving her a headstart in the fashionable world. George instructed her on how to dress and dragged her along to an endless round of dinners and dances. Virginia felt out of place talking about fox hunting; she did not want to be George's protégé, but she could not think how to escape him. Nor could she think how to

"Walk like a normal person, dear. I promise you won't break you mother's back."

escape George's wandering hands. Taking advantage of his role as chaperon, George sometimes groped Virginia in public, and occasionally he carried on his fondling in her bedroom. Whatever happened there (and no one knows), it only added to Virginia's distress.

The Greek slave period lasted approximately nine years. There was a good deal of normalcy mixed in. There were trips to Europe and long stays in the country; Thoby went to Cambridge and brought back interesting friends; Vanessa became an accomplished painter; Virginia studied Greek and started writing her diary. But life remained largely unpleasant until 1904. In that year Leslie Stephen finally died and Virginia suffered a second breakdown, throwing herself out of a low window in an attempt at suicide. As Virginia was recovering she heard the good news that George Duckworth was getting married and shipping out. George married Lady Margaret Herbert and when the engagement was announced Virginia cabled her congratulations. The cable was meant to read "She's an angel" and Virginia signed off with her childhood nickname, Goat. Unfortunately the cable got mangled and when it arrived at Lady Herbert's house it read: "*SHE'S AN AGED GOAT.*"

Towards the end of 1904 the Stephen children sold Hyde Park Gate and together they moved to a new house in Gordon Square where they were determined to live more freely. This house quickly became a meeting place for Thoby's university friends and the group

known as Bloomsbury took shape. With the Stephen children at its center, the Bloomsbury group achieved notoriety because while they rejected the old Victorian values, they were still closely enough associated with high society to be talked about by Duchesses. One rumor had Vanessa making love to the economist Maynard Keynes in the middle of a cocktail party.

Most of what was said was untrue, but Virginia and her friends did enjoy a new sort of sexual frankness. For one thing, Virginia found out that most of her best friends were buggers. For another, she realized she didn't care. Virginia said the floodgates first opened when Lytton Strachey pointed to a stain on Vanessa's dress and asked her if it was semen: "*Can one really say it? I thought & we burst out laughing. With that one world all barriers of reticence and reserve went down.*" It was an exciting time for everyone, but although Virginia was a bawdy talker and she heartily approved of others' sexual escapades, she herself kept staid. According to her brother Adrian, on the one occasion when Virginia got up the courage to go skinny dipping she was very vexed that it did not create more of a sensation than it did.

In 1906 Thoby died of typhoid fever and the following year Vanessa married Clive Bell and left Gordon Square. In combination these two events drained the energy out of Bloomsbury and in a desultory fashion Virginia began looking around for a husband of her own. She had a number of suitors but the man she accepted was Leonard Woolf.

Leonard had gone to Cambridge with Thoby, but he was not a typical member of the Bloomsbury group. Not only was Leonard a Jew, a fact which Virginia thought quite remarkable at first, but he had actually had a real job. After university, Leonard spent five years as a British civil servant governing a large section of Ceylon and he was a good deal more serious than most of the young men

Virginia knew. His earnestness comes through in one of his love letters: *"It isn't, really it isn't, merely because you are so beautiful – though of course that is a large reason & so it should be – that I love you: it is your mind & character – I have never known anyone like you in that – won't you believe that?"*

Virginia and Leonard were married in 1912. Virginia was in the midst of finishing her first novel *The Voyage Out.* She was deeply wrapped up in her work and the honeymoon in Spain was not a success. It is uncertain whether Virginia and Leonard ever made love, probably they tried; but after six months, the marriage was chaste and Virginia was plunged into madness. She tried for a second time to commit suicide and swallowed a heavy overdose of veronal tablets. She had to have her stomach pumped in hospital, and for the next two years her mental health was touch and go. Some days she refused to eat and was incapable of speech. Other days she blabbered nonsensically. There were long stretches of clarity in between but it was a rough way to start a marriage, and Leonard remained nervous about Virginia's health for the rest of her life.

Perhaps Leonard worried too much. Reading his autobiography one feels that Virginia teetered permanently on the brink of collapse. Leonard's anxiety is understandable but we would be wrong to believe that Virginia's life hung from so thin a thread. In fact, once the crisis passed, Virginia succeeded through more than twenty-five years of society, politics and hard work.

By 1940 Europe was at war. Fearing a German invasion and Leonard's subsequent persecution as a Jew, the Woolfs discussed the possibility of killing themselves. At first they settled on carbon-monoxide poisoning and Leonard made sure to keep a sufficient supply of gasoline on hand. Later, Adrian Stephen gave Leonard a lethal dose of morphia to carry with him. As the months passed, the German threat diminished, but Virginia kept the thought of suicide in her mind. In 1941 she began to have headaches and Leonard believed that she was on the verge of another collapse. He insisted that she agree to treatment. Vehemently opposed to hospitalization but afraid of insanity, Virginia could think of nothing else but to kill herself.

She left behind two short letters, one for Vanessa and one for Leonard. I quote from her letter to Leonard:

"Dearest,

I feel certain I am going mad again. I feel we can't go through another of those terrible times. And I shan't recover this time. I begin to hear voices, and I can't concentrate. So I am doing what seems the best thing to do. You have given me the greatest possible happiness. You have been in every way all that anyone could be...

I don't think two people could have been happier than we have been.

V."

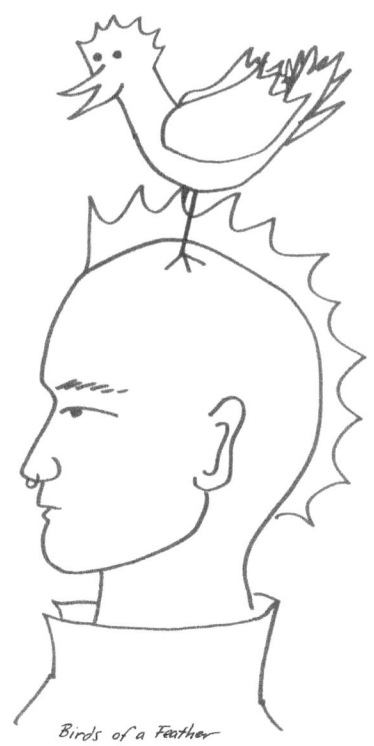

Birds of a Feather

Reviews

A Dance To The Music of Time, 1st Movement

by Anthony Powell

Chicago University Press, 1962

Some men are born wanting to change the world. Others are content simply to watch as the world changes. Anthony Powell is clearly in the latter camp. He is not a preacher and he has no great message to drive home; and for a book like *A Dance to the Music of Time* that is a very good thing. All told, *A Dance to the Music of Time* runs through twelve novels (though this review only covers the first three) and more than 3,000 pages. It is impossible to imagine any argument that could sustain itself for that long.

A Dance to the Music of Time is a difficult book to classify, but as much as anything, it is a social history of England's middle class. Powell's narrator is the shy and appealing Nicholas Jenkins, and the *First Movement* takes us from his schooldays during World War I to the time of his early middle-age in the 1930's. The story revolves around Jenkins and three of his close associates, each of whom touch a slightly different boundary of his social circle. There is Stringham, the dissipated aristocrat; Templar, the son of a business man; and Widmerpool, a hopeless drone who brings to mind Richard Nixon and who makes himself interesting only through sheer force of will.

Powell's action is tightly worked. A review of the plot reveals little that is extraneous and incident follows upon incident as if by logical necessity. At the same time, however, not much happens. A schoolmaster gets arrested by mistake; one boy goes to university whereas another does not; there is a dance, and a cocktail party, and Barbara dumps sugar on Widmerpool's head. It is mundane stuff and in synopsis it might sound wearisome, but somehow Powell saves it from being dull.

Part of the excitement is due to Powell's ability to draw out certain social truths that are widely known but seldom expressed. Here is the lowly Widmerpool trapped in the driveway of Sir Magnus' grand country estate with a

car that won't start. Sir Magnus asks absently whether anything is wrong. Widmerpool is flustered and terribly upset: *"However, obeying the law that requires most people to minimise to a superior a misfortune which to an inferior, they would magnify, Widmerpool thrust his head through the open window of the car, and, smiling reverentially, gave an assurance that all was well."* Such laws as this really do exist, and it is largely because Powell is so good at identifying them that we keep reading.

But it is not all plain sailing. As one can see, Powell's style is unusually loose. He writes baggy sentences. He loves the colon and the semi-colon, and he is not the least afraid of qualifiers or the extra phrase, even in his shortest sentences. Speaking of Templar's love life, Jenkins says: *"In the past he has sometimes spoken of his love affairs to me, but I had never before seen him, as it were, in action."* This is Powell at his most direct, but can anyone imagine an English teacher today reading that sentence without drawing a big X through the phrase *"as it were"*?

Powell's style is not what we are used to (those who insist on nothing but subject, verb, object should stick to *Dick And Jane*), but personally, I like it. His willingness to linger is a sign of his self-confidence and once one catches his rhythm, he is very easy to read. More importantly, his words are not window dressing; they carry meaning. For example, cut out *"as it were"* and you cut out a small irony. Powell is making fun of the fact that men so often behave like idiots around women, and *"as it were"* is just a small part of a larger joke that runs throughout the work.

A Dance To The Music of Time is never far removed from the comedy of the sexes and here Powell is often at his best. As regards women, Jenkins is by turns ignorant, curious and bewildered, but he is always honest. Towards the end of the second novel Jenkins discusses women with his artist friend Barnby: *"'Most of use would like to be thought of as the kind of man who has a lot of women,'* he said. *'But take such fellows as a whole, there are few enough of them one would wish to be at all like.'"* Quite right, I say.

As a rule people are wise to fear very long books. *A Dance to the Music of Time* is the brilliant exception.

Shakespeare: The Invention of the Human

T.E. MacVeagh

Harold Bloom's thesis in the *Anxiety of Influence* was that great writers are formed in the struggle with their mentors. "Strong poets" must confront and overcome the dread of being mere "imitators" of their literary masters and predecessors. The process of overcoming this dread involves both an active rebellion against the master's aesthetic and a renunciation of some part of the student's own imaginative strength. Bloom believes his analysis applies to all of the great poets of the English language, except the greatest of them all, William Shakespeare. Shakespeare's accomplishment, Bloom believes, so outstrips that of his immediate precursors (in particular Marlowe), that Shakespeare cannot really be thought to have struggled against any influence at all.

In his most recent work, *Shakespeare: The Invention of the Human*, Bloom tries to explain the unique magnificence of Shakespeare's accomplishment. Bloom argues that although Shakespeare did not invent a new literary form, he did invent an entirely new subject for literature, namely, humanity. As Bloom says, *"Personality, in our sense, is a Shakespearean invention, and is not only Shakespeare's greatest originality but also the authentic cause of his perpetual pervasiveness."* To ask about Shakespeare's influences, it seems, is as nonsensical as to ask about God's influences. Prior to both God and Shakespeare, *"the earth was without form and void, and darkness was upon the face of the deep."*

The problem with this argument is just that it is obviously wrong. Shakespeare was talented enough, but he was not the towering, inexplicably gifted, god-like intellect that Bloom and many others, envision him to have been. If you look directly at Shakespeare's plays (rather than the all the literature surrounding them) you see a series of fairly lame dramas saved by some strong characters, a few great speeches, and a neat ability to portray people with all sorts of different motivations, interests and backgrounds. Nothing that any good writer of science fiction cannot claim.

Okay, perhaps most science fiction writers cannot claim even these modest accomplishments, particularly the ability to write more than one or two characters. But many writers can. Dickens, for example, has a range and humanity just as broad as Shakespeare's; so does George Eliot; yet neither Dickens nor Eliot are held up as touchstones of our civilization.

What makes Shakespeare seem so much more significant than other writers is that he is constantly being reproduced and reinterpreted, and each new production imbues the plays with wider and more contemporary meanings. But all of this modernity and wisdom is not in Shakespeare himself. It is brought to him by his countless interpreters. And it is absurd to think that these interpreters have added nothing to the plays, only seen angles that were already there. Set design alone can bring an eerie contemporary feel to a very old-fashioned story.

I am not saying that Shakespeare is no good; just that he is not more brilliant than many other writers. The perception of his unique literary supremacy is largely because of the fact that he is at the foundation of our canon. As a result, we have many clever people all thinking about Shakespeare, talking about him and reading their own set of interests and concerns into him. It is not Shakespeare, but the entire English-speaking world as a whole that is always relevant; that anticipates every trend; and that evinces a universal sympathy. Shakespeare seems to encompass the wisdom of humanity only because he is constantly being recreated with the aid of the combined wisdom of humanity.

In this way, Shakespeare's work has taken over from the Bible: another fairly lame collection of stories, with a few strong characters and some nice moral insights, into which people used to read a divine intelligence. And it is interesting to think why Shakespeare, rather than any of our other literary giants, should have taken the Bible's place (which lost its role because religion lost any credible claim to be a unifying force between people and cultures) as the foundation to the canon.

Of course, it helps that Shakespeare really was quite good. And that he was prolific, leaving lots to interpret. It probably also helps that he wrote in English, given the growth of English as the *lingua franca*. But I suspect that the most decisive factor is the time period in which he wrote. Writing in the late 1500s, Shakespeare is safe. He comes after the Middle Ages and the Reformation, ruled by the rejected religious sentiments of Augustine and Aquinas, but before the creation of the new disputes in the 17th century, between rationalists and empiricists, between free-trade and protectionism, between democracy and socialism, which continue to divide us. Shakespeare is the foundation of the canon because no one has a reason to reject him. We can all speak to each other in Shakespeare, and our collective love of the plays shows us the joy of having a communal literature in a day and age when there is so little shared cultural experience.

When we are amazed at the brilliance and relevance of Shakespeare, we should understand that it is not the works themselves which hold us in their grip. Rather, it is the sum of the interpretation of the works. The superlatives which Bloom and his fellow enthusiasts mistakenly reserve for Shakespeare alone, should be directed towards our entire literary and intellectual culture.

Some people will think this a mean argument – as if I am robbing western civilization of its one true genius. But in case we thought that our last spiritual soul mate died in 1612, I see it as encouraging to realize that the delightful shock of recognition we experienced in last seeing or reading a Shakespeare play may connect us with a fellow, living human being, with our society at large, and not just with a dead man in a lost world. Shakespeare did not invent humanity, humanity invented Shakespeare. We can all take credit for his genius.

Reminiscence

Busted

Lincoln MacVeagh

I walked down the corridor past Jamie Boyce's study and heard him sobbing behind the closed door. My friend Peter told me what happened: Jamie had been busted for cocaine.

Jamie was the tallest of 48 boys in my class at Groton. At thirteen he was six foot two and he was decidedly unpopular. He was good at sports, a point in his favour, but he was goofy and his characteristic attitude was that of innocent enthusiasm. Charming in an old man, but deadly to a ninth grade boy.

Jamie wanted friends generally but there were three people in particular whom he sought after. Two of these were our classmates Greg and Thad. These two shared a study and together they were at the head of a small but respectable clique. Jamie went to the same grade school as Greg and felt he had a claim on him. As a result he was constantly pestering to be part of Greg and Thad's group.

The third person whose attention Jamie wanted was Mark Stryker. Stryker was one of the senior prefects in our dormitory and he was a star of the football team. He was an odd character who he made himself stand out by saying that he wanted to join the Green Berets instead of going to college. I imagine that to the other seniors he was a figure of fun, but seen from below, by boys four years younger than himself, Stryker looked impressive. On the wall in his bedroom he had pinned up three pairs of girls' panties. I admired Stryker's panties and I remember wondering whether it was customary for girls to leave their underwear behind as a souvenir.

Greg, Thad and Stryker all shared in common the idea that Jamie was a nuisance, and one night after study hall, Greg and Thad burst into Jamie's room and explained in hushed whispers that they he had bought an ounce of cocaine. Jamie was excited and very flattered to by included, but naturally, he was nervous. Drug offences were treated harshly at boarding school and although marijuana and alchohol were commonplace in the upper school, they were a rarity among the freshmen, and cocaine was not even thought of. To get caught doing it would mean certain expulsion.

Jamie put up a weak struggle but he dared not alienate his friends. Greg took out a small shaving mirror and a razor blade and placed them on Jamie's desk. Thad pulled a foil gum wrapper from his wallet, dropped a small pile of white powder on the mirror and began cutting lines. Greg busied himself rolling a crisp dollar bill into a short straw. It all happened very quickly.

"Who goes first?" said Greg.

Thad wanted to go first and the three of them worked out a security scheme. Greg and Jamie would stand guard outside and when Thad was finished doing his lines he would knock quietly on the door, telling the others to come back in. The scheme worked nicely. Greg and Jamie left the study and after a minute or two Thad's quiet knock was heard. When all three were back inside, Greg said it was Jamie's turn next. He and Thad went to stand in the hall, leaving Jamie alone in his study with the cocaine.

I don't know if Jamie actually snorted a line but certainly he didn't want to give himself away and he waited a decent while before giving the knock to say that he was done. As he did so, the door opened and Stryker walked in. Greg and Thad were nowhere to be found. Stryker looked at the white lines on Jamie's desk and said in his deepest voice: "You're busted!"

Jamie pleaded with him, but Stryker appeared to be very angry. He swept up the mirror with the cocaine on it and said he was taking all the evidence directly to Mr. Browne, our dormitory master. He refused to listen to Jamie's tearful assertion that the cocaine belonged to Greg and Thad. Stryker said that Jamie had clearly been alone in his room, and he told him he'd better start thinking about what he would tell his parents.

For the next hour Jamie was in a panic. He ran to Greg and Thad's study and found them sitting at their desks with their geometry books open. They wouldn't let him past the door and they told him that whatever he said they would deny it. So Jamie went back to his study alone and cried until it was time for lights out. Then, along with the rest of us, he marched upstairs to get ready for bed.

The news of Jamie's downfall spread quickly. No one spoke to him as we undressed and all along the corridor the cubicles were unusually silent. At ten-thirty Mr. Browne came out and told us to draw our curtains and lie down. He turned off the lights and in the dark he walked over to Jamie's cubicle. Jamie got out of bed and the two of them went down to Mr. Browne's office.

I have never fully understood what happened next because it seems to suggest that Mr. Browne was in on something, or at least accepting of it. As a boy I could not believe that a grown man could be such an ass and still I have trouble believing it. But in any case, once he got Jamie into his office, Mr. Browne told him it was all a fake. The white powder was not cocaine, it was powdered aspirin. Greg, Thad and Stryker had arranged the bust amongst themselves as a practical joke. Jamie did not have to worry about being expelled or telephoning his parents. He could go back to bed and rest easy. "But I hope," said Mr. Browne, "You have learned a lesson."

"I guess I never feel comfortable with casual Friday."

Games

Sir Laffalot

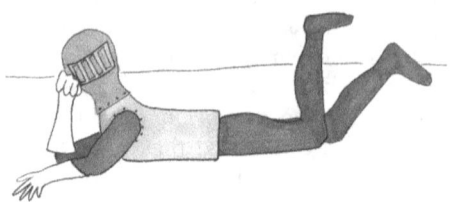

The ad in the *Village Voice* sounded promising: *Models wanted. Big $$$. No experience necessary. No portfolio req'd.* Sir Laffalot winked at himself in the mirror. What better for a man of such bracing sexual appeal? Besides, Sir Laffalot knew a thing or two about working with the camera: relax your body, concentrate your energy and let the power shine out from your eyes.

Eyes afire, Sir Laffalot was soon riding an 8th Avenue elevator next to a squat young man with bleached blonde hair. Joe was very self-conscious about his height. "You're tall," he told Sir Laffalot, "That's lucky." Sir Laffalot smiled graciously and Joe took out a few snapshots of himself in bikini briefs.

Joe was interviewed first and after just a few minutes he came out and flashed Sir Laffalot a big thumbs-up. Then Joe was led away to another back office for a second interview and it was Sir Laffalot's turn. The talent agent was a middle aged woman who fell in love with him on sight. "You're perfect for what we need," she cooed, "You'll be working within a week. Big dollars. All you need is a portfolio. Where are your head shots?" Sir Laffalot confessed that he didn't have any head shots and he showed the woman the ad from the paper: *No portfolio req'd.*

For some reason this sent the talent agent into a rage. Of course he needed head shots! What model didn't? How could he be so stupid? Fortunately, she had a solution ready, and she gave Sir Laffalot the address of a photographer where he could get four pictures of himself for just $500. It was a great deal, and after he got his head shots he would start getting placements right away. Still, Sir Laffalot wasn't sure, and when he balked at paying the $500, the talent agent threw up her hand in disgust.

Leaving the building, Sir Laffalot ran into Joe again. Joe was very excited. "I just need a few more head shots," he said, "And I'll be working by the end of the month."

Sir Laffalot's heart was heavy. Now he knew that his dream of finding fame on the pages of *Vogue* was shattered and he was bitter. Celebrity, he said to himself, is a game for fools. But somehow the words didn't sound right. Suddenly he remembered: *Celebrity* is a game for eight or more players!

Celebrity: How to Play.

1) Dividing into teams, everyone writes down ten famous names. The names are all put into a hat.
2) Each player gets 90 seconds to make his teammates guess as many names as possible. For example: *A writer with the nickname Papa – Earnest Hemingway!*
3) You may use rhyming clues but you must make your teammates guess the rhyme (if the name is *Bill Blass*, you can't just say, "*Designer, rhymes with Fill Glass*"). Once a name is pulled out there is no "passing". If time runs out before a name is guessed that name goes back in the hat.
4) Teams get one point for each name they guess. The team with the most points wins.

Sir Laffalot says: TOODALOO!!

Continued from page 16

shadows beneath Caribou's window. The Eskimo inviting his prey to the igloo for some nose rubbing!

How could she put up with it, I wondered. In the morning, Joey and his studly pals would make agricultural sound effects in her direction (Joey loudest of all), and at night the same evil boy would slip through the shadows like he was Lord Byron.

One morning the sun rose on something ugly in the neighborhood. In gigantic fuzzy letters, someone had spraypainted the word COW on Caribou's family's garage door. I went over to console, and overheard Caribou's mother insisting on calling Joey's parents. Caribou wailed to forbid it, but the following Saturday saw Joey sanding and repainting the garage in view of everybody. Becky and I got lemonade and watched.

Then they started dating.

They dated for ten more years: years of infidelities, violent couplings, drinks spilled in laps, bitchslaps, changed locks, and teary reconciliations. Meanwhile

Caribou rampaged through a career in Public TV and Joey leveled off into regular guy land. Finally they split up.

They hadn't spoken for nearly a year when Kara's Grandmother passed away. The whole family was down in Florida for the funeral when Joey showed up unexpectedly. After the ceremony Becky and her mother went back to the hotel to change, while Kara and Joey took a long walk on the beach. Hours passed. Becky was starting to worry when she saw her sister stomping up the path from the beach alone. Still in her funeral dress, her face all flushed, Caribou flung open the door like an avenging angel. She squared her hips, pounded her foot against the floor, thrust her fist into the air and cried, "YES!" Joey had popped the question.

At the wedding, Becky pulled out the old notebook with the words *Kara Clayton Kara Clayton Kara Clayton* madly scrawled and everybody cried.

The last time I saw Caribou was at Becky's own wedding a few years ago. I couldn't help thinking that she seemed like a woman caught in the grip of an anti-climax.

"I'm glad the Summer's over. The truth is Billy, fishing bores me to tears."

The high life

Caribou

David Garcia III

One day I was in Becky's room listening to the latest flute solo she was perfecting in hopes of wresting "first chair" from the dreaded Amy Spangler, when she realized that one of the pages of sheet music was missing. We searched high and low, and ended up in her sister Kara's room. Listening for footsteps, we found Kara's music folder. Scrawled on the back of it – the pen having dug into the cardboard violently – were the words: *Kara Clayton Kara Clayton Kara Clayton*. To an outsider these words meant nothing but to us they signified a shocking truth: Kara was secretly in love with Joey Clayton. Her nemesis. The boy down the street. "We can't tell anyone we found this," said Becky.

TUKTUJAKSNEOKIK-PUNGA!

It was the one Eskimo word they taught us that year. It means "the caribou are coming", and it led us to christen Becky's older sister "Caribou". Kara-boo. She hated it, but even she had to admit there was something fitting about it. Something in keeping with Caribou's booming voice and generous regal nose, which, combined with a fully developed woman's body (at 16), gave her an indelible impression of emotional largesse. Attributes which would have let her shine in almost any situation. Outside, that is, of an American High School.

At Huron High (home of the River Rat – don't ask), Caribou was a figure of some controversy. She was always storming out of Spanish class, her face all red, and Señor Regenstreif calling her "Sin Verguenza", which he said meant "without shame" and was the worst possible insult in the Spanish language. If it wasn't that, she was campaigning against IQ tests (on the grounds that they favor those who take tests well) or plotting to overthrow the student government.

The worst of it, though, was the way they made fun of her. Every day she would walk proudly down the hall and when she passed the pack of jocks – led by Joey Clayton – they would begin to "moo" at her. Really long, lowing "moooo's", which escalated every day, until you thought you were in the Corn Belt. All she could do was toss her hair and strut away. Proud Caribou shot with arrows.

About that time I discovered oil painting and was often up late splashing about. One night as I turned off my lamp, I thought I spied someone lurking in the dark across the way. My eyes adjusted to the unlikely sight of Joey Clayton whispering in the dappled

Continued on page 15

The ECLECTIC

November 1999   Volume 1 Number 9   Free

CONTENTS

Quotations

"In a temper, he took out a large Bible, opened it at random and wrote 'Irony' down the margin in red biro." A schoolboy takes his revenge on a library book in Stephen Fry's *The Liar.*

"There is nothing like desire for preventing the thing one says from bearing any resemblance to what one has in one's mind." Marcel Proust in *Remembrance of Things Past.*

"Like many wealthy people, it was Miss Crawley's habit to accept as much service as she could get from her inferiors; and good naturedly to take leave of them when she no longer found them to be useful." William Thackeray in *Vanity Fair.*

"But there is something in stooping to justification that the pride of innocence does not at all times willingly submit to." Sir Walter Scott ends with a preposition in *The Heart of Mid-Lothian.*

The Eclectic is owned and published by Linoleum Palace, Inc., 43-05 31st Ave., #2, Astoria, NY 11103. Copyright © 1999 by Lincoln MacVeagh. All rights reserved. Unsolicited submissions will not be considered or returned.

Chester Saves Ecuador

Lincoln MacVeagh

I'm afraid this is going to read rather like a shaggy dog story. There's a big set-up, a small middle and practically no finish at all. However, that's the way this story runs so we'll just have to hope for the best. Here goes.

Chester Wallace is a heavy set, retired Texan, who lives in Quito and who never wears anything but cowboy boots, black jeans and four-pocket Mexican shirts. Chester says he's the savior of democracy in Ecuador. I'll get back to Chester in a moment, but first, a brief introduction to the country of Ecuador and its recent political crisis.

Ecuador is a small mountainous country in South America. It is roughly the size of Colorado and its population of eleven million is less than that of the five boroughs of New York City. Ecuador is famous, if it is famous at all, as the home of the Galapagos Islands, a popular tourist destination and the place where Charles Darwin conceived his treatise, *The Origin of the Species.*

Ecuador won its independence from the Spanish King in 1824 when General Mariscal Sucre defeated the royalist troops in the Battle of Pichincha, and ever since the country has called itself an autonomous republic. The word "republic" brings with it the happy thoughts of freedom and pluralism, but Ecuador has never been particularly free or pluralistic. For the last 150 years the country has been run in much the same way that the Mafia might run a dog track. A few people win, most people lose, and periodically the whole charade gets busted up by the police. In Ecuador, political strongmen have been followed by popular uprisings, have been followed by military dictatorships, and although there has often been talk of democracy most everyone knows the game is fixed.

The most chaotic period in Ecuador's history was in the years 1931-1940. Presidents were like hit songs on the billboard charts and the country went through fourteen of them in just nine years. Then things settled down and for the next three decades the country was ruled by Jose Maria Velasco Ibarra. Velasco Ibarra was a charismatic demagogue who got himself elected President five times but never once managed to complete a full term in office. Whether he was in or out, however, it hardly made a difference. He always made sure that either he or one of his cronies held power, and his reign didn't end until 1972.

By that time almost everyone hated him. The liberals hated him because he shut down the universities and dissolved congress; the conservatives hated him because he was friendly with Fidel Castro and pretended to be a communist; and even the US government hated him, not only for his communism but because

he used his naval warships to threaten American fishermen working within Ecuador's territorial waters. In 1972 the US cut off economic aid and the country started spiraling towards depression. Finally the army decided it had had enough. With clandestine help from the CIA, and with objections from practically no one, the army ousted Velasco Ibarra in a bloodless coup.

The military Junta that followed was corrupt, haphazard, greedy and unjust. But to be fair, the Generals were not much worse than their predecessors and at least they had the good grace to step aside when their time was up. In 1978 the Junta wrote up a new constitution, had it ratified by popular vote, and the next year a civilian president was elected and put in place.

No one would pretend that the army's departure initiated a golden age in Ecuadorian politics. The country's ruling class has always had a reputation for stupidity and frivolity, and for the most part it is well earned. Take, for example, President Sixto Duran's decision to institute daylight savings time. For some reason, Sixto thought of daylight savings time as the symbol of modernity and civilization and he insisted that his country adopt it. He did not stop to consider that turning the clocks back makes little sense when you live on the equator, where the sun rises and sets at exactly the same time all year round. Obstinate, Sixto pushed his legislation through, and for the next three months no one in Ecuador could tell you whether it was eleven o'clock in the morning or twelve noon. If you asked someone on the street what time it was they would shrug their shoulders, laugh and say "¡Es la hora del Sixto!" – *It's Sixto time!*

So Ecuador's new era of civilian rule was not an unparalleled success, but the country did manage five peaceful elections in a row and with each clean transfer of power its democratic institutions grew stronger. More and more of the impoverished Indians and Blacks started to vote and the politicians slowly started responding to their needs. After 18 years, some optimists even began to believe that Ecuador's democracy had become healthy enough to perpetuate itself.

Then came the presidential election of 1996. The winner of the '96 election was Abdala Bucaram, a balding, populist politician from the coast. Around the desperately poor neighborhoods in Guayaquil Bucaram was sometimes called the "Arab Christ" but his own pet name for himself was "El Loco" and it was no joke. He really was crazy.

Once in office Bucaram focused most of his energy on promoting his recently recorded rock 'n roll CD and he appeared frequently on television variety shows as a singer and stand-up comedian. Once he had a girl in a bikini shave off his famous moustache for charity. He also created a new cut-rate brand of milk "Abdalact", and announced plans for building a million low-income houses "Abdalcasas", and meanwhile he told the press he was busy on an economic austerity program that would forever solve Ecuador's inflation problem. His dream was to do away with the national currency, the sucre, and replace it with the US dollar. Then he wanted to re-write the constitution so that presidents could get elected to more than one term.

All in all Bucaram's government was a disaster. Far from building a million low-income houses, the government could not even provide more than 12 hours of electricity a day. In just four months Bucaram created a state of intense confusion. Then the value of the sucre plummeted and in order to shore up his finances, Bucaram raised the price of gasoline 300% overnight. Confusion turned to outrage and riots broke out everywhere. What will the President do? The press flocked to his house but suddenly Bucaram was nowhere to be found. He'd disappeared.

One rumor said that Bucaram had fled to Panama; another said that he'd been murdered by the CIA (the Ecuadorians blame everything on the CIA). In any case, the country was without its head of state and Ecuador's political future was hanging in the balance. The entire country was waiting to see what would happen next...

And that's where Chester Wallace comes in. Or at least that's what Chester says.

I first met Chester in 1990, seven years before Bucaram's disappearance, when I was teaching school at the Colegio Americano de Quito. I met him playing pool in the back room of the Adam's Rib restaurant. He was a friendly, gregarious man, and a big talker. I found him entertaining, though I also thought he was a bit of a nut job. Chester was full of conspiracy theories and had grandiose ideas about himself that didn't really make sense, but there was something about his utter lack of self-consciousness that I liked, and sometimes he could be disarmingly sweet. I often saw him buy dinner for homeless children he'd met on the streets.

Chester's business cards at the time, one of which I have saved, said he was an international private investigator, specializing in cases of murder, kidnap and global larceny. "Will Travel The World!" He also talked about a side business of selling rubber truncheons to the Quito police force. The truncheons were manufactured in the States and Chester's idea was to make money teaching the Ecuadorians how to use them. It was never clear to me that you needed much training to use a rubber truncheon ("Right, now whack him over the head,") and I guess the Quito police felt the same way because I don't think Chester ever sold any truncheons. Nor, I imagine, did he get many jobs as a private investigator, and my own best guess was that Chester lived off his social security checks and whatever little money he could pick up playing pool.

Chester was a very good pool player. He had a fish-eyed Ecuadorian partner named Luis who was said to be a sergeant in the army but who dressed like an accountant, and the two of them used

to hang around the pool table for hours, waiting for unsuspecting tourists to bet against. Chester called it hustling, but if there was any hustle involved it was a rudimentary one. Chester and Luis were simply good players and when they played for money they usually won. I used to enjoy watching the games but I never saw more than $30 change hands.

So that was Chester in 1990 and I did not see him again until 1997 when I went back to Ecuador for a short vacation and ran into him at the Taberna Piemonte. The Taberna Piemonte is a beautiful Italian restaurant overlooking Quito's central valley. It's an expensive place and I was surprised to see Chester there. I was even more surprised when he offered to buy me dinner. Evidently Chester's circumstances had changed, but he was no more reserved than when we first met and it didn't take much prodding for him to boast about his new found wealth. Apparently his mother had died some time ago and left him an estate worth $300,000. Being a sharp operator, Chester liquidated the estate

immediately and invested all the proceeds in an indexed mutual fund pegged to the NASDAQ. In five years his investment more than tripled in value and Chester now owned his own house, his own car, and a small country place outside Otovalo. Chester was living large.

"I'm a lucky man," he said philosophically, "But the important thing about a man is not how much money he has, but what he does with it. How much do you know about Ecuadorian politics?"

This was not a question I expected from Chester. I'd never known him to care a fig about Ecuadorian politics. And yet he must have studied up since I last knew him because he launched into a long account of the country's recent troubles, covering more or less the same ground that I have already gone over. He talked about the 1978 constitution and the growth of democratic institutions, and he had just reached the point at which President Bucaram went missing, when he leaned back in his chair, took a long drink of beer and said, "Not many people know it but I saved this goddamn country from a military dictatorship."

When I asked him for details, this is what he told me:

On the second night after Bucaram's disappearance, Chester was eating dinner at Adam's Rib when Luis Arroja, his old pool playing partner, burst in and rushed over to his table. Luis, who was now an army colonel, was dressed in full uniform and he appeared very excited, anxious, and almost out of breath. He told Chester he had an enormous favor to ask of him, something on which the future of the country depended.

Luis then gave Chester an up to the minute account of the political situation. According to Luis, Bucaram was in Panama and even if "El Loco" returned it was unlikely that he could reclaim power because Congress had already agreed amongst themselves to vote him out of office on grounds of mental incapacity.

After Bucaram, there were only two

serious contenders for power. One of these was General Javier Sanchez, the head of the armed forces in the province of Pichincha; the other was Mr. Fabian Alarcon, the President of Congress; and in the battle between these two men General Sanchez clearly had the upper hand. Sanchez had the full support of his army and if it came to a fight, he was sure to win.

But according to Luis, Sanchez did not want a fight. He was a democrat at heart and he believed in civilian rule. Sanchez would only sanction a military government as a last resort, but the trouble was, he did not want to hand power over to Alarcon. The two men hated each other, and while General Sanchez was be happy to step aside in favor of someone else, he refused to give way to Alarcon. Alarcon meanwhile could not be persuaded to give up his chance at the Presidency and he clung to his constitutional rights.

Thus a stalemate. And the longer the stalemate lasted the closer to chaos the country drifted, and the more likely that General Sanchez's hand would be forced into declaring military rule. Even if Sanchez himself did not want power, the army would not stand idly by while the country degenerated into lawlessness.

"There is only one solution," Luis told Chester, "I am asking you this favor because I know that you are a wealthy man with a good heart and you can help save the constitution of Ecuador."

Luis said that the cause of the conflict between Sanchez and Alarcon was a business deal dating back to the early 1980's in which Sanchez believed himself to have been cheated. Sanchez was a man with a long memory and the only way he would allow Alarcon to become President was if he repaid the money he had stolen. According to Sanchez's calculations this amounted to $90,000. Not an enormous sum given that the future of the country was at stake, and yet Alarcon would not pay. He refused both on point of honor and because he really didn't have the money.

Luis said that for the last twenty-four hours he had been working as the go-between for Sanchez and Alarcon, trying to negotiate a deal, but he was at the end of his rope. He needed Chester's help. He wanted Chester to give congressman Alarcon $90,000 with which to pay off the debt to Sanchez. The General would save face because the debt had been paid; Alarcon would save face because the debt would not have been paid out of his own pocket; and only in this way could Ecuador avoid a new military dictatorship and preserve its constitution intact.

"$90,000," Chester said to me, "I almost spit my beer. But then again, Luis was right to say it wasn't much for saving a country's constitution. So the first thing I asked him was, why me? Why didn't he go to one of those rich banana bastards and tell him to save the country? You know what Luis said? He said he'd knocked on the door of every rich man in Quito. He said he'd been calling on the mucky-mucks for two days straight and they wouldn't even let him past the door. Not one single Ecuadorian was willing to pay up to save his own lousy government. You see, the way these rich Ecuadorians think, they'd just as soon get rid of democracy. Keep the peasants down. All they're interested in is cheap labor anyway. Luis said I was his last chance and I believed him. I said I'd think about it."

But this answer wasn't good enough. Luis insisted that time was of the essence. Chester had to make up his mind right away. If he was willing to pay off Alarcon's debt, good, but if not Luis had to move on and start looking for someone else. Every day that the political situation remained in flux, the country was pushed closer to military rule. There was no time to lose.

"So I rolled the dice," said Chester, "Hell, seven years ago I was broke. Now I'm almost a millionaire. What's $90,000 either way? And I figured that if I had the chance to help the cause of freedom in this country I sure had to give it a try. The only thing, I insisted on meeting with Alarcon first. If Chester Wallace was going to save his ass, I wanted him to know who saved it…. Yeah, I know what you're thinking. Dumb Texan, pissing his money away, but I've known Luis for fifteen years. I trusted him and I was right to trust him. Look at this."

Chester reached into his jacket pocket and took out a photograph. It was a picture of Chester standing next to Fabian Alarcon taken on the same night Luis met him at the restaurant. As soon as Chester agreed to put up the money, Luis took him downtown to the Congress building. The place was a mad house, swarming with politicians, reporters and armed guards, but everyone stepped aside as soon as they saw Luis' uniform and Chester and Luis marched right into Alarcon's office. Luis quickly explained that Chester was offering to pay off the debt to General Sanchez. Alarcon's face broke into a wide smile. He walked over to Chester, took his hand and made a short speech in Spanish commending Chester's heroism.

"He's a nice man," said Chester, "He called me an Ecuadorian patriot. A benefactor of the republic."

The next morning Chester woke up early and spent all day with Luis figuring out how to get $90,000 from his brokerage account in the States wired to the Banco Popular. At two-thirty in the afternoon they had a cashier's check made out to cash and later that evening they returned to Alarcon's office. Chester handed over the money in person.

Two days later General Sanchez held a press conference to announce that there would be no military intervention in the political situation. Congressman Alarcon was to step in as interim president and he would be given the full backing of the army.

"That's about it," said Chester, "That's how I saved democracy in Ecuador. And if you don't believe it, go out to the army base on the way to the equator. They put up a plaque for me. It's right there at the entrance for everyone to see. Luis and I went to a special dedication ceremony six weeks after President Alarcon took office."

I really have no idea if anything that Chester Wallace told me is true, but I did take a bus out to the equator the next day. I got off the bus at the army barracks and Chester was right about the plaque. It's a foot-square piece of bronze sunk into a large slab of concrete and it says, "Dedicated to Chester Wallace. A true friend of Ecuador."

Of course, anything is possible in this world, but I can't help thinking it's the most expensive bronze plaque ever purchased.

Reviews

Good-bye to All That

by Robert Graves

Chicago University Press, 1962

Long before the success of *I, Claudius*, Robert Graves was an unhappy man, desperately in love with a clever, young poet named Laura Riding. The two of them shared a tumultuous life in Hammersmith, and one day in 1929 Laura drank some disinfectant and hurled herself out a fourth story window. Graves followed her from the floor below. Both Robert and Laura survived and afterwards, in an effort to wipe clean his slate, Graves sat down to write his autobiography. *Good-bye to All That* ends before it reaches Hammersmith, but by the time it's over we have seen enough of trouble that Graves' suicide attempt no longer comes as a surprise.

Robert Von Ranke Graves was born in 1895 into a upper-middle class family of ten children. *"I have often been called: 'Phillip, Richard, Charles, I mean Robert.'"* His father was a schools inspector and sometime poet; his mother was a German aristocrat with high morals; and together they created a household that was both intellectual and priggish. *"My sister Rosaleen put up a printed notice in her corner of the nursery – it might just as well have been put up by me: 'I must not say bang bust or pig bucket as it is rude.'"*

There is nothing wrong with teaching your child not to say "pig bucket" but once having done so it seems a nasty trick to pack him off to an all-boys boarding school, and that, of course, is what Graves' parents did. Robert was sent to Charterhouse where he did not fit in. He was tortured mercilessly and eventually nervous tension led to heart trouble: *"This was low water. My last resource was to sham insanity. It succeeded unexpectedly well. Soon nobody troubled about me except to avoid any contact with me."*

From Charterhouse Graves won a place at Oxford, but he feared that university would be too much like school, and when World War I broke out he enlisted immediately: *"...only a very short war was expected – two to three months at the very outside – I thought that it might last long enough to delay my doing to Oxford, which I dreaded."*

The bulk of Graves' autobiography is an account of his life in the army and it is in large part a story of innocence lost. His introduction to war came from two wounded officers he met at training camp. *"Neither would talk much of his experiences. All that one of them, Emu Jones, would tell us: 'The first queer sight I saw in France was three naked women hanging by their feet in a butcher's shop.'"*

Graves makes no attempt to explain or understand the war's wider history but focuses instead on his own two years in the trenches. Graves' stories are always interesting and sometimes gruesome, but they are all told with a surprising coldness of manner. For Graves, it was a war without passion and there was not even the pleasure of fellowship. After being severely wounded, Graves' final verdict on the front is this: *"What I most disliked about the army was never being alone, forced to live and sleep with men whose company I would have run miles to avoid."*

There is enough lyricism in *Good-bye to All That* to suggest that Graves knew the wonder of life, but the great weight of his book shows the world a horrible place. At times one is tempted to protest his pessimism. But before one starts singing Yankee Doodle, one is stopped short by the thought that Graves has watched men stuff grenades in each other's pants for fun. It is hard to know what to make of such a world and it is harder still to preach sunshine to a man who has lived through it. In the end one admires him simply for having survived.

Commentary

A Short History Of Philosophy

T.E. MacVeagh

What is philosophy? Well, let's consider the traditional questions which philosophy tries to answer. How should we live our lives? What is morality? What is beauty? How can we know anything? Is there an external world? How do we know we are not just brains in vats? What exists and what does not exist? What is causation? Is there a God? Why is there something rather than nothing? What is the point of life? How do words mean? What is language? These questions cover the basic topics in philosophy of ethics, aesthetics, epistemology, ontology, metaphysics, existentialism and philosophy of language.

Philosophy began as an eminently practical pursuit. The very first philosophical question was: "How should I live my life?" Socrates asked the question hoping to answer difficult but routine questions of daily life: how to pass the day, when and what to eat, who and how to fight, where and with whom to sleep. These questions require introspection but, at least at first, no conceptual analysis. We may conclude that we should be courageous, temperate and just based on our everyday understanding of these virtues.

But as philosophers attempted to answer the question of how to live more precisely, they confronted the traditional questions of ethics and aesthetics. If we are to live our lives in pursuit of justice and beauty, then let us be sure that we know exactly what these concepts mean. What is Justice? What is Beauty?

I would say that epistemology, the study of how we know things and what knowledge consists in, became part of philosophy as a result of the problems with trying to figure out what morality and beauty are. Concepts like morality and beauty are complicated and multi-faceted. If we run into difficulties defining them, it makes sense to cut our philosophical teeth on easier questions. Physicists, after all, do not start off studying relativity. First they learn how fast a ball falls in a vacuum. So, when philosophers found that they had a hard time defining the concepts of beauty and morality, they retreated to easier questions.

At least, the philosopher says, I know that there is a table in front of me and a sun in the sky. And if we can understand how we know these things, we can use it to help us approach the more difficult questions of how to recognize beauty and morality. But it turns out that explaining how we know even the most obvious facts is quite tricky. And the philosopher found himself so tangled up trying to show that there is an external world, that any attempt to define "hard" concepts like morality and beauty was necessarily delayed.

Epistemology gives rise to ontology and metaphysics. In the struggle to explain his knowledge of the table and the sun, the philosopher found himself needing to define what it meant to exist, and to determine what exists and what does not. This is ontology. The philosopher also becomes involved in metaphysics, the search for unimpeachable "first principles" on which we may base our confidence in sense experience, experimentation and induction, and our understanding of causation.

Eventually, investigations into ontology and metaphysics give rise to a realization: perhaps there is no truth; perhaps God does not exist. The question "Is there a God?" is tinged with anxiousness because it arises in the context of rigorous skeptical arguments which have somehow managed to cast doubt on the existence of the very chairs in which we sit. And it seems impossible that the vague, amorphous concept of God will survive exposure to such corroding skepticism.

The conclusion that there may not be a God, that there may be no such thing as truth, leads to a revisiting of the original philosophic and moral questions with a desperate aspect. Whereas previously it was assumed there was such a thing as morality and beauty, and an answer to the question of how a person should live their life, if only we could find it, now the fear arises that there are truly no answers to these questions. Existentialist philosophers face this "crisis of rationality" and ask: Is life worth living?

Is life worth living? To some people this sounds like a weighty question but to others it just sounds silly. "Of course it's worth living," they answer, inadvertent existentialist heroes, "Next question?" Philosophy of language arose from the impatience of hard-minded rationalists who were tired of what they perceived as existential nonsense. Epistemological, ontological and metaphysical problems, they insisted, could be circumvented if only we could get a clear understanding of how language worked.

At first this approach looked like it would raise skepticism to new heights: not only can we not find any connection between what we think and the way the world is; but also, we cannot establish a connection between what we say and what we think. In fact, philosophers of language believe that by cutting out the middle-men between language and the world, the murky realms of thinking and meaning, they can solve the epistemological problems of philosophy. Epistemologists got confused because they mistakenly looked for a connection between the nature of reality and what we <u>think</u> about it. Once you realize that the connection is between the nature of reality and what we <u>say</u> about it, things get much

"I think you're gonna love it."

clearer. A little common sense can clear up the head-spinning mess that the debates over epistemology, metaphysics and ontology have wrought.

Logical and linguistic analysis had several early successes, clearing up a number of confusions which had crept into philosophical debates. Buoyed by early success, it was perhaps natural that some philosophers of language mistakenly believed that they had found a miracle cure. But in the end, the great questions from the history of philosophy were left untouched by the philosophy of language. After the mechanism of language is fully understood, we will still want to know how and whether to live our lives. And we will still wonder how on earth to go about figuring these things out.

So it seems as if our quick tour through the history of philosophy has left us in a dark place; in the impenetrable thicket of epistemological and ontological questions and the desperate, imponderable contortions of existential philosophy. How do we know we are not brains in vats? Is there any such thing as truth? Does anything matter at all?

All I can suggest is that we remember where we came from. We have to go back to the original question that needed answering: How should we live our lives? If we can figure out a practical answer to this question, perhaps it will not matter so much if we cannot find a precise definition of virtue or if we cannot prove the existence of the external world. If we can find a satisfactory way to live our lives, we may be able to cut off the vicious cycle of analysis which seems inevitably to end in the crisis of rationality.

So we start the philosophical journey again and see if there was a path Socrates and Plato missed. Can we determine how to live life without getting into messy definitional questions? Or can we answer those definitional questions in a practical way without invoking a full-fledged ethical theory? There are two preliminary difficulties to watch out for. First, to a large extent, we have all had our philosophic intuition shaped by the history of the subject. We must fight the tendency to see the previously-trodden pathways down which philosophy has traveled as the only and inevitable ones. Second, it is a fair question whether we can ask anymore how to live without resolving the prior question of whether to live. Can we recapture that naïveté which allowed the Greeks simply to ask which life had the most value? Or, once raised, must the challenge of nihilism be met before the word "virtue" can be uttered in a non-ironic fashion?

The best thing to do with these difficulties is probably to steamroll over them. The doubts cast on the reliability of our intuition and the value of existence are theoretical. When we ask, "What is the good life?", the answers we want are practical. When should I wake up? When should I go to sleep? (Is Ben Franklin right: Early to bed, early to rise?) And what should I do in between? Do not be put off that the term "the good life" is ambiguous between a life good for us, and a life in which we are good to others. This ambiguity mirrors the ambiguity of our own hopes and desires. We can live with the ambiguity knowing that any answer must satisfy our conflicting impulses.

And if we do not find answers that are satisfying? Well, one of the joys of philosophy is that there is always virgin territory to explore. No matter how often an intellectual path is supposed to have been traveled, it is always made new for the new adventurer. The grass unbends, twigs unbreak, the snow is made fresh again. The very contours of the terrain shift and move about. Old maps are useless and new tracks must be forged. Everyone is Lewis and Clark in the search for the good life.

Games

Sir Laffalot

Sir Laffalot once met a pretty girl who was in the Army Reserve and since he had the weekends free, he decided to sign up himself. All the ladies love a uniform. Even the ones who are wearing uniforms themselves.

The recruitment office was in Southcross Plaza, next door to a dry cleaner's. The walls of the office were covered in army posters and in the back there was video running on permanent loop that showed a high-tech missile blowing up two tanks in the desert.

Sergeant Aguilla greeted Sir Laffalot with a firm handshake and immediately gave him a form to fill out. Name, address, date of birth and reason for joining the Army Reserve. Reason for joining… Sir Laffalot thought of his pretty girl, but then he thought better of mentioning her and instead he put down that he wanted to better himself.

"Excellent!" said Sergeant Aguilla, "Now let's see what we've got. Got high school? Got some college?" Sir Laffalot answered yes to both and Sergeant Aguilla went on to explain that, going forward, the first activity step in terms of enlisting was to run through some preliminary evaluation procedures. He took Sir Laffalot into a back room and gave him two thirty question tests. The most difficult question on the math test was this: *Which is the highest number? A) ½ B) 0.75 C) 0 D) -½.* Sir Laffalot aced it.

Sergeant Aguilla was very impressed: "Oh man, you got every question right. Maybe it's time we talked Officer's Candidate School. You could be on the Joint Chiefs of Math!" Sir Laffalot giggled modestly. He could already feel the weight of four stars on his shoulders and he sank into a brief reverie.

AttennnnTION! Sir Laffalot pictured himself leading a squadron of fifty crack troops into a massive game of *Samurai Swords* against the Japanese. Stealth and quickness, men. Remember the Alamo! Sir Laffalot was born to lead.

"Any questions?" said Sergeant Aguilla.

"Just one," said Sir Laffalot, "Do you get to play a lot of *Samurai Swords* at the Officers School?"

Apparently it was the wrong question to ask. Sergeant Aguilla had never even heard of *Samurai Swords*, and by the time Sir Laffalot was finished explaining the rules he was out the door and back in the Southcross Plaza parking lot. What a pity, though. The guns and missiles boys don't know what they're missing.

Samurai Swords: How to Play.

1) Clear the Ming vases from the table tops (or go outside) and establish a decent sized field of play.

2) Each player gets a sword made out of rolled-up newspaper and once everyone is blindfolded, the game begins. Players must try to avoid being touched by the sword of another. If you're touched, you're out. The last player standing is the winner.

3) Those watching the game should help the blindfolded players to stay in bounds.

Sir Laffalot says: TOODALOO!!

Continued from page 16

announced, "Florescent paints will NOT impress the judges at RISD!" and they both laughed heartily. I was sure Matthew could overhear, and I wanted to crawl under a rock. I went through the motions of putting an application together, but soon gave up.

Two weeks later I stayed after school one day and my mother was late picking me up. I found myself drawn to the deserted art room, and the corner where Matthew kept his famous painting, which surpassed Vermeer in my imagination. I stood before it with my eyes closed, steeling myself for my own eclipse. I opened my eyes and drank it in, imagining myself Salieri confronting Mozart.

Instantly I could see it was painted with precision. The flowerpot was round, and accurately terracotta. The leaves were the exact size and shape of the actual, palpably waxy, and dull light shining with consummate technique. These impressions swam in my head, then began to gather, then recoil. I could feel the thoughts shoot out at the canvas from my narrowing eyes: "You are stagnant though, aren't you? You aim to impress the viewer, not to inspire. You are sunk in murk and irrelevance."

I was shaking and then it was if the painting spoke back: "Yes, and as of now you are in this until the bitter end." Like a vow that made itself. I heard my mother beeping her horn and left the room in a hurry.

Over the next few nights I got my application drawings together and mailed them to RISD. Near the end of the year I heard the art teachers saying how disappointed they were that "Matty" got rejected. I figured I didn't even merit the courtesy of rejection, and prepared to go to the University of Michigan, which had accidentally accepted me into their School of Dentistry. I would study teeth but secretly take art classes at every opportunity.

Absurdly late in the game, I came home to find a letter from RISD, mercifully stuffed too fat to be a rejection. I never told anyone at school that I got in and afterwards I heard that Matthew had decided against college and was working full time at the hardware store.

"Honey, how come we never go south for the winter?"

The high life

Taking The Veil

David Garcia III

When I was seven I married Susan Foley under a pine tree and Matthew Gorman acted as best man. Matthew was my best friend most of the time. He was overweight, with a kind of medieval look that would have made him the perfect choice to cast as Friar Tuck in an all-boy version of *Robin Hood.* He steadfastly refused to learn to learn to swim or ride a bike, and his disdain for kid-like pursuits caused most of the tension between us.

I should mention that Matthew was a genius. One day at school the teacher asked us all to draw the sun. Everyone (including me) drew the exact same smiley yellow sun with the same yellow spokes. Everyone except Matthew, whose drawing would not have been out of place in Leonardo's notebooks. Matthew drew a pulsing sphere without distinct outlines burning at the center of the page. Beautiful snaky lines radiated out from the center, growing larger as they left the paper for parts unknown. I wasn't jealous, really, just in awe.

Matthew's identity was based on art, and I became a fixture in his basement, watching him draw minutely detailed Renaissance-style portraits of characters from *Planet of the Apes.* I drew cartoons at home, but I never presumed to show them to Matthew.

When I was nine we moved to the Midwest. Eight years (eons in kid time) later, my Dad unexpectedly announced that we were moving back to our hometown. I was replanted back with all those kids who had been together their whole lives, and I was a stranger. Nobody wanted to play catch-up, and it was a lonely year.

By that time Matthew was firmly ensconced as the school artist and I ran into him on the first day of art class. It seems strange to me now that we never spoke to each other. Not one word. I think we took one look at each other and realized there was no point. He was fatter than ever, with shaggy long hair, ripped jeans and a Grateful Dead T-shirt. I had short hair and one of those shirts with the little alligator sewn on. I heard that he played in a rock band, and worked part time at a hardware store.

That first day we were all given dusty old houseplants to paint. These plants were our only project for the whole semester, as it turned out, and Matthew and I instinctively set up easels at opposite corners of the room. The two teachers clustered around Matthew, their superstar, who they said was going to be the first local kid to get into the Rhode Island School of Design.

I didn't tell anyone that I did art and I was too intimidated to go over and look at Matthew's picture. I didn't want him to look at mine either. I was convinced that he would laugh if he saw it. It didn't look much like reality, with its unreal greens and crazy tendrils waving at you, but I kind of liked it.

Near the end of the semester, the unfortunate happened. My Grandmother announced that it was her dream that I go to RISD, and consequently, my parents insisted that I show the things I had been doing at home to the art teachers to get their opinion. I brought a big portfolio of stuff in, and when I knocked at the door they didn't know who I was. They were salty codgers with white hair, and very devoted to Matthew. One of them

Continued on page 15

The
ECLECTIC

December 1999	Volume 1 Number 10	Free

CONTENTS

Quotations

"At fifteen, appearances were mending; she began to curl her hair and long for balls." Jane Austen introduces her heroine, Catherine Morland, in the transsexual classic *Northanger Abbey*.

"Human life does not come to its natural close with this people; but when a man grows very old, all his kinfolk collect together and offer him up in sacrifice; offering at the same time some cattle also. After the sacrifice they boil the flesh and feast on it; and those who thus end their days are reckoned the happiest." Customs of the Messagetae as described by Herodotus in *The Persian Wars*.

"She had a pretty gift for quotation, which is a serviceable substitute for wit..." From Somerset Maugham's story *The Creative Impulse*.

"When you walk in the street, smile at people, and if someone says good morning, answer back, because you'll always benefit from it." Albert Camus' advice to Anne Gallimard, the young daughter of his friend Michel.

Books

Don Juan In Paris

The Life of Albert Camus

Lincoln MacVeagh

"I must express what fills my heart and express it quickly."
"Every day write something in this notebook. In two years time, write a work."
"Don't give way to conformity and to office hours. Don't give up."

Albert Camus was a determined young man, and in the years between 1942 to 1947 he published three remarkable books: *The Stranger, The Myth of Sisyphus* and *The Plague.*

Camus lived to be famous and wealthy, but he was always ambivalent about his success. As a poor twenty-three year old he'd written in his diary, *"My joy is endless."* As a celebrated novelist in Paris, a friend once wandered into Camus' office and found him answering fan mail: a man had written to say he wanted to kill himself. It was Camus' tenth suicide letter that week.

Albert Camus was born in 1913 in Mondovi, Algeria. His father was a vineyard foreman who was conscripted in 1914 and died two months later in the first Battle of the Marne. As a result, his wife left the countryside and moved to Belcourt, a working-class quarter of Algiers.

Albert and his older brother Lucien grew up in a dark three room apartment dominated by their ill-tempered grandmother. Camus never went hungry but

"My joy is endless."

there were other privations. There was no running water or electricity, and only a Turkish toilet – a hole with a drain – on the landing. Grandmother gave the children one pair of new boots each year and regularly inspected the soles for wear. The boys were whipped if she suspected them of playing football in the street.

Camus' mother was only a silent presence in the household. She was partially deaf and rarely spoke. She worked long hours as a charwoman and had taught herself never to laugh or cry, but always to maintain an expressionless face. She was illiterate and there were no books in the apartment. In her old age, Camus' mother never fully understood what her son was famous for.

At home Camus was timid and quiet, but away from it he was a bright and energetic boy. *"Your pleasure at being in class,"* wrote his grammar school teacher, *"was always apparent and your face was so optimistic that looking at it, I never guessed your family's real situation."* At age ten Camus won a scholarship to the lycée in Algiers and in his mother's eyes he'd become a grown-up: *"I can still remember the despair that overwhelmed me when my mother told me that 'now I was old enough, and would get useful presents at New Year's.'"*

Camus was seventeen when he suffered his first severe attack of tuberculosis and after his recovery in hospital he left home for good. Afraid of infecting his brother Lucien with whom he shared

a bed, Camus went to live with his uncle Gustave and continued his studies. Camus did well at the lycée. He was a good scholar and although he could no longer play football because of his lungs, he loved to swim and he made friends easily with his middle-class schoolmates.

While still working on his B.A., Camus left Gustave's apartment because he wasn't allowed to bring girlfriends up to his room and for the next decade Camus lived as he could. Sometimes he stayed with friends, but for the most part he slept in bedsits rented by the week. The bedsits in which Camus lived did not have space for writing tables, and throughout his university career and beyond Camus carried his books and papers with him wherever he went. Almost all of his early works were composed on the run in cafes, in restaurants or in the houses of friends.

Camus once called solitude a luxury of the rich. Being poor, he had to teach himself to concentrate and there is no better evidence of his intensity than his early diaries. Camus began writing his diary in 1935 and he kept it until his death in 1960. In the end, the diary became a somewhat conventional record of daily events, but in the beginning, Camus' diary was unusual for its intellectual purity. Reading it, one is immediately struck by what is left out.

In the period 1935-1942 Camus left his first wife and married his second; he joined and was thrown out of the Communist Party; he spent three years directing and acting in his own theater company; he struggled with money and friendships; and he worked countless jobs from selling car parts on commission, to private tutoring, to collecting data from Algerian weather stations.

Yet none of all this bears mention in the diary and it would be quite impossible to draw up even the sketchiest biographical outline based on his entries. Instead, they are made up almost entirely of practice passages, reading notes, aphorisms and plot ideas. *"Short story: A priest, happy with his lot in a country parish in Provence. By accident, has to succor a man sentenced to death just before his execution. Loses his faith because of it."*

Forgetting the particulars of his own life, Camus devoted himself to the universal and in the few places where experience does intrude, it has been filtered down to its essence so as to turn into an idea: *"In the movies, the little woman from Oran sitting next to her husband, the tears streaming down her face at the misfortune of the hero. Her husband begs her to stop. In the middle of her tears she says: 'But let me make the most of it.'"* Camus rarely sets a scene or describes the people he's met because he only wants the nut: *"'I', he said, 'am the olfactive type. And there is no art that addresses itself to the sense of smell. Only life.'"*

Camus' early diaries give the sense of a life lived in isolation, but as he grew older his attachments to the world grew stronger. Unlike many of his comfortably placed friends Camus had no interest in being a bohemian. He wanted to earn a living, and in 1938 he found journalism. He got a job at the newly founded left-wing paper *The Alger-Républicain* and struck up a close friendship with the paper's editor, Pascal Pia. When *The Alger-Républicain* folded with the outbreak of World War II, Camus followed Pia to Paris.

Rejected by the military because of his health, Camus found work as an editor at Gallimard. It was the height of Vichy France, and although *The Stranger* was published in 1942 without objection, *The Myth of Sisyphus* met with trouble from the government censors because of its frequent references to Kafka. Kafka was a Jew and his work was banned. Camus was outraged but such were the facts of life. Everything in Paris had been politicized, and late in 1943, feeling no longer capable of remaining neutral, Camus once again followed his friend Pia, this time into the French Resistance.

Camus was not the most active member of the Resistance. He edited the underground newspaper *Combat*, but except for one close call when he was stopped by the Germans while carrying a *Combat* layout page (he slipped it to his lover who was not searched), he avoided personal risks. Nor did he have any involvement in the movement's dirty work. However, he was a recognizable name, and in 1944, with the liberation of Paris and the first legal edition of *Combat*, Camus became an important symbol of French courage. Willingly or not, he got pegged as the moral conscience of France and he could no longer escape the role of public figure.

After the war, Camus allowed himself to get increasingly wrapped up in the intellectual battles of his era. He fought with Francois Mauriac about the treatment of collaborators; he split with Pascal Pia over De Gaulle; and finally he lost his friendship with Sartre over a ridiculous argument about the progress of history.

Camus was sometimes wrong but often right. Generally, he preached decency and moderation: *"It is better to be wrong by killing no one rather than to be right with mass graves..."* But even when Camus won out, he took little pleasure in the victory. *"I've become pessimistic,"* he told his friends in 1948, *"I'm becoming an old crab... and the best thing would be to retire from the world and stop writing."*

It's easy to sympathize with Camus'

"Honey, if you don't fall asleep, Santa can't come."

frustration and it's depressing to think of his vitality slowly draining away in the backstabbing world of Paris politics, but in fact, the troubles of Camus' later life were not only those thrust upon him. Most of Camus' difficulties were of his own making. To put it simply, he was a ladies man and throughout the late forties and fifties he spent a great deal more time bickering with his women than he ever did fighting with Sartre.

Charming and handsome, Camus married twice, the first time at age twenty. Simone Hie was both beautiful and charismatic, but she was a morphine addict and the marriage ended when Camus discovered she was sleeping with her doctor in exchange for drugs. Seven years later, Camus married again to Francine Faure, but by that time, though Francine probably didn't know it, he had long since given up on any thought of faithfulness in marriage.

From his early twenties onwards, Camus kept busy with an almost endless string affairs. Women threw themselves at him and he had few scruples. He would sleep with the wife of a friend as willingly as he would with a single girl, and he could be quite brutal about his more casual sexual encounters. At one party he never spoke to a girl with whom he had just had sex; with other girls, he would leave his secretary to clean up the mess; and once he described a break-up to a friend by saying, "*I made her understand that she really wasn't up to the class of the establishment.*"

Camus was not thoroughly cynical about romance, but you can only fall in love so many times before the sentiment begins to ring false, and even in his affairs of the heart Camus lied constantly. Camus' longest lasting affair was with Maria Casarès, a young actress he met in Paris in 1942. The affair was tumultuous because Maria often flew into a rages about Camus' infidelities. He used to comfort her with the stock phrase, "*I deceived you, but I never betrayed you,*" and this worked passably well until the War ended and Camus' wife Francine came to live with him. Camus told Maria not to worry about losing her place. "*Francine is like my sister,*" he insisted, but shortly afterwards

"*I'm sorry, Mr. Peterson is going wee wee. Can I take a message?*"

Camus' "sister" got pregnant with twins. The timing of Francine's pregnancy is worth noting, because while wooing the respectable English lover of his friend Arthur Koestler, Camus told her he'd only married Francine because she got knocked up.

Camus said many different things to many different women, but more tawdry still was the fact that he kept repeating himself: *"For instance, the scene of the incomprehensible attraction, of the 'mysterious something,' of the 'it's unreasonable, I certainly didn't want to be attracted, I was even tired of love, etc...' always worked, though it is one of the oldest in the repertory."* Or else: *"Above all, I had perfected a little speech which was always well received and which, I am sure, you will applaud. The essential part of the act lay in the assertion, painful and resigned, that I was nothing, that it was not worth getting involved with me, that my life was elsewhere and not related to everyday happiness..."*

The passages above come from Camus' novel *The Fall*, but they were written knowingly and they bear at least some resemblance to a note Camus made in his diary upon meeting the twenty year old Catherine Sellers: *"It's the first time in a long while that I am touched in my heart by a woman, without any desire, any design, or game playing, and I love her for herself, with a certain sadness."* Within weeks Catherine was his mistress.

Camus met Catherine in 1957, and later in that same year his wife went insane. *"All she did was cry, sleep, and talk obsessively about Maria Casarès, her husband's lover."* Perhaps Francine didn't know that Maria was just one of many lovers; in any case, she threw herself out the hospital window and badly fractured her pelvis. *"I am the first one responsible,"* wrote Camus dolefully, *"because part of me has never stopped thinking instinctively that human affairs are not serious. It's also that I have hurt so many people around me... And really I don't know how to get out of it, when I think that Francine may continue to* be what she is right now." Crocodile tears perhaps.

Camus was a Don Juan and it's hard to be Don Juan. I've always been fascinated by such men. On the one hand, it's glorious to take an interest in every woman one meets, and there is a great deal of truth, both philosophical and sexual, in the insistence on universal attraction. One the other hand, the real world practice of keeping lovers on a string is usually a nasty business and it seems naive to think that it can be otherwise. I imagine Camus saw both sides of the problem. More than most he understood, *"The peculiar vanity of man, who wants to believe and who wants other people to believe that he is searching after truth, where in fact it is love that he is asking this world to give him."*

Albert Camus died in a car crash in 1960.

Reviews

The Eden Express
by Mark Vonnegut
(out of print)

Mark Vonnegut, son of the author Kurt, graduated from Swarthmore in 1969. His ambition was to be a good hippie: *"For me and a lot of other people a good hippie was something very worth being, if not the only thing worth being."* Vonnegut's memoir, *The Eden Express*, is a chronicle of both his modest success and his spectacular failure.

The book begins with Vonnegut determined to avoid service in Vietnam. First he applied for conscientious objector status but when this was denied him, he convinced the draft board at his physical that he was insane. Vonnegut was given a psychiatric 4F and shortly afterwards he and his Swarthmore girlfriend, Virginia, head north to British Columbia in search of land, peace and grooviness.

Vonnegut and Virginia were joined by a handful of other Swarthmore hippies and together they bought an eighty acre farm on a distant peninsula, some two hours by boat from the nearest town. The lived humbly, ate meagerly and worked hard, and for a short while Vonnegut felt he had discovered a true physical and spiritual freedom. But it was a freedom with limitations. *"Hell,"* said Sartre, *"is other people."*

As described by Vonnegut, the hippie culture in which he lived was a strangely rigid one. On the one hand everything was groovy, but on the other hand, it *had* to be groovy. There was little room for solitude on the farm and consensus was vital in all things. Self-discovery was transformed into a group activity and new hippie orthodoxies sprang up to replace the old. Vonnegut soon found himself chaffing against them.

Among the strongest of the hippie orthodoxies was the belief that phsycadelic drugs were an unqualified blessing. Vonnegut himself, however, was not an experienced tripper. Before moving to the farm he had taken hallucinogens only once and the experience terrified him: *"I never called it a 'bad trip'...If you had a bad trip it was because you were a bad person. If you weren't a bad person, then at the very least having a bad trip indicated that work was needed on this or that part of your head; a*

Why I like the MIDWEST Great Lakes! Jello Salad

by H. Seidel

lack of wisdom or something like it was at the root of your bad trip."

Vonnegut's bad trip weighed on his mind like a guilty conscience, so he was delighted when one spring morning he took mescaline again and enjoyed himself thoroughly. The world was beautiful, the farm was beautiful and for a day Mark Vonnegut knew grace. For an entire day Vonnegut managed to forget that his girlfriend Virginia had left him, that his parents were divorcing and that his father had recently attempted suicide.

Unfortunately, he did not come down well. The day after his beautiful trip Vonnegut saw *The Face*; three days after, he stopped eating and sleeping; and in less than two weeks he was a patient at the Hollywood Hospital in Vancouver. He was stark raving mad.

Vonnegut went on to suffer three severe bouts of schizophrenia (the second time he was admitted to Hollywood Hospital he was in a strait jacket accompanied by four Royal Canadian Mounties) and the meat of *The Eden Express* is his attempt to describe what happened to him. Occasionally disjointed and repetitious, the story is nonetheless well told. Vonnegut is an intelligent observer. He captures both the promise and horror of hippiedom and at the same time he gives a good account of his own insanity.

It's hard to know what to make of the insanity. Sometimes Vonnegut seems merely depressed, but at other times he appears to be in the grips of a prolonged epileptic fit. The cause of his illness is not easy to pin down and nor is its cure. Vonnegut himself believes that he benefited from large doses of vitamins; he also appears to have no faith whatever in "talking cures"; but beyond that, his own experience, combined with his later research, yield little but common sense advice. Eat well, sleep well, and avoid drugs. *"Coffee,"* writes Vonnegut in summation, *"is nearly always bad for schizophrenics. Grass, hash, and especially the hallucinogens and speed can be real trouble."*

One wants to know more and it is easy to get frustrated with such banal proscriptions, but one has to admire Vonnegut's refusal to preach simple doctrine. *The Eden Express* appears to have two distinct theses. On the one hand it says that schizophrenia is a treatable disease; on the other it says that madness is ineffable. Vonnegut's book is interesting.

Initial Public Offering

THE ECLECTIC

3,876,000 Shares
Common Stock

This is The Eclectic Magazine's initial public offering. We are offering 3,876,000 shares of common stock to the public. **Investing in the common stock involves risks. Please see the "Risk Factors" below.**

Neither the Securities and Exchange Commission nor any other regulatory body has approved of disapproved of these securities or passed on the accuracy or adequacy of this prospectus. Any representation to the contrary is a criminal offense.

	Per Share	Total
Public Offering Price	$23.00	$89,148,000
Underwriting Discounts and Commissions...	$ 1.15	$4,475,400
Proceeds Before Expenses to The Eclectic....	$21.85	$84,690,600

MORON STANLEY, DENSE WITTER
MORAL FLINCH INTERNATIONAL

ABOUT THE ECLECTIC MAGAZINE CORPORATION

The Eclectic was founded in February, 1999. One would expect that publishing and distributing a free magazine on the streets of New York was a way to meet and impress girls. But in fact, of the four founders, two had steady girl-friends and one was a girl-friend. Accordingly, one must conclude that the Magazine was founded out of the self-less desire to bring the highest quality writing and analysis to the reading public.

RISK FACTORS

You should consider carefully the following risks outlined in this prospectus before you decide to buy our common stock. An investment in our common stock involves risk. The trading price of our common stock could decline, and you may lose all or part of your investment. However, we are planning, shortly after the completion of the initial public offering, to launch an **INTERNET** version of the magazine, the ElectricEclectic.Com. As a **WEB-BASED** business, the risk factors described below can probably be ignored.

The Inscrutability of Mr. Lincoln MacVeagh. Since graduating from college, Lincoln MacVeagh has not held any job for more than a twelve month period. Indeed, it is rare that he has lived in one country for more than a twelve month period. This February will be the one year anniversary of the Eclectic. If Mr. MacVeagh suddenly decides to run off to somewhere like Bolivia, it would have a substantial negative impact on the Company's ability to continue to produce the Eclectic.

The Relationship of Ms. Seidel and Mr. Lincoln MacVeagh. In addition to being editors of the Magazine, Ms. Seidel and Mr. Lincoln MacVeagh are also romantically involved. Any damage to the romantic relationship may result in a situation adverse to the Magazine. If Ms. Seidel were to refuse to illustrate the magazine, it would have a substantial negative impact on the quality of the Eclectic.

Mr. T.E. MacVeagh is Getting Married. On February 19th, 2000, Mr. T.E. MacVeagh is getting married. If this marriage were to result in issue any time soon, the penetrating philosophical and political analysis for which Mr. MacVeagh's columns are widely admired may well be replaced by banal, insipid "insights" about the joys and tribulations of fatherhood.

Mr. Garcia and The Law of Averages. It is clear from Mr. Garcia's columns that he has met an unusual number of wacky individuals, or normal individuals to whom wacky things have happened. The law of averages suggests that sometime Mr. Garcia will start meeting nothing but boring people who have only had boring things happen to them. If this occurs, Mr. Garcia's column may become filled with tedious accounts of bankers and accountants watching HBO at home with the wife and kids.

Some of the Cartoons. Even the most dedicated and friendly readers have sometimes been baffled by certain cartoons, and the cartoonist is notoriously scornful of other people's perfectly funny suggestions. If readers cease to find the cartoons funny, this may have a substantial negative impact on the circulation of the magazine.

The Cash-Flow Limits. The editors of the Eclectic do not currently accept advertising, and have no plan to accept advertising even if they form an Internet version of the magazine, the ElectricEclectic.Com. As a result, the only source of income is from subscriptions. The editors do not intend to ever distribute more subscriptions than Mr. Lincoln MacVeagh can comfortably send out in an afternoon, around 100. As it is hard to imagine charging more than $3.00 per issue, it is equally hard to see how the Magazine could ever generate more than a maximum of $300 in income each issue.

USE OF PROCEEDS

The Eclectic will receive approximately $90 million in net proceeds from this offering. We expect to use the entire amount for general corporate purposes, including an aggressive launch into the Internet magazine market with the *ElectricEclectic.Com*. Also, there will be lifestyle adjustments for the major contributors to the Magazine. We believe that, among other benefits, the ability to throw around vast quantities of cash may allow us to meet celebrities. If the stories and essays in the Eclectic were peppered with insights into the lives of celebrities (rather than long-dead writers and poor Latin Americans), the editors believe that circulation may increase substantially.

DIVIDEND POLICY

We have not paid and do not intend to pay dividends on our common stock in the foreseeable future. Instead, we will retain our earnings to finance lavish vacations and parties for the principals. Our Board of Directors will have the authority to declare and pay dividends on the Common Stock at any time, but don't hold your breath.

MANAGEMENT DISCUSSION

Overview. Once we develop our WEB-BASED version of the Magazine, the ElectricEclectic.Com, we expect to be golden.

Sales, Marketing and Distribution. Our distribution relies chiefly on placing copies of the Magazine at Shakespeare and Co. bookstore in New York, and hoping curious shoppers pick them up. We have tried other distribution outlets, including West Village cafés and pizzerias, but our chief distributor has never seen a Magazine picked up at these locations. Indeed, he suspects that they are thrown in the trash as soon as he turns his back. Thus far actual sales of the Magazine have been restricted to friends, relatives, relatives of friends, and friends of relatives.

Competition. Our sole competition is the New Yorker. The Eclectic has several advantages. It is smaller and fits in the pocket more easily. It has less advertising. And Tina Brown has never edited it.

Intellectual Property. Not only does the Eclectic continue to own all rights to all of the stories and artwork already produced, but each of the contributors is a hothouse of ideas, and should be deemed the owner of a great variety of valuable ideas not yet produced.

Employees. Many readers have volunteered for the position of proof-reader, stating that they would do a better job than whoever has that responsibility currently. The Eclectic editors do not disagree with this, but are reluctant to go through the extra hassle for the sake of a few typos.

Year 2000 Disclosure. If our computers, or Mr. MacVeagh's scanner, fail as a result of the Y2K bug, the January, 2000 issue of the Eclectic may be delayed. Our impression, however, is that nobody would notice.

MANAGEMENT

Executive Officers and Directors

Chairman and Editor-in-Chief: Lincoln C. MacVeagh founded the Eclectic in February, 1999. Mr. MacVeagh received a grudging bachelor of arts from Harvard before spending a tortured several months writing advertising copy, including a well-received rap for the Wonderland dog track. Thereafter he misspent several years boozing and teaching in obscure Latin American countries. Mr. MacVeagh has sold short stories in front of the Metropolitan Museum of Art and played Algernon in the *Importance of Being Earnest*. In addition, he has served hors d'oeuvres to Sigourney Weaver.

President and Executive Illustration Editor: A. Hollace Seidel received her artistic training at The Waldorf School, where all subjects are treated as grist for the artist's mill. She is an accomplished singer, dancer, choreographer and painter; however, she rarely finds jokes about the overemphasis on arts at Waldorf Schools amusing. Moreover, she emphatically does not believe that all modern dance is a metaphor for sex. She has recently cut her hair to an attractive and sassy shoulder-length, and is currently considering a multi-hued dye-job.

WHERE TO SEND THE CHECKS

Please make checks payable to Lincoln C. MacVeagh or Theodore E. MacVeagh. Mail the checks to: The Eclectic Magazine, Linoleum Palace, Inc., 43-05 31st Avenue, Apt. #2, Astoria, NY 11103. A minimum purchase of 1,000 shares will be permitted. Share certificates will be delivered to you upon the exhaustion of the funds received and the removal of the principals from the jurisdiction of the United States.

Good luck with your investment. (God, don't you love the 90's.)

Reminiscence

What Time Is It?

Lincoln MacVeagh

Tonya was my landlord's maid in Mexico. She was short and stocky, and had long black hair which she wore in a plait running down her back. I think she was about thirty, but she had long since given up any idea of marriage and she already thought of herself as a spinster.

Tonya was extremely shy. When I first knew her she always called me "Hombre." I thought it was her version of formality, but it turned out she just didn't know what else to call me. Three months after I moved in I overheard a woman on the bus ask Tonya my name. "How should I know?" she replied curtly, "Ask him yourself!"

Tonya was from a tiny village in the mountains. The village was a four hour walk from the nearest highway and everyone there spoke Xapoteca instead of Spanish. She said the language was in the water. Her father was a peasant laborer and an alcoholic who died when she was six. Her mother also used to drink but gave it up when her husband died. Tonya herself never touched alcohol but whenever she thought I was coming down with the sniffles she gave me a shot of hot mezcal with lime for breakfast.

Tonya was cautious with me for a long time but she enjoyed talking about her village and she enjoyed teaching me about plants, and some time in January, I must have won her over because she decided to start doing my laundry. I can only think it was a sign of affection but Tonya was incapable of expressing it that way. She waited until she caught me washing my jeans one afternoon and then she came running outside to yell at me: "What are you doing? Leave that alone! That's woman's work! You should be reading your books!"

Tonya never understood how I could spend so much time reading. Sometimes she would ask me what was in the books, but mostly she thought books were a waste of time. She said that she'd gone to school only once

"Hello, Mr. Right!"

when she was nine. There was a government teacher who'd been sent to the village and on the day Tonya showed up at school the teacher looked right at her and asked her a question in Spanish. Tonya didn't understand Spanish and turned to the girl next to her to ask what the teacher had said. This made the teacher angry because no one was allowed to speak Xapoteca in the classroom, and to get her point across she hit Tonya on the wrist with a ruler. Tonya immediately jumped up from her seat and ran home. She never went back, she explained, because only her mother was allowed to hit her.

Tonya and I usually ate dinner together at seven o'clock, and at nine I would go back to the house to fill up my water jug before going to bed. Very often when I went to get water Tonya would ask me what time it was. My landlord came home at ten and I suppose she was interested to know when to start cooking his dinner.

It always surprised me that Tonya asked me the time because there was a digital clock sitting in plain sight on top of the refrigerator. I pointed it out to her once but Tonya wasn't interested, and then it dawned on me that she couldn't tell time. I suppose I should have guessed as much but I never thought of it.

A few nights later I asked Tonya if she wanted to learn how to read the clock. I'd been thinking about this offer for some time and I was quite excited about it because for some reason I thought teaching Tonya would say something important about myself. For different reasons, Tonya was excited too, and as soon as dinner was over we started work.

On a piece of paper I wrote down the numbers one through twenty.

Tonya already knew how to count so it was just a matter of matching the words to the symbols, and after a while she was able to identify most of the numbers. But she had difficulty with the two digit numbers and I had lots of trouble explaining why "17" wasn't "one, seven." I told her that she mustn't ask too many questions, that she must be patient and memorize.

We went back to my number line the next night but Tonya quickly got bored. She wanted to know how to tell time and she couldn't see how studying the pencil symbols would help. It was no use arguing with her so I put the paper away and asked Tonya to read the numbers off the digital clock instead. Suddenly all was confusion.

07:45. None of the numbers on the clock looked anything like my handwritten numbers. My seven had a bar in it whereas the digital seven didn't; and the digital clock put a confusing zero in front of the seven and a colon after it; the number forty-five hadn't even been on our number line.

We had to start over at the beginning. I set the minutes to ":00" and asked her to concentrate on just reading the hours. It seemed to me a simple thing to memorize the numbers 01-12 on a digital clock, but Tonya couldn't get it; she was distracted and grew irritable. "This is stupid," she said.

The following night I asked Tonya again if she wanted to study the clock but she said she was busy. I think she was just embarrassed to take up more of my time, but in any case I was relieved when she said no. I was tired of my little project. I was frustrated with Tonya and I realized that if I were to teach her how to tell time it might take weeks. I never offered Tonya any more lessons and she never dared ask for them herself.

Sir Laffalot

Last month Sir Laffalot signed up with an entertainment company in the city. Balloons, gorillas, birthday girls – that sort of thing. The work's been good so far and he reports only one real horror story. The fur coat and g-string woman was mistakenly sent to a children's party in Bronxville and Sir Laffalot got stuck with fifteen Smith, Barney brokers in a private room downtown.

Sir Laffalot doesn't do tricks with cigars, but the evening wasn't a total flop and everyone had a good time playing *Telephone*. The brokers laughed hysterically when "The S&P is up 400 points" turned into "Stephanie is up for a hundred boinks," and Sir Laffalot made good money on tips.

Sir Laffalot likes the cash, but the great drawback of the workaday world is that it leaves him so little room for his social obligations. Every holiday season Sir Laffalot receives hundreds of invites, but now that he's employed he can't possibly accept them all, and as a result, he spends much of his free time RSVP'ing regrets. A sampling from last week's mail bag:

Dear Liza,

Thanks so much for the charming. A quiet night of Y2K snuggles and Chablis sounds delightful, but sadly Sir Laffalot is previously engaged and won't be able to make it. Until next time, mon cheri. XXX OOO. Sir L.

Dear Rudi:

Love your New Year's resolution. The pencil moustache is a great idea. Unfortunately, however, Sir Laffalot will not be able to join you in the festivities. Best to Donna and the kids. Yours etc., Laffalot.

Sir Laffalot hates writing these letters. He knows that no matter how tactfully you word it, people take rejection badly. So in order to avoid hurt feelings Sir Laffalot would like to announce once and for all that he's busy this Dec. 31. He's already working a party. He hopes his many friends will understand, and for those who wish to be with Sir Laffalot in spirit, he has two suggestions.

First, when you pop the champagne save the wire that wraps around the cork. Hold the wire at arm's length with the larger circle closer to you and the little circle further away. Focus on a point two feet beyond the wire and keep staring for twenty or thirty seconds. Suddenly you will see the wire invert itself and it will look as though the little circle is closest and the bigger circle further away.

Sir Laffalot's second suggestion for New Year's fun is a game that he himself will be playing. It's called *The Balloon Game* and it's marvelous.

The Balloon Game: How to Play.

1) All players tie balloons around each ankle.

2) When the music starts players try to pop each other's balloons.

3) If both your balloons get popped you're out. The last player standing is the winner.

Sir Laffalot says: HAPPY NEW YEAR!!

The high life

Apricot Cookie

David Garcia III

When last we spoke, my friend Laura had returned to the family home in Pittsburgh. Withdrawing from the world, her life devolved into a Russian roulette of mouse-clicking, Prozac, cigarettes, coffee, and watching sitcoms with her (recently retired) father. She woke up in the afternoon, and when she got to the kitchen there would always be an apricot cookie waiting for her on the table. Her father bought them each day at the bakery.

Laura's father started talking about building a wing on the house for her to live in... *forever*. Laura imagined herself playing the role of "crazy old lady down the block, who never worked, and inhabits her dead parents increasingly dilapidated home." She said she might have to bury a kid or two in the backyard, just to keep the legend going.

When she told me that she had begun to spend her few waking hours cruising the Internet Personals, I thought I had lost her. She started in Pittsburgh, but then expanded on to California, London, and Berlin, periodically forwarding me copies of the detailed questionnaires that they make you fill out – primarily about your appearance, but also about preferences. "If white, are you willing to consider a black man?" One of the key questions was, "Have you ever imagined being romantic with another woman?"

At one point, Laura withheld her age from the questionnaire (she's 34 now), and got into an extended cyber-flirt with a monosyllabic 28 year old. Eventually she revealed how old she was, and he wrote back, "Sorry to hear that. I thought you were really cool, and I wanted to keep going." As if she had died. As if Cindy Crawford wasn't in her 30's.

After a few similar misfires, a software guy from California hooked onto her. One of those atonal Gatesy (as opposed to Gatsby) types who went to college at 12 and make scads of money munching code. Things progressed and they graduated to phone calls where she learned he's in his 40's, has three kids, and is divorced. They started e-mailing photos back and forth (he looks kind of like John Belushi) and having six-hour talks where he would play entire Steely Dan songs for her on the piano. He sent her a plane ticket.

She agonized over the trip, and at the last minute cancelled out, fearing he was getting "too-close-too-soon," and also that he might be a serial killer who would bury her in a ditch along the highway. She broke off all communication, and he responded by hopping on his motorcycle (he collects them), and driving all the way to Pittsburgh to meet her in the flesh.

It was too weird to have him there with her parents, so she felt pressured into taking a ride on his bike. They cruised down the interstate, and then stopped at a truckstop to chat. He pulled out a halter-top for her to wear, and she (who usually wears fishing vests and baggy clothes) consented to putting it on as a lark. After a couple of hours on the open road, they stopped at a Red Lobster and ate Surf n' Turf.

Out in the parking lot, they started to make out in the hot sun. Then they just kept going from hotel to hotel all through Vermont and Canada. After a few weeks he took her home, and flew back to California. She's booked on a flight there in a few days time, to give it a go with the three kids, and perhaps to have one of her own. She thinks March is a good month for a wedding.

**FOR SUBSCRIPTIONS
TURN TO PAGE 7.**

The
ECLECTIC

| February 2000 | Volume 2 Number 1 | Free |

CONTENTS

Quotations

"*There on a Holy World hilltop, I realized how very dangerous it is for people to hold any human being in such esteem, especially to consider anyone some sort of 'divinely guided' and 'protected' person.*" Malcolm X explains his break with Elijah Muhammad to Alex Haley in *The Autobiography of Malcolm X.*

"*One of the luckiest things that can happen to you in life is, I think, to have a happy childhood. I had a very happy childhood.*" Agatha Christie in *An Autobiography.*

"*The only reason I was eager to be a hero was so that Irena would finally go to bed with me.*" Danny points to the source of all courage in Josef Skvorecky's *The Cowards.*

"*You can't just shout at them. First you have to learn to ignore them.*" Roald Dahl advises his wife about children.

The Eclectic is owned and published by Linoleum Palace, Inc., 43-05 31st Ave., #2, Astoria, NY 11103. Copyright © 1999 by Lincoln MacVeagh. All rights reserved. Unsolicited submissions will not be considered or returned.

Don't Bother About Tomorrow

A Portrait of Roald Dahl

Lincoln MacVeagh

Roald Dahl (pronounced Roo-ahl) liked food, wine, sports and gambling. He also wrote children's books. *The Fantastic Mr. Fox* is the first book I ever read cover to cover in a single day and by 1980 Dahl was selling an average of one book a year for every third child in Britain. In 1939, however, he was just another young man working for Shell Oil in Tanganyika, East Africa.

Dahl had skipped university in favor of adventure and when the second world war broke out he was drafted into service by the local authorities. Tanganyika was previously a German colony, so most of the Europeans living there were Germans, and on the day England declared war, Dahl was ordered to set up a road block along the main highway leading out of Dar Es Salaam. He was given a red arm-band, a machine gun and twenty native troops, and told to round up all the Germans attempting to flee the country.

"I am really not trained for this sort of thing," said Dahl, "I'm just a chap who works for Shell."

"Rubbish!" barked his superior.

So Dahl put his arm-band round his arm and drove a few miles out of town. He parked two trucks across the highway to block traffic; hid his troops and the machine gun in the woods on the side of

"I'm just a chap who works for Shell."

the road; and he stood by himself in the hot sun waiting for the Germans. They came in a long convoy, carrying wives, children and furniture, and when the lead car reached the road block a burly man got out and told Dahl to shove off. Dahl refused and soon an angry crowd gathered around him. Many of the Germans carried pistols and they started waving them around defiantly. In a signal to his troops, Dahl put his hands over his head and a volley of gunfire exploded in the air above the highway. Dahl told the crowd that they were outnumbered and would all be killed if they tried to pass on. In desperation, one German lunged at Dahl, grabbed his arm, and stuck a Lugar in his chest:

"What came next happened very suddenly. There was the crack of a single rifle shot fired from the wood and the bald man who was holding me took the bullet right through his face. It was a horrible sight. His head seemed to splash open and little soft bits of grey stuff flew out in all directions. There was no blood, just the grey stuff and fragments of bone. One lump of the grey stuff landed on my cheek. More of it went all over my khaki shirt. The Lugar dropped on to the road and the bald man fell dead beside it."

After leading the Germans back to prison camp, Dahl went home, drank a glass of whiskey, and the next day he rushed happily off to join the R.A.F. He wasn't the least troubled by thoughts of mortality. From pilot's training school in Kenya he wrote to his mother, *"Dear Mama, I'm having a lovely time, have never enjoyed myself so much. I've been sworn in to the R.A.F. proper and am definitely in it now until the end of the war."*

After a hideous plane crash in the Libyan desert which destroyed his nose and left him blinded for more than three weeks, Dahl finally saw combat in Greece and it was an immediate disaster. Vastly overmatched by the German Messerschmidts, Dahl's squadron was decimated within just ten days of his arrival and the few survivors had to be withdrawn to Palestine. The fighting continued with intensity and in five short weeks Dahl flew over forty missions before being grounded because he started to suffer frequent blackouts in the air. Still in Palestine, Dahl wrote home to his mother:

"They may even send me to England, which wouldn't be a bad thing, would it. It's a pity in a way though, because I've just got going. I've got 5 confirmed, four Germans and one French, and quite a few unconfirmed – and lots on the ground from groundstraffing landing grounds. We've lost 4 pilots killed in the Squadron in the last 2 weeks, shot down by the French. Otherwise the country is great fun and definitely flowing with milk and honey..."

Otherwise the country is great fun.

Roald Dahl was exceptional among writers for being nearly incapable of melancholy. He had an inquisitive mind but not an introspective one. He never published a work of philosophy but he did write a cook book. Above all, he liked fun and he was never ashamed to admit it. As a boy he loved games, and even as a middle-aged man he still played razor golf regularly each morning, trying to shave himself in as few strokes as possible.

Dahl was born in Wales in 1916, the son of a prosperous Norwegian businessman. Harald Dahl made his fortune as a ship's broker in Cardiff and he believed in getting on with life. He lost his left arm falling off a roof at fourteen but he learned to tie his shoe laces faster with one hand than most people could with two, and his only complaint was that he couldn't cut the top off a boiled egg.

Roald's mother Sofie was also Norwegian. She was Harald's second wife, nineteen years younger than her husband, and together the couple had five children. The eldest of the these, Astri, died of appendicitis at age seven and

"At first I thought he was sensitive interesting, but then I realized he was sensitive boring."

Harald died a short while later of pneumonia.

Sofie was seventh months pregnant at the time. She was still much happier speaking Norwegian and she had no family in Wales to support her, but she didn't go back to Norway because she'd promised her husband to educate his only son in England. For some reason Harald had an inordinate faith in English public schools, and according to his father's wishes, Roald left home when he was nine.

Dahl disliked boarding school. He spent two years at St. Peter's and another four at Repton, but though he was a fair student and very good at games, he was not much for discipline and he often landed in trouble. He was so unhappy at St. Peter's that he once faked appendicitis in order to get sent home, and he remembered Repton mostly for the beatings he was given. In his glorious memoir *Boy*, Dahl described the headmaster at Repton as a vicious sadist who delighted in lecturing boys on morality while slowly caning their buttocks so hard as to break the skin. The headmaster's name was Geoffrey Fisher and later he became the Archbishop of Canterbury.

When Dahl left school he went on to Shell, and then to the war, and skipping forward to 1941, Dahl was back in England. He was twenty-five years old, he'd seen combat with the R.A.F., and walking round London in his pilot's uniform he was treated like a hero everywhere he went. Dahl enjoyed the attention and soon he parlayed it into a job as assistant Air Attaché at the British Embassy in Washington D.C..

Tall, handsome, sophisticated, and funny, Dahl was an instantly popular dinner guest in Washington and he quickly set about cultivating influential friends. The most important of these was Charles Marsh, a millionaire oil man who remained his patron for years afterwards, but according to many accounts Dahl's best success was with rich women of a certain age. Charles Marsh's daughter said of Roald, "*I think he slept with everybody on the East and West coasts that had more than fifty thousand dollars a year.*" Dahl himself liked to show off a gold house key given to him by the Standard Oil heiress Millicent Rogers. He also had an affair with Clare Booth Luce, the wife of the *Life* publisher Henry Luce: "*That goddam woman,*" Dahl told a friend, "*Has absolutely screwed me from one end of the room to the other for three goddam nights.*"

In Washington, Dahl earned a reputation as a good storyteller and with interest in the war at its peak, he was asked to write about his plane crash in Libya for the *Saturday Evening Post*. Dahl called it *Shot Down Over Libya*, and although the shot down part was fiction, the story was a success and he began to write more regularly. Starting out with propagandist war stories, Dahl's work kept getting better and in 1945 he published his first collection.

By the end of the war Dahl had devoted himself to writing. He divided his time between New York and London and filled in spare hours buying wine and artwork for Charles Marsh. After a bad novel, Dahl came out with his second collection of short stories in 1953 and suddenly he was famous. Confoundingly, however, it wasn't the stories that got the world's attention, it was his marriage to the Hollywood starlet Patricia Neal.

Other than good looks and ambition, it's hard to see what Pat and Roald had in common. After Roald's first visit to Pat's family in Tennessee, he went home and asked for a divorce. When Pat went to England to meet the Dahls, she was upset to find that no one kissed her or embraced her. She got nothing but a cold hello from Roald's mother, and she was further disturbed after dinner because Roald's brother-in-law started lighting his farts. Pat was a southern belle

accustomed to being pampered while Roald was a stern minded Englishman incapable of flattery. He once caught her admiring herself naked in the mirror. Instead of complimenting her figure, he shouted, *"My God, will you stop that! Put some clothes on."*

Dahl seems to have been ashamed of his wife's lack of culture and he often insulted her in public. Pat got back at him by telling her friends that Roald looked like Virginia Woolf in drag, only bald. Incredibly, however, the two of them stayed married for thirty years and through most of that time Dahl lived in his wife's shadow.

In 1965, Dahl was asked to write the script for the James Bond film, *You Only Live Twice*. He was given the job not because the producers loved his books, but because they felt sorry for his wife. Pat had recently suffered a massive stroke and Hollywood was reaching out to her through her husband. One might think that Dahl would be offended by the offer, but in fact he jumped at it. He was a practical man, and horribly enough, he'd already learned to live with disaster.

Eight years earlier Dahl's infant son had been hit by a car on the corner of 82nd and Madison, leaving him permanently brain damaged. Three years after that his oldest daughter died overnight from an attack of the measles. Dahl was certainly upset by his wife's stroke, but he was long past agonizing over it. It is one of the macabre little details of his life that when his wife was re-learning the alphabet at age 39, his six year old son was delighted because it meant that he and his mother had the same homework.

Pat's stroke left her partially paralyzed and unable to speak, and her husband's reaction was to institute a rigorous rehabilitation regime. Some people were appalled to see that Dahl would not help his wife out of a taxi, but it was his view that if once she got used to assistance, she would never be independent again.

Dahl's regime worked. Pat was pregnant when she went into her coma and five months later she gave birth to a healthy baby girl. At the same time she slowly recovered her ability to walk, to speak, and even to read. Naturally, there was trouble along the way. On one occasion Pat broke down in tears because she couldn't understand her Beatrix Potter book. "*You mustn't worry about it,*" said Roald sincerely, "*Pigling Bland is Potter's toughest book. It's not at all easy to follow.*"

Kurt Vonnegut once said that nothing dissolves a marriage faster than a spouse who gets religion. In Dahl's case the solvent was brain damage, and though it worked more slowly it was equally effective. Before the stroke, Pat was the family star; after the stroke, she was just another dependent. Her incapacity made her cranky, and moreover she was jealous of her husband's growing popularity.

By 1971 Dahl's second children's book had been made into a movie (*Charlie and the Chocolate Factory* was re-titled *Willy Wonka and the Chocolate Factory* because Hollywood said that "Charlie" was black slang for the white man) and Roald was fast becoming the best-selling children's author on the planet. Dahl's success grated on Pat, and for his part, Dahl grew tired of playing nurse maid to a woman he no longer needed. Years after her stroke Pat still had trouble concentrating, but Dahl showed little patience. When Pat faltered playing bridge he rebuked her sharply saying, "*You must answer your partner with a bid if you've got some points in your hand. You do know how to count points, do you not?*"

Surely Dahl could have been more forgiving, but he had other problems to deal with. His eldest daughter was addicted to heroin and his second daughter was addicted to cocaine. He was also suffering from terrible back pain. When he went into the hospital for his operation, he came out with a severe limp in his right leg. Since Pat still limped on her left leg, whenever the two of them walked together they now had to choose between knocking shoulders every other step, or else coming apart like a pair of scissors. In 1983 Dahl and Pat divorced

and Dahl remarried to a younger woman named Felicity Crosland.

Dahl lived another seven years after his second marriage. Throughout his life he'd maintained a regular writing schedule, working two hours in the morning and two hours in the afternoon, and he kept up the pace in his dotage. He published his two best books, *Boy* and *Going Solo*, in 1984 and 1986 respectively, and he even wrote one last children's book, *Matilda*, just shortly before he died.

Many people have said that in old age Dahl was a mean, grasping, and paranoid alcoholic. It's true that he wrote nasty letters to his publishers and drank a good deal more whiskey than was healthy, but it seems churlish to hold such sins against him. Dahl's great gift was to enjoy life and it's not surprising he got grumpy when he finally realized his life was to end.

Reviews

The Naked Civil Servant

by Quentin Crisp

Penguin Books, 1997 (reprint)

Quentin Crisp believed that squalor was his natural setting. He lived thirty-three years in a dirty, one-room Chelsea flat and he didn't like cooking, cleaning or foreign travel. He struggled to boil a kettle, believed that only a fool would make his bed every day, and he saw no glamour in visiting Europe: *"I don't hold with abroad and think that foreigners speak English when our backs are turned."*

Quentin Crisp was also inescapably queer. *The Naked Civil Servant* is his autobiography and in the book's first sentence he puts the matter quite simply: *"From the dawn of my history I was so disfigured by the characteristics of a certain kind of homosexual person, that, when I grew up, I realized that I could not ignore my predicament."*

Born Dennis Pratt in 1908, Quentin was a boy who brought a pack of cards to birthday parties so he could play solitaire. At school he was bright, but he was a desultory student and made no effort. *"I was at boarding school for four years. During that time I learned only one thing that I was ever able to use in adult life. I learned that my great gift was for unpopularity."*

With no chance at university, Quentin's mother pressed him into a course in commercial art and this led to work in advertising. Crisp liked getting paid because it meant he could live on his own, but the time he spent at the office passed slowly: *"The other members of the staff adopted the ruse of filling in the hours by doing the work well. This ruse never occurred to me."* He got fired from a number of jobs and ended up supporting himself as an artist's model. *"When stripped I looked less like 'Il David' than a plucked chicken that died of myxomatosis."*

Crisp was an artist's model for most of his adult life, but his real career was that of being a homosexual. For three decades he was the most famous, if not the only, openly gay man in England. When Crisp came of age, homosexual-

ity was so taboo as to be nearly invisible. *"It was thought to be Greek in origin, smaller than socialism but more deadly – especially to children."* In 1930, gay men stayed in the closet as a matter of course, but Crisp refused. He possessed the courage of the damned and knowing that he would never be able to disguise his high pitched, lisping voice or his mincing walk, he chose to trumpet them.

At eighteen he started wearing make-up in public. He henna'd his hair, grew his fingernails and wore colorful scarves. Then he marched through the streets as if all of London were his private confessional. *"Almost every living being seems to feel that if all were known he would be admired, and even I was never able to rid myself of the idea that if all were known I would be forgiven."* Predictably, Crisp was not forgiven and he got a lot of beatings for his trouble. His only means of self-defense was walking quickly but it was by no means foolproof and he was often left for dead on the pavement. Strangely though, he never learned to despise his attackers: *"I regarded all heterosexuals, however low,*

as superior to any homosexual, however noble."

As tragic as it sometimes is, *The Naked Civil Servant* is not a self-pitying book and Crisp is much too good a writer to let his anger dominate. He doesn't rant or lecture. He aims to entertain, and he tells his story simply, but with charm and a light touch. *"I now know,"* he says, *"that if you describe things as better than they are, you are considered a romantic; if you describe things as worse than they are, you will be called a realist; and if you describe things exactly as they are, you will be thought a satirist."*

By his own definition, Quentin Crisp was a satirist. As a result he sometimes runs the risk of sounding hollow or superficial, but it's a mistake to insist on tears from a man just because he's been kicked around a bit. Crisp has earned his sense of humor, and at the close of his book he hints at the hard work behind his laughter: *"Even a monstrously undeviating path of self-examination does not necessarily lead to a mountain of self-knowledge. I stumble toward my grave confused and hurt and hungry..."*

Commentary

Is Literature Lying?

T.E. MacVeagh

Plato claimed that fiction was just a bunch of lies strung together. In *The Republic* he went on and on about how Homer's poetry was filled with falsehoods and he banned it from his ideal city. I think those people you sometimes meet who say they never read fiction generally agree with Plato. They pretend embarrassment about not being well-read, but I suspect what they really want to say is: "I'm not taken in by the nonsense people call *literature.*"

One argument in the defense of literature runs something like this: the events in a piece of fiction may be lies, but the work as a whole expresses emotional truths. Sure there was not a person called Anna Karenina who actually threw herself under a train. But the emotions described by Tolstoy are real and true to life.

I always used to think that this defense granted too much to a meritless accusation. To say that fiction is "lying" doesn't make sense. It is like saying that a table is "intelligent" or an auto mechanic is "parallel". It is a category mistake. Not all adjectives apply to all nouns. Is the statement "The present king of France is bald" a lie because there is no present king of France? The word "lie" doesn't seem to apply.

And as for those people who never read fiction, I have always felt kind of sorry for them. Lacking a sense of literature, they seem handicapped and shut off from a beautiful world. Like blind men who don't understand the joys of painting, or deaf men who cannot appreciate music.

However, I am rethinking this position. A little while ago I read several books about concentration camps and, after a little while, I realized that I had begun to find the tropes of the genre comforting. I found myself at home in the soup line holding that stale piece of black bread, jostling for the place in line where the soup doled out would be thickest. After the initial shock of the stories, I returned to them for enjoyable escapism. Perhaps you will say I was a particularly callous reader, to be able to read Holocaust literature for pleasure, but I suspect this is a fairly normal reaction.

Stories do not affect us like real life. We are much more willing to endure horror in a novel than horror in real life. Of course, part of the reason is that in novels bad things happen to other people. Not to us. And in real life too, we are always much better able to endure horrors to other people than to ourselves. But still, the terror of novels is just not that terrifying. The experience of novels is not real experience. It is false, unthreatening experience, to be enjoyed in front of a fire.

Why is the "experience" gained in novels so different from that of real life? It seems to me that the constant, pervasive emotion accompanying reading literature is a sense of calm. Literature does not reach either the range or the intensity of emotions experienced in even the most ordinary life: real desperation, painful loss, true joy or awe-struck love. Perhaps, my first defense of literature has it backward. Literature does not contain factual lies because it is not trying to be an accurate portrayal of events; but it is filled with emotional lies. You think because you read a work of Primo Levi that you understand the Holocaust; you think because you read Anna Karenina that you understand why a Russian aristocrat might throw themselves in front of a train. But you don't. The emotional experience you gain from reading is an illusion. A lie.

As well as emotional lies, novels also contain lies about possibilities. Writers write about time travel, mind-reading, post-death experiences and sudden transformations into cockroaches. They suggest to us that we understand what these things would be like. But do we really? Borges has a story about a contemporary Spaniard who rewrites Don Quixote, "meaning" each sentence of the text as it would be meant by a contemporary Spaniard. Describing such a feat is not only a far cry from performing it, but a far cry from even understanding what the performance would require.

Literature is also filled with more mundane lies: the spy who is impossibly cool; the hero who never has a wicked thought; the sexpot who is always willing. And here it may be that these lies of literature are as damaging as Plato claims.

Literary and fictional images are central in the construction of our self-images. Look around the subway one day and try to identify which combination of characters from film and literature have gone into the images that your fellow passengers are trying to project. The man across the aisle shows a hint of Holden Caufield, a little Keanu Reeves from the *Matrix*, and heavy Gordon Gekko. The woman next to him is part Jane Austen heroine, with a bit of Melanie Griffith from *Working Girl*. It can be fun and interest-ing to pick out the cultural references but it is also a little sad to realize that the models upon which we base our lives are illusions. These characters are driven by emotional falsehoods; they are a collection of qualities that cannot be brought together in real life. And the goals and interests we have adopted on the basis of these images are more appropriate for fiction than reality.

All of these points admitted, let us moderate our criticism of fiction. How different is fiction from autobiography, history or journalism? Concentration camp literature, to take one example, is often in the form of memoir or first-person reportage. It is history. History, just as much as fiction, is read calmly while sitting in front of cozy fireplaces. If fiction is filled with emotional lies, so are most other forms of writing.

In fact, I would argue that the calm that overtakes us when we are reading is the dominant emotion of abstract thinking in general. This is why abstract thinking is such an effective balm for pain and misery. It is much more tolerable to reflect on the general nature of pain than the particular-ized agony of your own toothache or heartache. To say that fiction contains emotional lies may be right, but is it a criticism? After all, it is the calm con-sideration of a subject, free from the prejudices of passion, fear and hatred, which we value in abstract thinking. Is there any reason not to value them in fiction as well?

Reminiscence

Dirty Words

Lincoln MacVeagh

Between the ages of five and ten I went to a preparatory school in London called Tower House. There were one hundred boys in the upper school and another forty or so in the lower school and we all wore grey flannel trousers, grey cotton shirts, and a matching blazer, tie and cap which were navy with light blue stripes. I was very proud of my Tower House uniform. I was a proper English schoolboy and I even had trouble pronouncing my R's. I said *wight* instead of *right*.

My best friend at Tower House was Jeremy Hughes. Jeremy was the cleverest boy in the class and he used to bring sweets to school every day which he doled out to his friends after lunch. He was small and skinny, with mousy brown hair and soft brown eyes, and when Jeremy and I were both eight years old we discovered dirty words. We could entertain ourselves for hours simply by whispering bum and willy back and forth to each other. We were interested in all sex words generally but my personal favorite was cobblers. I think it derives from the cockney rhyming slang, cobbler's awls – balls.

By the time we reached Form II, Jeremy and I started keeping a notebook full of dirty rhymes and limericks. Our work was illustrated with naughty pictures and most of our inspiration came from a popular rugby song about a woman named Dinah. *"Dinah, Dinah, show us your legs / Show us your legs / Show us your legs / Dinah, Dinah, Show us your legs / Yard above the knee luv."* This song always puzzled me because it was my assumption that a woman's midsection was the most interesting part of her body and thus

I always pictured Dinah to be a sort of giantess.

Jeremy and I spent lots of time writing new lyrics in our notebook about Dinah. We had Dinah floating in a punt, Dinah fixing a lock and Dinah in the city, and one day during science class Mr. Price caught me reading the notebook and asked me what I was doing.

Mr. Price was my favorite teacher. He coached rugby as well as teaching science and I always wanted desperately to please him, so when he caught me with the notebook I was very upset. I blushed red and went perfectly mute. Mr. Price picked up the notebook and started flipping through it. A momentary expression of shock came across his face but then he collected himself and calmly placed the notebook in a drawer in his desk, confiscating it. He gave me a stern look and went on with his lecture.

Although I didn't much like the idea of Mr. Price possessing a book full of dirty rhymes written in my handwriting, I got over my embarrassment quite quickly, and soon Jeremy and I went on to other forms of sport. The best of these had to do with Mr. Price's wife. Mrs. Price was blonde and beautiful and she taught second years in the lower school. I remember that her father owned a patent on the first microwave oven, but I can no longer remember her name so I will have to call her Annie. Jeremy and I fell in love with Annie.

The lower school playground was separated from the upper school playground by a big shed and the school auditorium. You couldn't see from one playground to the other but sound carried over the low buildings and during play time Jeremy and I used to wait behind the shed, listening for the lower schoolers to come out of their classroom. When we heard the younger children screaming, we knew that Annie would be outside watching them and the game of declaring our love would begin. *I love you, Annie!*

The game developed quickly and Jeremy and I dared each other to say dirtier and dirtier things in louder and louder voices. Mostly we sang the rugby songs we remembered from our notebook, cleverly substituting Mrs. Price's name for all references to Dinah. We asked Annie to show us her legs and ride in a punt and so on. We screamed these songs at the top of our lungs in high-pitched schoolboy voices and there was a good amount of real sex feeling in it. There was also the pleasant thrill of misbehaving, but I never much worried about getting found out. Because of the shed and the auditorium, it was impossible for Mrs. Price to see us and since it never occurred to me that she would recognize our voices, our game kept up throughout the Spring term.

When we got back from holidays, however, Jeremy told me the most awful thing I'd ever heard. Over break Mr. and Mrs. Price went to a dinner party at Jeremy's house and Jeremy's mother called him out to shake hands with the guests. After introducing him round, Mrs. Hughes turned to Mrs. Price and said:

"Annie, you know my son, don't you?"

"Of course," said Mrs. Price smiling, "He and his friend Lincoln have lovely singing voices."

Jeremy didn't seem to understand the awfulness of this story. He thought it was funny but I didn't think it was funny at all. When I heard it my heart began to beat wildly and a horrible pit took shape in my stomach. I hated the idea of Annie laughing at me, but more than that I was terrified to think that she might tell my parents all the dirty things I'd said.

I was so scared that the story would get back to my mother that after school I made a deal with God. I promised on my side never to use any more bad words, if only he would make sure that the history of my love affair with Annie stayed under wraps. This deal made me feel slightly better but it turned out that neither side kept up the bargain. The very next day I caught myself swearing again, and years later I discovered that my mother had known about my thing for Mrs. Price all along.

"You'll lose a little dexterity in the left eye, but you're gonna look great."

Games

Sir Laffalot

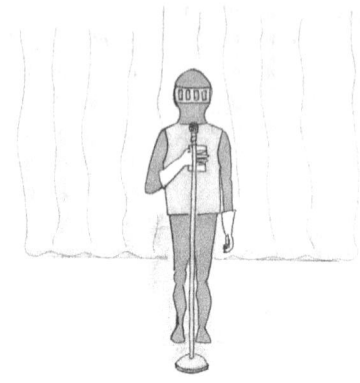

Sir Laffalot's life as a children's entertainer came to an end last month after a particularly unpleasant outing in Montauk. The birthday girl was an aggressive young thing, ten years old and four feet tall, who demanded that everyone play Barbie. The girl's mother seemed to think her daughter was a real spitfire. "Isn't she lively?" she said beaming, but Sir Laffalot's patience was exhausted. "Indeed, she is like life itself," he replied, "Nasty, brutish and short." He was terminated the very next day.

Fortunately, however, Sir Laffalot has already chosen his next career path. He aims to be a poet and Tuesday night was the first meeting of his new poetry group. The leader's name was Mr. Lewis. He was a wiry, energetic man in jeans and a black turtleneck and he started the evening off with a simple exercise in appreciation. He had everyone in the group read a haiku out loud and then he went through the room asking people how they felt about it. Sir Laffalot's haiku was all about ice and snow and he said it made him feel cold. There was an awkward silence for a moment and then Sir Laffalot looked up and saw that everyone in the group was staring at him. Their mouths were slightly open and they were all nodding their heads slowly up and down. "Good," said Mr. Lewis, "*Good.*"

Mr. Lewis went on to explain that the trick to understanding poetry is *listening* to the *words*, but as far as writing it is concerned, he said there's only one unbreakable rule and he asked people to guess what they thought it was. Sir Laffalot suggested it might be a matter of replacing verbs with gerunds, but the secret to poetry turned out to be less technical than that. Mr. Lewis' eyes went all shiny and his voice quavered when he said it: *Write what you know.*

Sir Laffalot jotted the dictum down in his notebook, but he couldn't help but feel a little disappointed. Sir Laffalot doesn't know anything about anything but playing games and you can't write a lot of poems about that. Or can you?

Categories is a game in which players are asked to come up with a long series of related objects. It is a leisurely game suitable for long trips. It's also good practice for a poet in search of synonyms, and since Sir Laffalot has to come up with something in time for Saturday night's poetry slam, he's decided to set the rules of *Categories* to verse. The title of the poem is inspired by a line from Joyce and it's called *Categories: How to Play.*

Categories: How to Play.
Pick a category with which to start,
Like African countries or flavors of Pop-Tart.
Then go round in a circle with each player saying,
A thing from the category with which you are playing.
Failure to think of a word means a "P",
A "P" as in pig, as in pig-snout you're OUT!
Pick a new category and keep up the fun,
The last player left is the winner who won.

Sir Laffalot says: TOODALOO!!

Continued from page 16

when I got home I would throw off my filthy clothes and sink into the deepest depths of sleep. Each morning, the clothes would be in the same spot as I had dropped them, magically cleaned and folded by my stealthy Grandma. Grandma came and went, and I never heard a sound.

Often, however, the door at the top of the stairs would creak open at some absurdly early hour and with an infinite, agonizing slowness, the sound of slippers would make itself known on the stairs. Sluff, sloof. Sluff, sloof. It seemed to last hours. Grampa took forever to shuffle through the dark maze (I had eliminated most of the light bulbs to discourage him) of pool tables, weight benches, old furniture, and boxes of clothes, until he found my remote corner. He would pause, and just stand there breathing, like a life-size chess piece from medieval Spain. I knew if I acknowledged his presence with a groan, he would start nudging and poking. If I didn't acknowledge him, he would hit me with his hat.

"Macheen."

"Whuuu?"

"Macheen. You star de macheen."

"Macheen, macheen," he kept saying until I put on my clothes, stepped into the hot sun and pulled at the cord that brought the lawnmower fitfully to life. He was too old to start the machine himself, but despite having lost three toes to a lawnmower in the 1970's, he insisted on mowing daily. I would crawl back into my cave and try to fall asleep despite the noise but I couldn't stop myself from listening for the engine to stall.

To my pleasant surprise, though, this ritual came to an end two summers later, when Grampa abandoned "de macheen" to embark upon a mysterious new project.

Each day he would shuffle out past the extreme right hand corner of the backyard with a wheelbarrow full of rakes and tools, and disappear into the woods. I asked my Grandmother what he was up to, and she said, "All I know is that it's quiet. Maybe he's digging a hole to China."

He had devoted untold hours to this undertaking by the time I was finished with school and before graduation, I brought a girl named Gwen home for the weekend. I drove her around town and gave her a tour of the house. We were in the backyard when she said she saw a deer moving in the woods. I told her it was Grampa, and explained that he was busy with some mysterious excavation.

Later that night, we ran into my Grandfather as he was shuffling off to bed. "This is my Grandfather," I said, "Grampa, this is Gwen." He grunted and Gwen (true to form) confronted him.

"Hey, *Grampa*. David wants to know what you do all day in the woods."

"So you can dance," he replied gruffly, but with perfect clarity. Gwen laughed until I thought she would hurt herself.

It was dark outside, but a fairly clear night and Gwen insisted we investigate Grampa's project. The property had been a tree nursery 100 years ago and the trees were all organized in even rows. Walking into the woods we followed one long row until we came to a large area that looked like it had been cleared away to prepare for some Druid ceremony.

Little by little, Grampa had eliminated all the vegetation from a section of woodland about the size of two tennis courts. Hundreds of pounds of twigs and vines, small trees and weeds and plants had been carted away, leaving only the smooth ground. It was like finding an empty ballroom in the middle of a huge cluttered mansion. The open area held all the sounds of the woods (cicadas and birds and frogs and branches) like an acoustical chamber, and the fireflies stood out like party lights.

We took off our shoes, giggling, and did our best to waltz.

Green Thumb

David Garcia III

Spain was the darkness they stepped out of, and the photo was the one document of their migration to America. It was antique by the time I saw it, and what fascinated me most was the sight of my father's father as a handsome, dapper boy. This boy was rare and dangerous. I looked hard but I couldn't find a trace of him in the man I knew as Grampa.

He couldn't have known it when the photo was taken, but he was heading for decade after decade in the furnace level of a West Virginia coal mine, followed by decades more near the furnace in a Ford factory in Detroit. He never learned more than a few words of English, and of my four grandparents, I have to admit that he was my least favorite when I was a kid. We referred to him as "Mr. Curious" and "The Mole".

Around the time I was finishing High School, my Grandparents moved in upstairs to help my parents pay for the house. It was quite a deal for us, because my Grandmother took over the cooking (superbly), and my Grandfather did all the yardwork. To call him an avid yardworker was an understatement of huge proportions. No matter what time of year, he would suit up and head out to the yard (happily a vast one) like he was punching a clock and heading down to the mines.

He wore one or two flannel shirts over a T-shirt, a button down sweater, tweed slacks (yes, belted at the rib cage), a porkpie hat on his shiny head, nylon socks and slippers. When it was cold he would add a coat and scarf to the ensemble, and the slippers would give way to boots. In winter there was snow to shovel, in autumn the constant fall of pine needles to sweep, and summer was all lawn. There were several rectangular lawns on all sides of the house, and these were surrounded by woods in the back.

When I was home for the summer from college, I worked at the family business, which was a motel with a bar/restaurant attached, to help pay for school. My hours were 10 a.m. to 1 a.m. and my job entailed changing kegs, hauling cases of beer up from the basement, and whipping up pizza, subs and burgers for various bikers, softball teams, and the omnipresent "regulars."

The small kitchen was hot as the Gobi, and waiting for pizzas to cook I used to stare at the brand name of the oven: Vulcan. By the end of those nights I was ready to go in the oven myself. My hair and skin got seasoned with a spicy layer of beer, sweat, pizza sauce and blood from trying to cut sausage quickly while under the influence of heat exhaustion and pop music. When I walked home after work the local dogs would strain at their chain link fences, mad with the smell of this giant passing snack.

My room was in the basement, and

Continued on page 15

**FOR SUBSCRIPTIONS
TURN TO PAGE 7.**

The
ECLECTIC

| March 2000 | Volume 2 Number 2 | Free |

CONTENTS

Quotations

"One can always impress a Native by wasting more time over a matter than he does himself, only it is a very difficult thing to accomplish." Isak Dinesen shows her impatience with the Kenyans in *Out of Africa*.

"We'd really love to get you on board. If you signed on it would add a credibility to the whole house." A New Yorker at a cocktail party overheard talking to his more popular friend about a summer house share in the Hamptons.

"To survey with wonder the changes of one's own self is a fascinating pursuit for idle hours." Joseph Conrad in *A Personal Record*.

" 'There is no man,' he began, 'however wise, who has not at some period of his youth said things, or lived a life, the memory of which is so unpleasant to him that he would gladly expunge it. And yet he ought not entirely to regret it...' " The painter Elstir advises Proust's narrator in *The Remembrance of Things Past*.

My Little Booby

Marcel Proust Before Thirty

Lincoln MacVeagh

We begin with three quick scenes from Proust's youth. In the first, he is eighteen and preparing to go out for the evening. He's chatting with a young friend and struggling to get dressed. He's hoping to hide a sweater underneath his dinner jacket and quoting Racine, he bends down to buttons one button on his boots. When he stands up his cravat has just come undone again, and just then Mme. Proust sticks her head round the door:

"I've done nothing."

"*Will you soon be ready, my little booby? You're soirée is at ten and it's eleven already.*"

"*Mamma, little Mamma, don't hustle me...*"

"*My God, my dear Marcel, how scruffy you look!*"

A year later and Proust has joined the army. He's not cut out for the life but he's proud of his uniform. At least he learns to fire a pistol and he's happy to be surrounded by so many vigorous young men. The military is like a charming, rustic hotel, and Proust's only complaint is the occasionally shoddy service: "*One evening I was dining with a captain and he offered to put me up for the night. When I got into the guest room I found that the bed hadn't been made up – there was just a pile of sheets and blankets. I was annoyed because I had never made a bed, and I got myself all entangled with the sheets. I ended up sleeping on the bare mattress.*"

Now Proust is twenty-five. He's back at home and tensions are starting to show. He has an afternoon appointment with a popular society hostess and he's just had the worst fight of his life with his mother. He's so angry that he slams the door behind him and smashes to bits the Venetian glass she once gave him as a present. Why is he so upset? Mme. Proust has returned from the store with a pair of grey gloves. He had specifically told her *pale yellow.*

The most precious of creatures, Marcel Proust was born in Auteuil, outside Paris, in 1871. Proust's father, Adrien, was the son of a small town grocer who went on to become a prominent doctor. Adrien Proust made his name fighting the cholera epidemic of 1866 and later he rode through Persia on horseback studying the disease. A popular figure in the highest government circles, Dr. Proust was an energetic and ambitious man. Marcel was afraid of him, but he was by no means an ogre. When Dr. Proust walked in on his son masturbating, he did not scold the boy as expected, but simply asked him to hold off for four days before going at it again. Marcel appreciated the kindness but he preferred his mother just the same.

Jeanne Weil was fifteen years younger than her husband and she was the handsome daughter of a very rich Jewish stockbroker. Reserved and bookish, she was a meticulous housekeeper and a loving wife, but by far her greatest passion was her children. Mme. Proust had two sons, Marcel and Robert, and she liked nothing better than to curl their hair and dress them in extravagant costumes. She doted on her children endlessly and Marcel loved her for it: *"She thought of everything. In winter, when she sent us for a walk in the Champs-Elysées, she used to tell Félicie to bake some big potatoes in their jackets, which we put in our fur muffs to keep our hands warm."*

Growing up deep in the bosom of the family, Marcel and Robert competed fiercely for their mother's love, but Marcel, the eldest, always had the upper hand. He was *mon petit loup*; Robert was *mon autre loup*; and just in case his victory was ever in doubt, Marcel sealed it at the age of nine when he suffered his first debilitating attack of asthma. The attack was so severe that his father

didn't think he'd survive, and the most immediate result of it was that Marcel was ordered to have his nose cauterized more than a hundred times.

Dr. Proust thought the cauterizations would prevent hayfever, but although painful, they were entirely useless, and the more lasting result of Marcel's sickness was that it gave him the perfect lure for his mother's affection. Young Robert became a mere afterthought and Marcel developed the dangerous habit of falling ill whenever he felt neglected. This habit stayed with him even as a grown man and the following comes from a peevish letter Proust wrote to his mother in 1902: *"I caught cold last night; if it turns to asthma, which it's sure to in the present state of affairs, I have no doubt that you'll be good to me again, when I'm in the same state as this time last year. But it's sad, not being able to have affection and health at the same time."*

As a child Proust knew only his parents and his parents' friends, and he did not begin to meet boys his own age until he was pushed off to school at

"A lot of people have asked what inspired me to write my book on the television documentary about the making of the movie."

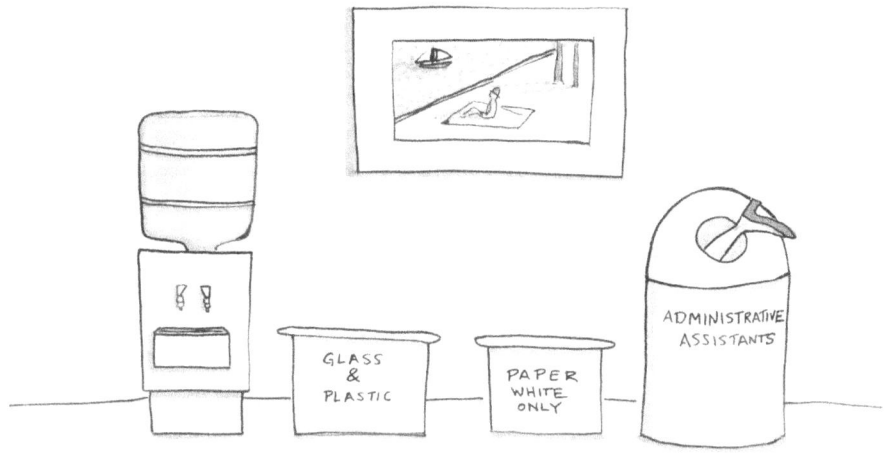

eleven. Health permitting, he attended the Lycée Condorcet for the next seven years. Effortlessly good at his studies, Proust was well liked by the teachers, but he was less popular with the students and he was teased mercilessly. One of the boys Proust tried to befriend was Daniel Helevy; Daniel didn't like him and he seems to have spoken for the crowd: *"There was something about him which we found unpleasant; his kindnesses and tender attentions seemed mere mannerisms and poses, and we took occasion to tell him so to his face. Poor, unhappy boy, we were beastly to him."*

Part of Proust's difficulty was sexual. Proust was gay and his sexual interest scared many boys away. The above mentioned Daniel Helevy was probably among them. After the initial rebuff, Proust wrote to Daniel to patch things up: *"If you are delicious, if you have lovely eyes which reflect the grace and refinement of your mind with such purity that I feel I cannot fully love your mind without kissing your eyes, if your body and mind, like your thoughts, are so lithe and slender that I feel I could mingle more intimately with your thoughts by sitting on your lap, if, finally, I feel that the charm of your person, in which I cannot separate your keen mind from your agile body, would refine and enhance the 'sweet joy of love' for me, there is nothing*

in all that to deserve your contemptuous words..."

Those are not the words with which to reassure a timid fourteen year old, and Proust was generally left to himself as a teenager. But the Lycée is not the world and soon Proust was to learn an important new fact about life. Whereas schoolboys do not care for perfect manners, clever conversation and goo-goo eyes, rich old ladies love them.

Leaving school behind, Proust moved on to the salons of fashionable society and he courted his new acquaintances with the most unctuous flattery. When the Comtesse de Noilles published a book of poems his letter says: *"Madame, I was awaiting your poems with the anxious certainty of one who knows he will have a new beauty to admire."* And to please the Count Robert de Montesquiou, Proust proposes to write an essay about him: *"In it, if 'Your Grace' agrees to help me, I would show how very much you differ from the run-of-the-mill decadents of our day. I would show your strength of will, the richness of your intellect, and how much of the seventeenth century there is in you, in short, everything that I have already taken the liberty of saying to you."*

The same compliments that made young students wince were received by men like Montesquiou without a blink.

Fashionable people took Proust's flattery as their due and a great many of them took Proust under the wing. His rise up through society happened with remarkable speed. In May of 1889 Proust had written a gushing, anonymous fan letter to Anatole France: *"With the memory of the hours of exquisite delight you have given me I have built, deep in my heart, a chapel filled with you."* Just a few months later Proust was chatting with the novelist at the house of Madame de Caillavet.

Proust was delighted with his success and over the next decade he worked hard to preserve it. He developed a reputation as a dandy. He spent his summers at the Grand Hôtel in Cabourg and in winter he was a welcome guest at the best houses in Paris. Proust flitted about the city with a camellia in his buttonhole and a smile on his lips. He was charming, handsome and funny, but although few people knew it, he was often just acting the part.

Many of Proust's burdens stemmed from his living at home and among the most difficult of these was the need to keep his homosexuality hidden. Proust was adamant that no one should know his shameful secret and he once fought a duel with a journalist who hinted at his love affair with Lucien Daudet. Two shots were fired in the air and the duel was reported in *Le Figaro*, but though he could silence a journalist with a pistol, it was not possible to relieve his mother's doubts in the same way. While still at the Lycée, Marcel had a bad scare when the father of a friend called on his parents to complain about his evil influence. On that occasion Proust was young enough to disown his friend with a light heart, but seven years later when he fell in love with Reynaldo Hahn, he was no longer able to walk away so easily. Proust felt trapped. He could not live apart from his mother, but nor could he abandon his lover and his only release was resentment.

Money troubles increased the resentment. Although Proust cared nothing about money for its own sake, he spent it at an alarming rate, and it was a constant source of conflict with his parents. Paying for a short cab ride to his brother's house, Proust tipped the driver five francs and his father exploded: *"I warn you Marcel – at this rate you will end up dying in rags!"* Proust's pride sometimes prompted him to offer to pay rent for his room, but as he had no income except his allowance, his offers only made him look ridiculous.

Proust had no money because he had no job and this too led to fights with his father. Dr. Proust was not happy with his son's life in society; he insisted that Marcel find a career. To put him off, Proust joined the army, but it was not a permanent solution, and when he returned home he was pressed into studying law. Proust spent three years studying for his law diploma but as soon as he earned it, he gave up the profession. He wrote to his father: *"I still believe that anything I do outside of literature and philosophy will be just so much time wasted. But among several evils some are better and some worse. In my most desperate moments I have never conceived of anything more horrible than a law office."*

In the end, Proust took an unpaid position at the Mazarine library and it was probably the only job in Paris that was suited to him. His first order of business was to apply for a two months leave of absence and he kept on applying for leave until he'd been at the library for five years, almost without ever setting foot in it.

Proust's notional job at the Mazarine quieted his father, but it did little to allay the single greatest fear of his early life. This fear had nothing to do with sex or money or work. Rather it was the fear that his talent would prove to be worthless. Proust was secretly ambitious and he wanted desperately to write great books, but with each passing year there seemed less and less hope that he would ever do so.

In 1896 Proust published his first book of essays, *Les Plaisirs et les jours,* and it was ignored. Next he began work on a novel, *Jean Santeuil,* but though he worked on it for four years he never came close to finishing it. When he told friends that the book was complete, he meant only that he'd thought of an ending; he still hadn't written a middle. Proust went on to translate Ruskin and to write pastiches for the press, but the work never satisfied him.

Distracted by life in high society, Proust felt his genius wasting away. He did not want to be remembered as a dandy but he had no solid accomplishments to offer the world. On his thirtieth birthday he was ready to admit defeat: *"I'm thirty today, and I've have done nothing."*

Continued Next Month

Reviews

The Garden of Eden

by Ernest Hemingway

Charles Scribner's Sons, 1986

Hemingway began work on *The Garden of Eden* in 1946, but the novel remained hidden until his estate published it forty years later. Loosely biographical, *The Garden of Eden* tells the story of a young American writer named David Bourne and his new wife Catherine travelling in the South of France. They go to the beach, meet kindly hoteliers, and drink an enormous variety of cocktails. Then Catherine announces she has a surprise. Catherine wants to be the boy and she wants David to be the girl.

David accepts the arrangement because he knows that love has no rules, and the couple ends up at a styling salon in Nice where they both get their hair cut and dyed in identical fashions:

After she was asleep David got up and looked at himself in the bathroom mirror...

"So that's how it is," he said to himself. "You've done that to your hair and had it cut the same as your girl's and how do you feel?" He asked the mirror. "How do you feel? Say it."

"You like it," he said.

He looked at the mirror and it was someone else he saw but it was less strange now.

"All right. You like it," he said. "Now go through with the rest of it whatever it is..."

Catherine's surprise is so genuinely surprising that the first hundred pages of *The Garden of Eden* fly along beautifully. Unfortunately, however, just when David discovers that he likes looking like a girl, the novel backs off. A beautiful French girl named Marita is introduced and the plot changes course. Catherine sleeps with Marita; then David sleeps with Marita; then Catherine gets jealous and starts to go crazy.

By the end, the novel has turned into a somewhat conventional love triangle. David no longer worries about looking like a girl, he only worries about having two girls at the same time: *"He did not have to examine his conscience to know that he loved Catherine and that it was wrong to love two women and that no good could ever come of it. He did not yet know how terrible it could be."*

There is a lot of wood in *The Garden of Eden* and I imagine it's mostly because Hemingway never finished editing the manuscript. But it may also have something to do with his style of writing. Hemingway insists on simplicity, but he cuts so relentlessly that sometimes there is nothing left at all. Here David and Catherine are drinking on the terrace:

"Do we want another?" David asked.

"I think so. Don't you?"

"Sure."

"Do you want a fine?"

"No. I'd rather drink the wine. Do you have to work tomorrow?"

"We'll see."

In passages like this Hemingway wants us to imagine that there are great emotions bubbling beneath the surface, but since he never lets his characters speak eloquently or at length, it's hard for us to see into the depths. Despite the sense of gravitas that comes with the short, punchy sentences (we can almost hear the actors spitting out each word), there is only so much we can read into a line like, *"We'll see."*

The Garden of Eden is still a good book. It's always readable and it's also interesting for what it tells us about Hemingway himself. At one point David goes to Spain. He buys some American newspapers, but he's embarrassed to be marked as a tourist: *"He bought some bullfight weeklies to wrap the English language papers in and then walked down the Carrera San Geronimo to the cool friendly morning gloom of the Buffet Italianos."*

Who knew that Hemingway was so intimidated by the Spanish?

Commentary

Insignificance
And Justice

T.E. MacVeagh

Have you ever sat in a crowded train station at rush hour and watched the people stream by? Thousands upon thousands of them, in seemingly endless waves. They walk, alone or in groups, lost in their thoughts or in their social units, scarcely aware of the crush of other people around them. Full of ambition and determination, headed for mysterious destinations for mysterious purposes.

And have you ever been struck with the sudden, vertiginous revelation that the destinations and purposes of these people are not really so mysterious at all? They head to suburbs and cities; they come from jobs and schools and appointments; they are joyful, they are indifferent, they are confident, they are happy, they are sad. They possess every characteristic that you prize and disdain in yourself and in your friends. Only, because there are so many more of them, they almost certainly have each and every one of these characteristics in greater quantity and greater quality.

And have you ever thought through the terrifying implications of the brute fact of the existence of so many people? It is said that gazing at stars makes people feel insignificant. But it is hard to put the heavens on the scale against humanity. If you want an apple, one thousand oranges will not help. But what is the value of one apple in a pile of a billion?

How can we afford to accept the humanity of the multitudes? If these numberless specimens are "just like us", then we must admit that each of them has his or her own special claim to pride. But then what of ourselves? Which of our talents retains its significance against such intense competition? Perhaps we are cleverer than one, better at dealing with hardship than another, better humored than a third. But if you sit and watch enough people walk by, eventually your pride will be overwhelmed by the numbers. The qualities you have treasured in yourself seem insignificant; your self-image rings false and hollow. It is sobering, and not very pleasant, to realize how trivial a thing your own life or death is against the vastness of humanity.

People who study genocides say that an important first step taken by the perpetrators is to "dehumanize" the victims. Because humans hesitate to commit acts of cruelty against their own kind, genocidal leaders start by convincing their followers that the intended victims are not really human. This makes sense and seems historically accurate. But we should not overestimate the difficulty of dehumanizing someone.

Dehumanized, after all, is the normal state in which we regard most of humanity. We can manage a few relatives and friends intruding on our sense of self, demanding recognition of their own separate identities, but we are not capable of extending this privilege to the hundreds of strangers who cross our paths every day. We discount the existence of our fellow commuters rushing shoulder to shoulder with us to and from work. We do not make eye-contact with the others and we do not speak to them. We sit, absorbed in ourselves; alone, isolated, even lonely, in a sea of humanity.

This is not to condemn society as inherently genocidal. Those of us who are not sociopaths switch our point of view quickly enough when confronted by someone who demands recognition. When we are forced to converse with somebody, even just to borrow the paper, we extend a small, contingent acceptance of that person's humanity. One reason we do not notice the extent to which we dehumanize the people around us is that we generally do not dehumanize them while we are interacting with them. But we need no very great excuse to deny the humanity of people who are and remain essentially strangers.

Reflecting on this fact may help us to understand the difference between justice and virtue, and also the value of justice. Justice was the great virtue of the Greeks and the Old Testament judges. However, the advent of Christianity brought the conviction that it is not enough to judge justly, one must judge mercifully. And once one embraces the duty to be merciful, the old idea of justice seems wanting. Justice is cold and unforgiving, even cruel. There seems little use left for it as a virtue. If anything, it seems a fancy dress for the sin of callousness.

In many ways, justice is a second-best to mercy. Empathy, fellow-feeling and love are the wellsprings of mercy. We are not merely "fair" to those in whom we recognize ourselves. We do not treat those we love "even-handedly". Rather, we make deep and irreversible sacrifices. We share our kidney with our brother not in the name of justice, but in the name love.

But this does not mean that justice is a negligible virtue. As anyone can see while waiting for a train: we do not empathize with everyone who crosses our path. For the most part we view our fellow commuters as abstractions. They seem like automatons, the humanity of which we can accept intellectually, but which we cannot intuit. Justice is a virtue of the intellect. It insists on fairness and equal treatment for all those we know to be equivalent without regard to how or what we may feel towards them. If mercy is the great virtue of the judge, who must look the condemned man in the eye and pass sentence, justice is the great virtue of the legislator, who must weigh the interests of large groups of society, impartially and impersonally.

We all have our strengths and weaknesses. Some men are braver than they are wise, others wiser than brave. Similarly, some men are better at mercy than at justice, others more just than merciful. Those who are good at mercy can extend their fellow-feeling more broadly than the rest of us, and are ready to make extraordinary sacrifices for those we might believe they hardly know. But a man or a woman who is merciful, may be unjust. When at last the limits of his fellow-feeling are reached, he may act capriciously and unfairly. Indeed, a merciful man may have little practice at acting justly. Connected emotionally to all who surround him, he may never have considered the need to act fairly for intellectual reasons alone. He may even have come to believe that his own gut judgments are beyond reproach. There is danger in those charismatic politicians who confuse the limits of morality with the limits of their empathy; they may become cruelly dictatorial as legislators for a supposedly "common" good.

We are more familiar with those men and women who have a sense of justice but none of mercy. They treat everyone fairly, but none with understanding. It is easy to criticize the shortcomings of such people. But as we have seen, it is difficult not to dehumanize most of the people most of the time. In such circumstances, we should all be thankful for those who remind us of our obligation to behave justly.

Reminiscence

Fear of Friends

Lincoln MacVeagh

Perhaps it was cowardice or maybe just common sense, but when I lived in San Antonio I was very cautious about making new friends. In six months in Texas I received exactly three offers of friendship and although I was often lonely, I turned them all down. Only a small part of me regrets it.

The first person to offer me friendship was an attractive thirty year old woman I met in a bar called *100 Grand*. I was sitting by myself in the back when Georgia strolled over and introduced herself. She wasn't a drunk and she didn't ask me for money. She started talking about her job and her apartment. She said the best thing about life was meeting interesting people. She talked for five minutes straight.

"So what about you?" said Georgia, "You look pretty down and out."

I was wearing green work pants, an old T-shirt and a pair of Brooks Brothers black oxfords with no socks. It hadn't occurred to me that I looked down and out, and I asked her what she meant.

"Look at you! You can't even afford a pair of socks! Don't be insulted. I want to help." Georgia wrote down her address and telephone number on a bar napkin and handed it to me. "If you ever need a decent meal, you can come over to my house. I know how hard it can be."

For a brief moment I wanted to explain to Georgia that wearing dress shoes without socks was quite common among the rich, prep school crowd in New England.

"I'll leave you alone now," said Georgia, "But don't forget. You give me a call."

I pictured Georgia's house teeming with vagrants eating large plates of mashed potatoes. I thought perhaps she was a born-again Christian evangelist but she didn't look like an evangelist. In any case, I never called to find out.

My second offer of friendship came from a girl at work. I had a job grading standardized tests at the Psychology Corporation, and for two months a large group of us waded through 150,000 tests taken by eighth graders in Wisconsin. I was assigned to the Social Studies room: What are two reasonable conclusions that can be made about the ancient Egyptians based on the fact that they built the pyramids?

Ron, our room director, was a fat, jolly man and at the end of each week he picked a different bar where people could gather after work on Friday night. It never occurred to me to go to these gatherings. I was perfectly happy to grade my tests and go home.

I usually graded about 300 tests a night. The tests were handed out in packets of forty and when you were finished with one packet you raised your hand and a cute high-school girl brought you another. One night after I'd been working for six weeks, I raised my hand and when the packet girl came over, she leaned down and whispered in my ear: "First row. Third from the back."

I noticed there was a post-it note stuck on the outside of my new test packet. I've saved the note so I can quote it exactly. It said: *Lincoln, Are you going to the party Friday night? You should. There will be lots of good food and plenty of fun. I should know I partied with these guys at Taco Cabana. I'd also like to meet you. I'm kind of embarrassed to send you this note but I see no other way to get to know you. If you're not interested I'll understand. Sincerely, Reader 586, Mariana.*

I had long since studied the room thoroughly and I knew there were only two vaguely attractive women in it. Neither of them sat in the first row, and for a while I considered playing dumb and not looking up at all. Curiosity, however, got the best of me and as nonchalantly as possible I turned my head towards the wall. Mariana caught my eye immediately. She was a sad-faced Mexican girl with sallow skin and bleached blonde hair. She smiled and waved her fingers and I smiled back. She pointed to her watch and mouthed the words: *See you at break?*

"I'm glad you got my note," said Mariana, "I hope you don't think I'm too forward."

"Not at all."

"What do you do? Do you go to college?"

I told Mariana that I was graduated from college and that I used to teach school. She was tickled. She went to college too, and she was studying to be a teacher.

"Do you like reading?" she asked.

When I said yes, Mariana slapped my forearm playfully.

"We have so much in common!"

Mariana went on to say that she'd lived in San Antonio for four years but she wasn't from Texas and she had a hard time meeting people and sometimes she was lonely and didn't I understand?

The third and final offer of friendship that I received in San Antonio came from the Bengalese man who ran the Kwik-Fil next to my apartment complex. His name was David and one night when I got up to the counter he caught me looking distracted. I was trying to decide whether to buy three beers or four, and I was staring vaguely into space.

"What are you looking at, my friend?" My mind was blank. "I see you are wanting something. Don't be embarrassed. You can ask me. You mustn't be ashamed."

I suddenly realized that I'd been staring directly at the condom selection behind the counter.

"What kind you want? Reservoir tip?" David laughed and pulled a packet off the rack.

"No, no," I said, "I was only wondering whether to buy more beer."

""Don't be afraid. You can buy some condom. What you got? You got married? You got girlfriend?"

The awkward expression on my face somehow told him that I was neither married nor had a girlfriend. David's eyes twinkled happily.

"Aha, you go outside! You go outside? Don't be shy. Everyone goes outside. I'm married, but sure I go outside. And you really need a condom for outside!"

I couldn't figure out whether he meant boys or hookers but I didn't think to ask.

"Okay, fine," said David, "I'm from Bengal and you are an American. I like to be friends with an American. Let's be friends. We can go outside together. On Saturday night my wife thinks I'm at work. You can meet me right here. I have a very good place. It's fun."

I told David that I would think about it.

"Don't be afraid!" he called out as I left the store. "Don't be afraid, my friend!"

Sir Laffalot

Sir Laffalot has been on jury duty. He marched into the waiting room at the Queens County Courthouse just in time for the morning's first announcement. A female official stood up from behind her desk in the back and clapped her hands: "Good morning. My name is Brenda and I'm an officer of the court. I know that many of you are immigrants from weird countries but don't come up to me telling me you don't speak English. I can't do anything about it. Thank you."

An hour later another official showed up and started reading out a long list of difficult names: "Maria Mericano, Chu Phat, Nikki Kariafitis..." Sir Laffalot was assigned to a sixty-five member jury panel in the courtroom of Judge Daniel Roth. A man in a beige suit was on trial for second degree murder.

Prospective jurors were interviewed in groups of fourteen and the first person to get excused was a young black banker whom Sir Laffalot had sat next to in the waiting room. The banker had been making cell phone calls to his secretary and he had a clipped English accent just like Cary Grant. Everyone thought he'd get picked, but then the judge asked him if any of his friends were in trouble with the law. The banker answered that both his brothers were in jail on drug charges and the prosecutor had him dismissed.

Next there was an incident with an Indian woman who refused to say where she lived. Judge Roth got very angry. "You're a shirker!" he shouted, "You will tell me where you live!" After a short battle of wills the Indian woman broke down in tears and said she lived in Jackson Heights. Still crying, she said that she'd recently been raped outside her front door and that's why she wanted to keep her address secret. Judge Roth let her go and the selection process dragged on.

By the second day, the jury panel was so bored that Sir Laffalot needed to liven things up. He decided on *Wink Murder* and as luck would have it, he drew the murderer's card just as he was called up to be interviewed. All eyes were upon him. A quick wink at the defendant and BOOM! Then the defense attorney and two old Spanish ladies. Sir Laffalot was on a good roll until he ran into Judge Roth. Sir Laffalot winked at him but nothing happened. He winked again. "No fair!" cried Sir Laffalot, "When I wink, you have to die!" Judge Roth refused to play along but at least Sir Laffalot got out of jury duty.

Wink Murder: How to Play.

1) Draw lots to pick the murderer.
2) The murderer kills people by catching their eye and winking at them.
3) If you get murdered, count silently to three before saying, "I'm dead!"
4) You can stop the game at any time and say, "J'accuse!" If you accuse wrong, both you and the person you accused are dead.
5) When the murderer gets caught, everyone draws lots again and the game starts over.

Sir Laffalot says: TOODALOO!!

Continued from page 16

he complimented my shoes, he gave me free soap samples, and would certainly have zipped up my fly for me had I let him.

It made me sad that they put this man in a little outfit, and stationed him in the bathroom (probably with no hourly wage) to earn tips by assisting in an activity that no one needs or wants to be assisted with. We were there late drinking, and I made a few more trips to the bathroom, each one resulting in an increased effort on the part of the attendant to extract a tip. How could I tell him that I was broke, and drinking on my friends' expense account?

When we finally left the restaurant, it was snowing, and I shared a cab with Alan, and one of his bosses, a woman named Marti. We headed towards the hotel, and as we turned a corner, a figure darted in front of the cab, and made contact. The driver screeched on his brakes, we slid, and Marti screamed, "Oh my God! We didn't just hit someone?"

After a few moments of confusion, we were all relieved to see the young man standing on the corner, cursing us, but apparently unscathed.

Our cabdriver was a big, tough-looking Jamaican man, and after the incident was over, he drove half a block, and pulled over without saying anything to us. He cried out. "They trying to take my life away! I got <u>kids</u>! They take away you <u>life</u>! I work hard, but it's no matter – they take away YOU LIFE".

Marti reached over the seat and began rubbing his shoulders. "You poor man" she said softly, "It's alright – nobody was hurt." The man kept repeating "They took my life away" over and over as if he had actually killed someone. He started crying, and then we were all crying like only drunk people and distraught cabbies can cry.

"I'm going home," said the cabbie, "I'm <u>done</u>." Then he just sat there, blubbering like a jellyfish until we silently paid him, got out of the cab, and walked through the snow to the hotel.

"Just try it, honey. It's part of the high-protein, low-fiber diet."

The high life

MPOTIBY*

*Medeival Peasant of the Internet Boom Years

David Garcia III

I've always been prone to Februcholia but this February was a little extreme. Not only was I broke, but my phone was shut off, and the moment I was incommunicado the lives of my friends spun out of control, leaving me both powerless to commiserate, and unable to keep current on the gossip.

Laura flew home to Pittsburgh after two months living in California with the guy she met on the Internet, only to discover that she was pregnant. She announced this to her parents at breakfast saying, "I've made an appointment with a doctor, because I'm late, which either means I'm pregnant, or I have a cyst." Her father's response was, "If it's a cyst, what will you name it?" In light of the child's unique provenance, Laura decided it should be called either Wee Willie Dotcom, E-Sp@wn!, or @lb@ tro$$.

Simultaneously, in Vermont, Alan's boyfriend decided to move out after 10 years of codependent bliss, and I was unable to share in the distress. A week later, however, Alan came to town for a trade show and treated me to dinner with his company. Having been out of touch, I assumed that he would be a complete wreck and my mind's eye conjured visions of a haggard, bloated Alan, dressed in a frayed peasant shawl, black rivers of mascara running down his cheeks, and Billie Holiday playing on his walkman. Nothing of the kind. Alan was lighting up the room with golden smiles, as fresh and rosy as ever.

There were a lot of people at our table, and I didn't have a chance to really talk to him until dessert was being served. I leaned over and asked him, "Is he gone? Are you okay?"

He told me that his boyfriend had ransacked the place, packed up his car, and taken off for a new life in Provincetown. Halfway to his destination, the boyfriend became suddenly ill and his car broke down. The poor guy had to have his stomach pumped, was hospitalized twice, and couldn't even keep a glass of water down for the next week. He was forced to move back in with Alan to recover, and I'm not sure if they ever found out what was wrong with the car.

"Okay, where did you bury the chicken heads, and how much goats blood did you drink?"

"Oh, no," said Alan, taking a spoonful of brownie dripping with cherry sauce, "I don't need props anymore. I just will these things to happen."

I ordered another cocktail, and went to find the bathroom. The restaurant used to be called Lucky's, but was now called Rue 57, and it had been extensively redecorated to resemble a turn of the century riverboat whorehouse, complete with gilded chandeliers, a red velvet spiral stair, and an old fashioned restroom attendant.

On my first visit to the bathroom, I was disconcerted to find a large man, obviously drunk, offering a much smaller man in livery a fifty dollar bill. The smaller man was from India, and he started cleaning a spot on my jacket while I was relieving myself at the urinal. I asked him to stop, but he did not speak English, and began rubbing with increased vigor. When I finished and pulled away to wash my hands, he lunged for the sink with a huge grin, and started squirting me with liquid soap, his eyes darting toward the tip tray suggestively. He dried my hands,

Continued on page 15

The
ECLECTIC

April 2000   Volume 2 Number 3   Free

CONTENTS

Quotations

"*The reception one meets with from the women of a family generally determines the tenor of one's whole entertainment .*" Thomas De Quincy advises us to be nice to the hostess in *Confessions of an English Opium Eater.*

"*Men of sixty experience wet dreams and spontaneous orgasms (an extremely unpleasant experience, agaçant as the French say, putting the teeth on edge).*" William Burroughs describes the life of a withdrawing heroin addict in *Queer.*

"*A conscience stricken – and anonymous – thief has returned the faded paperback with a bankers note for £500 which also covers a few pens he stole. 'It was,' he wrote, 'a terrible act and I have to answer for my actions.'*" A sinner repents of a sin committed twenty years ago, as reported in *The Times of London.*

"*All that I grasped was that to repeat what everybody else was thinking was, in politics, the mark not of an inferior but of a superior mind.*" Proust marvels at the conversation of the diplomat M. de Norpois in *Remembrance of Things Past.*

Proust Goes To Bed

The Last Twenty Years

Lincoln MacVeagh

In 1913 a Paris chauffeur named Odillon Albaret went back to his home town of Auxillac to marry a country girl. Celeste Albaret was twenty-two when she married. She'd never left her village before and starting her new life in the city she felt lonely and out of place. Odillon saw that his wife was bored and thinking that work might cheer her up, he arranged for his employer to offer her a job. Celeste had to be talked into it: *"You'll see,"* Odillon told her, *"Monsieur Proust is a very nice man. You must be careful not to displease him because he notices everything. But you'll never meet a man more charming."*

"Last night I wrote 'The End.' Now I can die."

Odillon seems to have been right on both counts. Proust was certainly a demanding employer and the one day Celeste failed to change his sheets he noticed right away. Celeste protested that the sheets were still clean but Proust disagreed: *"I think they may be damp – there is always some dampness and a little sour smell after they have been used. You don't realize it, but what you have done is awful. You know I can't have it. Even if I go out every day, the sheets have to be changed every time."*

It sounds like torture to work for such a picky man; however, Celeste adored it.

Starting out at as an errand girl delivering copies of *Swann's Way* to Proust's friends, she went on to run his entire household. She was Proust's cook, his maid and his confidante, and though it's said that no man is a hero to his valet, she was also his most passionate admirer.

In her memoirs, she attributes Proust's appeal to his extraordinary kindness and intelligence, but there must also have been something in Celeste that loved mystery and circus freaks. The description she gives of her first encounter with Proust in his bedroom recalls nothing so much as Dorothy's first meeting with the Wizard of Oz.

Celeste had been working for Proust for more than two months before she was finally allowed the great responsibility of delivering to Monsieur a croissant. This was a task usually performed by Proust's manservant Nicolas, but Nicolas had to go out and in the emergency he called on Celeste. Before leaving the house Nicolas gave her detailed instructions, and he added with special emphasis: *"Whatever you do, don't say anything unless he asks you a question."*

All afternoon Celeste waited in the kitchen for the bell. When at last it rang she took the croissant upstairs and nervously opened Proust's bedroom door. Inside, the room was dark and oppressively hot. A fire raged in the fireplace. The walls of the room were lined with blue cork to keep out noise, and the windows were tightly shuttered and curtained so that neither air nor sunlight could seep in from the street. The only light came from a small bedside lamp, but even this was obscured by thick clouds of white smoke that hung in every corner of the room. The smoke stung Celeste's eyes and nearly blinded her:

"All I could see of M. Proust was a white shirt under a thick sweater, and the upper part of his body propped against two pillows....Fortunately there was the gleam of the silver tray and coffeepot on the table by the bed. I made for these without looking at anything else...I bowed toward the invisible face and put the saucer with the croissant down on the tray. He gave a wave of the hand, presumably to thank me, but didn't say a word. Then I left."

For Proust it was just the start of another day. He was a man of peculiar habits. Sensitive to noise, he lined his walls with cork. Sensitive to cold, he kept a fire burning in his bedroom throughout the year and asked that his underwear be heated in the oven before he got dressed. Afraid of fragrance Proust never washed with soap and turned away friends with the whiff of perfume on their clothes (*"...I'd be glad to have an opportunity of seeing you from time to time. Unfortunately, my health makes that difficult, especially as you wear a lot of scent..."*). Terrified of germs, he ordered that incoming letters be soaked in disinfectant before he read them. But the most striking thing of all about Proust's later life is that he spent the vast majority of his time in bed.

Proust himself believed that he stayed in bed out of medical necessity and he got snippish if the point was questioned: *"Doctors used to say that a pessimist is a man with a bad stomach. Now Dr Dubois says outright that a man with a bad stomach is a pessimist."* However, despite that he was sometimes very sick, Proust was not so much of an invalid as he led others to believe and he lived in bed not because he had to, but simply because he was happiest there. *"You're very lucky*

"Ouch."

to have been born rich, monsieur." Celeste once told him. *"I don't know how you'd have survived if you'd been born poor."*

Proust's typical day began in the early evening. He used veronal to put himself to sleep, and as a result he woke up slowly. The first two items on his to-do list were fumigations and coffee. Proust burned medicinal powders each morning for his asthma (hence the thick white clouds of smoke in his room), but coffee was his most important drug. He drank two cups and insisted that the water be poured through the grounds one drop at a time so as to produce the strongest essence possible. He not only needed the caffeine, but the milk in his café au lait was also a principle source of nourishment.

Except for his daily croissant, Proust ate very little. Sometimes he could be talked into a bite of fried potato, and sometimes he would send Celeste running out to Larue's restaurant for a special dish, but the sight of food tended to kill his appetite.

"Just a little bit more, monsieur. What am I going to do with the rest?"

"Just throw it away, Celeste."

Having drunk his coffee, the burden of existence would lift and Proust's workday would begin. Proust wrote countless letters along with his vast novel and though he employed a variety of young men he was keen on as secretaries, he did most of his work alone. With a sweater wrapped around his shoulders, he worked half lying down in bed with only his knees as his desk. If his sweater fell off his shoulders he rang for a servant to give him another one, and he kept a large supply of pen-holders on the table next to him because if he dropped one on the floor he couldn't pick it up for fear of disturbing the dust. Practically motionless, Proust could work for hours at a stretch and on many days he worked himself straight back to sleep without ever getting up at all.

Proust was not entirely without

his entertainments. During one phase he used to listen to the opera over the telephone through a service the French called Théâtrephone. He also accepted occasional visitors and he continued to go out from time to time (which I'll get to later), but he never allowed his attention to wander too far from his notebooks. Having given his first thirty years to the life of society, Proust devoted his last two decades to the most intense introspection imaginable.

The turning point in Proust's life was the death of his mother in 1905. Her death was important for two reasons, the first of these being that it made Proust rich. One biographer estimates his inheritance at today's equivalent of $6 million, but this figure seems small. Another way of looking at it is to consider that shortly before World War I, Proust sustained a stock market loss of 800,000 francs (*"...shares are generally like old mistresses whom one is fond of precisely because of the trouble they have caused one..."*); meanwhile Celeste earned only one hundred francs a month and she considered the sum reasonable.

The death of Mme. Proust was also signicant because she was the only person her son ever loved. Proust had many friends but friendship didn't touch his soul: *"No doubt to every man the life of every other extends along shadowy paths of which he has no inkling."* Proust's mother was the only exception to this rule; she was his only tie to the world outside his

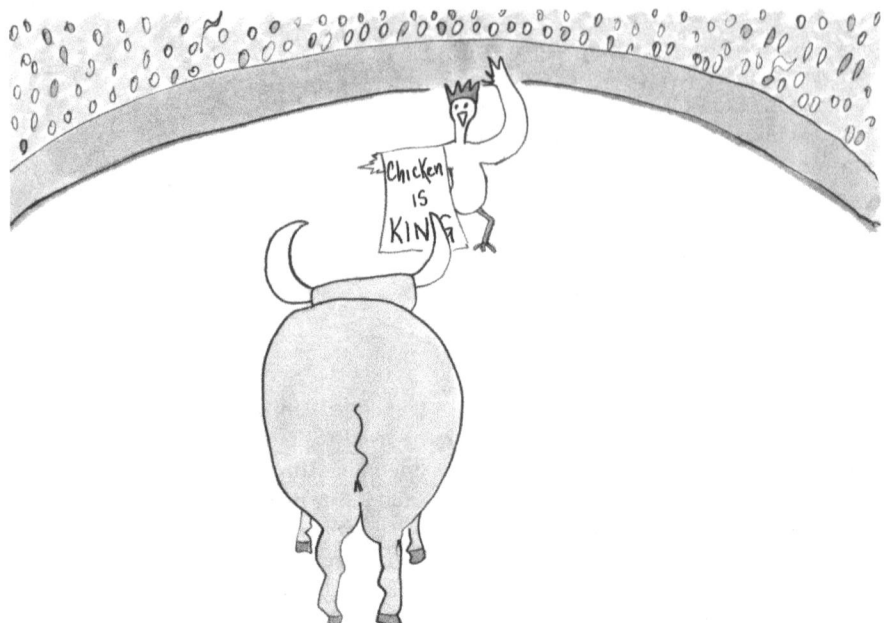

own thoughts. When she died the tie was broken and Proust retreated into an isolation from which he never came out.

Proust's retreat began with a long period of mourning. He declined all invitations and put off visitors with claims of illness or a difficult schedule: *"It's impossible to see me before eight o'clock in the evening and difficult after that!"* His mourning lasted two years and before it was over he'd conceived the plan for a book that would end up pulling him even further into himself.

This book was *Remembrance of Things Past* and it was originally envisioned as a shortish novel to be read in conjunction with a literary essay about the critic Sainte-Beuve. The combined length of both works was to be approximately 450 pages. However the proposed book was rejected by a number of publishers and having no definite publishing date to work towards, Proust allowed his ambition to expand. Dropping the essay, Proust let his novel grow longer and longer. By the time the first volume was printed, it was more than 900 pages and the pattern of Proust's life was unalterably set. He would be writing his book

until he died.

During the last fourteen years of his life Proust went out less and less, but though his excursions were infrequent, especially during the war, he was never a total shut-in. So let's now imagine that it is eleven o'clock at night and Proust has decided to leave the house. A mad rush of activity would ensue: *"And could you warm my underwear and send for the barber? And you will have to order a cab..."* It took Proust ages to get ready, but he was surprisingly unconcerned about his appearance. He never seemed to care if his ties were flecked with toothpaste: *"Do you think people want to see me for my ties?"*

One favorite destination was the Ritz where Proust was on good terms with the staff. He once borrowed a large sum of money from the doorman only to turn around and gave it back to him as a tip. Proust liked to meet his friends at the hotel, but as a rule he was not interested in casual conversation. When Proust went out it was with one of two purposes in mind. Either he was doing research for his novel, checking facts or hairdo's or styles of dress; or else he was out looking for sex.

Once he started writing his novel, Proust no longer had time for love affairs with his social equals and his tastes turned towards young men of the working class whose affections he could win more easily. He was friendly with a number of the waiters at the Ritz, some of whom he took as lovers, and he was also a frequent guest at the male brothel run by his friend Le Cuziat. Proust invested money in the brothel; he even donated his mother's furniture to the place; and according to a number of sources, his nickname amongst those who worked there was "the rat man." Proust once told Andre Gide that he needed many disparate visual elements brought together in order to achieve orgasm, and apparently (though he didn't tell this to Gide) he liked to masturbate while watching a naked boy stick needles into a rat. Another story has Proust masturbating while spitting on a photograph of his mother.

Of course we can't be certain about the rats or the photograph of his mother, but we can be quite sure that Proust went to Le Cuziat's brothel because when he got home he told Celeste about his visits. "*My dear Celeste, what I have witnessed this evening is unimaginable. Le Cuziat told me there was a man who goes there to be whipped, and I saw the whole thing from another room, through a little window in the wall.*"

For Celeste's benefit, Proust maintained that he only watched such scenes in order to be able to write about them. This was not strictly true, but neither was it wholly false. Everything Proust did went into his work. Whenever he came home looking pleased with himself, Celeste knew it was because he'd found something worth adding to his novel: "*Did you get a good haul monsieur? What sort of honey are you going to make for us today?*"

Proust's great fear towards the end of his life was that he would die before completing *Remembrance of Things Past.*

It is a wonder that he held on. With his health declining rapidly, Proust overdosed on veronal in late 1921 and in early 1922 he overdosed again on the stimulant adrenaline. But somehow he survived long enough to tell Celeste that he was finally done: "*Last night I wrote 'The End.' Now I can die.*"

Suffering from pneumonia, an abscess burst in Proust's lung and he died in November of 1922. Celeste was horribly stricken and much of Paris cried with her. Even the Comte Greffulhe's butler was sobbing. "*But why are you grieving? Did you know Monsieur Proust?*" asked the count. To which the butler replied, "*Oh yes, every time there would be a ball here, Monsieur Proust would come by the next day and quiz me about who had come, what they said, how they were related to one another and so on. Such a nice man – and he always left such a generous tip!*"

Reviews

The Enormous Room
by E.E. Cummings
Viking Penguin, 1999

When the United States entered World War I, Edward Estlin Cummings was recently graduated from Harvard and painting cubist paintings in New York. Vaguely pacifist, Cummings joined the ambulance service to avoid conscription and shortly afterwards he was sent to France. He was a driver in the Section Sanitaire XXI and although close to the Front, there was little to do.

So Cummings and his friend Walter Brown passed their time gossiping with the French soldiers assigned to their unit as menials. Because French morale was low, the soldiers talked defeatism and Brown made the mistake of repeating what they said in his letters home. When these letters caught the attention of the censors, Brown was arrested as a spy. *KEW-MANGZ*, as the gendarmes pronounced it, was arrested as Brown's friend. Both men spent the next four months in a French prison camp called La Ferté Macé and neither of them knew when, if ever, they would be released.

The Enormous Room is Cummings' account of camp life and when it first came out in 1921, the book was considered noteworthy in large part because of the way it's written. Cummings is loose with his punctuation; he makes free use of slang; and he invents words when he sees fit. Today, these innovations are less striking and it wasn't until I read the Afterword that I realized Cummings doesn't put spaces after his commas ("*However,my...*" instead of "*However, my...*"). I still can't see the significance of this particular device, except to save time for Cummings the typist, and since the no-spaces rule is followed consistently, it doesn't seem irregular and goes unnoticed. The same happens with Cummings' other stylistic quirks. One gets used to them quickly and it turns out that the real interest of *The Enormous Room* is not in the gram-

mar but in the life it describes.

As in other prisons, this life revolves around food, money, fighting and punishment, and Cummings develops his book as a series of jaunty character sketches. La Ferté Macé provides plenty of material: *"For who was eligible to La Ferté? Anyone whom the police could find in the lovely country of France (a) who was not guilty of treason (b) who could not prove that he was not guilty of treason."* Thus we meet a Dutch soldier in jail for reporting a day late back from leave, a Russian woman in jail for saying that she missed the snows in Russia, and three beautiful innocents whom Cummings refers to collectively as *"The Delectable Mountains."*

Cummings is an excellent observer of others, but his own personality is rather a puzzle. While he has the utmost sympathy for the suffering of his friends, he hasn't an ounce of pity for himself and he seems to view his own ordeal as a great lark. After he's first arrested the French police ask if he has anything in his shoes: *"'My feet' I said, gently."*

Cummings is constantly having epiphanies in unusual places. En route to La Ferté he gets locked in a miserable cell overnight, but he insists that he is happy to have escaped his ambulance unit: *"An uncontrollable joy gutted me after three months of humiliation, of being bossed and herded and bullied and insulted. I was myself and my own master."* Later, an exhausted Cummings is travelling on foot with two armed guards: *"I was somewhat sorry to find the way hilly, and in places bad underfoot; yet the unknown adventure lying before me, and the delicious silence of the night (...) boosted me into a condition of mysterious happiness."* And when Cummings finally reaches La Ferté, he declares himself fully pleased: *"'By God,' I said, 'this is the finest place I've ever been in my life.'"*

In the face of such heroic optimism, it comes almost as a relief to hear Cummings say, of his departure from prison, *"When finally I made my exit, the part of me popularly referred to as 'mind' was still in a slightly bent if not twisted condition."* Crazy or not, Cummings was an interesting man. His memoir is worth reading.

Out On A Limb: Politics in 2012

T.E. MacVeagh

Let us assume that Gore defeats Bush for the presidency. He is likely to be a one-term president. The economy will falter at some point during the next four years and Gore does not have the political skills to escape bad news unscathed. He will prove a velcro-president, to whom every unfair charge sticks.

Though Gore will be the Democratic nominee in 2004, he will face a strong challenge from his left, and he will lose to the Republican in the general election. Who will that Republican be? George W. will have been labeled a loser and his brother Jeb will want to wait before inflicting another Bush on the country. The raft of Republican governors will have had their reputations tarnished by the economic downturn. The nomination will be sewn up early by John McCain.

McCain has tasted national campaigning and he clearly loves it. Over the four years of the Gore administration, he will rebuild his ties with the Republican majority. He may not make up with Trent Lott or Pat Robertson, but he will woo those within the RNC whose support he sees as essential. And he will play the conservative heavy in Congress to confirm his right-wing credentials. Also, some of the tension between McCain and his party will diminish after the Gore administration passes a watered-down campaign finance bill and the Republicans discover that their fundraising edge is unaffected.

Having mollified the conservatives, McCain will run from the center, as he did this year, and again he'll win the support of liberals and the media. He will be elected with a great sense of hope: a strong leader to clean up the mess of the Gore administration and to make us forget the moral failings of Clinton.

Unfortunately, despite a long honeymoon, things will not go smoothly. The economic down-turn will worsen, not improve, and by the time McCain is elected in 2004, it will be a full-fledged recession. McCain will be frustrated. He won't be interested in the details of domestic policy. He will try to be a world statesman just as the rest of the country is clamoring for him to "focus on the economy." McCain will be tempted to ignore economic issues, on the theory that the president can't do much about the economy anyway, and this common sense will be seen as callousness both in the press and in popular opinion.

In addition, McCain will face a hostile Congress. Although he will have won over the moderate Republicans, the right-wingers will treat him as an anathema and oppose everything he does on principal. Meanwhile, the Democrats, who will hold Congress in 2004, will be anxious to practice the same "politics of personal destruction" as used by the Republicans against Clinton.

McCain is not a patient man. The opposition of Congress and the perceived unfairness of the press will enrage him. When he finally tries to respond to the economic situation, it will be with grand programs which Congress will delay and defeat. McCain will respond with temper tantrums and vituperation, which will just harden Congress and the press against him further.

McCain will try to ignore Congress, using the presidency to make direct contact with the people. It will work for a while and some of the press will continue to admire his "growth" in office, meaning his tendency to move closer to the center. But such support will not protect McCain from the economy. By his third year, McCain's "temper" and "grandstanding" will have begun to wear thin. It will become obvious that he too is a one-term president. People will begin to consider his successor.

Sick of his party, and unwilling to kowtow to the electorate, McCain may decide not to run for a second term. Even if he does, he will lose to a challenger from the right-wing because his move to the center and his disdain for fellow Republicans in Congress will have angered too many in the party establishment. The religious conservatives will pull out all stops to regain their prominence within the Republican hierarchy, and the broader electorate, terrified by the prospect of a long recession, will prove willing to embrace extremist solutions. The evangelicals, led by Ralph Reed behind the scenes, will finally win their long-sought prize: the Republican nomination for president.

On the Democratic side, the left-wing of the party will win the nomination. The economic down-turn will galvanize the labor unions and quasi-socialists, and Al Gore's collapse will be remembered as the failure of Clinton/Gore centrism. The nominee will be a charismatic leftist firebrand, perhaps Andrew Cuomo.

Setting extremists in both parties against each other, and taking place in the wake of huge economic disruption, the 2008 presidential campaign will be volatile. There will be mass protests, with occasional violence, against each of the candidates wherever they appear.

In the end, faced with the choice between a Democratic socialist and a Republican evangelical, the United States will choose the Democrat. Religious freedom (and not capitalism) has always been America's most important principle. And the threat to religious freedom represented by a right-wing evangelical will be more frightening than the threat to capitalism represented by a left-wing socialist. The high-water mark that social conservatives reach by winning the Republican nomination

in 2008 will turn out to be their last hurrah. Thereafter faith-based politics will slowly disappear from the American political scene.

But voters will not have handed their future to a socialist president without precautionary measures. The Democratic president will be facing a fiercely antagonistic, Republican-controlled Congress. After a period of significant social unrest, and many predictions of doom, each side will pull back from the brink. The president, despite his rhetoric, will govern from the middle, and the Congress will support him. Each side will find, in the cozy way of Washington insiders, that they have common interests.

About midway through the new president's term, the economy will surge forward and the full potential of the technology we toy with today will begin to be realized. This new technology will be controlled by Gen-X and Generation Y, the members of which will finally be taking over economic and political control from the Baby-Boomers. The Baby Boomers will be aging in a world of technology they barely recognize and many of them will have few resources to help them understand it, having been over-leveraged and over-invested in equity markets when the recession hit.

The presidential race of 2012 will be a generational battle. A popular young president, credited with restoring the U.S. economy, will face the boomer backlash. The boomers aided by social conservatives, who will not have forgiven the rhetoric of the new president, will run a nasty campaign. But in the end, the strength of the economy and the new post-boomer generations will ensure reelection of the president in a land-slide.

Thereafter, things become harder to predict.

Reminiscence

Archimedes

Lincoln MacVeagh

In Costa Rica I taught earth science and mathematics to the sixth grade. The great difficulty I had teaching earth science was that I knew nothing about it. In mathematics, I had a firmer grip on the subject and the trouble was simply one of pacing. I had two classes of roughly twenty students each and the children varied widely in ability. The trick was to move quickly enough to keep the clever students interested, without moving so quickly as to the leave the less clever ones behind. I never quite managed it. Try as I might, Amber was always bored, and the notorious Karim was always hopelessly muddled.

Karim was a Lebanese boy. He had shoulder length black hair and fat, puffy cheeks. He was the smallest boy in the sixth grade. Only his toes touched the ground when he sat in his desk, and whenever I saw him with his knapsack on it looked as though he were about to fall over backwards. Nevertheless, his presence in class was enormous. Karim hated to feel left out, and although he couldn't follow the math, he had a knack for digging out my vulnerabilities.

When I started teaching at the school I was clean shaven. Over Thanksgiving break I grew a beard and on the first day back someone asked me why. Karim's hand shot up. He waived his arms in the air for silence and climbed onto his chair to make an announcement. He told the class that I'd grown a beard in order to make myself appear more grown-up and authoritative and he added that, as far as he was concerned, it didn't work.

The beard didn't work and I shaved it off a few weeks later when we started working on simple algebraic equations.

One day I was trying to explain the distributive property of multiplication when Karim's hand shot up again. I was pleased whenever he showed interest in class and I called on him right away. Karim furrowed his brow and made a serious face.

"Mr. Mac, when was the last time you had sex?"

Taken off guard, I listened just long enough for the question to register and then suddenly I felt stuck. I didn't have the sense to move on quickly. I was startled and I blushed. The class erupted and I threw Karim out in a fit of anger, but I was unable to stop the laughter and for the next fortnight I was the subject of countless whispered jokes and pointed fingers. I was even dragged into a meeting with the evil school principal Mrs. Battle. She called me aside to say she'd heard rumors I was discussing my sex life with my students. Through clenched teeth I told her that was not the case. She casually waved her hand in the air as if to say she didn't want an argument: she only wished to state on the record that sexual discussion of any nature was inappropriate.

Such are the trials of teaching. I was terrible at it, and as the year progressed both Karim and I waded further and further out of our depths. Unable to keep discipline in my classroom, I became increasingly short tempered; unable to keep up with the work, Karim became ever more difficult to manage. By the time we reached the section on geometry we were just about equally fed up. The radius of a circle is two inches long: what is the area of the circle? Karim stood up on his chair and said peevishly:

"This is so stupid. Why do we have to learn it?"

Perhaps because I myself was so frustrated I had already given the question some thought. The stock answer is that children have to learn boring things because they may turn out to be useful later on. However, this answer has never much appealed to me and I didn't think it would appeal to Karim either. Though it's true you can't be an engineer without some knowledge of geometry, Karim wasn't destined to be an engineer, and so instead of arguing the practical merit of mathematics, I told him the story of Archimedes.

Archimedes was the great geometer of ancient Syracuse and he loved knowledge for its own sake. When Syracuse was besieged by the Romans, Archimedes was urged to give up his theorizing and set his mind to the invention of war machines. Archimedes, however, was too much enthralled by the pure science of mathematics to bother with finding applications and while the Romans attacked the walls of his city, he stayed put in his garden, drawing figures in the dirt and studying the strange relationships between them.

Eventually the Romans broke through the walls of the city and a great cry of anguish rose up from the citizens of Syracuse. Archimedes didn't hear it. He was so lost in contemplation that he didn't realize his city had fallen. In time, a Roman soldier came upon him in his back yard. The soldier commanded that Archimedes march out to meet the conquering general. Unconcerned, Archimedes answered that first he must finish demonstrating the solution to the problem he was working on. Whereupon, the enraged soldier drew his sword and cut off his head. Archimedes died without ever realizing his life was in danger.

I concluded this story by telling Karim that one studied mathematics because it was possible to fall in love with the subject, as Archimedes had done. The argument was flawed like any other, but at least it had the benefit of being longwinded. By then I'd learned that the best way to deal with impossible questions was by means of distrac-

tion, and in this instance the technique worked nicely. Karim's eyes glazed over with boredom and I finished out the period without further interruption.

The next three weeks were something of a golden era. Karim was moderately well behaved and he even passed a few of his quizzes. It wasn't until after Easter that we had our last big fight.

This fight came at the end of a class, during the ten minutes in which the students usually started their homework. The rule was that they could talk quietly amongst themselves on condition that they did not leave their seats, but I'd hardly finished writing the assignment on the board before Karim jumped up from his desk. I told Karim to sit down but he ignored me. "Sit down!" I shouted (I never knew what else to do).

Karim was indifferent. He thrust his arms straight out in front of him and he was goose-stepping around the room like a zombie. Turn and march, turn and march. "Sit down!" I yelled as loudly as I dared, but to no effect. Karim was now walking towards me. His knees were locked, his arms held straight out in front, and his eyes were rolled way back in his head. Then he opened his mouth and said in a robot-like monotone:

"I am Archimedes... I am Archimedes..."

Sir Laffalot

Strolling through the Metropolitan Museum, Sir Laffalot was inspired. "Jolly nice to paint like Rembrandt," he said to no one in particular. "A strong hand," muttered the gentleman behind him. "Such a delicate touch," whispered his date. "Composition," said the man. "Chiaroscuro," purred the woman, "the brilliant juxtaposition of light and dark." This last remark closed discussion and everyone moved on to the impressionists, but by then Sir Laffalot's fate was sealed. It was only a short walk downtown to the Art Student's League.

Sir Laffalot signed up for a life drawing class that met twice a week. Life. It seemed rather a big subject to take on all at once, but one has to start somewhere. Sir Laffalot rushed out to buy some paper and a big box of colored pencils and the next morning he was back on 59th street waiting for his first class to begin.

Sir Laffalot's fellow students were not as he had pictured them. No one smoked Galoise. The woman sitting beside him was at least sixty years old and drank V-8 juice instead of espresso. The girl next to her had blonde hair in pigtails. In the corner was a middle aged man who looked like an accountant. Sir Laffalot left his beret in his knapsack and he strolled over to introduce himself to the girl with the pigtails.

"Mind if I look through your work?" he said cheerfully.

Sir Laffalot was met with the iciest of stares and he hurried back to his easel just in time to see the model walk in. She was a tall, brown haired woman with a pierced eyebrow, and she wore a long silk kimono belted at the waist. She stepped onto the short stage and turned to face the class with a faraway look in her eyes. The expression was perfect. Sir Laffalot grabbed a pencil and started drawing furiously.

"Hold on a minute," said the V-8 woman. Sir Laffalot's hand went still and when he looked up from his sketch pad he saw the most remarkable thing. The tall, brown haired model had pulled at the belt of her kimono and was now standing arms akimbo in the middle of the room, STARK NAKED!

"You dropped your pencil," said the V-8 woman.

"Does this happen every class?" asked Sir Laffalot. Somehow he couldn't help himself from grinning. Life is a lovely thing to draw.

Sir Laffalot hasn't missed a class since, and hoping to encourage the artist in everyone, this month he presents a doodling game for children. It's perfect for long journeys and it's called *Squiggles*.

Squiggles: How to Play.

1) Track down a pencil and some paper.
2) One player draws a random squiggle on a piece of paper.
3) The other player tries to makes sense of the squiggle by incorporating it into a larger drawing. Use your imagination!
4) Players switch roles and start over.

Sir Laffalot says: TOODALOO!!

Continued from page 16

and yowled, while she turned red, and ran off in tears. They were afraid of a lawsuit, and they videotaped my interview. It was my big moment, but I'd told the story one time too many and I performed terribly.

I'd never quit a job before, but as soon as the interview was over, I walked over to Human Resources. I was so tense that I got a spontaneous nosebleed on the way. Blood started pouring down my face and I rushed up to the executive floor, where the men's room was usually empty. I washed my face and applied a paper towel to my nose, and just then, Lew Glucksman came in.

Lew Glucksman was famous for his temper, and for keeping a section of tree, with an axe in it, mounted above his desk. He looked kind of like an ulcer come to life, and I assumed he was going to bite my head off for using the executive washroom, but he surprised me by saying "Come with me" in an authoritative tone.

I followed him to his sprawling, gleaming office and he took some ice out of a pitcher, folded it tenderly in a cloth napkin, and applied it to my nostrils. He told me to stay put until the bleeding stopped, and meanwhile we shot the breeze. I was beginning to feel guilty about quitting, until he said, "Say, aren't you the fella that walked in on that blow job?"

Blood or no blood, it was time for me to see the HR manager. Her name was Laurel Rund, a plus-size woman with orange hair and suits tailored to give her the sleek look of an overfed tabby. She and her assistant Andrea (pronounced "And-ray-uh") always had the upper hand in our dealings, but this time, I told myself, it was going to be different. They were going to beg me to stay.

Andrea showed me into the office, and Laurel gave me a brisk, "So, what's on your mind?" as soon as I sat down.

"I – I quit," I said, expecting another blood vessel to blow.

Laurel reached for her intercom.

"Andrea, call back that guy – Carlos? – who interviewed today. Tell him that we have an opening after all."

I was replaced before I even got up from my chair.

The high life

Night Secretary

David Garcia III

One Friday night, when I was the night secretary for the investment banking group at Smith Barney, I ended up staying late to conjure up some word processing magic for Ralph "The Source" Watts, an old-school investment banker complete with slicked back hair, dyspepsia, and suspenders. It was past midnight, and all that remained for me to do was to print out the documents and distribute them to the executives on the top floors.

Ralph made a point of telling me (slowly, as if I spoke no English) how important it was that I try the office door first. If the door was unlocked, I was to leave the report on the chair inside. If locked, I was to slide it under the door. By no means was I to leave the report outside the door or on a secretary's chair. Ralph slipped me a $50 and called himself a car service.

I had finished the top floor, and was almost finished with the floor below, when I reached the office of one of the biggest wigs. I opened it and found that I had accidentally walked in on a private meeting. The woman was fully dressed, but the man had his shirt and pants undone, and she was performing oral sex. It was dark, and I couldn't make out their features, only that they were alarmed. I quickly closed the door, slid the document underneath it and hustled down the spooky corridors, thinking that if this was a movie, I would have to be killed before I left the building. On second thought I decided that I approved of the couple's behavior, and I resolved not to mention it to anyone.

When I got back downstairs, one of the young analysts, Gregg (with three g's), was still there crunching numbers.

He wandered out of his cube (in stocking feet, his tie slightly loosened) and the first thing out of my mouth was, "You'll never guess what I just saw." He asked me a few casual questions, but he seemed to regard my story as very blasé-blah, the kind of thing that happened all the time.

On Monday, there was a Post-it-Note on my computer which said that I should see John (who I was friendly with) ASAP. I met him in a conference room, having no idea what he wanted, and he said that the girl from Friday night was embarrassed, and asked me to please promise not to tell anyone. I told him it was too late and he said, "Shit!" and left (taking his Seven-Up can with the cigar balanced on top) without saying goodbye.

It turned out that Gregg had been busy spreading the intelligence. He'd figured out the location of the office and checked it against the sign-out sheet in the lobby. I never knew the couple's names, but he did. They all did. And for the next two days I was pulled into a maze of offices and cubicles and asked to provide the details. I couldn't help being intimidated by these people – seduced – by their bonuses, their salaries, and their preeminent role in the social construct. I was suddenly popular and I found myself polishing the story to make it more entertaining for my audience.

By the end of the week the girl had resigned, and I got a call from the Diversity Coordinator. The Coordinator told me that there had been a previous problem involving the same girl. Apparently, someone had rigged her computer to play the famous Meg Ryan orgasm scene from "When Harry Met Sally". She tried to turn it off, but that was rigged too, and all the guys hooted

Continued on page 15

The
ECLECTIC

May-June 2000 Volume 2 Number 4 Free

CONTENTS

Quotations

"The flatterers of Dionysius, whose sight was failing, used to bump against one another and upset the dishes at dinner." From Plutarch's *Moralia, vol. 1.*

"According to your photo it does not look as though it is very long since you left your cradle so I think you would be wise to go home and suck your titty. The Electors of Chelsea want a man of experience to represent them." William Philpott, constituent, responds to a mailing from Bertrand Russell's campaign for parliament, in volume 2 of *The Autobiography of Bertrand Russell.*

"It's very simple. You must give way to them in every respect." Nancy Mitford explains how French women keep their lovers in *Love In A Cold Climate.*

"The three geniuses of whom I wish to speak are Gertrude Stein, Pablo Picasso and Alfred Whitehead. I have met many important people, I have met several great people but I have only known three first class geniuses and in each case on sight something within me rang. In no one of the three cases have I been mistaken." Go Gertrude! Stein writes about herself in the deceptively titled *The Autobiography of Alice B. Toklas.*

The Thin Girls

Lincoln MacVeagh

Sonia had a moon face and light hair. Hillary had a pointy face and dark hair. They were students in their second year of business school and they shared a two-bedroom apartment on the Upper West Side of Manhattan. They got on well together.

The perfect roommate doesn't need to be witty or charming. A constant charm can be very tiresome. It's much better that the girl you live with be dull and reliable, than brilliant and flaky. A good roommate is someone who agrees with you on little things like when to turn off the TV, when to tidy up, and when to buy more toilet paper. In all these respects Sonia and Hillary were perfect for each other. But what made the girls real friends was that they also agreed on the two most important aspects of life. They both felt the same way about diet and exercise.

Sonia and Hillary were slender as toothpicks and they worked hard to maintain their physiques (which is why Sonia thought it so unfair to be born with a round face rather than Hillary's chiseled features). The girls went to the gym together at seven o'clock each night and they were extremely careful about what they ate.

Hillary lived on salad, fruit, steamed vegetables, yogurt and rice cakes. Once a week she ate fish for protein. Sonia's diet was nearly identical, but she didn't like fish so she ate rice and black beans instead. Sonia believed in food combina-tions. She ate rice and beans because she said that they created a complete protein in your body that you wouldn't get from eating them separately. Hillary did not believe in food combinations, and she didn't eat rice and beans because they were too high in carbohydrates. It was a point of contention between the girls but only a small one. For the most part, minor disagreements were forgotten in the face of a broader philosophical con-sensus.

I'm not sure just when thinness and spirituality first became linked in the public consciousness, but for Sonia and Hillary the correspondence between a strong mind and a narrow waist was an idée fixe. They accepted it wholeheart-edly.

To Hillary, staying thin was a straightforwardly logical proposition. "They've done studies," she said. "If you take two mice and feed one a great deal and the other just a little, the mouse that eats less will live twice as long and be twice as active as the mouse that eats too much." Besides, being fat made you miserable, and since the goal of life is happiness, why would you want to be fat?

Sonia, who was less coldly rational than her roommate, was more willing to admit that she stayed thin in order to look nice, but she also believed that the care you took of your figure was a metaphor for the care you took of your soul. If pressed, she was likely

to mention Buddhism, Gandhi and the unity of mind and body. However, Sonia's ideas about Buddhism and oneness were not clearly worked out in her head, and since Hillary had little patience for mysticism, she generally kept them to herself.

The other thing Sonia kept to herself was Claude Davis. Hillary knew something of Sonia's feeling for Claude but she didn't know the full extent of it. Sonia had a massive crush. Claude was a first-year student at the business school and he was clever, kind, handsome and marvelously built. In a perfect world, Sonia dreamed of herself waking up next to him every Sunday morning. Claude would kiss her awake, bring her a glass of orange juice in bed and then the two of them would go running round the Park.

Sonia and Claude had as yet shared nothing more intimate than a cup of coffee, but Sonia's hopes were high and the weekend coming up would be telling. Sonia, Claude and Hillary were all invited to the glamorous wedding reception of another business school friend at the Waldorf on Saturday night, and although Sonia was not going as Claude's date, she knew from her sources that he wasn't bringing anyone else either.

Hillary wasn't so worked up about the wedding reception as Sonia, but she too was looking forward to the week ahead. Her cousin June was coming to stay. She and Hillary had once been best friends and they still wrote letters back and forth from time to time. June was a journalist in Chicago and when she wrote to say that she had a job interview with NBC in New York, Hillary urged her to take a whole week's vacation and spend it in the city.

"What's she like?" asked Sonia.

"She's full of stories. She's very funny and writes the best letters. I'm going out to the airport after school tomorrow to pick her up. Why don't you come along?"

"I'd miss the gym."

"But I'm missing it too." Hillary didn't like to go without exercise any

James James, Morison Morison, Weatherby George Dupree,
Took great care of his Mother, though he was only three.
James James, said to his Mother, "Mother," he said, said he;
"You must never go down to the end of the town without cell-phoning me."

more than Sonia did and she would have preferred that they miss the gym together.

"I'm sorry, but I can't. Not with the reception on Saturday."

Sonia didn't need to mention Claude. Hillary understood. No one wants to go to the Waldorf feeling frumpy.

So on Monday evening, while Sonia sweated up and down on a stairmaster, Hillary rode the Carey bus out to Laguardia by herself and waited at the arrivals gate, watching a horde of plus sized Midwesterners file through the exits past her.

Hillary hadn't seen her cousin in ages but she remembered her as a tall, stringy teenager with curly blonde hair and a big smile. No one she saw fit the description and Hillary was quite startled when a young woman of medium height with breasts, large hips and the distinct beginnings of a double chin walked up and embraced her. Hillary was so small and scrawny in comparison to this woman that she could barely touch her arms around the woman's chest. It was like being smothered by a walrus.

They stepped back to examine each other.

"Skinny as a rail," said June cheerfully. "You haven't changed a bit. You look beautiful."

"So do you," chirped Hillary. Her smile was frozen on her lips. Even the unpracticed eye could see that June was at least twenty pounds overweight.

Anyone else might have said that June was very pretty and that she carried herself well. Hillary couldn't help noticing the stiff roll of fat around June's waist. June's tummy had escaped her jeans and was hanging over her belt like batter rolling over the side of a muffin tin. Hillary was disappointed to see her favorite cousin so changed and she wondered what could have happened.

"Have you eaten?" said June. "I'm starving."

Hillary told her there was food in the apartment and suggested they get back. "I'm dying to introduce you to Sonia," she said.

In fact, Hillary was now somewhat nervous about the introduction. She knew how much Sonia relied on first impressions and she hadn't imagined the possibility that June would look so heavy. Hillary worried that the shock might start things off on the wrong foot.

Sonia was just home from her workout when the girls got in, but if she was at all surprised by June's appearance she didn't show it. Sonia had already made up her mind to like June. She kissed her enthusiastically on the cheek and volunteered to make dinner while Hillary gave June a set of keys and showed her how the sofa folded out.

Hillary explained that she was busy with classes during the day, and she told June that she'd have to fend for herself on Saturday night (the wedding reception), but at least they would see each other in the evenings and perhaps they would all go to the Metropolitan Museum on Saturday morning.

June didn't mind. "I'm perfectly capable of entertaining myself," she said.

Sonia announced that dinner was ready.

Neatly laid out on the kitchen table were three tall glasses of water and three plates of food. Upon each plate were five carrot sticks, two rice cakes and a good sized bed of lettuce with a tablespoon of fat-free Russian dressing on the side. There were bananas for dessert.

"My goodness. I almost forgot," cried June. She fetched a bag from her pile of luggage and pulled out a large Wisconsin cheese basket overflowing with candied apples, hard sausages and a wide variety of cheese. It was her housegift. "I hope you like cheese."

Hillary looked over at Sonia.

"I love the taste of cheese," said Sonia.

She was too polite to add that cheese is animal lard and that she'd never in a million years eat a piece.

"Good," said June, "Because I love it too." She squeezed the cheese basket onto the table and cut herself an inch thick piece of salami and a large slice of white cheddar. "Of course, what we really need is some good bread."

Hillary nibbled a carrot and spoke briskly. "I know, but all we can get around here is the store bought kind and everyone hates store bought bread." She felt intruded upon. She didn't like to eat staring at an enormous basket of cholesterol and again she glanced at Sonia to gauge her reaction.

Sonia, however, refused to catch Hillary's eye. She was pretending that everything was normal and she was asking June about life as a reporter in Chicago. June told a story about one of her editors, whom she called The Lecherous Mr. Collins.

"The Lecherous Mr. Collins acts like Don Juan and he's a terrifying bore. Worst of all he recently developed a crush on me. Three times a week he'd stop by my desk hoping to make conversation but all he could think to do was ask me what time it was. Finally I got so sick of him that I bought him a watch. Now he's started bothering the poor girl who writes the obituaries."

After dinner Hillary and Sonia cleaned up while June was in the bathroom.

"What are we going to do with it?" hissed Hillary conspiratorially, pointing at the cheese basket.

"What can we do with it? We can't just throw away."

"Why not? It makes me sick. We could find a roach in it and tell June it's infested."

"Ssshhh," whispered Sonia. "Don't be silly. If I can stand it, so can you. She's *your* cousin."

Sonia and Hillary left promptly the next morning for classes and June woke up by herself. She was thrilled to be in Manhattan. She went out to explore the neighborhood and in no time at all she discovered Zabaar's. Knowing that the girls were low on groceries she bought smoked salmon, bagels, cream cheese with chives, eggs, butter and mayonnaise. Three blocks away she found a real bakery (how could Hillary have missed it?) and added two crusty loaves of French bread. She ate an omelet for breakfast, packed a sandwich for lunch and spent the afternoon at the Cloisters. That evening, she persuaded Hillary to walk with her through the park while Sonia was at the gym and they ended up at a café on the East Side drinking chablis on the sidewalk. It was heaven.

The following day June visited the Statue of Liberty and bought three tickets to a Broadway play at the cut rate tickets booth in Times Square. Sonia got home with enough time to workout before the eight o'clock show but Hillary was late and had to be whisked off to the theatre the moment she stepped in the door.

On Thursday June spent the whole day in the shops. She bought a charcoal grey interview suit at Saks; she had an informative chat with the sales lady at Henri Bendel's make-up counter ("You should wear silver eye shadow to highlight your fair complexion"); and though she didn't need it, she found a sexy green dress at Bloomingdale's that was so becoming she couldn't resist.

June's interview with NBC was on Friday and it lasted all morning. In the afternoon she got a call from the news director and he told her they'd decided to hire someone in-house.

"I'm so sorry," said Hillary, "Don't take it too hard. Television isn't for everyone."

June replied that it wasn't as bad as it sounded. The news director was very encouraging and had told her to keep in touch. There would be other openings soon.

"Should we be commiserating or congratulating you?" asked Sonia.

"I don't know, but in either case the interview's over and I think we should celebrate." June took a bottle of champagne from her shoulder bag. "I've made reservations for seven o'clock. I'm taking you both out to dinner."

Sonia clapped her hands together. She had anticipated that June might want to go out and she had just returned from a run.

Hillary hadn't anticipated going out and she wasn't nearly so pleased. Hillary desperately wanted to workout. Three out of four days that week she'd missed the gym and it didn't help Hillary's mood to think that Sonia had kept up an exercise schedule without her.

To make matters worse there was a half-eaten cheese basket on the kitchen table and every morning when Hillary opened the fridge for her rice cakes, she'd found herself confronted by a jar of mayonnaise and a dozen eggs. The prospect of watching her cousin stuff down a large bowl of pasta in public was horrid. But there wasn't much Hillary could do. She wanted to be a good hostess and if June offered to take her out to dinner, she had to go.

Hillary woke up Saturday morning feeling bloated as a tick. When June suggested making pancakes for breakfast, she put her foot down. "No," she said firmly. "We haven't time. If we're going to the Metropolitan we must get there early. The crowds are terrible later in the day, and Sonia and I have to get home in time to prepare for the wedding reception."

Hillary was cranky, but fortunately the Met is a good place to regain one's equilibrium and after five minutes standing in front of the El Greco's, her troubles slowly melted away. Hillary took June to see her favorite painting in the museum, a portrait by Modigliani, and then Sonia dragged everyone to look at the Giacometti statues.

The girls were passing through a photography exhibit when a voice called after them and a roly-poly young man named Eddie Switzer rumbled up to say hello. Eddie was at the business school with Sonia and Hillary. It turned out he'd also been to college with June. He punched June playfully on the arm.

"What are you doing in town? Did you come for the wedding?"

"Just visiting," said June.

"She's my cousin," said Hillary.

"But you should come to the wedding," said Eddie. "It's going to be a fabulous party."

"Not invited," said June

"Well, I am and my invitation says *and guest*. You can come as my date. I can't remember the last time I had a date."

June gave Hillary an inquiring look. Hillary smiled. Having recovered her spirits, she was now feeling slightly guilty about leaving her cousin alone that night and Eddie's arrival seemed like a stroke of luck. She looked at his fat boyish face and thought that he and June would make a nice couple.

"You can wear your green dress," said Hillary.

"Alright," said June. "But you mustn't keep me out too late. I have an early plane to catch tomorrow morning."

"I plan to make sure you're still drunk when you get to the airport," said Eddie.

It was settled and the girls went home to get ready.

June had the easiest time of it. She only had the one green dress; she added a touch of silver eye shadow as per Henri Bendel and was done. Sonia didn't suffer much either. She'd already tried on her

dress countless times since Monday and all that was left to do was fix her hair so it wouldn't keep falling in her face.

Hillary went back and forth for hours between a tiny black cocktail dress (can you wear black to a wedding?) and a long purple gown that made her feel elegant but too matronly. At last she decided on the gown and the three girls took a picture of themselves in front of the sofa just before Eddie showed up. They all told each other how nice they looked. June batted her eyes and pursed her lips playfully, and Hillary couldn't help thinking how attractive she'd be if only she lost a few pounds.

Everyone shared a cab to the Waldorf and once inside the ballroom Eddie and June broke off. The girls had skipped lunch because of the reception and June dragged Eddie straight over to the hors d'oevres. She was famished.

Sonia and Hillary were also hungry but they were both too nervous to eat. Especially Sonia. She drank a glass of wine and looked around the room wondering whether Claude was there yet. She saw him leaning against a wall talking to a girl in his study group. Sonia waved.

Sonia drank a second glass of wine when Claude came over to say hello. They talked for a long time and soon it was eight o'clock and the party was in full swing. Claude asked Sonia to dance and afterwards they sat down at a large table of friends. Sonia had a third glass of wine. She still hadn't eaten anything

but she felt so blissful sitting next to Claude that she happily accepted a fourth drink.

Suddenly Sonia felt faint.

Worse than faint, Sonia was about to throw up. Without saying anything to Claude she leapt up from her seat and ran off in a frantic search for the bathroom. Hillary saw her reeling past the bandstand and rushed in to help. Sonia made it to the ladies room sink just in time and after that Hillary took her home as quickly and discretely as possible. It was really frightful. Sonia kept nodding off in the cab and the moment she flopped onto her bed she passed out cold.

Since there was nothing more Hillary could do, she decided to go back to the Waldorf to pick up June. It was midnight and the ballroom was almost empty. Hillary ran into Eddie at the coat check. He was on his way out.

"I hope Sonia's alright."

"She'll be fine," said Hillary, "But where's June? Why aren't you with her?"

"June and Claude went out for a nightcap. I couldn't do it. Too tired, and I'm drunk enough as it is. It sure was great to see June again. Isn't she fun?"

Hillary didn't answer. She marched straight past into the ballroom, but as Eddie said, June was already gone. Hillary was upset. She was angry at Sonia for being so stupid, she was angry at herself for coming back to the Waldorf for no reason, and she was angry

at Claude for taking off with June. What on earth would Hillary tell Sonia if she found out? Hillary hoped she wouldn't find out and went home to sit up for June. She ended up falling asleep in front of the television.

She was still on the sofa the next morning when June bustled in and woke her up. June was wearing her green dress and Hillary thought she heard a man's voice outside the door. June gave her a devious smile and silently mouthed the words "Oh my God" while pointing over her shoulder.

Claude poked his head around the corner. "Good morning, Hillary," he said sheepishly.

"We had the most wonderful night," bubbled June. "Now I just have to pick up my bags and go. Claude's driving me to the airport."

Hillary was stunned. Sonia, who was awake in her bedroom and suffering from a dreadful hangover, heard Claude's voice and almost burst into tears.

June kissed Hillary on the forehead, "Don't get up. I just want you to know how much fun I've had. Tell Sonia I say goodbye. I hope she's not feeling too rotten after last night. I'd love to say goodbye to her, but I've got to catch my plane." June handed a piece of luggage to Claude. "Thanks again. See you soon!"

Hillary went to peek into Sonia's bedroom. As soon as Hillary turned the door handle, Sonia rolled violently over in bed and faced the wall, refusing to look at her. There was nothing to say so Hillary left her alone. How could a healthy young man pick a fat cow like June over Sonia? It was ghastly.

Hillary dressed quickly and went out for a cup of coffee. She sat in the cof-fee shop feeling tired, flabby and glum. She didn't want to go home and face Sonia. She lingered as long as she could but eventually she found herself climbing the stairs back up to the apartment.

On the landing Hillary heard a terrific crash. She ran into the kitchen and saw Sonia standing there with a large black garbage bag at her feet. Sonia lifted up the bag so Hillary could see inside. At the bottom of it were the shattered remains of mayonnaise jar.

"I hate mayonnaise!" Sonia said fiercely, "You know what else I hate? I hate eggs. One egg has as much saturated fat as a small order of McDonald's french fries!" Sonia took an egg out its carton and smashed it into the sink. "Care for an egg?"

Hillary knew just how Sonia felt. She picked up an egg in each hand and smashed them both into the sink.

"Cheese basket!" Hillary exclaimed. Using a salami as a bat she tossed a hunk of cheese in the air and whacked it across the kitchen.

"Bagels!" cried Sonia. In quick succession, she threw the bagels like frisbees straight into the garbage. Next went the butter, the bread and what was left of the smoked salmon. Sonia and Hillary worked feverishly until every last fatty calorie had been thrown into the trash. The garbage was double bagged and triple knotted.

"I feel so much better," said Sonia.

"Better than better," said Hillary, "I feel glorious."

The girls looked at each other across the kitchen table. Their eyes were shining. They both spoke at once.

"Let's go to the gym."

Reviews

My Story
by Isadora Duncan
Norton Ww, 1995 (reprint)

Isadora Duncan was beautiful, brilliant and seemingly possessed by fire. She was born in San Francisco in 1878 and her mother was an Irish-American piano teacher. Mrs. Duncan was a divorcée who taught her children that their father was a devil with horns in his head.

The family was extremely poor and as a schoolgirl Isadora wrote the history of her life as follows: *"When I was five we had a cottage on 23rd Street. Failing to pay the rent, we could not remain there but moved to 17th Street, and in short time, as funds were low, the landlord objected, so we moved to 22nd Street..."* At ten she left school to make money teaching dance.

Isadora's noble goal was to express the mysteries of ancient Greece through movement and she believed she could do it. When she turned fifteen she dragged her mother to Chicago to offer herself to the world. The world wasn't interested and Isadora was forced to take a job in pantomime to survive. *"Now pantomime to me has never seemed an art,"* she says sniffily. *"When I was told that I must point to her to say YOU, press my heart to say LOVE, and then violently hit myself on the chest to say ME, it all seemed too ridiculous."*

Isadora moved to New York where she danced in a show starring Ada Rehan. One day there was a note on the cast bulletin board: *"The company are informed that they need not say good-day to Miss Rehan!"* Again Isadora was miserable. Her talent was being wasted and she spoke to the show's manager: *"'What's the use of having me here with my genius,' I said, 'when you make no use of me?'"*

Despairing of the United States altogether, Isadora gathered up her family and moved them to London. They were still poor but they were all so in love with Art and classicism that they barely noticed their hardships. They ate penny buns, and spent their days in the British Museum. At night the Duncans offered group performances to the ladies of society: *"My mother played for me; Elizabeth read some poems of Theocritus, translated by Andrew Lang, and Raymond gave a short conference upon the subject of dancing and its possible effect on the psychology of future humanity."* Isadora's presence could make anything worth watching.

Indeed, one can hardly imagine a more attractive girl. At first even her faults are charming. She is too much in love with her own genius, but this seems merely an expression of exuberance. One assumes she will become less self-involved as she grows up.

But Isadora doesn't grow up, and as a result *My Story* bogs down. Part of the trouble is simply that the book goes on too long. Once Isadora becomes famous her autobiography loses its narrative force. The rest is anti-climax, and reading it is a bit like reading a long postscript to *Pride and Prejudice* about the married life of Mr. and Mrs. Darcy.

The more serious trouble is that Isadora herself loses vigor. *"Gone were the days of a glass of hot milk and Kant's 'Critique of Pure Reason.' Now it seemed to me more natural to sip champagne and have some charming person tell me how beautiful I was."* Her magnificence slowly dies away and is replaced by a tawdry celebrity. One ceases to trust her. Even Isadora's love of Art becomes suspect. Perhaps it is just a love of doing as she pleases.

Isadora closes *My Story* with a parallel between the stages of her life and the stages of her sexuality: *"I was once the timid prey, then the aggressive Bacchante, but now I close over my lover as the sea over a bold swimmer..."* She has written a fascinating book but by the end of it one feels sorry for those bold swimmers.

A Visit to Germany

T.E. MacVeagh

It is often said that the 20th century was the "American Century." What is meant, I suppose, is that the history of the century is, most significantly, the history of the rise of the United States to world dominance. This view strikes me as giving too much weight to recent events. Looking at the last one hundred years as a whole, it seems more accurate to say that the 20th century was the "German Century."

The skeleton around which the century unfolded consists of three wars: World War I, World War II and the Cold War. The obvious focus of the two World Wars, Germany was also a central participant in the Cold War. Though the main combatants were Russia and the United States, Germany was the battleground and prize over which the Cold War was fought. The wall running through Berlin and the divided Germany was the most important symbol and the most important fact of the war. And the Cold War ended, symbolically and actually, when the Berlin wall was torn down.

In addition, the intellectual life of the century was overwhelmingly German. The most significant political and cultural struggles were based around the ideas of the German Marx and the German-speaking Austrian Freud. A German, Einstein, discovered relativity, and another, Heisenberg, discovered quantum mechanics. The most important philosophers of the century were Heidegger, a German, and Wittgenstein, a German-speaking Austrian. German expressionism was among the dominant artistic movements, and one could even argue that the flowering of American intellectual life in the middle of the century, particularly in Hollywood, owes no little amount to the influx of Jews of German heritage.

Obviously not everything was accomplished by Germans. They have no special claim to Darwin or Jazz or computer technology. Still, it is not surprising that when Time Magazine elected its man of the century, it chose a German, Albert Einstein. Einstein's life seems representative of the century itself. He grew up in Germany, did his ground-breaking work in German-speaking Switzerland, and he arrived in America only after his most important accomplishments were behind him. Similarly, America itself arrived only after the most significant events of the century had passed. Einstein is an appropriate symbol of the century in another way too. He was German, but also Jewish. As many German Jews cannot be reconciled with their German heritage, so history has been uncomfortable with the dominant role of Germany.

This history makes Germany a fascinating place to study and visit, but a difficult place to love. The countryside is green and lush. It is dotted with towns and villages which look like the Hollywood sets for Medieval fantasies. Collectively, its art museums – every third village seems to house a collection of some surprising significance – are surely the finest in the world. Its people welcome travelers speaking even the most mangled German. In stunning contrast to France, the admiration and respect for Americans in Germany is palpable. (This is mostly out of grateful memory for the "deliverance from Hitler" and the aid in reconstruction provided under the Marshall Plan). Weary tourists can restore body and soul at conveniently spaced beer gardens, offering simple but well-cooked meals and the freshest beer in the world.

And yet, somehow, for all of this, Germany fails to spark love or passion.

Few Americans visit compared with the numbers that flock to France, England or Italy. The fact that I intended to go to Germany for my honeymoon was met with astonishment. Those that do visit may leave appreciative and impressed, but they are rarely moved or inspired. Tourists in Germany never give you the sense (as expressed in Peter Mayle's books about Provence or Bill Bryson's book about England) that they have found their home, the geographical equivalent of a soul mate.

The Germans themselves are deeply connected to their country. Most Germans I know feel a painful homesickness when they are away too long. The bars, hotels and restaurants are filled with signs of "gemütlichkeit," a particularly German form of hospitality, and everywhere there are affirmations of "Heimat," the vision of Germany as a home and shelter to its people. Architecture, costumes, antiques, bric-a-brac, and most of all menus, are all designed to say you are at home in Germany now. You can relax.

But whereas French or Italian kitsch touches something in the American soul, the German equivalent leaves us cold. The furniture is too dark and heavy. The keepsakes are too sticky sentimental. The architecture is filled with awkward stairstep patterns or comical peaks. The clothes look uncomfortable. As for the menus . . . well, they are just funny. Ten kinds of wurst for breakfast? Ten kinds of potatoes for lunch? Ten kinds of cabbage for dinner?

Of course, the most important reason for the foreigner's uneasiness is the unavoidable history of the Holocaust. Most non-Germans retain a deep-seated suspicion that the Holocaust was a uniquely German evil. For better or for worse, Americans who visit Germany wander around constantly on their guard against signs of Nazi revanchism. Local customs that in Italy and France would be accepted as merely adorable (such as wearing Lederhosen) are scrutinized for fascist tendencies. The very experiences that are the most likely to build good will and fellow feeling between tourists and Germans, such as swilling beer and swaying to the sound of waltz music in the Hofbrauhaus, are enjoyed as guilty pleasures. The Americans smile knowingly at one another as if to say their enjoyment of the scene is merely ironic. They know that it is precisely such drunken revelry, such debauched togetherness, that produced the mobs for Kristallnacht and the Beerhall Putsch.

But I suspect that there are reasons that reach beyond and below the Holocaust as well. Except perhaps for a brief period prior to World War I, Germany was always treated as a backwards and uncivilized neighbor by the rest of Europe. It has simply never served as a beacon of taste for the Western world. Accordingly, we are not taught to have the same respect for the German sensibility and the special German flair that we are taught to have for Italian or French style. Indeed, the notion of German flair may strike us, *a priori*, as an oxymoron.

It is sad to see a country so eager to please so disparaged by its visitors, so incapable of inspiring the love for which it yearns.

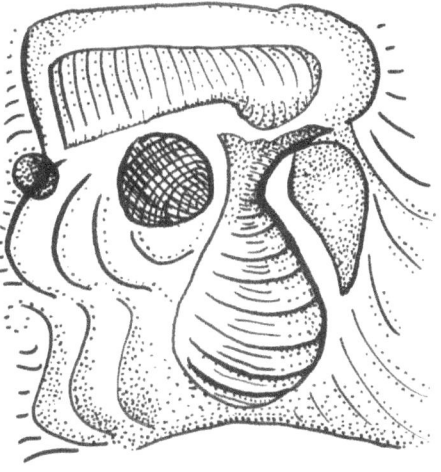

Games

Sir Laffalot

Quick with a smile and a *bon mot*, Sir Laffalot is known as the perfect party guest, but he also has a serious side. He is a student of history.

Sir Laffalot thinks of history as a giant picture book. He likes to flip through the pages and marvel at the funny hairstyles and silly outfits. Sometimes he tries to draw himself into the book and he wonders how he would have behaved as a Spanish inquisitor or a suffering Jew.

Sir Laffalot believes that it is edifying to test oneself against the lives of other men in other centuries. In his view the lessons of history are moral lessons and he is suspicious of those who would study the picture book in search of more practical wisdom.

History is a slippery thing. After winning the first war against Carthage the Romans took pity on the city, believing that their kindness would be remembered and thus prevent future wars. After the second war with Carthage the Romans destroyed the city and killed all its inhabitants, thinking that mighty vengeance would succeed where mercy failed. Carthage rose again, and if nothing else, subsequent wars proved to the Romans just how difficult it is to interpret the past.

At this point in the discussion Sir Laffalot usually pounds his fist on the desk and thunders, "The nature of causality does not change over time. Trying to explain history is the same as trying to predict the future!" Sir Laffalot loves making this analogy and he used to think it ended the argument. He took it as a point of faith that the future is impossible to predict.

Recently, however, his faith has been shaken. Last week he met an old woman in a purple scarf who confidently claimed that she really could predict the future. She pointed out that scientists have long been able to foretell the positions of the stars and she said that in the same way she was able to foretell the state of men's souls.

The old woman asked Sir Laffalot if there was anything he wanted to know about his own future. He thought for a moment, shifting uncomfortably in his chair: "Will I ever run out of games?"

Happily, the fortune teller assured him that he would not, and just to make certain, she taught Sir Laffalot a new parlor game. It's called *Predictions*. It's very popular with the psychic set but it's fun for normal people too.

Predictions: How to Play.

1) Players take ten minutes to write down a prediction about the world 10 years from now. Be as detailed as possible and offer as many good arguments as you can.
2) Read all the predictions out loud and discuss them.
3) Take a group vote to determine which prediction is most likely to come true.

Sir Laffalot says: TOODALOO!!

Continued from page 16

this patient he had never seen, and they arrested him.

The Doctor said he would understand if she dropped him, but that was the last thing on her mind. At this point she was dangerously unhappy, and about a week away from the point where an abortion becomes a risky procedure. She had no idea what to do, and practically begged him to make a decision for her. He said his personal opinion was that she should leave California right away, and have the abortion as soon as she could. He even called her parents to talk them into taking her back.

For someone who sleeps all day and has never worked, Laura can be scarily efficient when she sets her mind to something. As soon as the guy left the house the next morning, she made plane reservations, called a car service, and caught the first flight to Pittsburgh. The guy came home early, and raced to the airport on his motorcycle, but he just missed her.

Laura's parents drove her home in silence. They never asked her what she was thinking, or if she had second thoughts or doubts. She didn't call me

for fear I would talk her out of it again, and the baby was gone the next day.

On the way home from the abortion, Laura and her Mom were hit by a car, and had to go back to the same hospital to get checked out. A few days after that, her Dad got chest pains, and had to have surgery on his heart, which of course convinced Laura that she's being punished by God.

It's been a few weeks now since the operation, and she hasn't left the house. She stays up all night watching television until the sleeping pills kick in, and then she sleeps all day. She uses all her creativity to dwell, and has convinced herself that she made a mistake. Every time she sees a baby on TV she starts to tear up.

I've been on the phone with her a few times since the operation, and a couple of times I've managed to make her laugh. It's hard though. Sometimes when I'm talking to her its like I can see a specter. The specter of someone hopelessly in love with her own tragedy. I said, "Come to New York and become a famous artist!" but she only sighed. She's very tired, with a long haul of mourning ahead.

The high life

The Story Ends

David Garcia III

As soon as I got to the running track it decided to pour rain. I went running anyway and it was exhilarating. Everyone had taken shelter except for me and a man in a green sweat suit who was standing motionless in the middle of the soccer field.

Just like in a story, I came down with a cold the next day. I stayed home sick from work, and that's how I was home when Laura called.

By this time her pregnancy was in its third month, and she was back at her parents house again, having fled from a failed attempt to establish herself as a Soccer Mom with the baby-to-be's father in California.

She let me babble on about my life for a while before she dropped the news that the abortion was scheduled for the next day. At first, I did my job and played the supportive friend, but as we kept talking I found myself trying to talk her into keeping the baby. The conversation lasted all day, and by the end of it she had decided against the operation, and was considering giving California another try.

After we hung up, I collapsed on the floorboards in exhaustion and started to drift off to sleep. I imagined meeting the unborn boy/girl at their high school graduation. I was sitting in the bleachers seventeen years from now, and wanting to tell them about the time I went jogging in the rain, and how it helped to save them from oblivion.

In the following days Laura negotiated terms with the baby's father, booked a flight, and even mailed her computer to his house. She flew to California the same day that I flew to Florida (for my yearly visit to Grandma), and our planes were in the air at the same time. She was doing so well that I didn't think to give her my Grandmother's phone number.

At first things were fine. She unpacked her stuff, went on some family outings (the father has three kids already), and watched lots of bad TV. She tried out some maternity clothes, and started cutting back on her chain-smoking/antidepressants. Then she started to cry. She cried all day, and she couldn't say why.

One of the problems was sleeping. Laura likes to sleep alone (with sleeping pills, earplugs and eyeshades), but the guy insisted she sleep with him. Naked, in his waterbed, no less. He's large, and when he lay on the waterbed, he would sink in the middle. This made a kind of ravine that she would tumble into. "Every night I would lay there, wide awake, naked and pregnant, wedged up against his fat body. I would start crying, and he would hold me. When I cried harder he would hug me that much harder. It was supposed to be comforting, but I felt like I was in a cage."

What made matters worse was that her psychiatrist, Dr. Z, had been missing since before she was pregnant. She had left frantic messages on his machine, but he never called back, and she assumed that he had just grown tired of her. Then he called out of the blue, telling her that he had been in jail for a few months. Apparently it was all over the papers. The Police sent an undercover agent to Dr. Z's office posing as the husband of a severely depressed woman with a foot injury. The Cop said his wife couldn't come to the office, and he asked Dr. Z if he could write her a prescription anyway. The good Doctor ("never stingy with the pills" – Laura's favorite thing about him) promptly wrote out a generous prescription for Zoloft to

Continued on page 15

The
ECLECTIC

| July 2000 | Volume 2 Number 5 | Free |

CONTENTS

Quotations

"We stood in a biting wind outside the gate, waiting – so we were informed – for some Ethiopians. I said to Mr. Bennett: 'Do tell them it is quite useless to wait for Ethiopians' – and, in fact, they never turned up." Nancy Mitford voices impatience during a Cold War visit to the Kremlin in *The Water Beetle.*

"One should never tell people one loves them without asking their forgiveness." Henri de Montherlant in *The Girls.*

"'I would stay on the mainland if I could be certain that the new government will allow people to dress properly...'" An aristocrat explains his reasons for choosing Taiwan over Maoist China in Yuan-tsung Chen's *The Dragon's Village.*

"How could I have foreseen, in America, with all those firecrackers they put up your ass to give you pep and courage, that the ideal position for a man of my temperament was to look for orthographic mistakes?" Henry Miller celebrates life as a proofreader in Paris, from *Tropic of Cancer.*

The Man Who Said Fuck

The Life of Henry Miller

Lincoln MacVeagh

Norman Mailor published *The Naked And The Dead* in 1948. It's a decent book, but anyone who reads it today can't help but notice the falseness of much of the dialogue. The story is about a desperate band of GI's and the word constantly on their lips is "frig." Were it not for Henry Miller soldiers might still be saying "frig" today.

Miller was the first thoughtful man to use the word "fuck" in print. It sounds like an easy thing to do, but it took nerve. Respectability can be hard to shake off and Miller spent years writing with a thesaurus at his side before he learned to say what he wanted with simple four-letter words.

Henry Miller was born in 1891 and he grew up in a lively, middle-class section of immigrant Brooklyn. His family was German on both sides. Miller's father was a genial and unambitious tailor who drank too much. His mother was a high-strung woman who felt put upon. Miller's younger sister Lauretta was retarded.

Miller's childhood was a mixed bag. On the one hand he was an energetic boy, popular with his friends and doted on by his parents. Whatever he asked for he got, and at times he suspected that the world was in a vast conspiracy to please him. Overwhelmed by his good fortune he once spent an afternoon distributing all his toys to other children in the neighborhood.

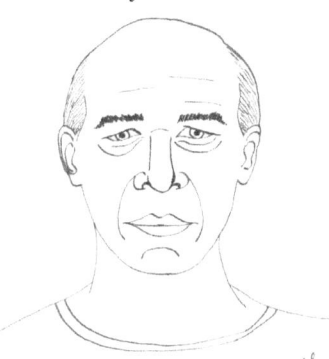

"Keep off the grass! That's the motto people live by."

But life at home could also be dreary. Miller's mother made him go back and collect all his toys and he remembered her as a cold-hearted and difficult woman: *"I'll never forget my mother standing over Lauretta in the kitchen, trying to teach her the simplest things on a little blackboard. In one hand she had a piece of chalk, in the other a ruler... It always ended up with a beating, then mother would turn to me with this exasperated look on her face, and she'd throw her hands up in despair."*

It was equally depressing when Miller's father returned from work: *"Every night he'd come home drunk and have constant rows with my mother. There were always scenes at supper, and it wasn't long before the two of them would start to scrap. And I'd begin to gag. It's a disorder I've suffered from for years; I'd start eating and my throat would get constricted."* Miller invented much of his own suffering for effect, but this story about gagging at the sight of food appears to be true.

Not surprisingly Miller liked to get out of the house, and at school he was an excellent student. Although his family was not remotely literate – Miller's father confiscated his copy of Balzac's *The Wild Ass* thinking it was dirty – Miller was an avid reader. As a young child he used to read out loud while his grandfather worked cutting cloth in the tailor shop, and as a teenager

Miller developed a vision of himself as an intellectual. *"I can't quite believe,"* he wrote to a friend, *"that I am capable of writing anything worthwhile and yet, for the life of me, I can't repress the desire to put my thoughts down on paper."*

Leaving high school, Miller applied for a scholarship to Cornell but was turned down and went to City College. Perhaps because his pride was hurt, Miller did poorly and he dropped out after only one semester in favor of a variety of odd jobs. Miller's parents pushed him to become a tailor but he was determined not to. He gave piano lessons instead and it was through the mother of one of his students that he met Pauline Chateau.

Miller had been with hookers before but Pauline was his first girlfriend. She was ten years older than Miller and he lived with her for almost two years. He liked her but he was never much good with women. To be more precise, Miller was strong on the thrust and weak on the parry. When he finally grew tired of Pauline he couldn't think how to break it off. He told her he was off to pan for gold in Alaska and went to hide out in his parents' house.

Miller's next girlfriend was Beatrice. Beatrice got pregnant and Miller paid for her abortion. He did not think of marriage until the first war came along. In *Tropic of Capricorn*, Miller records a friend's advice: *"'Get married, you silly bastard, and you'll be deferred.'"* Miller took the advice and Beatrice got pregnant again. Now with a wife and a daughter, Miller was aiming at respectability and he wangled a job as the hiring manager for Western Union in New York.

Miller was a company man for five years and for the most part he was a reliable employee. Though he went on to deny any interest in business, one surviving memo suggests that he took his job fairly seriously. The memo outlined a number of initiatives that could help keep more messenger boys on staff: *"... as a policy of business, not as a matter of sentimental humanitarianism, the Company must make the boy feel that he is more than*

"Dina, will you marry me?"

a mere cog in the wheel. He must be made to feel that the Company is concerned with his welfare."

During a vacation from Western Union Miller wrote his first novel. It was a surrealistic version of the Horatio Alger story. At the time, and for many years afterward, Miller believed in the romantic notion that great art must be purely spontaneous and he was so eager to prove his genius that he worked himself into a frenzy. He used every ten dollar word he knew and he wrote at the pace of eight thousand words a day. The book was finished in less than two weeks and even Miller knew it was unreadable: *"Everyone I showed it to said it was terrible."*

Nonetheless, the effort fired his imagination and made him increasingly impatient with his routine. He came to loathe his work, and he was unhappy with his wife. Miller and Beatrice were ill-matched and they fought constantly. Among other things, Beatrice didn't like his use of foul language during sex. Miller started looking for a way out.

In the summer of 1923 he found his escape by falling violently in love with a beautiful taxi girl named June Edith Smith. He promptly divorced his wife, quit his job, and married June. Unlike Beatrice, June was contemptuous of all things bourgeois and one of her great attractions was she encouraged Miller to think of himself as a brilliant writer. Another attraction was that she didn't wear panties.

Miller married June to save himself from a death by inches, but having done so it turned out that he wasn't best suited to the bohemian life either. He found it impossible to bring June to heel. He argued about her smoking in public and he complained about her not cleaning the apartment. June only laughed at him. Eventually June brought a lesbian friend home to live with them, and desperate for attention, Miller swallowed some sleeping pills in a half-hearted suicide attempt. June came home, read the suicide note, and woke Miller up. Straightaway she lit a cigarette and started chatting with her friend.

Lesbians aside, Miller's greatest worry was money. He continued to write but no one would buy his work. He sold encyclopaedias door to door; he sold chocolates at nightclubs; he opened a speakeasy. Everything failed and Miller had to rely on the money June made as a professional flirt.

June could always find rich old men to fall for her and one of them was Pop Roland, a joke writer for the *New Yorker* cartoonist Peter Arno. June told Roland she was a writer and sold him Miller's stories as her own. She even persuaded Roland to buy the full manuscript to Miller's inane second novel *Molloch*. Roland paid June enough to finance a trip to Europe and then he quietly killed himself for want of her affection.

Miller traveled to Paris with June in 1927. They stayed six months and when they got back to New York it was clear to both of them that their marriage was all over but the shouting. In 1929 June sent Miller back to Paris by himself.

Miller was forty years old and for the first time in his life he was alone. He examined himself. He had little money and few friends. He'd tried life as a working man and hated it. He'd tried life as a bohemian and hated it. He was about finished with his third novel and it was just as awful as the last two. He was a failure and the future in front of him was as bleak as the past behind. Some people would have reached for the knife, but Miller kept looking and finally he saw something startling. He was happy:

"Somehow the realization that nothing was to be hoped for had a salutary effect upon me. For weeks and months, for years, in fact, all my life I had been looking forward to something happening, some extrinsic event

that would alter my life, and now suddenly, inspired by the absolute hopelessness of everything, I felt relieved, felt as though a great burden had been lifted from my shoulders."

Miller had finally found his subject and in the years roughly between 1931 and 1938 he produced three remarkable books: *Tropic of Cancer, Tropic of Capricorn* and the short work *Quiet Days In Clichy*. In these books Miller writes under control. He no longer trusts his writing to spontaneous inspiration. Having learned the value of editing, he goes so far as to mock his earlier aesthetic pretensions. In *Tropic of Cancer* Mr. Wren is the man who thinks as he goes along: " '*He thinks as he goes along' – very charming, charming indeed, as Borowski would say, but really very painful, particularly when the thinker is nothing but a spavined horse.*"

At the center of Miller's best books is the idea that nothing matters in life except his own enthusiasm for it. "*One can live without friends, one can live without love, or even without money, that supposed sine qua non.*" It's a beautiful idea, but the obvious corollary is that one can live without good books as well, and Miller seems to have recognized this.

Almost immediately after finishing *Tropic of Capricorn*, he abandoned his

control and returned to writing whatever gibberish he pleased: "*I obey only my own instincts and intuitions. I know nothing in advance. Often I put down things which I do not understand myself, secure in the knowledge that later they will become clear and meaningful to me.*" Charming indeed, but really very painful.

The rest of Miller's life is little more than a story of celebrity. In 1940, after a decade in Europe, Miller returned to the United States and went to live high up on the cliffs in Big Sur, California. He entertained himself with writing, painting, ping-pong and falling in love.

Miller married three times in California. The wives were Lepska, Eve and Hoki. Miller was seventy six when he married the twenty seven year old Hoki. Much to Miller's disappointment, the marriage was never consummated but there were always other girls. At the age of eighty-three, Miller struck up an erotic correspondence with the young actress Brenda Venus (her real name). He wrote her more than 1,500 tripey letters: "*God give me the power, the strength, and I will kiss you endlessly.*"

Miller had little trouble finding women because he was already famous when he arrived in California. *Tropic of Cancer* and *Tropic of Capricorn* were both published in France in the 1930's, and although the books were not publicly available in America, imported copies were sold under the counter throughout country. The obvious intelligence of the books, along with the ban on their publication, made Miller into a minor cult figure.

"*Listen*," says Kronski in *Tropic of Capricorn*, "*why do you run around with all these dumb bastards you pick up? You seem to have a genius for picking up the wrong people.*" Even as an unknown in Brooklyn, Miller attracted his share of hangers on and as a censored writer living on a cliff top he was inundated with admirers. Alfred Perlès, Miller's old Paris flatmate, was unimpressed. He once described Miller's Big Sur crowd as a bunch of "*genial morons.*"

Miller seems not to have minded. He liked people generally and he thought it natural to be surrounded by acolytes. One gets a sense of Miller's new regime from an interview conducted by his friend Georges Belmont:

Belmont: The least that one can say is that you have an awe-inspiring facility for hearing the world's echo, and that of other people, in your own inner resonance.

Miller: Yes, that's true.

Miller was by no means as tiresome as the above snippet makes him sound, but he did like acting the sage and he was always open to the possibility that he possessed special powers of insight. This led to all sorts of nonsense, most notably a growing interest in astrology. Writing about the war, Miller says: "*The date most commonly agreed upon (by professional prophets) for the end of this war is the fall of 1947.*" He goes on to analyze Hitler from an astrological perspective: "*With Hitler Pluto came out into the open.*"

Far from hearing the world's echo, Miller was singularly deaf to any voice but his own. He couldn't see past his own nose. He had no sense at all of other people and the funniest proof of his obtuseness is the story of a visit he once paid to Eudora Welty.

When Miller first returned to the States he was still hard up and he supported himself partly by writing erotica for private collectors. Miller found the work easy and he called on Welty with the intention of letting her in on the business. He wrote to Welty of the money to be made and of the "*unfailing pornographic market.*" Welty and her mother were horrified. Miller stayed three days in Mississippi, and the prim Miss Welty made sure there were always at least two chaperones with her whenever he was around.

Self-absorption is the only possible explanation for a man who tried to sell Eudora Welty on writing pornography. Miller was an egotist first and last. In the right light Miller's egotism looked like genius; in the wrong light it looked like mere boorishness; and Miller was enough of an egotist not to care about the difference.

Reviews

The Worst Journey In The World

by Apsley Cherry-Garrard

Carroll & Graf, 1997 (reprint)

In 1909 Captain R.F. Scott announced plans for his second Antarctic expedition. He aimed to reach the South Pole, and more than 8,000 volunteers signed up to join him. Apsley Cherry-Garrard was the youngest and least experienced of the twenty-five men chosen. *The Worst Journey In The World* is Cherry's record of the expedition.

Although everything about Scott's polar expedition was pretty awful, Cherry's title refers specifically to a short, exploratory trip he undertook with Bill Wilson and Birdie Bowers in search of an Emperor penguin's egg. Wilson was the leader of the trip. He was the expedition's naturalist and he wanted to collect embryonic eggs from the Emperor penguins because he believed that they might contain important clues about the history of evolution.

The difficulty was that the only known Emperor rookery was some seventy miles away and the penguins nested in winter. There's no daylight in the Antarctic winter and no one had ever tried winter travelling before. Collecting an egg meant a three month trek through perfect darkness and horrible cold. After two weeks out, Cherry notes down the thermometer readings: "*That night the temperature was −75°; at breakfast −70°; at noon nearly −77°.*"

Remarkably, the men made it back to camp with a egg in tact, and the last scene in the drama of the penguin's egg took place at the British Museum of Natural History. Back in London, Cherry went to present the museum with his egg. The first custodian he met with wouldn't have it. Nor would the second. Finally Cherry found the right curator, but the curator was busy with other things. Distracted, he told Cherry to leave the egg on his desk. He didn't have time to write out a receipt.

There is something very English about risking death for the sake of a penguin's egg and there is something very English about all the men Cherry intruduces us to. Titus Oates, for example, was Scott's expert on animal husbandry. Cherry first describes him as follows: "*Titus Oates was the most cheerful and lovable old pessimist that you could imagine.*"

Later we see Titus at a Christmas party celebrating the first grueling year in Antarctica: "*Titus got three things which pleased him immensely, a sponge, a whistle, and a pop-gun which went off when he pressed the butt... 'If you want to please me very much you will fall down when I shoot you,' he said to me, and then he went round shooting everybody.*"

The last we see of Oates is with Captain Scott on the tragic journey back from the South Pole. Oates, Scott and three others marched 81 days to reach the pole. When they got there they discovered that the Norwegian explorer Roald Amundsen had beaten them by more than a month. They turned home exhausted and on the return, Oates got frostbite in his foot.

The foot became gangrenous and Oates was no longer able to keep up the march. Afraid of holding the others back, he woke up in the middle of the night: "*A thick blizzard was blowing, and he said, after a bit, 'Well, I am just going outside, and I may be some time.'*"

Oates killed himself on March 17, 1913. Two weeks later Scott and the rest of his men died frozen in their sleeping bags. A search party went out to look for them the following spring and found their bodies just eleven miles away from the base camp. Cherry-Garrard tells the whole story brilliantly.

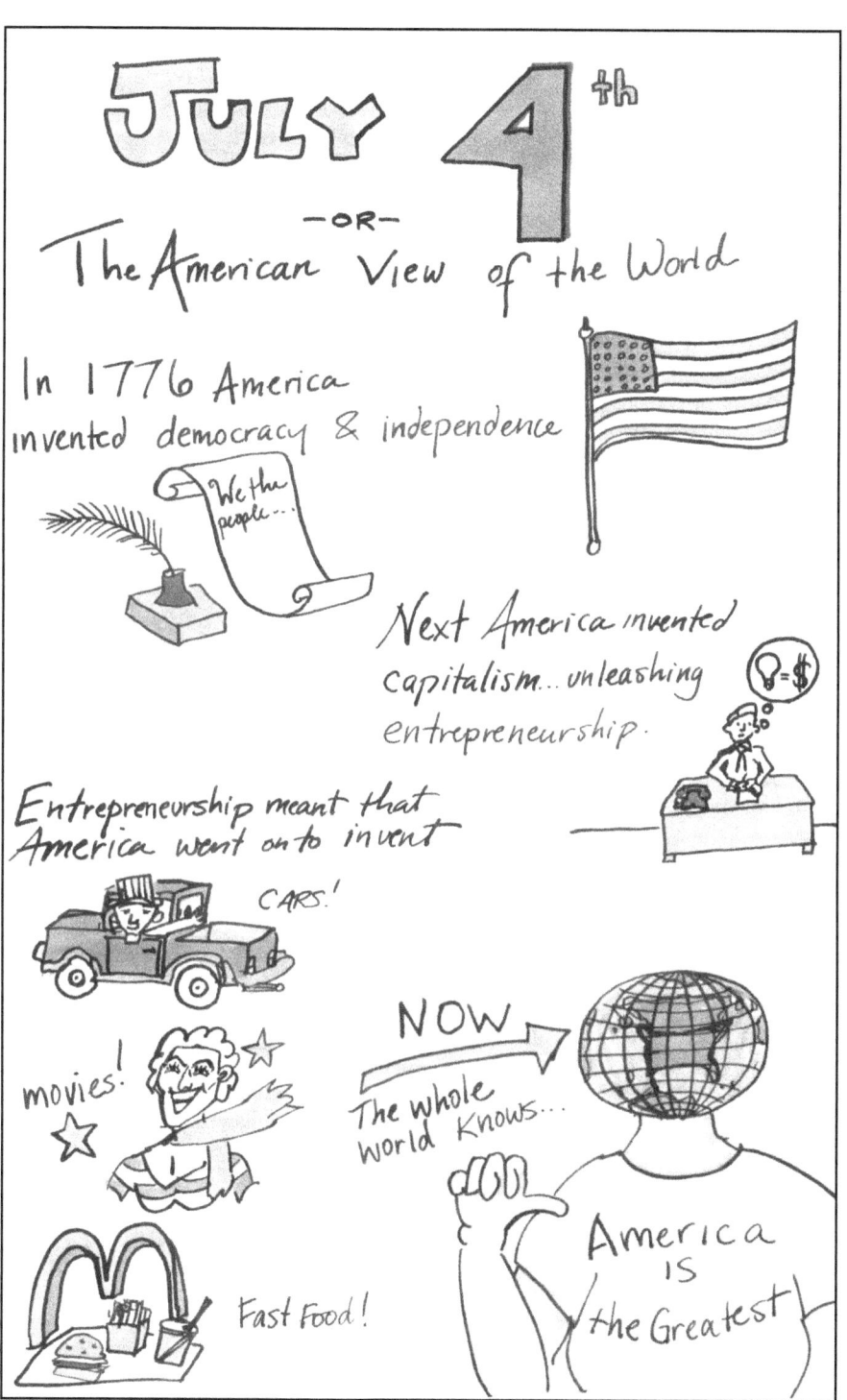

Commentary

The Perfect Life

T.E. MacVeagh

There is a myth that many believe although few admit. It is the myth that wretchedness, desperation and humiliation are experiences that may be avoided. It is the myth that failure need play no part in one's own life. It is the myth of the "Perfect Life."

The professional résumés of the educated elite are structured like graphs showing constant growth. A stellar high school record leads to an elite college. College achievement precedes an impressive graduate school. Each subsequent job is but a stepping stone to a new position of greater influence. Slowly but inevitably, everything leads to professional preeminence and a role of leadership within the community.

Personal résumés are created to show the same logarithmic progress: from good friends to a better spouse; from a happy marriage to happier kids; from a couple of children to multiple adorable grandchildren.

The myth of the Perfect Life is that the details of an actual life can mirror such an uncomplicated chain of successes. It is the myth that the movement from point to point goes in a straight line, inching upwards at each step. Believing in the myth, one imagines that one can achieve a life without rejection or self-doubt. A life free from hurt. A life in which one is never forced to start from scratch, never pursued by the black dog of depression, never stand exposed in one's folly to the scorn of the world.

If the myth seems ludicrous, it is also compelling. Only by achieving the Perfect Life can we justify the tremendous resources that have been spent on us, the love that has been showered on us, the education we have been granted, and the material benefits we have enjoyed. The Perfect Life also confirms our congratulatory estimates of our own self-worth. And only the Perfect Life can prevent the burning jealously we would otherwise feel towards those who are more successful or fortunate than ourselves.

Indeed the myth is so compelling that not only do people arrange their lives so as to achieve some version of the Perfect Life, they constantly rearrange their memories so as to be able to perceive their life as a constant series of forward progressions. Did they fail to make their high school varsities? Very well, athletics were of little interest to them. Have they been less successful in amorous adventures than their fellows? Their high moral standards required fidelity to one person alone. Did they hate their internship at the investment bank? The work clashed with their socialist ideals.

If we are sophisticated enough, perhaps we realize that embracing the myth does us no credit. Believing in the Perfect Life is as silly as believing in the tooth fairy. It would be hubris to strive for it. We understand that a Perfect Life is a boring one. Our friends and associates do not want to hear the litany of our successes. Our failures and flops make for more amusing stories.

And yet, for all of that, it is hard to let go of the myth. We live tensely, filled with a lingering dread that the Perfect Life is passing us by. The quest for perfection wizens and deforms us. It squeezes our ambition into narrow paths; it shrinks our social lives to safe and known circles. Success does not bring happiness because it seems like the minimum due, and in our fear of failure, we miss rich opportunities and rewarding experiences. In our terror of the average, we lose our natural resiliency.

Belief in the Perfect Life stems from a failure of imagination which is very hard to overcome. It is the same failure of imagination which makes it so difficult to make career choices. Do you want to be a fireman or a corporate lawyer? One thinks something like: "Well, would I rather be a simple-living stud muffin, jumping through burning windows to save infants, or would I prefer to lounge around air-conditioned New York skyscrapers in double-breasted Freeman-Hickey suits while powerful business interests hang on my sage advice." Never mind that it would be more relevant to ask whether you would rather spend your nights driving to false alarms in a ridiculous plastic suit or photocopying documents in order to make a 3:00 a.m. courier-service deadline.

The remarkable thing is that this decision-making process may change little even if we have actual experience as both a fireman and a lawyer. We continue to judge on the basis of these absurd, flattened stereotypes. It is strangely difficult to view life three-dimensionally.

Similarly our image of success and happiness is often little more than a snapshot of a résumé. We picture Bill Gates fleecing IBM, or Tiger Woods pumping his fist after the Masters. We do not imagine them lying awake at night, in panic or misery, crying about their own inadequacy. Even if we do, we cannot believe these parts of their lives are terribly important.

It is the same with our own lives. It is difficult to integrate the good and the bad into a single picture. Rather, we see the good and believe our lives might be perfect. Then we experience the bad and believe all is lost. The process of turning our experience into a single rich and varied story is an important step in gaining wisdom, but it is not easy.

Great novels can help. One of the ways you can distinguish between real and escapist literature is to ask yourself whether the story manages to present a vision of the world in which good and bad are hopelessly intermingled, or whether, in contrast, it presents a battle between the poles. Authors like Tolstoy, Proust, Woolf and Maughm provide models of the integration of experience which we should seek in our own lives.

Friend, Girlfriend, Maid & Flan

Lincoln MacVeagh

My friend Andrew used to live in a cozy duplex apartment on East 76th Street. The place was bursting with furniture and the walls of the apartment were decorated with pictures, antique guns and a few swords in their scabbards. Two stuffed ducks hung from the ceiling downstairs and there was even a stuffed armadillo on the floor next to the sofa. The whole apartment was littered with countless silver trinkets. It must have been a nightmare to clean.

Fortunately, Andrew had a maid. Her name was Carmona and she was Spanish, from Madrid. She was industrious woman and she kept Andrew's apartment in very good order. He felt he was lucky to have her.

Ingrid, Andrew's new girlfriend, felt differently. Ingrid moved in with Andrew after the first few months and it soon became clear that she and Carmona didn't get on. It wasn't Ingrid's fault. Carmona simply didn't like her.

One day when Andrew was out Carmona found a cheap gold bracelet on the floor.

"Is dees your bracelet, sweetie?" Carmona looked very pleased with herself and waved the bracelet in front of Ingrid's face.

"I've never seen it before."

"But I find it under the sofa." Carmona smiled condescendingly and tossed her head. "Never mind. It must belong to a different girlfriend."

Carmona could be quite poisonous and since she felt certain that she would outlast Ingrid, she behaved without compunction. One morning the phone rang and it was Andrew's mother. Ingrid was in the bathroom when Carmona picked up.

"Andrew not here," said Carmona. "Who? You want to speak with the girl? Which girl? There is a girl, but I can never remember their names."

On another occasion Ingrid baked Andrew an apple pie. Ingrid left the apartment and Carmona came in to clean. Andrew offered Carmona a piece of pie.

"Where you get this pie?" she said. "It's deeleeecious."

"Ingrid made it."

Carmona laughed at his naiveté. "Nooooo... Ingrid never make this pie."

"She did. She made it with her own two hands."

"That's what she tell you? And you believe it? No, Ingrid never make this pie. It's so deeleeecious."

Ingrid was frustrated by the fact that her boyfriend's maid didn't like her and she tried to win Carmona over. She was unfailingly polite and she took to cleaning the apartment thoroughly on the mornings before Carmona came. Carmona warmed up a touch.

In December Andrew threw his annual Christmas party. The party was set for a Thursday night and Andrew made special arrangements with Carmona to come twice that week, both on Thursday to clean before the party and on Friday, to clean up afterwards. Carmona was agreeable. She even seemed excited by the idea of a party.

"I make you a flan. I make you a beautiful flan."

"You mustn't trouble yourself."

"Is no trouble. I make you a beautiful flan. You will love it."

Fair enough, thought Andrew. He had no idea that Carmona was planning to make flan for sixty. When she showed up on Thursday morning, the flan was so big she needed help carrying it up the stairs. It was five gallons of stiff yellow custard in a large white plastic bucket.

"How kind of you," said Ingrid.

That night, Ingrid set up for the

party. She put the drinks on one table and the food on another. She laid out a few cups and spoons and put the bucket of flan next to the oers d'oevres.

The Christmas party was a great success. It was a young crowd and everyone drank and smoked too much. Andrew went to the office feeling quite groggy the next morning and he left Ingrid in bed recovering from a hangover.

Ingrid didn't need to be at work until later in the day and she rolled lazily out of bed at ten thirty. Carmona was coming to clean at eleven and the apartment was in such a dreadful state that for once Ingrid was happy to have her. Ingrid showered and dressed, and she was just about out the door when she took a last glance around at the mess. She gasped.

Carmona's bucket of flan looked awful. Only one of the five gallons of custard had been eaten and there were big divots in it where people had dug their spoons in. Much worse, someone had used the bucket as an ashtray. A thin pool of red wine had collected on the surface of the yellow custard, and cigarette butts floated lazily about in it.

Ingrid put her bag down and sprung into action. The bucket had to be cleaned out before Carmona arrived and Ingrid faced a daunting question. How does one get rid of four gallons of flan?

She lugged the flan into the kitchen and threw some of it into the sink. This was a bad idea. The sink clogged immediately and Ingrid realized that it would take hours to stuff the whole thing down the drain. She rushed to the bathroom and tried flushing it down the toilet.

The flan, however, was stubborn and refused to go without a fight. The whirling flushing action broke up the large chunks of custard into small pieces and a thick crust of flan stayed floating on the toilet water even after repeated flushes. Ingrid's heart was racing.

She scooped the crust of flan out of the toilet and ran to the cupboard for a garbage bag. She dumped the bucket upside down into the bag but the flan wouldn't budge. It clung to the sides of the bucket and Ingrid had to dig it out with her hands to get it loose.

Task accomplished, Ingrid rinsed out the bucket, washed her hands and she once again was about to leave for work when she realized that the garbage bag, being white, was completely transparent. She couldn't leave it in the apartment. She had to take it outside immediately.

The garbage bag was very heavy and just managing to pick it up, Ingrid carried it awkwardly downstairs. Still holding the bag at arm's length, she stepped backwards through the front door onto the street. She turned around and almost hit Carmona square in the stomach.

"Hi!"

Carmona walked directly past her without saying a word.

The rest of the story is something of a mystery. When Andrew came home at five o'clock, the apartment was still in a shambles. Carmona had not lifted a finger to clean it and though in subsequent weeks he tried repeatedly to contact her, he never managed to get in touch. Carmona never worked for Andrew again. Ingrid didn't mind at all.

Games

Sir
Laffalot

Sir Laffalot once sat for a job interview with an advertising agency. He wanted to be a copywriter. After making very little money off his masterpiece of suspense, *The Darkness of the Duke's Back Passage*, it seemed to him a wonderful thing to get paid a living wage for writing simple three word sentences like Coke Is It, and Carlton Is Lowest.

"Point of purchase," said Sir Laffalot, "Consumer direct. A go-getter. A self-starter. Work well in a group. A real people person."

The man in the seersucker suit was impressed and he flipped through Sir Laffalot's portfolio with a thoughtful smile on his face. He asked about salary requirements and work experience, and having received satisfactory answers on both points, it looked like the job was in the bag. Then the man leaned back in his leather swivel chair and hit Sir Laffalot right between the eyes.

"What is your greatest weakness?"

Sir Laffalot gulped. He'd never given the question much thought, and now that it was staring him in the face he couldn't come up with anything. Vanity, gluttony, body odor? Sir Laffalot felt that he needed something more commonplace. Bingo!

"I drink," he said cheerfully, "I like to sneak a glass of whiskey before lunch."

"Oh dear," said the man, "You're meant to say you're too much of a perfectionist. Or else obsessive attention to detail. I'm afraid sneaking whiskey isn't in the cards. Thanks for coming in."

Sir Laffalot felt cheated, especially since he'd made up the drinking just to have something to say. He slammed his portfolio in the trash, left the build-ing in a huff, and hoping to forget the interview, he jogged over to a *Mr. Softee* truck. Still, however, he couldn't stop pondering the question of his greatest weakness. Sir Laffalot wondered what it was.

How does one discover one's own failings? The cynic says the solution is simple: just ask a friend. Sir Laffalot, however, is a sensitive fellow and he's wary of losing his friends. Although he knows that everyone has faults, he doesn't like to have his own faults pointed out. Not even in a nice way.

Let that be a warning. This month's game is *Greatest Weakness Charades* and when playing it, one must proceed with caution.

Greatest Weakness Charades: How to Play.

1) Everyone writes down their greatest weakness (such as forgetfulness, randiness, snobbery) on a strip of paper. The papers are put into a hat and jumbled up.

2) As in charades, players pick a paper from the hat and act out the weakness for the group.

3) Once the weakness is guessed, the next step is to guess whose weakness it is. Be careful!

4) Continue playing until all the weaknesses have been acted out.

Sir Laffalot says: TOODALOO!!

Continued from page 16
with dogs and as if on cue, the dogs ran out the door (back to the hell that spawned them). Brad caught his breath on the edge of my bed. He was sweaty and covered in dog slobber. His Pittsburgh Pirates boxer shorts were imprinted with rows of little pirate heads, each with its own moustache and eye-patch. He asked softly if I was okay, and seemed to want to stay, but I told him I was exhausted, and started putting my pajamas on.

Before I turned off the lamp by my bed, I noticed a photo in a gilded antique frame. I figured it must be of the man that Tony used to own an antique store with. The man was sporting a handlebar moustache, and I remembered hearing that he died of an unnamed ailment in the early 1980's. I could hear the TV going downstairs as I sneaked down the hall to peek into Brad's bedroom. There was no bed, just a set of drums that looked like they hadn't been played in a while, and some dumbbells.

The next day, I slept in while Tony and Brad went to buy my Grandmother a mink coat. The house was empty when I woke up, and I decided to heat some coffee, and search the bookshelves for some definitive clues. I wasn't sure what I was looking for, maybe *The City and the Pillar* by Gore Vidal, or Edmund White's *A Boys own Story*, or *Down there on a Visit* by Christopher Isherwood. Something to put my curiosity to rest so I could pursue more worthwhile obsessions.

All I found, however, was titles like *Tobacco Road, Cannery Row,* and *War and Remembrance.* I managed to unearth *Other Voices, Other Rooms* by Truman Capote, but it looked as though nobody had ever cracked the spine. I was still reading in a high backed chair when they came home. I heard my Grandmother excuse herself to the bathroom, while Tony and Brad took off their coats in the foyer. They couldn't see me, and they started to trade cruel impersonations of the effeminate man who sold them the mink coat. They started lisping and prancing and swishing to beat the band, but it wasn't funny. I put the book back on the shelf, thoroughly confounded.

The next day was my Grandmothers birthday, and we spent the afternoon with Tony, visiting the Smithsonian and the Washington Monument. Afterwards, we had reservations at a posh restaurant (Tony lent me a suit), and Brad was supposed to meet us there.

Brad was late and we ordered drinks. Grandma and I were happy as clams, sipping our drinks and munching breadsticks, but Tony was very tense. An hour passed. Tony said he didn't want to order until Brad arrived because it would ruin the special day he had planned.

Tony's anxiety was contagious, and we were relieved to see Brad finally come through the door. He wasn't dressed up like we were, (just a Polo shirt and jeans), and he didn't have the flowers that Tony had asked him to bring. He sat down as if he wasn't late at all, and Tony went ballistic, slamming both fists down on the table.

"I can't believe you're pulling this crap again!"

"What crap?"

"No respect! I'm disappointed in your behavior!"

"I don't have to take this!"

"It's the last time!"

They went on and on, and all my Grandmother and I could do was stare ahead in mortification. All the other people in the restaurant had stopped in mid-bite to watch the spectacle.

And it was a spectacle. Two strong men – Air Force men – fighting like only a husband and wife can. And that was how I knew for sure.

After we got back to the house I went to give my Grandmother a kiss goodnight. On my way out the door she gave a bemused sigh and said, "Tony has a houseboy."

The high life

WONDER

David Garcia III

My father has two brothers, Bob and Tony. My whole life, Bob was constantly over at our house (he actually lives with my parents now), but Tony kept his distance. Bob was like a happy dog always wanting to play; Tony was the mysterious cat that peeks in your window and runs. We received Christmas gifts from Tony, and talked on the phone occasionally, but not much else. He was always a source of curiosity for me.

When I was fresh out of college I was invited to tag along with my Grandmother to spend a week visiting Tony in Washington D.C.. Tony had been a Major in the Air Force before he retired young to work "in computers." He had a lovely house stocked with tasteful antiques, and two enormous Chesapeake Bay Terriers (dogs originally bred to hunt polar bears off ice floes). He also had a housemate named Brad.

Brad was younger, but also retired from the Air Force. He didn't have a job, unless you counted playing with the dogs, driving Tony's BMW, and watching videos. He was hyperactive, had a gravelly voice, and a thick-necked build like a weightlifter. I thought that Tony and Brad might be boyfriends, but I decided that they were just too macho.

The first night of our visit we got all dressed up to see *Les Misérables* at the Kennedy Center. The play was enjoyable enough, but it couldn't compare with the intermission. After hitting the restroom, I stopped at the top of a staircase to stare down at an enormous clay head. It was supposed to resemble JFK, but was really one of the most putrid examples of public art that I had ever seen. I turned to go downstairs, and there at the bottom of the staircase was Linda Carter (TV's Wonder Woman) staring up at me. She was dressed in black, seemed about eight feet tall, and was stunningly beautiful. She glanced over at the sculpture, rolled her eyes, and hit me with the kind of smile that a young man takes to his grave.

After the play, we went back to Tony's house to look at slides of statues and flowers that he had taken with his expensive camera equipment. When it was time for bed, Brad decided to stay up and watch horror videos. Brad told us that he had his own room, but he usually wound up crashing on the couch after a night of TV.

I was getting undressed in my room, and the moment I was down to my underwear there was a huge commotion coming up the stairs. It sounded like the running of the bulls in Pamplona. A second later, the door burst open and the two dogs came barreling in, knocking me onto the bed. As they started to maul me, in came Brad, clad only in boxers. He pulled me from the grip of the beasts, and then jumped on the bed and began wrestling with them.

The dogs were biting down on his arms, and for a second I was afraid that they were going to hurt him. Then I realized that this is just what jocks do

Continued on page 15

The
ECLECTIC

| August 2000 | Volume 2 Number 6 | Free |

CONTENTS

Quotations

"Truth and reason are common to everyone, and no more belong to the person who first spoke them than to the man who spoke them later. It is no more according to Plato than according to me, since he and I understand and see it in the same way." Montaigne in his essay *Of the education of children.*

"Thinking – as General Conyers used to insist – damages feeling. No doubt he had got the idea from a book. That did not make it less valid." Anthony Powell echoes Montaigne in the 4th volume of *A Dance To The Music of Time.*

"Now it cannot be denied that the homosexual has a narrower outlook on the world than the normal man." Somerset Maugham discusses El Greco's sexuality in *Don Fernando.*

"You see, I was a quarter normal and three-quarters queer, but I tried to persuade myself it was the other way round. That was my great mistake." Maugham discusses his own sexuality with his nephew Robin in *Conversations With Willie.*

The Eclectic is owned and published by Linoleum Palace, Inc., 43-05 31st Ave., #2, Astoria, NY 11103. Copyright © 1999 by Lincoln MacVeagh. All rights reserved. Unsolicited submissions will not be considered or returned.

Books

Somerset & Mrs. Maugham

The Untold Story of a Marriage

Lincoln MacVeagh

Somerset Maugham wrote more good books than anyone else in the 20th century. His last book was a collection of autobiographical anecdotes called *Looking Back.* Maugham started writing it in his late eighties and he is said to have written it twice. After finishing an initial draft, Maugham decided the book was too revealing and he burned it. Later the publisher Lord Beaverbrook got wind of the missing manuscript and he offered Maugham £75,000 to rewrite it. The money persuaded him.

"She made my life utter hell."

Looking Back first came out in three issues of the American magazine *Show.* It ran from June through August of 1962 and attracted little attention. Later it was serialized again in London's *Sunday Express* and this second serialization caused an uproar. Maugham's old friend Noel Coward was so offended that he said of the author, *"I don't think I want to see him again."* Maugham's publisher began to worry that *Looking Back* would hurt Muagham's public image and dampen sales of his other books. A libel suit was threatened. Under pressure, Maugham withdrew his memoir and it has never appeared since.

For the most part *Looking Back* is innocuous. Maugham talks briefly of his mother; he remembers Winston Churchill; and he repeats much of what he'd already said about Christianity. The controversy surrounding the book centered solely on Maugham's comments about his ex-wife, Syrie. Syrie had been dead for seven years but she was still a popular figure in London society and those who remembered her fondly, Noel Coward among them, were shocked by Maugham's unflattering depiction of her.

The shock was the greater because in all Maugham's other books he steers clear of Syrie. When her name does come up, he invariably describes her as a physically attractive woman, vivacious and with exquisitely good taste. In *The Summing Up* he says only that Syrie was an interior decorator, and he commends her for having been the first person to design all white interiors, a style which became a craze in the thirties. Maugham leaves the impression that his marriage ended amicably, and for the same reason that most marriages do, simply because husband and wife had grown apart.

In *Looking Back* Maugham paints a different picture. Syrie is still beautiful and she still has good taste, but she's also breathtakingly shallow and almost criminally dishonest. Maugham tells of giving Syrie an expensive jade necklace from China. She took it to Paris with her and returned to England sobbing. She'd lost her necklace in the Louvre:

"'Fortunately, you'd insured it,' I said. The insurance people paid up. About a year later one of the officials in the insurance company was in Paris and happened to stroll along the rue de la Paix. He stopped to look at the window of a jeweler's shop. The first thing he saw, handsomely presented, was the jade necklace. He went in and asked the salesman how they had come by it. He was told that it had been sold to them by Madame Maugham." Syrie comes off as a money grubbing social climber and Maugham seems determined to make it clear that his marriage ended not simply because he grew apart from his wife, but because he detested her.

I have always been curious about Maugham's marriage. Although he never admitted it in print, Maugham lived the last forty-five years of his life as a homosexual. I always thought that Maugham's marriage was a straightforward business proposition, a sham designed to protect his reputation. It was more complicated than that.

To begin with, Maugham was not exclusively homosexual. The sex lives of other people are hard to understand and to make it easier on ourselves we tend to assume that people must be either straight or gay, and those who claim to be bisexual are widely thought to be faking half of it. Whether or not this analysis is generally true, in Maugham's case it doesn't seem to fit. "I'm bisexual," he once said to his nephew quite straightforwardly, "but for the sake of my reputation I don't care to advertise the fact. But as you know, I've loved boys and I've loved girls, I've loved women and I've loved men."

Maugham had good reasons for not wishing to be an out and out homosexual. He was born in 1874 and he was twenty-one when his idol Oscar Wilde was sent to prison for sodomy; a short while later his older brother, also a homosexual writer, committed suicide by swallowing a bottle of nitric acid. Undoubtedly these tragedies persuaded Maugham to fight against his taste for men, but at the same time, his taste for women does not look like a simple put on. In a number of his books Maugham described a youth busy with heterosexual affairs, and in *Looking Back* he writes convincingly of his long running involvement with the actress Ethelwyn Jones, whom he calls "Rosie."

Maugham's affair with Rosie was a happy one. "One evening, after we had dined together at a restaurant, I took her

"You're saying they buy and wear clothes they can't even wash?"

back to my single room in Pall Mall. I became her lover. On the way back in the hansom to where she lived she asked me how long the affair would last. 'Six weeks,' I answered flippantly. It lasted eight years." By the end of it, Maugham was nearing forty. He thought it was time to be married and after looking around, he settled on Rosie. He didn't care that she had slept with all his friends. He was fond of her. Maugham bought her a ring and proposed. To his dismay, Rosie turned him down. One imagines that his pride was wounded.

It was just a few months later that he met Syrie Wellcome. Syrie was the wife of a American financier, but she was much younger than her husband and she did not live with him. *"She had lovely brown eyes and beautiful skin. She was very nicely dressed in the height of fashion and wore on her fingers large cabochon emeralds. I did not then know that they were false."* Syrie was worldly and gregarious and she told amusing stories about her rich admirers. She batted her eyelids at Maugham and he was flattered. Syrie said that the terms of her separation agreement allowed her absolute freedom to do as she wished. Maugham became one of her lovers.

The affair seems to have progressed rapidly. *"One day when we had driven to Richmond and were strolling in the park she took me aback by suggesting that we should have a baby. I thought she was joking. I pointed out the difficulties it would entail. She brushed them aside. She had a younger brother, recently come back from Canada with his wife, and, since they were childless, when the baby was born they would be glad to take it and we could go to see it whenever we wanted. After three or four years she could adopt it and no one would know that she was its mother. I must confess that I was tempted; she made it all so simple and easy, and the idea of being the father of a child amused me."*

Unwise as this sounds, Syrie soon got pregnant. Her first pregnancy

ended in a miscarriage but she got pregnant again just at the start of World War I. Maugham asked her to have an abortion but Syrie refused and she went off to Italy for her confinement. Maugham resigned himself and was sent to France as an interpreter with the ambulance service. Whilst there he met a charming American drunk, eighteen years younger than himself, named Gerald Haxton. Maugham fell passionately and permanently in love, and suddenly his life became very difficult.

In 1915 Maugham went to Italy to watch Syrie give birth to their daughter Elizabeth. When the three of them returned home, Gerald joined them in England. Then Syrie's husband filed for divorce naming Maugham as co-respondent. Maugham was aghast. It turned out that Syrie's separation agreement did not give her such complete freedom after all. Custom now obligated him to marry her.

Maugham's lawyer suggested that Syrie be paid off with £30,000 but Maugham dithered. He had been an orphan himself and he was, he says, chiefly concerned about his baby: *"I could not bear to think what its future would be if I didn't marry its mother."* While he struggled to make up his mind, Syrie took the opportunity to attempt suicide by swallowing a slight overdose of veronal. Maugham was convinced. He believed that Syrie was deeply in love with him, and he promised to marry her at the end of the war.

It probably wasn't such a difficult promise to make. The end of the war must have seemed a long way off and over the next several years Maugham was kept busy with his work as a secret agent. He went to Russia with the remarkable assignment of trying to prevent the Russian revolution. He was brought close to death by an attack of tuberculosis and had to spend six months in a Scottish sanatorium. Upon recovering, he met up with Gerald and rushed off on a long trip to Tahiti. All the while, however, Syrie was waiting for him. She finally caught up with him in New York on his way back from Tahiti. It was 1920. The wedding took place at a town clerk's office in New Jersey.

It is difficult to know what Syrie thought she would get out of marrying Maugham: money probably, and the status that comes from being a famous author's wife. It's even possible that Syrie loved her husband and believed that her feminine attractions would eventually prove strong enough to win his heart back from Gerald. If so, she was mistaken. Maugham steadfastly refused to give up Haxton and the result was a state of constant tension. Maugham's nephew describes a typical scene: Gerald moves an armchair to get it out of the way. Syrie notices the chair has been moved and demands that it be put back. Gerald makes as if to rise but Maugham commands him to sit down, saying that the space makes the room more comfortable. Whereupon Syrie snaps: *"It makes the room look vulgar and suburban. Put the chair back, Gerald. Now, if you please."* And so on.

Love triangles are rarely happy and Maugham's version seems to have been particularly unpleasant. The centerpiece of *Looking Back* is his account of the nightmare and Maugham presents it in the form of a letter which he claims to have written to Syrie towards the end of their married life. Maugham claims to have found the letter in an old notebook. It seems unlikely that the letter is genuine, and in some respects it is fundamentally dishonest since it completely brushes over Maugham's relationship with Haxton, but it does gives us a very good idea of how Maugham felt about his wife. Some excerpts:

"I married you because I was prepared to pay for my folly and selfishness, and I married you because I thought it the best thing for your happiness and for Elizabeth's welfare, but I did not marry you because I loved you, and you were only too well aware of that. Why now should you torment with reproaches that I do not love you?"

"Do you know that no one in all my life has said the things you have said to me? No one has ever complained of me and nagged me and harassed me as you have. How can you expect me to preserve my affection for you? You have terrorized me. Just think that at the age of forty-six, a strong, healthy enough man, I should often have to go and have a cocktail in order to face you. My dear, I was forty-three when I married you. I was too old to be treated in that way. I am too sensitive. You have lived all your life among people who say the most awful things to one another, but I haven't. It humiliates me. It makes me miserable."

"You tried to enter in my life as Madeleine W. thought she could acquire taste when she lived with Arthur Cohen, and you thought you had only to wish to become artistic and literary. I am afraid it is not as easy as that. You lacked what was essential, an interest in the things of the mind and the spirit, and your pretenses could

deceive nobody. My poor Syrie, when people are talking about books and you say, 'How extraordinary,' in different tones, do you really think you persuade them that you are using words that have any meaning to you?"

"You see, you have no resources of your own. It seems to me tragic. I am very sorry, but how can I help it. I have often thought that your attitude towards life is shown by the way you take a man's arm. Most women just rest their hand on it and the gesture is pleasant and friendly, but you throw your whole weight on the man so that in a little while he grows tired and releases himself."

"You are constantly saying that you must have this and must have that, but do you ever think of what you offer? I wonder if it occurs to you ever what a man has a right to ask of his wife and how little you give. When it comes down to brass tacks about all you do is to sit about in beautiful clothes and look picturesque. It isn't very much, is it?"

"There are only two courses open to us now. You must either accept the claim I made then for freedom to go and come when I liked, for as long as I liked and as often as I liked in peace and without scenes; or else separation. Really I am not strong enough to live a life of unhappiness, scenes and complaints, I haven't the physical strength, I should only die; I have said little enough of Elizabeth, but you know how constantly she is in my thoughts, and how much I have done in these last years for her sake. For her sake, as well as for yours and mine, I should like us to continue to live together if you can only bring yourself to a willing compromise."

The anger and sadness evident in Maugham's remarkable letter to his wife make it impossible to believe that he meant it when he wrote that he wanted to continue living with her. Obviously, he didn't want to at all. Maugham and Syrie separated and after nine years of marriage they were divorced in 1929. Syrie got a lump sum of £12,000, £2,400 a year as alimony,

a house on King's Road and a Rolls Royce. Maugham got his freedom and bought himself a new house on the French Riviera where he lived with Gerald until the start of World War II.

Gerald died in 1944 and Maugham returned to the Riviera after the war. He found a new companion in Alan Searle and Searle stayed with him for the rest of his life. It was a long life, but in all the decades after his divorce, Maugham never quite managed to forgive his ex-wife. They met only three or four times. One day during the war he ran into her in the lobby of the Dorchester Hotel. Syrie was about to sail for America and she told Maugham that she was terrified of being torpedoed. *"Then,"* he is reported to have said, *"I have only one piece of advice to offer you. Keep your mouth open, and you will drown the sooner."*

Reviews

Down There On A Visit

by Christopher Isherwood

Farrar, Straus and Giroux, 1959

It is possible to admire a book without accepting the author's judgement of his characters. You might see churlishness in Holden Caufield, or a comic side to Captain Ahab, but the important thing is that the characters come to life. In this respect *Down There On A Visit* is a great success. Isherwood draws a convincing picture of his world and his characters are undeniably real. Strangely, however, he doesn't understand them at all.

Down There On A Visit is an amalgam of four separate episodes from Isherwood's life. It spans young manhood to middle age, and in the first episode Isherwood is invited on a trip to Germany by an elderly friend of his mother's. Mr. Lancaster is full of bluff and he arranges for Isherwood's rough passage aboard a tramp steamer. *"It might just possibly make a man of you,"* says Mr. Lancaster heartily.

This is the sort of phrase that infuriates Isherwood. Mr. Lancaster is a narrow minded buffoon: *"It was very dangerous for me to stop regarding him as a grotesque and start thinking of him humanly, for then I should hate him for bullying me."* Mr. Lancaster's sins include serving Isherwood sausage for breakfast, dragging him to a businessman's gala dinner, and taking him on a fishing trip. At every step of the way Isherwood reacts as if he's under attack. He's convinced that Mr. Lancaster's only interest is to knock the sissy out of him.

It never occurs to Isherwood that Mr. Lancaster is a lonely old man. It never occurs to him that *"make a man out of you"* is a meaningless stock phrase, or that gala dinners and fishing trips might be Mr. Lancaster's idea of a good time. Isherwood has a different idea of fun, but that hardly makes Mr. Lancaster a venal man.

In the book's second episode Isherwood travels to Berlin, where he meets up with a handsome young man named Waldemar. Waldemar is constantly cadging money, but he is such a great friend that Isherwood doesn't mind: *"It was really very pleasant, dealing with people like Waldemar. I knew in advance that, whatever I did or didn't do, he would never bear me any grudge."* Again it looks like Isherwood has misunderstood the relationship. Waldemar is not a bad fellow, but he is more mercenary than Isherwood recognizes. He may be incapable of holding a grudge, but if Isherwood stopped paying out, he would soon enough find a new friend.

Isherwood has no talent for seeing the man in full. He's a perceptive writer but, as the title of his book suggests, he habitually holds himself at a certain distance. Thus removed, he is constantly analyzing the people around him and because analysis demands resolution, he ends up idealizing some of his characters (Waldemar) and demonizing others (Mr. Lancaster).

In the final section of the book Isherwood travels to California and becomes the follower of a Hollywood guru. This baby spirituality fits Isherwood nicely. It feeds his self-absorption and encourages him in his incessant search for meaning. *"Does anything happen by accident?"* Isherwood thinks not.

I disagree. As far as I know, things happen willy-nilly. People do not live intentionally. They often act for no real reason and for the most part they talk just to have something to say. Isherwood takes himself too seriously to accept that. He has no sense of the absurdity of life. As a result, *Down There On A Visit* is an engaging book and an honest one, but Isherwood is wrong about almost everything in it.

Commentary

Post Postmodern

T.E. MacVeagh

The outstanding characteristic of the contemporary art world is fragmentation. There is no longer a single canon to be imposed, imitated or made anathema. Each new Whitney biennial leads to a series of articles puzzling over the lack of an emerging theme. Literary journals regularly diagnose the impossibility of writing the great American novel amidst the diverse influences of multiculturalism, feminist literature, queer studies and genre fiction. In music, the very fineness of the distinction between styles (*e.g.*, "This record is an outstanding example of latino-influenced white jazz fusion") makes it clear how disjointed the scene has become. The pattern here is the absence of pattern.

Indeed, whether we are talking about painting, music, theatre, dance or literature, the most significant trend of the last twenty years is the disappearance of a dominant school. Contemporary art and thought is dominated by the absence of the traditional cycle from orthodoxy, to rebellion, to a new orthodoxy. (That is, the absence of the Hegelian pattern of thesis, antithesis and synthesis.)

Orthodoxy remains, not as a singular orthodoxy but in multiple orthodoxies, between which we are free to choose. Rebellion, which used to be a vertical concept, a movement surging from below up to dominance, has become a horizontal matter, a shifting of loyalty from one existing orthodoxy to another. Why build an alternative system if one already exists? If you are unhappy with one school of thought, another one down the road meets your requirements.

This fragmentation marks the final end of postmodernism, seemingly the last dominant "ism" of our age. Postmodern art is art that remains ironically aware of its status as art. Postmodernist theorists would have us believe that in the age of postmodernism, it is impossible not to be postmodernist. Once the self-referential stance is possible, it is impossible to avoid. Every act is the self-conscious decision to do that act rather than another one.

In this view, even a traditional sea novel is inevitably a postmodern and ironic commentary on the nature of narrative because both the writer and his reader know that each hackneyed line of plot represents a conscious decision not to use non-linear story-telling techniques. As such, the work is at once a parody of the tradition and a commentary on the writer's technique and audience expectations. (I am not making this up; a recent review of the fourth Harry Potter book noted Rowling's "sly postmodern play" with the traditional stereotypes of children's fantasy.)

It is not unusual for a critic to believe that his theory is somehow privileged. But neither the art world nor its interpreters are dominated by post-modernist messages or sensibilities. Artists are saying all sorts of things in all sorts of ways, postmodernist and not.

The current state of fragmentation is, however, partially an outgrowth of postmodernism. The concept that every work of art is perfectly self-conscious suggests that whatever the artist's thesis, it "always already" includes a meta-commentary on the possible antitheses. Which is simply to say that no straightforward antithesis is available. There is no longer a call and response in the art world. Rather, there is only a series of highly nuanced calls.

But a more important factor by far is the ever-increasing wealth and democratization of society. A gigantic expansion in the of number of people with the

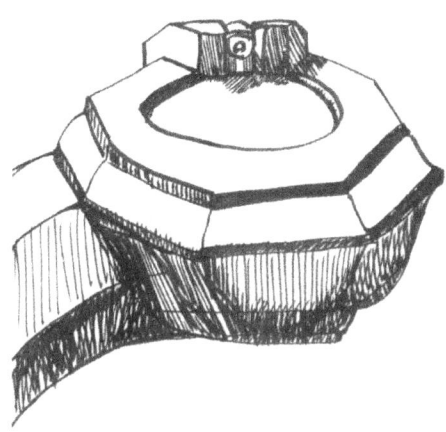

time and money to take an interest in art has inevitably led to a corresponding growth in the number of artists and art authorities. Instead of having matters of taste decided by 100 or so patrons in Paris or New York, there are probably several thousand rich, opinionated art impresarios in the Dallas-Fort Worth area alone.

All of this democratization is for the good, but it puts the artist trying to make a universal statement in a difficult position. The artist is no longer understood as someone who can reveal "Truth" in all its glory. The most he can do is give you a glimpse at one aspect of it. Indeed, the artist ends up losing his role as the privileged spokesmen for artistic truth. Art consumers take the task on themselves, becoming meta-artists of a sort by carefully choosing what mix of artistic statements to endorse. One person chooses expressionist prints, science fiction and Broadway musicals. Another reads 19th century literature, loves pop art and listens to classical Indian music. The consumer uses the fragmented art world as a supermarket in which to purchase the ingredients for a satisfying home-cooked stew, and considers it far preferable to the rarified fare available in the posh restaurant down the street.

This too, of course, is an outgrowth of postmodernism, which considered art as a commodity, and urged artists and critics alike to give commercial objects the same scrutiny as was previously reserved for works of art. Now, not just critics but every consumer can create their own intellectual décor by mixing and matching art products the same way they choose furniture for their living rooms. (Consider the museum curator as a prototype of a new sort of meta-artist: Creating an artistic statement by combining the work of other people in her own tasteful fashion.)

When people survey the chaos of the contemporary artistic scene they often mourn a simpler age when the art scene was dominated by undoubted giants who could be dethroned only by the genius of rebels who had first absorbed the lessons of the masters. This misty-eyed nostalgia for an artistic golden age should make us suspicious: was the art world ever as tidy as this? Also we should be wary of our attraction. While we may be entranced by the power wielded by kings, we would be fools to yearn for an end to democracy.

Still, the writer in his study trying to write the Great American Novel, the artist hoping to become the heir to Jackson Pollock, may legitimately wonder: once fragmentation has occurred can it end? Or is the history of art like an egg that is easier to break than reconstitute?

It is almost always foolish to predict that change will not occur. Possibly a transformative artistic genius will emerge from obscurity, the magnitude of whose achievement will demand universal deference in the same way as did Einstein's scientific achievements. More likely, the fragmented art world will be brought together by a momentous event occurring outside the artistic realm which breaks down the differences between our existing subcultures: a nuclear war, environmental disaster, the discovery of an alien intelligence. Some such event will no doubt happen eventually. But best not to hold back one's novel until it occurs.

Reminiscence

Strange Men

Lincoln MacVeagh

I was a boyish looking twenty-five. I had only just started to shave. I had blonde hair and an innocent face, and in Mexico I got used to being approached by middle-aged men offering to buy me a bottle of beer. Some of the men wanted to practice their English; others asked how to get a job in the United States; and it was my sense that most of them were trying to pick me up. I rather enjoyed the attention.

Mr. Serrano, however, was not my type. He was short, fat and balding, and he had a thick black moustache and a greasy manner. He sneaked up next to me on a park bench in Oaxaca and put his arm around me. He told me that I was a handsome and intelligent young man. He had a proposition for me. How would I like to earn $600 a month?

As rudely as possible I told him I wasn't interested, but I had misread the situation and Mr. Serrano quickly explained that he was an English teacher from the small town of Tlaxiaco. He wanted to start an after hours language institute and he'd taken the trip to Oaxaca in search of a native speaking gringo who could teach conversation to the advanced students. He gave me his address and I said I would consider it.

Two months later I wrote to Mr. Serrano to say that I was coming to Tlaxiaco. It was an ugly, desolate town, but I was full of romantic notions and I was quite happy to be in the middle of nowhere. It was then my belief that a strong mind should feel at home in any surroundings. I took a room in a hotel next to the market and when I went to buy breakfast the next morning I saw a large crowd gathered around a man selling herbal remedies. He claimed that he could cure everything from kidney disease to woman's pains and to prove the power of his medicine he wrapped a number of snakes around his arms and neck.

In the afternoon I went down to the elementary school to find Mr. Serrano and he walked me back to town to show me the building that would house his language institute. He talked excitedly about the money we would make together, but when I pressed him for specifics it turned out that my $600 a month had suddenly dwindled down closer to $250. Moreover, whereas Mr. Serrano had at first said that the two of us would share the teaching duties, it now came out that he viewed himself more as an executive partner. My job would be to teach class eight hours a day; his job would be to look after the accounting.

By the end of an hour I had lost interest in Mr. Serrano's language institute, and three days later I was entirely fed up with Tlaxiaco as well. I gave up on proving my strength of mind and hatched a new plan to try making it as a television star on the Mexican soaps. Late at night I boarded a bus for the twelve hour trip to Mexico City.

I was the last person to board the bus and I took the last row of seats in front of the bus toilet. There was a young couple cuddling together in the row in front of me and in the opposite aisle there was a strange man huddled in the seats at the very back of the bus. I noticed him when I hoisted my bag onto the luggage rack. He was wrapped in a dark poncho and he had a wide-brimmed felt hat pulled down over his face. I glanced at him and he made a quick motion with his hand as if to suggest that I should sit down next to him. I didn't want to at all and I was about to say something when he quickly put his finger to his lips to hush me.

It was a horrible bus ride and the road wound through the mountains in a long series of S curves, churning my stomach. At the same time, I couldn't stop thinking about the man in the poncho. He made me nervous. I couldn't see his eyes but I sensed he was staring at me.

I was envious of the young couple in front of me. They drifted off to sleep as soon as we hit the highway. I wanted to fall asleep very badly but I couldn't. I kept glancing over at the man in the poncho to see if he was still watching me. He never stopped, and after an hour or so he called to me from across the aisle. "Tsss, tsss." He patted the seat next to him where he wanted me to sit. Another hour later he called to me again. I pretended not to hear him and stayed frozen in my seat. The bus was pitch dark and silly visions of myself getting raped in the bathroom ran through my head.

Towards morning I finally started to doze and when I woke up we were pulling into the bus station in Mexico City. I chided myself for having had such cowardly thoughts the night before. The driver announced our arrival and turned on the interior lights. I was about to stand up. I glanced once more at the man in the poncho and incredibly, I saw him rip off his hat and pull a twelve inch knife from behind his back. He rushed towards me and I screamed. I thought he was going to kill me.

Instead, he attacked the young man sitting next to his girlfriend in the row in front of me. There was no time for a struggle. In a flash the man in the poncho was straddling the younger man's legs. He had one hand braced against the young man's forehead and with the other hand he held his long knife against the young man's neck. The man in the poncho looked to be about forty-five. He slapped the young man's girlfriend in the face.

"This whore," he proclaimed, "is my wife. This man has stolen my wife. Together they have stolen all of my merchandise. Now they are running away to escape justice. I won't let them. Someone must call the police or else I will cut both their throats."

Nobody moved. All eyes were fixed on the man in the poncho and he glared angrily back at the crowd as if to say: what are you looking at? Finally the bus driver volunteered to go find a policeman and as soon as he left the man in the poncho relaxed. He even seemed somewhat embarrassed.

"I promise not to kill anyone. I'll wait for the police. The rest of you can get off the bus. Take your belongings, remain silent and don't rush. I'm sorry to have interrupted your trip. Now go."

The passengers filed out quickly and no one lingered to discuss what had happened. Soon the parking lot was all but empty and the man in the poncho was left alone on the bus with his two captives. I never saw the police arrive.

Games

Sir Laffalot

The day a boy first learns to tie his shoelaces he is very excited. Two weeks later the thrill is gone. It's a pity that young children cannot relax in their bunk beds and content themselves with nostalgic thoughts: "Ahhhh, that was the day I got dressed all by myself..." But they can't. Children demand ever different challenges to distract them, and when nothing new appears on the horizon they all raise their voices at once and let out the signal cry of youth, "I'M BORED!"

I'm Bored Syndrome (IBS) is now recognized as a serious problem confronting today's youth and early data suggest that there may be as many as 500 million sufferers worldwide. Scenting profits, several large drug companies are busy at work developing psycho-active medications to combat IBS. Sir Laffalot finds this development worrisome. He believes that the pharmaceutical approach is wrongheaded and recently he participated in a panel discussion devoted to finding alternatives remedies.

Sir Laffalot's co-panelist was the sexy English theorist Dr. Mary Poppins, and debate was both lively and informative. Dr. Poppins advocated what she referred to as the "Spoon Full of Sugar" method. Sir Laffalot felt that her heart was in the right place, but he found her proposed solution wanting. "Spoon Full of Sugar" amounts to little more than telling children to sing songs when they're bored. Sir Laffalot argued that this was not enough to deal with the real world tedium facing children in the twenty-first century.

Take, for example, the simple problem of a playground see-saw. Up and down, up and down. A see-saw can be very dull. Does anyone really think you can make it more exciting simply by singing a song? Something more radical is needed. To bring a see-saw to life you have to stop sitting on it and try running across it from one end to the other a top speed.

Speaking without notes, Sir Laffalot went on to give an impromptu analysis of his own anti-boredom techniques. In general, he recommended that when children are bored they should try making up a game. With regard to the specific problem of the playground see-saw, he outlined the basic rules of an activity he called *Obstacle Course*. Notes below:

Obstacle Course: How to Play.

1) Obstacle courses can be set up almost anywhere but the best place for them is in an empty playground.
2) Start by mapping out of a course: up the slide, over the monkey bars, down the pole and touch the swing set.
3) Each player gets a practice run through the course, then each player goes through it again as quickly as possible.
4) The fastest time wins. A new course is established and the game starts over.

Sir Laffalot says: TOODALOO!!

Continued from page 16

in search of new kicks. But cleanliness was only half the story. Cindy also harbored a severe phobia about kitchen cabinets, and she didn't like putting food away. She had a thing about fruit as well. She would buy it, and if it started to go even slightly bad before she ate it, she couldn't bring herself to touch it, much less throw it away. Her bath was stocked with Aveda products, her bedroom was strewn with canned good and paper bags, and her refrigerator was bursting with malignant fruit.

Somehow in all this mess we forgot about Don Perry. He showed up one day, having obtained leave from West Point, and the three of us went to a forlorn Jersey City mall to see "Sleepless in Seattle." I wept when the couple in the film finally met on the roof of the Empire State Building, in marked contrast to the engaged couple, who sat stoically. Afterwards, Cindy and I made fun of Meg Ryan while Don walked on ahead. Back at the apartment, Cindy did all she could to make Don feel unwelcome and finally he went out to a comedy club by himself. He came home late and started to undress. I was sleeping on the floor and when Don got into bed,

Cindy said coldly, "Don't touch me."

He left early in the morning, and I thought that would be the last we would ever see of Don Perry. His name didn't come up much, and Cindy and I were busy trying to find new jobs. One day as we were on our way to my apartment to pick up a few things I asked what happened with the wedding. "Oh," she said. "I'm not really sure. Diamond Lil [Cindy's mother] has taken over. She's got the Martha Stewart book, and she's planning up a storm. She adores Don, but I'm going to call the whole thing off as soon as he finishes his final exams." Twenty seconds later I opened my mailbox. *Calligraphy.* The invitations had been sent.

Cindy got very depressed and left work. They gave her a generous severance package and an expensive cake, and suddenly she was gone. I was left alone with the maid, the chauffeur, and the creak of the descending dumbwaiter. Cindy gave up her apartment and disappeared to Weddingland, vowing that she would have it out with her Mom once and for all. Her last message on my answering machine before she disappeared was like the whisper of a dying woman.

The high life

Grunge Girl: Part I

David Garcia III

Cindy was part of the day pool of secretaries, and I worked the night shift, so we only overlapped by about an hour. This was enough time for me to take note of her pastel nails, matching pastel outfits, and little flip hairdo that fell forward into two soft tusks when she leaned down to write something. In conversation with a mutual co-worker, I made an offhand comment about her appearance, something like, "I could never be friends with someone so average looking." This got back to her and she began to regard me with the intense scorn that so often leads to lasting friendship.

One night Cindy was out at Texas & Arizona (T&A) with her friend Lisa, and a bunch of cadets arrived in full uniform. Jokingly, she pointed at one specimen and said to Lisa, "How come guys like that never come up and talk to *me?*" Then, as if summoned, the exact guy came up and talked to her. He was Don Perry, a big lonely boy from Ohio, and he liked Cindy enough to ask her to marry him before he returned to West Point. Half-jokingly she said yes, and then she half forgot about it.

Cindy moved to Jersey City (after breaking off with a longtime slug boyfriend) and stumbled onto an ideal new job – high salary with few responsibilities. She was hired to be the secretary of a woman on pregnancy leave. The woman wasn't sure she would ever return, but she insisted on having a private secretary to take the occasional call and forward her mail. It was an unusual company. It was housed in a beautiful townhouse right around the corner from Tiffany's and its purpose was to invest money in computer related businesses, but there were no deadlines and

no urgency, and the company executives rarely showed up. However, they felt that it was proper to have people on hand for appearance's sake and that's where Cindy came in. I soon followed.

At first it was great. Not only was there free lunch, but the company paid for our transportation and gave us periodic bonuses. We had our own maid, a Jamaican woman named Rosaire, and handyman/chauffeur named Osiris. Every afternoon Rosaire sent coffee, tea, and snacks throughout the building via dumbwaiter, and Osiris changed the light bulbs every day, whether they needed it or not. Cindy and I talked on the phone, played computer games, and threw mock tantrums: "Where the hell is Rosaire? My tea has gotten cold!"

After about a month though, the lack of work began to get to us. Each morning it became a little harder to walk through the glass reception area. There was nothing to do. It was nightmarish. Unable to face the increasingly Bergmanesque dread of preparing for work by myself, I moved in with Cindy. The alarm would go off, and one of us would groan, "I can't. There is just no way. Don't make me go." At night, we took the edge off with wine, grunge CD's, and videos. I did paintings of Cindy while she did her nails and read Dorothy Parker. We were trying not to become heroin addicts.

Cindy had some curious habits. On the one hand, she was obsessively clean, always washing and scrubbing and hoarding beauty products. Her favorite pastime was laundry, which she did every night without fail. "How about we do some laundry?" she would say, like a parent offering a treat to a child. Sometimes we used the huge industrial laundry machines in the building, and other nights we tried out local places,

Continued on page 15

The ECLECTIC

Sept.-Oct. 2000   Volume 2 Number 7   Free

CONTENTS

Quotations

"If you talk to a thoughtful Christian, Catholic or Anglican, you often find yourself laughed at for being so ignorant as to suppose that anyone ever took the doctrines of the church literally." George Orwell remarks on the slipperiness of religious intellectuals in *As I Please, Vol. 3.*

"I made the mistake, common in youth, of not understanding that people who like one for oneself, will overlook occasional lapses." Cyril Connolly regrets his childhood fear of the faux pas in *Enemies of Promise.*

"In Italy my name is Baroness, but in New York I'm just Sylvia." A fading beauty overheard introducing herself at a Manhattan cocktail party.

"In my experience, there was usually a relation to height, as Philip Rahv and Bill Mangold, both tall men, bore out. There may be dwarfish men with monstrously large organs, but I have never known one." Mary McCarthy reflects on the lessons she learned as a single girl in *Intellectual Memoirs.*

Soft Heart Sharp Tongue

The Life of Mary McCarthy

Lincoln MacVeagh

Hearts that are kind and forgiving, tongues that are neither: if that is the definition of good company, then Mary McCarthy was very good company indeed. She was a sympathetic woman, incapable of holding a grudge, and she was much too well aware of her own failings not to be forgiving of others. But you might never have known that to meet her.

McCarthy began her career in the 1930's as a theater critic for *Partisan Review*. She was clever and hard to

"Unfortunately, I am not discreet, and I do not seem to learn."

please. She didn't like *A Streetcar Named Desire* and summed up the plot saying it's about a man who fights with his sister-in-law because she is always occupying the bathroom. McCarthy quickly earned a reputation as a dangerous young thing and according to one of her editors: *"When most pretty girls smile at you, you feel terrific. When Mary smiles at you, you look to see if your fly is open."*

McCarthy ruffled feathers and couldn't help it. *"Unfortunately, I am not discreet and I do not seem to learn."* Her first novel poked fun at her friends from *Partisan Review* such that many of them stopped speaking to her and one former lover threatened to sue. *A Charmed Life*, about McCarthy's summer community in Wellfleet, made her husband so nervous that after its publi-

cation he insisted they sell their house. And McCarthy's most famous novel, *The Group*, caused a small tempest. McCarthy didn't mean to give offense, but it was her curse to live most of her life amongst people whom it was very easy to offend.

The Group follows the lives of eight Vassar girls from college to young adulthood and the book has a good deal to say about sex. The Vassar graduates were outraged. Two of them joined forces to blackball McCarthy's admission to a Stonington country club and the rest flooded the alumnae quarterly with angry letters. *"The only thing Mary learned to love at Vassar was the sound of her own voice."* Even the most diplomatic women had to struggle to find a kind word. At the height of her celebrity, McCarthy received the following note from her Vassar class correspondent: *"Loathed The Group, but loved your new hairdo on the Jack Paar show."*

McCarthy shrugged off the criticism. She liked respectable people but she could not become one. She had neither the right temperament nor the right background. She spoke her mind too freely and besides, one of her grandmothers was Jewish, and her father was an Irish Catholic ne'er-do-well.

Mary was born in Seattle in 1912. She was the eldest of four children and when she was six the family migrated back to her father's hometown in Minneapolis. Roy McCarthy had been unable to hold a job out west and it was hoped that he might do better in more familiar surroundings. That hope proved false. The McCarthy's boarded their train just at the height of the influenza epidemic and in the course of the journey both of Mary's parents came down sick. They died one after the other, on successive days, shortly after reaching Minnesota.

Roy and Tess McCarthy each came from wealthy families, but neither set of grandparents were willing to take on the children. Mary and her brothers were sent to live with fat Uncle Myers and timid Aunt Margaret.

Myers and Margaret were the poor relations. In all likelihood, they got a good stipend for looking after the children, but if so their charges didn't see its benefit. In her best book, *Memories of a Catholic Girlhood*, McCarthy recalls with horror the never changing diet of boiled turnips, rutabagas and potatoes. Uncle Meyers sliced peaches on his corn flakes while Mary and her brothers ate farina for breakfast.

Myers and Margaret seemed determined to teach the orphans the lesson of hardship. No toys were allowed, no books and no entertainment. Regular bowel movements were highly prized, and for some queer reason mouth-breathing was frowned upon. At night the children had their mouths clapped shut with adhesive tape to force them to breath through the nose.

"We were beaten all the time, as a matter of course..." It's odd to think of the sophisticated Vassar woman being beaten, but she was and Uncle Myers punished both good and bad behavior with equal force. At age ten Mary won $25 in a children's essay contest: *"...my uncle silently rose from his chair, led me into the dark downstairs lavatory, which always smelled of shaving cream, and furiously beat me with the razor strop – to teach me a lesson, he said, lest I become stuck-up."* The

"I was just over by the fruit and I swear someone was trying to kill me."

money was confiscated too, and over time Mary learned that her only means of self-preservation was secrecy: *"...for several years after we were finally liberated, I was a problem liar."*

Mary's liberation was the work of her maternal grandfather. Mr. Preston was a prominent Seattle lawyer and in 1923 he went to Minneapolis on a visit. Catching a moment alone with him, Mary poured her heart out. Mr. Preston did not seem much impressed by her troubles, but he was curious to know why she wasn't wearing her eyeglasses. Matter of factly Mary explained that she was being punished for having broken them in the school playground, and somehow this small detail took hold of her grandfather and enraged him. Uncle Myers' household was broken up; the brothers were farmed out to new relatives; and Mary went off to live with her Preston grandparents.

Mary was once again rich and safe, but as a newcomer to Seattle, she now faced the confounding problem of re-establishing her social position at school. Accustomed to popularity, Mary had become an outsider and she was jealous of the girl who sat next to her in study hall. She handled it badly: *"I took a piece of paper and wrote, 'In my other school I was popular too,' and shoved it over onto her desk... 'It must be very hard,' she wrote back, sympathetically. And that, to my amazement, was the end of it."*

McCarthy possessed a keen self-consciousness and for years it made her life more difficult than it might have been. Worried that her nose was too snub, she slept with a clothespin snapped upon it; worried that her grandparents were too stodgy, she tried to hide them from her racy friends and vice versa. She was always trying to appear more sophisticated than she was and occasionally she suffered for it. Embarrassed to admit she knew nothing about sex, at age fourteen she lost her virginity to an unpleasant twenty-three year old with

a didactic bent: *"...he became very educational, encouraging me to sit up and examine his stiffened organ, which to me looked quite repellant, all flushed and purplish."*

The cad stood her up at their very next meeting, but McCarthy survived, and in 1929 she won a place at Vassar, then one of the most prestigious schools in the country.

Prior to arriving at Vassar, McCarthy and her grandmother spent a week sightseeing in New York City. A spat at the Metropolitan Museum sent Mary out onto the street by herself and wiping her tears, she chanced to bump into Harold Johnsrud, an actor she knew from Seattle. Johnsrud was trying to make it on Broadway and that afternoon he took Mary out to tea. They became lovers, and four years and countless fights later they were married at a small church on Stuyvesant Square: *"I had a beige dress and a large black silk hat with a wreath of daisies."*

Johnsrud was a cold, self-important man and McCarthy was not in love with him, but she was an impressionable girl and she admired his capacity for angst. She was fully convinced of Johnsrud's genius and she hoped that might be enough. It wasn't and the marriage dissolved rather quickly.

In search of a lover for whom to leave her husband, McCarthy chose a wet young man named John Porter. She picked him almost at random and she tired of him immediately, but the divorce went through. By 1936 McCarthy was single again, and in an odd twist, both Porter and Johnsrud died shortly thereafter. Porter died of fever in Mexico and Johnsrud burned to death in a hotel fire. He had rushed back to his room to save one of his precious manuscripts.

Meanwhile, McCarthy took an apartment in Greenwich Village and wrote for *Partisan Review*. Her articles were widely admired but she was not much good at solitude. Even in middle-

age she preferred losing weight to eating at a restaurant alone, and as a girl in her twenties she seems to have had a horror of feeling left out. She hated leaving parties by herself, so she always asked someone else to take her home: *"It was getting rather alarming. I realized one day that in twenty-four hours I had slept with three different men."*

One drunken evening McCarthy allowed herself to be seduced by the famous critic Edmund Wilson. Right away Wilson proposed to her. McCarthy was aghast, but at the same time: *"I could not accept the fact that I had slept with this fat, puffing man for no reason, simply because I was drunk. No. It had to make sense."* She married him to salve her own conscience and moved to Massachusetts.

This second loveless marriage was as much a disaster as the first. Edmund Wilson was an intelligent man but he was also an old drunk with a violent temper. The benefits of marriage to him were that he fathered McCarthy's only child and that he forced her to start writing fiction. Like Collette's

husband, Wilson shut her in a room and wouldn't let her out until she'd produced *The Company She Kept*, an excellent collection of short stories.

The disadvantages of life with Wilson were more numerous. He was petty and boorish, he lectured Mary endlessly, and when he got angry he beat her up. She was once so badly injured that she had to be taken to the hospital. To cover up his crime, Wilson told the nurses that his wife had gone insane. McCarthy was placed in a mental ward against her will and she had to remain there until Wilson cleared up the matter the next night.

Remarkably, the marriage lasted eight years, but in the end McCarthy ran away and the bitterness of the separation came out in the court depositions. McCarthy: *"Since the birth of our son I have tried to see this marriage through but from the time of its inception to the present time I have been compelled to suffer physical and mental humiliation at the hands of the defendant."* Wilson: *"Plaintiff is the victim of hysterical delusions and has seemed for years to have a persecution complex as far as I am concerned."*

With Wilson gone, McCarthy now needed to support herself and she took a job teaching at Bard College. She moved back to New York and considered a new role for herself as a political activist in the fight Senator Joe McCarthy. *"I conceived the ridiculous idea of going to Harvard Law School."* However, McCarthy distrusted her own zeal, and instead she settled down to write her third novel, *The Groves of Academe,* which made fun of communists and anti-communists alike.

The Groves of Academe was published in 1952, by which time McCarthy was well into her third marriage with Bowden Broadwater. Eight years younger than McCarthy, Broadwater was an aspiring novelist who went on to become a teacher at St. Bernard's school for boys. Tall, slender and reserved, he was a very decent man. He was kind to McCarthy's son, devoted to McCarthy herself, and he took great care to see that she got the peace she needed to work. It was McCarthy's most productive period. She wrote *The Group* and published nine other books, including *Memories of a Catholic Girlhood.* She contributed regularly to the *New Yorker* and was finally able to make a living with her pen. She owed part of her success to Broadwater and she knew it and she liked him for it. Then she met James West.

It is widely believed that people go through life constantly repeating their past; women who have not found love by forty are assumed to be incapable of finding it. Mary McCarthy may have believed that herself, but it's not true, and in 1960 she went on a lecture tour in Poland and met an American diplomat for whom she fell head over heals. James West had a wife and three young children; McCarthy was still married to Broadwater; and they immediately set about getting divorces. It was folly

but love is folly. West left his post at the embassy in Poland, and he and McCarthy were married in Paris the following year.

McCarthy was thrilled. When she and West first met she wrote to a friend, *"...the whole thing has been kind of a revelation, as though I had never known the creature called Man before."* Ten years later, her letters show that she was still giddy: *"I cling to you"; "I love you more all the time"; "I am madly, crazily in love with my husband."*

McCarthy and West remained together until her death from cancer in 1989. In the intervening years, *The Group* made McCarthy famous. She appeared on television talk-shows; she took up the anti-war cause and made dangerous trips to Saigon and Hanoi; she wrote two more novels and a great many essays. Most of all, however, she enjoyed herself. Wonder of wonders, she became passionate about cooking and gardening.

Little that she wrote after her marriage to West was much good. The second volume of her memoirs is uneven, the third volume nearly unreadable, but McCarthy never complained about the diminution of her talent. She said it only made sense for young people to write better novels than old people, and she seemed not to mind about aging. *"I used long ago to come to New York to see a lover,"* she joked, *"then to see a psychoanalyst, then an editor or publisher, then a lawyer, and finally a dentist."*

Mary McCarthy died content, and what is wrong with that?

Reviews

Slackjaw

by Jim Knipfel

Jeremy P. Tarcher/Putnam, 1999

It used to be that only famous people wrote books about themselves, but lately the memoir has become accepted as a natural first step for young authors and I'm not convinced it's a good thing.

There are a number of reasons why memoirs are especially appealing to beginning writers. Most obviously, the material comes ready made. There is no need to tax your imagination and you needn't worry about verisimilitude because it comes built-in. A memoir is also easier to structure than a novel. The writer has but one choice of voice, the first person, and he is more or less restricted to laying out his plot in chronological order. Furthermore, a memoir does not require such strict attention to narrative continuity. No matter how much the anecdotes jump about, they will all be tied together by the presence of the central "I".

All of the above is for the good. The problem with the memoir is not a structural one; it begins earlier than that.

The hardest question facing a novelist is the first one: Why bother? It is such an extraordinary waste of energy to write fiction that a novelist must have something very important to say in order to justify it. The autobiographer does not face so stiff a challenge. His concern is to record the facts, and whether or not what he says is deeply important, he can always fall back on the excuse that at least he is writing the truth.

Truth, however, is not always self-justifying. If the autobiographer is Winston Churchill we may be curious to know what detritus floats in his head; if the autobiographer is not Winston Churchill we are less likely to care. It is not enough to write down the facts simply because they are facts, but that is what memoirs often do. And that's the problem with Jim Knipfel's first book, *Slackjaw.*

Jim Knipfel is a columnist for the *New York Press* and he's an interesting man. Despite repeated attempts to kill himself and despite going blind, Knipfel's work is never mawkish and it's often very funny. When he attends a seminar teaching blind people what to do should they fall onto the subway tracks, Knipfel learns that the best thing to do is to get someone on the platform to pull you back up. In a pinch, he's told, you can lie down flat on the tracks and the train will probably pass right over you. Knipfel accepts the advice with a wry smile. You might want to take off your backpack.

Slackjaw does best in its early sections, where Knipfel appears as an intellectually curious boy stifled by the hard-driving mediocrity around him. In suburban Green Bay all anyone cares about is football; in college it's the same; and everywhere Knipfel goes, bookishness is frowned upon. He draws a convincing picture of America's hostility to serious thought, but then *Slackjaw* breaks down and the book itself seems to share in that hostility.

Too often Knipfel falls back on the mannered pose and the false insight. One Christmas he spends drinking in a bar full of alcoholics: "*We all knew what the game was, and we all knew we had lost it big-time.*" At another point Knipfel presents us with the grand sum of his philosophy and all we get is the simple three word phrase, "*Deal with it.*"

To me this sounds shallow. Knipfel would probably argue that the shallowness is of no account because it's true to life. It's how he really thinks. That might be, but I say that "real" and "worthwhile" are two different things. Knipfel has to work harder to shape his material. Maybe he should try writing a novel.

Commentary

Why History?

T.E. MacVeagh

In high school and grade school they tell you that you have to study history to learn "to avoid the mistakes of the past." It's a nice idea and briefly appealing. It may win over uncooperative school children. But it does not hold up to much scrutiny.

History is such a mess that it is hard to draw many useful lessons. I can think of couple of old chestnuts: Don't humiliate a defeated opponent, and never launch a land invasion of Russia. Even if they were true, these "lessons" would have limited practical applications. But it also remains open to debate how true they are.

Napoleon and Hitler had trouble in Russia because their armies were caught in the Russian winter with supply lines cut off. A modern army, moving faster and supplied by air, might have better luck.

And there is at least one famous counter-example to the rule that one should not force an unequal peace on a defeated opponent. Cato insisted that Rome would continue to face military challenge from Carthage until the city was destroyed. After the Third Punic War, Cato got his way. Rome razed Carthage to the ground and sowed the ground with salt. Carthage never bothered Rome again.

If we could really "learn from the past" then history would be in much more demand than it is. In fact, history is remarkably out of demand. Fiction lovers consider history books to be badly written and poorly organized, offering little human depth. It is hard not to agree with them. Most "serious" history books do not have a compelling narrative. They load up mind-numbing facts at the expense of readability. They show little flair for character. Instead you read passages like the following:

In Merovingian Gaul, the functions of the grafio, *or count, had originally been identical with those which the Carolingian counts, three centuries later, exercised in the German provinces of the east. There was also a popular form of self-government, in which an elected* thunginus *(or 'thing man') directed affairs of the* Gau, *that had persisted for some generations after the Frankish conquest; and the* grafio *or count was simply the King's local agent, the local administrator of the King's estates and his military representative. But this dualism of function between the popularly-elected* thunginus *and the royal* grafio *was of short duration in Gaul.*

Phew! For all this, not only do I like reading history, but (and here it is) *I think you should too.* The question, however, is why? And I have to admit it is not all that obvious. Why read history when the lessons are iffy, the drama is tedious, and when novels offer so much more psychological insight?

One argument is that history can help us tell right from wrong. Any history of the struggle for civil rights in America inspires one to draw moral lessons. The right positions on the issues shine through so clearly in retrospect; the wrong positions are so thoroughly discredited. The history of civil rights seems a flaming arrow pointing to an important moral truth. But things get trickier if you try to decide exactly where that arrow points. Does it point to some truth beyond what we have already discovered, or simply to our current state of enlightenment? There will be no agreement with the former, and no magic in the latter. The problem with using history to draw moral lessons is that it only works where we are already convinced of our own moral correctness.

Nevertheless, one might suggest, history is an excellent source of moral example. We can use history as Plutarch did in his *Lives*, not to provide philosophical grounding for what constitutes morality, but to provide rich source material to illustrate moral lessons. Certainly history is full of "incident" that can be a benefit to a flagging imagination. But if this is the only value of history then it has no advantage over fiction. The imagination must be able to provide better source material for our reflections on the nature of morality. Unrestricted by the requirement of actual occurrence, the literary imagination can shape more complex, more precise and more varied incident for our consideration.

But surely it is an advantage that the stories of history are true, while those of literature are, at best, merely plausible. Literature, it seems, must be grounded in history. After all, how can we know what is plausible if we do not know what is true? It would seem that only an understanding of history lets us judge whether or not a fictional story has any moral relevance at all.

As tempting as this argument is, it cannot be accurate. A knowledge of history cannot help us judge the "plausibility" of realistic fiction because the subject matters are completely distinct. Literature examines individuals and their thinking. The vast bulk of history does not concern itself with individuals at all, but rather the rise and fall of nations and social structures; the birth and death of ideas and ideologies. Even a deep knowledge of history cannot tell us whether Elizabeth and Mr. Darcy were right for each other, or whether Hamlet was likely to have been so upset over his father's death. No amount of history can help us judge the "plausibility" of Marcel's recollections upon smelling a madeleine. (And historical biographies, focused on individuals and often relying on the techniques of fiction and psychoanalysis, generally have more in common with novels than with history.)

What history shows us is, in fact, unrelated to what literature reveals. In the study of literature we study our individuality, our psychology. In history we study that part of ourselves which is not individual. We study our membership in a community; we study our commitment to abstractions: What it means to be "American" or "Hispanic" or "Catholic".

We are social constructs as well as individuals. And it is clearly right that our judgments are powerfully shaped (and sometimes twisted) by the position in the social net into which we are born. The first step in controlling the effects of these forces on our thinking must be to understand them. The study of these forces, of what it means to be a certain race, religion, class or nationality, is the study of history. We study history like we study literature to understand ourselves and others. But where literature teaches us about our individuality, history teaches us about that part of ourselves which we do not choose. History teaches us what we think when we are not thinking, who we are when we are not being anyone. It teaches us our default settings.

The problems addressed in the study of history are not simple. If we are careless, our attempt at analysis falls into casual stereotyping. Perhaps this is why the historical tradition requires painstaking documentation and circumspection in its deployment of narrative force. The conclusions we are trying to reach are not just about Tom, Dick or Harry, but about much "bigger" matters: *e.g.*, the nature of Feudalism, the purpose of law, or the character of Chinese society in general. If one accepts the momentous stakes, one can even learn to enjoy the style of history, including its meandering accumulation of detail and its tepid conclusions. The style of history may seem dull compared to the style of literature, but only in the way that Bergman or Kurosawa may seem dull when you are used to Tarantino.

Reminiscence

School Rules

Lincoln MacVeagh

Major school rules were rules that you could get kicked out for breaking. Leaving your dormitory after curfew was a major school rule, as was entering a girl's bedroom. There were also stricter prohibitions against cheating and stealing, but neither of these rules played much part in our daily life. Cheating was unusual at Groton, and although petty theft was rampant, the sort of stealing that could get you expelled was rare.

There was really only one school rule that mattered and it was the rule against drinking. It was considered vital to enforce, but it was constantly broken, and it hung over the school like a giant cloud darkening even the sunniest spring day with the shadow of hypocrisy. On one side was the faculty, otherwise reasonable adults, who felt obligated to pretend that alcohol was a terrible and dangerous thing. On the other side were the students, who were forced to keep secret the simple truth that everyone already knew.

Perhaps at Eton boys were content to gather around the teapot discussing the relative merits of Blake and Tennyson, but at Groton they drank. There were fifty odd boys (I know much less about how the girls lived) in my senior class and at least half of them got drunk once a month or more. A bottle was the gold standard of cool; those who had booze were sure to find friends and those who had friends were sure to find booze. Among the more popular students drinking was a social necessity. There was no such thing as a teetotaler who kept his friends past the eleventh grade.

My aunt says that the acceptance of hypocrisy is a sign of maturity and she is probably right, but to my young mind it seemed appalling that drinking should be punished so severely when it was both so commonplace and essentially harmless. Few other students shared my sense of outrage. "If they made it legal, it wouldn't be any fun," was the ordinary argument. Indeed, it was the boys who drank most heavily who most readily accepted the ban on alcohol. They seemed to enjoy the cat and mouse game. They were content to hide away in their rooms, priding themselves on their ability to knock back shot after shot in quick succession.

At Groton we drank hard liquor because beer was too dangerous. Whereas a fifth of rum can be hidden almost anywhere, it is hard to fit a case of beer into a sock drawer. There was also the risk that a teacher might walk into your room at any moment, and you can't easily slip an open beer bottle into your trouser pocket. A shot glass is much more manageable, and because I learned to drink at Groton, one of the first things I learned was how to fight the natural gag reflex that comes from drinking four ounces of rum in ten minutes.

But I never did learn to enjoy the cat and mouse game. I got no fun out of breaking rules only for the sake of breaking rules, and while I liked getting drunk, I disliked having to lie about it and I was always afraid of getting caught.

I was never punished for drinking but I once came very close. On a cold Saturday night my friend Dikka and I split a half-pint of gin. As was the custom we drank it as quickly as possible. Dikka went off to the dance while I brushed my teeth, put a throat lozenge in my mouth and went out visiting. I wanted to see what Christian was up to.

Christian's room had two entrances. There was front door off the common hallway on the opposite landing and there was a back door opening directly into the room next to mine. I went through the back door. The alcohol hit me harder than I'd expected and I tripped over Christian's strong box, knocking over some books. Christian wasn't around. I bent down to pick up the books and was turning to leave when the front door opened and Ms. Youngholm walked in. Ms. Youngholm was just a teacher roaming around in search of rule breakers.

"Where's Christian?" she demanded.

At this point I must explain that the year previously I had very nearly failed French. I was determined to do better in the coming year and I had taken to repeating little French phrases over and over in my head. I was also very drunk.

"Je ne sais pas," I replied.

"What are you doing here?" Ms. Youngholm looked very angry, but it occurred to me that she, much more than I, was the fish out of water.

"Christian est mon ami," I said defiantly, "Qu'est-ce que *vous* faites ici?"

"Tell me why you're here!"

Suddenly I realized what trouble I was in and I ducked out of Christian's room and ran down to the woods where I threw up. Three hours later I went back to the dormitory for our mandatory eleven o'clock check-in.

Mr. Sackett, our house master, said that Ms. Youngholm had reported me drunk. He stood very close to me and asked to smell my breath. I opened my mouth wide and tried to feign exhaling without actually letting out any air. I'm sure I reeked of gin, but I was saved because Mr. Sackett was much angrier at Ms. Youngholm for having invaded his territory than he was at me for being drunk. Mr. Sackett took me aside into his apartment.

"I can't tell if your drunk and I'm not going to say that you are, but if you don't want this to go any further you will explain yourself to Miss Youngholm by next Friday at the latest."

My immediate reaction was one of relief but as day followed day during the subsequent week I grew more and more nervous about the prospect of confronting Ms. Youngholm. I finally caught her alone in the gymnasium.

"Mr. Sackett told me to speak to you. I wasn't drunk last weekend."

"You certainly looked like you were."

"Yeah, well I wasn't."

Every schoolboy has to learn how to drink but it was one of the special qualities of a Groton education that you also had to learn how to tell a bald-faced lie. It would be foolish to hold a grudge, and I don't think I do, but I still remember it as a humiliating lesson.

YE OLDE DENTIST SHOPPEE

Sir Laffalot

Conquering his way through the Germany, Julius Caesar once remarked that he would rather be chief of a barbarian tribe in the middle of nowhere than be a mere handmaid to power in Rome. Caesar liked to be the center of attention. If he were alive today he would have become an actor.

Indeed, he might well have been the young man sitting next to Sir Laffalot in his *Introduction To Dramatics* class. The young man was blonde, intense and frighteningly determined. He was Caesar with a soul patch.

"I used to have one of those," whispered Sir Laffalot, "But it tickled my chin." Caesar ignored him. He was concentrating on his lungs.

"Inhale... exhale... inhale... exhale..." Fiona Gardiner led her class through a three minute breathing exercise. She was an august woman, of indeterminate age; she had a sonorous voice and an unshakeable belief in the importance of proper breathing: "A sculptor's medium is clay, an actor's medium is air."

After breathing came trust and commitment. Each student was asked to find a partner. Sir Laffalot closed his eyes and prepared to fall backwards into young Caesar's arms.

"You won't drop me, will you?"

"That's not what I'm about."

It turned out that what he was about was performance. In the last section of the class everyone was asked to act out a speech they'd been working on and young Caesar chose King Lear's death speech from Act V. He rose from his chair and in the blink of an eye he transformed himself into an old man. Real tears welled up in his eyes as he looked down on the imaginary corpse of his daughter Cordelia.: "*Why should a dog, a horse, a rat, have life,/ And thou no breath at all? Thou'lt come no more,/ Never, never, never, never, never!*" The strength of the emotion was too much for him and his chest grew tight. "*Pray you undo this button. Thank you sir.*" Too late. He had a heart attack and collapsed dead on the floor.

Fiona Gardiner wiped a tear from her eye and indicated that it was now Sir Laffalot's turn. He announced that he would be performing something called *Chair and Cassette Tape*. He did it beautifully but Fiona Gardiner was unimpressed. "That's not acting, that's a circus trick."

"I know," said Sir Laffalot, "But it's jolly good fun!"

Chair and Cassette Tape: How to Perform.

1) Find a sturdy, four legged chair with no arms. Stand a cassette tape next to one of the back legs.

2) Going round the side of the chair opposite the cassette, players must pick up the cassette in their teeth and return to a sitting position without letting any part of their body touch the floor.

3) The fun is in watching people fall over, but don't worry, you won't hurt yourself. And remember, it can be done.

Sir Laffalot says: TOODALOO!!

Continued from page 16

boy has already gotten far more than he deserves."

Just then the dog strained toward the house and started bellowing. A light had been turned on upstairs, and we all screamed quietly in unison when we saw what it revealed. Cindy's Mother had hung up the wedding dress in front of the window and it made a silhouette, looming darkly over us, like the money shot in a cheap horror film.

The next morning was a nightmare of hungover adults jockeying for bathroom time. It was an early wedding, but not too early for Cindy's father to blatantly stare up Lisa's dress as they sat opposite each other in the limo. Charitably, Lisa refrained from beating him with her purse.

The wedding was held at a country club surrounded by miles of empty golf course. We congregated in the front hall, standing stiffly, with everyone half-expecting the bride to flee at any moment. Everyone except the groom, who made small talk with me, and looked as though he was on his way to the prom.

An organist began to play a warbly version of "Moon River," and we all took our places to watch the procession. The priest read his solemnities and when it was over, we shifted over to the reception hall, a huge white room full of circular tables, giving way to a large balcony out back. The Deejay announced that the bar was open, causing a stampede that made it look like a local bank branch on the day of the stock market crash.

Outside on the balcony, a rash of group photographs were being taken. At one point, Cindy took a break from smiling to grab a smoke and a martini. Her father charged over, grabbed the cigarette from her mouth, and threw it into the shrubs. Inside the hall, a rumor was circulating about the Best Man, Don's brother Jimmy. Jimmy, who was

also at West Point, had been caught leaving the base to go to a strip club. He was about to be expelled but he begged the disciplinary committee not to tell his parents until after Don's wedding and they agreed. Soon everybody at the reception knew the story.

Food was served and champagne was passed out. People started hitting their glasses with spoons to indicate that it was time for the Best Man to make a toast. Those terrible spoons chimed and chimed, and people started yelling, "Speech!" Jimmy just stared down into his boiled meat, turning red.

Jimmy finally stood up, looking like he was facing a firing squad, and after a pants-wetting pause, he began to croak: "First grade...nobody liked me...nobody wanted to play, but Donny. Donny always played with me..." Jimmy clenched his face trying to keep from blubbering. "Fourth Grade.....we.... moved to a new town....and there was nobody to play. 'Cept Donny. Donny.... was always there for me. Donny always....played."

Cindy interrupted loud enough for everyone to hear, "It sounds like he should be marrying Don."

Jimmy started to cry all over his epaulets like an expensive ice cream cone melting in the sun. Gigantic minutes passed with Jimmy just standing there in a vacuum of silence, unable to raise his glass to end his toast. Merciful relatives started clapping and somebody helped Jimmy off to the Men's room. We rushed through desert, and the dancing was cancelled. Lisa and I got back in our car.

I got a few letters from Cindy after she went to Germany. She liked walking her puppy through the wheat fields and giving hell to the army wives. I went to see her and we took off to Amsterdam for a week without inviting Don. After a year, Cindy divorced him, and returned to the USA to finish her last semester of college at age 29.

The high life

Grunge Girl: Part II

David Garcia III

Two months had passed since Cindy (Grunge Girl) had gone home to confront her Mother about canceling her wedding with Don. It was starting to seem that we would never hear from her again. Then, two days before the ceremony, Lisa and I both got frantic messages saying, "Please come and help me".

We rented a car and whipped up some outfits, but I didn't think we'd end up wearing them. As I envisioned it, we would pull up in front of Cindy's house and she would come tearing out, chased by her Mother, and jump in the car.

When Lisa and I finally made it to the house though, nobody came running. Some relatives answered the door and showed us into the living room. Everyone was making strained small talk and nobody seemed to want to be there. Cindy and her parents were at the rehearsal dinner with Don's family.

Long after conversation had started to flag in the living room, there was a commotion outside. A glossy black puppy came busting through the door, followed by a woman who looked to be Cindy's equestrian twin sister. Only it was *her*. Lisa and I were expecting the drugged out, flannel-clad ghost that we had known in New York, but what we got was pure tweed: red velvet jacket with black velvet cuffs, jodhpurs, and a Town & Country hairdo. "Oh my God," Lisa whispered, "She's wearing a brooch."

Cindy's manner was even more alarming. She whirled around, showing off her engagement ring and saying things like "So good of you to come." Then she sat down on the edge of the coffee table, and proceeded to *run the room.*

"Uncle Chuck, tell that story about how my Mother used to breastfeed me and smoke at the same time. I can't get enough of that one. Hahahahahha. Did you hear that Don and I are moving to Germany for two years right after the honeymoon? And I see you've met my new puppy. Hold still, baby!"

When I could barely take it anymore, Cindy turned toward Lisa and me and said crisply, "You two kids must be *drained.* Let me show you to your *rooms.*"

Lisa flopped on the bed in her room, and I was shown to Cindy's little brother's room, where he was sitting Indian style, watching the Simpson's. She told him to go watch TV in the den, and the minute the door was closed she burst out crying. She tried to talk, but all I could make out was choking sobs. There was a knock on the door and Cindy seemed to will her tears back into their ducts. She blotted her wet face on my t-shirt, and replied, "I'm on my way."

Once all the guests had gone, we raided the liquor cabinet and took the dog for a walk around the yard. Lisa and I tried to talk Cindy into getting into the car with us, but she sighed that it was too late. She seemed calmer. She told us of her recent travails, her myriad tantrums, and of an enforced trip to a shrink who gave her mega-medication and told her, "All I'm hearing is doom." Her Mother kept chanting that this was her last chance to get married before 30, and the wedding steamroller kept plowing ahead. She had tried calling Don at West Point to put a stop to it, but she'd lost her nerve.

"Basically, my Mother wants to marry Don and Don is desperate for a companion for when he gets sent to Germany. They're making me do it. I figure I'll wait a year, then I'll get it annulled." Lisa said that she thought they only gave annulments if there wasn't any consummation. Cindy shot back, "There will be none of that! After this hell? No, no, no, no, *no.* Not part of the deal. That *Continued on page 15*

Continued on page 15

The
ECLECTIC

| Nov. – Dec. 2000 | Volume 2 Number 8 | Free |

CONTENTS

Quotations

"As the old Chinese saying has it, 'You listen to the man who feeds you.'" Yuan-tsung Chen explains why she was so polite to her boring old uncle in *The Dragon's Village.*

"He imagined that to be a good general it was enough to give praise to those who did well and withhold it from those who did badly. The result was that decent people in his entourage liked him, but unprincipled people undermined him since they thought he was easily managed." Xenophon discusses the shortcomings of a Boeotian commander in *The Persian Expedition.*

"Death is not an event in life. Man does not live to experience death." Proposition 6.4311 from Wittgenstein's *Tractatus Logico-Philosophicus.*

"Scribbling on the walls of public lavatories is the futile revenge of minorities." Henri de Montherlant in *Chaos and Night.*

The Eclectic is owned and published by Linoleum Palace, Inc., 43-05 31st Ave., #2, Astoria, NY 11103. Copyright © 1999 by Lincoln MacVeagh. All rights reserved. Unsolicited submissions will not be considered or returned.

Dead and Forgotten

Henri de Montherlant

Lincoln MacVeagh

*"True greatness is greatness
that has no point."*

Paris, September 21, 1972 – Henri de Montherlant committed suicide this afternoon in typically thorough fashion. He swallowed a dose of cyanide then shot himself through the temple. His body was found by his secretary in Montherlant's apartment overlooking the Seine. He died sitting in his favorite chair, and he left behind three letters on the table next to him: a note to his secretary, his will addressed to the courts, and a short letter to a friend. Writing to his friend, Montherlant said simply, *"I am going blind. I am going to kill myself."*

Henry Montherlant's death showed the same stoic determination with which he lived, and thirty years ago his suicide was international news. He was among the best known writers in France. A best-selling novelist and for decades a popular playwright, Montherlant was perhaps the only man ever elected to the Académie française without writing the traditional letter of application. Montherlant vowed he would never submit to the formality; the Académie believed him and he was elected anyway.

Today, nobody cares. Montherlant is almost entirely forgotten. His work has long since gone out of print in English, and in France he is remembered only long enough to be dismissed for his lunatic misogyny: *"...one of the horrors of war, to which attention is never sufficiently drawn, is that women are spared."* Lines like that aren't considered funny anymore, so Montherlant's books get left on the shelves.

Obscurity would seem a sad fate for an author, but Montherlant was not much interested in fame: *"True greatness is greatness that has no point."* Reclusive and fiercely independent himself, Montherlant admired independence in others as well: *"Any man worthy of the name despises the influence he exercises."* A small, stiff man with a military bearing, Montherlant spoke to the world through pursed lips and he was most unusual among writers. He never asked to be loved.

Henry Montherlant was born in Paris on April 20, 1895. The date requires some explanation. In all the biographies published during Montherlant's lifetime, his birthday is given as April 21, 1896. This date was an invention. Montherlant chose it because he was an ardent classicist and April 21 was the founding date of Rome. Why he made himself a year younger is anyone's guess. Vanity perhaps.

Montherlant's parents both belonged to the minor nobility. They were queer fish and they were both terrific snobs. Socially exalted in her own mind, Mme

Montherlant wouldn't let Henry be an altar boy because she couldn't bear to have him sharing the vestments worn by boys of lesser families. There was even a question as to whether Montherlant's parents would let him take his baccalaureate exams. *"In their view, I think, it was not so much learning itself that was degrading as the fact of allowing their son to be 'examined' by strangers whose social origins were more than doubtful."*

Montherlant had a dull life at home. His father was man of leisure, cold and distant: *"...I am of the opinion that paternal love is a sentiment almost non-existent in nature."* His mother was an invalid who never left the house and spent her time shuttling from bed to chaise longue and back. Her husband visited her for a quarter of an hour each evening, but he was not in the habit of speaking to her, and he always left promptly when his time was up. Evidently a lonely woman, Mme Montherlant poured her love out on her son in buckets and Henry found it slightly wearisome. In *The Boys* he describes the ordinary relationship between mother and son as follows: *"Mme de Bricoule adored her son. He was fond of her."*

Ignored by his father and bored by his mother's love, Montherlant was nonetheless a child of enormous vitality. His three absorbing interests were literature, ancient history and bullfighting. Montherlant wrote his first novel at age eight. Two years later he fell in love with classicism after reading *Quo Vadis?* and rewrote his novel to give it a Roman setting. Then, at age fourteen, Montherlant accompanied his grandmother on a pilgrimage to Spain and saw his first bullfight. He secretly practiced in his bedroom, pretending his bedframe was a bull, and he started fighting in amateur corridas the very next year.

Meanwhile he still had to go to school. Montherlant's father wanted him to go to a Jesuit school, but Henry insisted on the École Saint-Croix because a young friend, whom he adored, was already in attendance there. A short battle of wills ensued, but Henry won it easily. Having recently had his appendix removed,

"And this is me on Wall Street, next to a real New York banker wearing the traditional native costume."

he kept re-opening the wound until his father gave in.

Montherlant left home for Saint-Croix in 1911. He was very happy at boarding school, but his happiness was short-lived. He was expelled from school after just fifteen months – probably because the masters were suspicious of Montherlant's attachment to his friend. The exact reasons for the expulsion are not known, but it's certain that Montherlant took it badly, and sixty years later he could still remember his anguish: *"To be suspected of what one has not done, to have one's word disbelieved, corrodes everything."*

Returning home, Montherlant made a brief attempt to study law but failed his preliminary examinations. His mother pushed him into society but he didn't like it. He consoled himself with bullfighting and writing. In 1914 he wrote the first drafts for two novels and a play, all of which were subsequently published.

1914 was also the year World War I broke out and the year Montherlant's father died. Montherlant's mother begged him not to enlist until after she was dead too, and he reluctantly agreed. She didn't last long and three years later Montherlant joined up. The Americans were already in France and he was sent to the Front as an interpreter.

"During the war, I refused to be anything more than a private, so as not to be cut off from the working classes and obliged 'to keep my distance'; and so as not to have to lead them to their deaths in accordance with plans that I myself had not drawn up."

Montherlant enjoyed the war, especially the camaraderie of men at arms, but it's unlikely he was ever really one of the boys. He was too wierdly removed and scarcely a quarter of his army notebooks deal with the fight against Germany: *"... at the age of twenty-two, I was only interested in myself and the contemporaries of Pelopidas; perhaps I might stretch a point and go as far as AD 200."* While

the bombs fell, Montherlant filled page after page with detailed drawings of Etruscan helmets and he lived through the war as if in a classical fantasy. When he was finally wounded, it seemed the perfect ending to his dream. He'd served his country he'd suffered for it, and no one need know that the shell that hit him was fired by French troops during training exercises.

Back in Paris, Montherlant kept his war memories alive by working as secretary to a memorial fund and he kept in touch with the lower classes by joining a suburban athletics club. He also continued to write. *La relève du matin*, Montherlant's first book, was published at his own expense in 1920. It was immediately successful and Montherlant quickly followed up with a novel, a collection of poetry and a new set of essays about sport.

He was rapidly making a name for himself as a clever young man, but Montherlant felt uncomfortable in the part. *"I saw a broad and easy path ahead of me and jibbed at it. So I disposed of hearth and home, put my remaining possessions into store and, completely relieved from now on of all earthly encumbrance of a place of residence, left France with two suitcases which, for nearly ten years, were to be my only luggage."*

It sounds like bravado, but it was the exact truth. For the next decade the trunks in Montherlant's apartment remained exactly where the movers left them. He stopped investing his money, he stopped pushing his literary career,

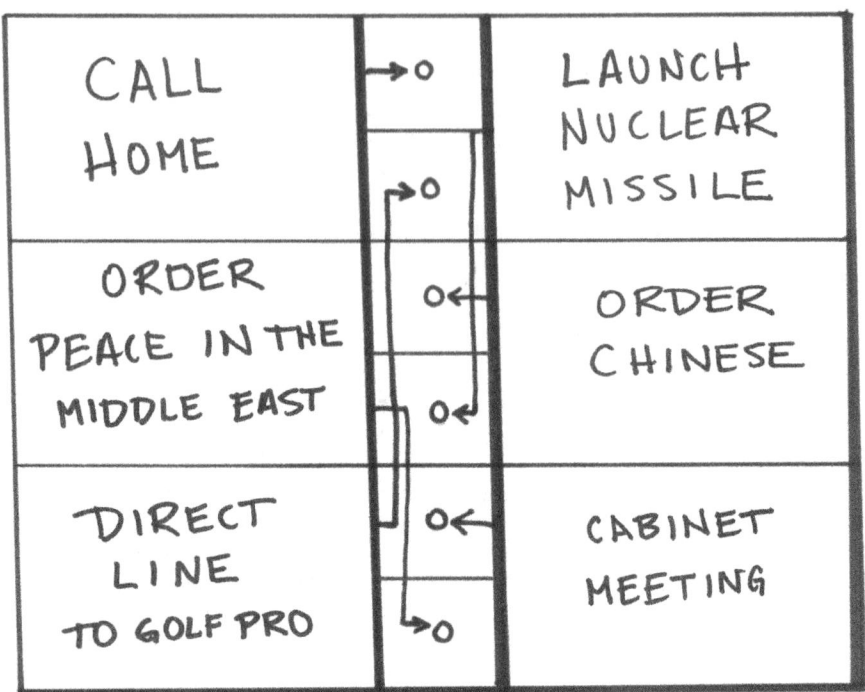

and he cleared out to roam through Spain and North Africa. *"In a word, I wanted (1) to live a life of enchantment; (2) to be uncommitted. In addition, I had a great lust for human beings."*

One immediate result of Montherlant's adventuring was that he almost died. Fighting bulls in Albacete he was gored and the horn nearly punctured a lung. The injury was complicated by typhoid and attacks of pneumonia, and the long months of debilitation provoked a spiritual crisis. By his own account, Montherlant emerged a new man, less enamored of the intellect and more determined than ever to enjoy the pleasures of the flesh while they lasted: *"Formerly, the question: 'What's the use?' would plunge me into despair; now it soothes me."* Required to give up bullfighting, he threw all his remaining physical energy into lechery.

Montherlant was the staunchest defender of sexual pleasure imaginable and he traveled tirelessly in search of it. He worked under a pseudonym,

making conquests wherever he went, and he was neither ashamed of his desire, nor shy about boasting of his success in his published journals. *"All the women who are weeping because of me. At the moment, I can think of four; it's a regular cascade."* Indeed, Montherlant was such a confident lover that it's sometimes hard for his readers not to feel a twinge of jealousy: *"I am sure of my pleasure and of my partner's pleasure. I experience no misgivings, no questionings, uneasiness or remorse."* Can it really be as simple as that?

For Montherlant it was. He roamed the Mediterranean in search of love and managed to keep writing novels at the same time. *The Bachelors* and *The Girls* were both written out of his suitcase, and in 1934 Montherlant won the French Academy's Gran Prix de Littérature.

He gave his prize money to the commander of the French troops in Morocco, asking him to divide it equally between the conquering French soldiers and the defeated Moroccans. Montherlant added: *"I fear these instructions may be cause of embarrassment to you. And so, please dispose of the money as you see fit."* General Giraud gave the money to the Red Cross.

Montherlant's years of wandering came to an end with the approach of the second war. In 1938 he went to the Maginot Line as a war correspondent, but ill health soon pushed him back to Paris and he stayed there for the rest of his life. During the war and for twenty years after it, Montherlant worked primarily as a playwright for the Comédie-Française. His life became quite settled and the habits he adopted at the start of the war never changed again. He worked with discipline every morning, and with equal discipline he pursued his love affairs in the afternoon.

Montherlant was a successful playwright and it was not until shortly before his death that he went back to writing novels. His very best novel, *The Boys*, was published 1969, but by then Montherlant was already going blind. Terrified of becoming dependent, Montherlant suffered a heart attack in February of 1972 and he killed himself eight months later.

It is intriguing to wonder what would be Montherlant's reputation if we knew nothing more about him today than was known at the time of his death. However, it's impossible to know because Montherlant's suicide is not the end of the story. The last chapter comes from a book written by Roger Peyrefitte.

For thirty years Peyrefitte was one of Montherlant's closest friends and in 1977, Peyrefitte published a memoir called *Propos secrets.* Montherlant, the great womanizer, turned out not to be a womanizer at all. Nor did he like men. Montherlant was a pedophile and his only taste was for boys with no hair on their cheeks.

The correspondence between Montherlant and Peyrefitte can be genuinely disturbing. For example, Montherlant writes about one of Peyrefitte's young friends who is holding out against sodomy: *"Why don't you make it official with this child? He deserves rough treatment, and that's what I'd do if I took him back..."*

No one can read such letters without reconsidering Montherlant's rapturous defense of sexuality. His standard line was that sex meant pleasure all around, but it's obvious that the boys Montherlant picked up didn't always enjoy themselves. They weren't even well paid. According to Peyrefitte, the first rule of pederasty was moderation in compensation and Montherlant accepted the motto wholeheartedly.

The inevitable result of Peyrefitte's revelations was that Montherlant's popularity died out. Montherlant believed that his sexuality offended only against society's prudery, but society disagrees and for that reason Montherlant no longer figures in the history of 20th century French literature. It's a pity, because his books are much better than most, and even after discarding Montherlant's sexual philosophy there is a great deal of intelligence left over.

Anthropologists often try to reconstruct the full skeleton of a dinosaur based on the evidence provided by just one or two bones. It's not always possible to do the same with human beings. As often as not, man is a jumble of contradictory impulses. Merits and vices stand side by side. It's not a question of one outweighing the other. They are apples and oranges; they exist independently.

Reviews

Resurrection

by Leo Tolstoy

Penguin Books, 1966 (reprint)

What is the purpose of a novel? Narrowly speaking, Tolstoy wrote *Resurrection* to raise money for a small sect of unorthodox Christians known as the Doukhobors. The Doukhobors preached chastity, vegetarianism, communal property and non-resistance to evil. In 1891 the Russian government began a vigorous campaign of suppression against them and in 1895 Tolstoy sent an article to the London *Times* condemning the suppression. As a result, the English Society of Friends petitioned Emperor Nicholas II to let the Doukhobors leave Russia. The Emperor agreed, but only on condition that his government bore none of the costs. A committee was established to help finance the emigration, and in support of it, Tolstoy finished writing *Resurrection*, pledging all his profits over to the Doukhobors.

Published in 1899, *Resurrection* was Tolstoy's first novel in more than twenty years. After *Anna Karenina* in 1877, Tolstoy gave up on imaginative work, deeming it frivolous. Instead he concentrated on pamphleteering and his own queer search for truth. *Resurrection* made him into a novelist again.

Tolstoy's plot was based on a report he once heard about a nobleman summoned to jury duty who discovers that the prostitute on trial is a girl he had once seduced. Nekhlyudov is the handsome, black bearded nobleman; Maslova is the buxom, young prostitute; and *Resurrection* is the story of Nekhlyudov's spiritual crisis.

Tolstoy became engrossed in the work and he soon conceived a very broad ambition for the novel. In particular, he wanted to write about the Russian justice system (which looks very much like our own), Christianity, and the land reform proposals of Henry George. More generally, however, the purpose of *Resurrection* was to express all the philosophical ideas that had preoccupied Tolstoy for the last two decades.

On the surface this seems like a reasonable aim. It makes sense to think that the purpose of a novel is the expression of ideas. But if so, what's the difference between a novel and a straightforward work of philosophy? In other words, what's the point of all the scenery? *"The sun shone warm, the grass, where it had not been scraped away, revived and showed green..."* Tolstoy scatters such passages throughout *Resurrection* and along the way he also tells us that Maslova's bosom in large and

that Nekhlyudov's beard is black. Why? After all, it's very difficult to coax a philosophical idea out of the color of a man's beard.

One obvious difference between novels and works of philosophy is that novels sell. Towards the end of his life, Tolstoy seems to have arrived at the conclusion that this was the *only* meaningful difference: *"Like a clown at a country fair grimacing in front of the ticket-booth in order to lure the public inside the tent where the real play is being performed, so my imaginative work must serve to attract the attention of the public to my philosophic teaching."*

That is to say, there is no difference. Philosophy is Tolstoy's goal and the novel is merely a device he uses to draw an audience. Why is Nekhlyudov's beard black? For the same reason that manufacturers of children's aspirin add sugar to the recipe.

It's a defensible argument, but it still strikes me as fundamentally wrong, and if *Resurrection* could be reduced solely to its philosophical teaching, it would be a failure. Indeed, Tolstoy is always least convincing in those passages where the message he wants to drive home is most clear.

At one point, for example, Tolstoy has Nekhlyudov deliver a lecture to his peasants about Henry George's land reform proposals. The peasants are enchanted and immediately won over: *"'He had a head on him, that Henry George,' said the imposing old man with the curly beard."* Obviously Tolstoy's readers are meant to be won over as well, but the real effect of the passage is simply to make us doubt Tolstoy's sincerity. Both Nekhlyudov's speech and his peasants' reactions sound horribly contrived.

If novels were merely a sort of window dressing for philosophy, then *Resurrection* would have to stand or fall on its effectiveness as a rhetorical device. Tolstoy's inability to persuade us of his conclusions about land reform, Christianity and so on, would mean that the novel as a whole doesn't work. But the novel does work and I suspect that it is precisely Tolstoy's success as a novelist that dooms him as a soap box preacher.

Nekhlyudov's spiritual crisis is believable because Nekhlyudov has life in him. As a result, Nekhlyudov can't serve as a mere peg on which to hang ideas. He is too real to be just a clown outside a tent, grimacing to attract attention.

This suggests another way of seeing the difference between a novel and a philosophical argument. Whereas a philosophical argument aims at the expression of thought, a novel aims at the depiction of a man thinking. These are different things. *Resurrection* achieves the latter goal brilliantly.

Money!

T.E. MacVeagh

I don't understand about money and I doubt I ever will. This is something of a disadvantage in my job as a corporate lawyer. Clients generally expect their lawyers to have a pretty firm grasp of not only how people make money but why, and of the whole, strange etiquette that surrounds financial transactions. When discussion turns to cash flow, price and profit, I can sometimes fake the appropriate response, but I still feel like a fraud. Like a deaf person who has learned to read lips and pretends he can hear.

It is not that I am an ascetic. I like expensive houses, antique furniture and fancy restaurants. I buy my groceries at Bread & Circus and I fight (not always successfully) the urge to buy high-octane gas. And I realize that there is a connection between being able to indulge these tastes and having a lot of ready cash.

But for all this, I just cannot bring myself to be *interested* in the money end of things. My eyes glaze over at the merest mention of interest rates, stock portfolios or, especially, tax savings. The animated conversations of others remain gobbledygook to me, like I am missing some vital decoder ring.

I don't even fully understand how I earn my own money. I work at a law firm and get paid a handsome salary. I know I wouldn't work if I wasn't paid. But it never feels like I'm working *because* I get paid. Etiquette motivates me more than money. I have (perforce) a relationship with my clients. When a person you know calls you up to ask a favor, it would be rude not to help him.

If I were genuinely to consider my services as given in exchange for money, it would seem that I should have an ethos according to which clients received greater or lesser attention depending on what I bill them. But I don't have that ethos. I feel obligation based on how well I know a client. New clients aggravate me because they are like strangers calling up to ask for favors.

I suppose that I am not alone among lawyers. Law has always been considered a "profession" rather than a business. What that means, as far as I can tell, is that a lawyer's duty to his clients does not depend solely on what they pay (like a doctor's duty to his patients). Rather, all clients are owed the best service possible in the name of one's duty to "Law" itself. Scoff if you like, but I would guess that the law attracts many of us types who don't understand the value of money. Business people have had to hit lawyers over the head again and again with the lesson that the more they pay the more they expect (part and parcel of which is that those who pay less must receive less).

It's true that I'm beginning to learn that it helps to do better work for clients that pay well. But the value of what I do remains a puzzle to me. What I do is so far removed from anything that anybody really wants. I do services for people who do services for people who do services for people who produce things people want. I can see how a ham sandwich or a compact disk has a value. I can see how a haircut or a massage has a value. But the services of a corporate lawyer?

How one should charge for a service so far removed from the appeal of a ham sandwich is a mystery. Or at least it would be without money. The point of money, I suppose, is that it is meant to allow us to compare apples and oranges. Everything can be reduced to dollars per unit. (Really everything! Chicago School economists tell us that this includes nonconsensual intercourse and civic pride.) Through the miracle of the money standard, we can say that an hour of my time as a lawyer is worth about 16 compact disks, five meals at a fancy restaurant or 14% of the monthly rent in a comfortable apartment in Cambridge.

Which is all very well if pricing is a tool in which you have confidence. But I don't have confidence in it. I feel like the mathphobe who cannot abstract from a word problem to see the underlying mathematical puzzle. Given a discussion of price, I keep wondering about value. Who cares that a day at the beach costs the same as a steak? The question is: what do you want, sun or sizzle?

Maybe flattening all our desires to their prices makes such questions easier to answer, but it also drains them of all vitality and interest. Money is just a means to an end, not an end in itself. And means are intrinsically boring. Athletes train to become good at sports, but it's the game that is televised, not the sessions in the weight room.

Besides, money doesn't really seem a particularly reliable indicator of value. If we just look at money as the determinant, then suddenly *Titanic* becomes the best movie ever made, and Tom Clancy is the greatest novelist in history. How often do I really perform work worth sixteen compacts disks an hour? Rarely I suspect. So not only is money just a means to an end, but it is an unreliable means to an end. It's beginning to sound like a real waste of time.

The most attractive thing about the money standard, as far as I can see, is related to the fact that it is so uninteresting. Money has no independent value. It imposes no morality. If the money standard tells us that *Titanic* is a better movie than *Manhattan*, well at least it is not imposing any sort of ideology. Money is not intrinsically Christian or Marxist. It's just money; stacks of greenbacks; numbers in a bank account.

An analysis of a controversial issue which points out that some course of action is economically inefficient is met with nods all around. An analysis which points out that the same course of action is at odds with Christian or Muslim values causes outrage all around. Money is boring enough to be acceptable to everyone.

But how can people spend so much time thinking about something the only advantage of which is that it is utterly boring? As I said, I just do not understand money.

"This is your Captain speaking. Sorry folks, looks like we've got some weather developing and we're gonna be on the ground until it clears up."

American Pangloss

Lincoln MacVeagh

After I quit my first job in San Antonio I saw a notice in the classifieds advertising a goverment sponsored carpentry training program. I signed up for the program and that's how I met Bob Steele.

Bob was an American Pangloss, an eternal optimist, and he was president of the Home Builder's Association. He was a barrel-chested man with an enormous head and sandy blonde hair which stuck in place like dried cement. He must have been in his fifties. When I first met him, he shook my hand firmly and told me the same thing he told everyone else. The future looked bright.

The training program Bob organized was taught by a genial out-of-work carpenter named Jim Downing. We spent our mornings in a classroom and in the afternoons we practiced snapping chalk lines on plywood and hammering walls together.

There were sixteen students in the class: thirteen Mexicans, two whites, and one African-American named Richard Lewis. Richard was a quarter Indian and he had startling green eyes. He told me he'd spent two years in reform school for lighting his mother's boyfriend on fire. Two weeks into the course, Richard got the nickname "Magnet."

The story behind the nickname was

that someone in the class kept stealing our building materials. A sheet of plywood would go missing, or else a hammer, or a box of nails. Jim, our teacher, regularly complained about the theft and his chief suspect was a fat Mexican named Roberto.

Roberto was the class clown. He never did his homework and he made it clear to anyone who asked that he was only enrolled in the training program for the sake of the credential. His motto was: "I just want my CERTEEFEE-CATE!"

Roberto didn't like being suspected as the thief, so whenever anything disappeared he put the blame on Richard. Roberto invented the nickname "Magnet" to suggest that, like a magnet, Richard would pick up anything that wasn't bolted down. The name caught on and Richard took it with remarkably good grace. Especially since, as everyone knew, it was Roberto who did all the stealing.

The training program lasted six weeks and our final class project was the building of a ten by ten tool shed complete with door, roof and window. Our construction site was the back of the Builder's Association parking lot and the trouble was that when it rained we couldn't work. That meant a visit with Bob Steele.

Bob didn't like to see us sit idle and whenever the storm clouds gathered he would call us all into his conference room for an inspirational speech. Standing at the front of the room, Bob took off his suit jacket and carefully laid his eyeglasses on the table:

"I want to talk to you about opportunity. Now I know that many of you have lived full lives already. In the past, maybe you haven't experienced success, but there's always a chance to start over. It takes hard work and dedication. Believe me. Today I'm president of the Builder's Association, but I know where you're coming from. I know what poor is. I was born in Oklahoma and my father was a farm hand. I never went to college. When I was nineteen years old I started working for an oil company. Long weeks on the road but I stuck to it. Five years later I was regional sales manager covering the entire Southwest. I came up from nothing to make a good living. I did it because I believed in myself and I believe in you people too. You can make life what you want it. Just keep focused and keep trying. You're good people, etc.."

Bob could talk like that for an hour straight and he always said the same thing. We heard the speech so often that many of us had parts of it memorized. Roberto did a beautiful impression. While the rest of us were working away, he'd call for attention, wipe his hand across his brow and start speaking in a thick Mexican accent: "I was born in Oklahoma and my father was a farm hand. I never went to college..."

Bob's lectures were heroically dull, and he antagonized his audience by talking down to us, but there was also something mesmerizing about the way he spoke. None of us believed in Bob's rags to riches fantasy, but his own belief was so fervent that it was almost touching. He was so achingly sincere that it was difficult to laugh in his face.

When the tool shed was finally completed, our course was over and we gathered for a last time in Bob's conference room. It was graduation day. One by one Bob called our names and handed each of us a blue certificate stating that we had completed apprenticeship training in the craft of carpentry. Roberto whooped. The rest of us waited for Bob's inevitable parting speech. He announced that he had two important things to say, both somewhat sad.

The first bit of news concerned Rawley, the youngest member of our class. Bob wanted us to know why Rawley wasn't at graduation. Three days previous, he'd run away from home and joined the navy. Bob had spoken to him on the phone and he was okay. We must wish him the best and keep him in our prayers.

The second item was about Bob himself. "As some of you may know, I have recently learned that this is to be my last week as president of the Builder's Association. The national organization has decided on a restructuring process so you will no longer be able to reach me at the number printed on my business cards."

Bob had promised to find us all jobs through his contacts in the construction industry, but now he too was looking for work. He insisted that we copy down his home phone number and told us to call whenever we felt like it.

Bob was obviously upset. He was afraid of letting us down on the job hunt, but more than that he seemed afraid that we would misinterpret his firing as evidence that all his talk about the value of hard work and dedication was just so much hogwash. He struggled with the thought for a moment before overcoming it. "No, it's just not so. It's the opposite. When I was speaking to you as president of the Association I had no way of showing you what I meant about opportunity. Now I can really prove what I was talking about. Two months from now I am going to have a new job, and it'll be a better job, and you know how I know that? Because I believe in myself. And I believe in you too. We can make our lives what we want. Just keep focused and keep trying. We're good people, etc.."

Sir Laffalot

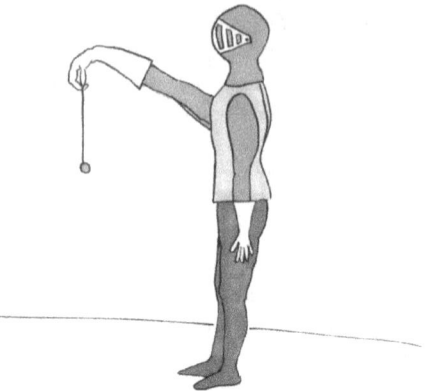

Imagine there was a special tree that gave balls and jacks for fruit. Now imagine if no one knew how to play jacks. What a lot of fun would go wasted!

Something similar is happening with the conkers in New York City. Each fall the precious conkers drop from their branches in Central Park and they are swept into the gutters simply because no one knows how to play conkers. Sir Laffalot has wiped the tears from his eyes and resolves to educate the masses.

A conker is a horse chestnut. Conker trees have soft, paisley shaped leaves and the conker itself comes wrapped in a spiky, green casing. It has a tough brown skin and a whitish meat. In size it is somewhere between a cherry and a golfball. Conkers are inedible. They don't even eat them in China.

The conker tree is native to Asia and the ancient Chinese used to plant them along highways for good luck. Many centuries later, Arab silk traders introduced conkers into East Africa where their novelty made them into a valuable status symbol. For a brief period in the twelfth century prosperous trading centers specializing in conker jewelry sprang up along the African coast.

However, the conker trees flourished all too easily and the short conker boom was followed by a very long bust. The jewelry business dried up and the conker sank back to anonymity. It was not until nearly four hundred years later that an Italian merchant brought the first conker back to western Europe, presenting it as a curiosity to the Pope in Rome.

Initially the Italians were very excited about conkers, but they were never able to put them to good use. The frustrated Pope was ready to declare conkers sacriligious but at the last minute a young bishop stepped in with the clever idea of selling them to the Irish.

Hoping to lessen Ireland's dependence on the potato crop, the Irish government encouraged their farmers to plant conker trees by the thousands. The Italian exporters made a bundle, but the Irish farmers were sorely disappointed after they discovered that conkers were inedible. It almost sparked a revolution.

Fortunately, calm was restored when a man in a pub realized that although you couldn't eat conkers, you could still play a jolly good game with them.

Conkers: How to Play.

1) 1) Make a hole through each conker with a skewer. Pull a string through the hole and tie a knot at one end.

2) 2) One player holds his conker still, dangling it at arm's length. The other player tries to hit it by swinging at it with his own conker. Then the players switch positions. Whichever conker breaks off the string first is the loser.

3) 3) A conker that wins a single battle is a onesie. Two battles and it's a twosie. If a twosie beats a threesie, it becomes a fivesie. The best conker ever was a one hundred and sixsie.

Sir Laffalot says: TOODALOO!!

Continued from page 16

hours he's got a pyramid of dirty wet cin-
derblocks in the middle of the floor, a case
full of empty beers, and he announces he's
in love. He tickles me until I mess up my
drawing, then he runs out into the rain
again. Later I hear that he broke Zoe Zim-
merman's window with a rock, passed out,
and needed to be helped back to her room.

It was pretty charming. I was different from John, but not seeing each other
every day allowed us to kind of bond.
He bought me a big Grolsch beer for
Christmas and sat with me when I had
my head in the toilet. I helped him down
from an acid freakout when he saw fuzzy
pink worms crawling down the walls.
And it was all cemented when we discovered that we shared an embarrassing
favorite song, "Calling Occupants of
Interplanetary Craft" by the Carpenters.

Meanwhile, school got more and
more intense. My friends and I wandered home in clouds of charcoal only
to stay up all night making three-
dimensional replicas of Dali paintings
out of papier-mâché. I wondered if
we were really getting anywhere, or if
we just lacked the courage and natural
vitality to be like John Walker, who was
failing architecture, but scoring off the
charts in boozing and fornication.

Towards the end of second term,
Kelly's 15-year-old sister came up for a
visit. John got her drunk, and sloppily
deflowered her while I tried to sleep in
the top bunk. The sister told Kelly and
in the aftermath, John spent every night
getting high in our room and working
on some kind of sculpture made of glass
and glue. He said it was a cityscape, but
it looked more like a jumble of jagged
icebergs. He also tried to stop drinking.

One night I knocked over one of
John's houseplants. I put the plant back
into the pot and patted the dirt down
as best I could, but John discovered it
the next day, and for some reason, he
lost his mind. He destroyed one of the
laundry machines, ripped the phone

out of the wall, and yelled that he was
going to kill me seriously enough that
my friends warned me not to go home
until he cooled down.

I went to a party, and stayed out late
enough so that John would be fast asleep
when I returned. When I got home, I
found him lying on the floor. Naked, and
covered in blood. Was he dead? A practical joke? Performance art?

John's glass sculpture was smashed
to bits, and there were shards all over
the floor. It looked like he'd fallen
on top of it, and then rolled over. I
couldn't see how badly he was cut
because he had smeared the blood all
over his body until he was literally red.
I called the dorm monitor, who called
security, who called the ambulance, and
they all rushed at once. Before anyone could touch him, John looked up,
started laughing, then passed out again.

His wounds turned out to be superficial, but the incident combined with
his bad grades got him kicked out of
school. He didn't go back to Alaska.
Instead he hung around campus and
got a job working in the school's computer lab. He gained 100 pounds and
smoked a *lot* of pot.

During my sophomore year, I saw
him from time to time, but we didn't
hang out. He was busy becoming one
of those campus characters, like Liver-
fish the bum, or Charlie the model. His
brain cells seemed to have been smoked
away, and in general he acted like a
burned out hippy, despite the fact the he
wasn't even drinking age yet. He asked
me to be his roommate again at one
point, but I told him I couldn't afford it.

The only reason I thought about
John Walker was that I saw him
recently. I was taking a cab uptown,
and around 57th street I passed him;
I recognized him immediately. He was
walking briskly, rail thin, with long
slicked back hair, and his cream colored
Armani suit was flapping in the wind.
Maybe he was on his way to breakfast.

The high life

Johnny Walker Red

David Garcia III

At art school I was assigned to room with Francisco Fernandez, an actual Spanish kid from Spain. We had nothing in common beyond ethnic surnames and dark hair, and within a few minutes of our meeting he had hauled out snapshots of his summer spent in Ibiza on jet skis with bikinibabes.

Francisco lived to siesta and this was a problem because our noisy first floor room was just inside the entrance and across from the dorm telephone. Luckily, one of the guys on the third floor (Julian, a would be sculptor) started wandering outside naked at night. Julian was removed to a nearby facility, and Francisco jumped at the chance to take the quiet upper room.

For a few weeks I had a huge room of my own and it was a dream. Then I heard rumblings of trouble elsewhere on campus. Word was that Andrew Weinberg was being terrorized by his roommate, John Walker. Andrew was threatening to sue the school and the head of Student Services called me in to explain the situation. He asked politely if I would consider letting John Walker be my roommate. I was surprised to have a choice in the matter, and a little suspicious when he offered to lower my tuition. I told him I needed a few days, and I decided to do some detective work.

I already knew that John was the resident jock at the school. At someplace like Ohio State, he would be just another BMOC, but at art school he had the Frat Boy niche to himself. Every girl I spoke to had either slept with him or been propositioned. I learned that he was an Army Brat from Alaska, that he was studying Architecture, and that he

got wasted every night. I also learned that he ate breakfast in the cafeteria every morning. This last fact set off alarm bells – no one I knew ever made it to breakfast.

Everyone seemed to have an opinion about John Walker, and it amused me to find that it wasn't the puking and groping that bothered people – it was his personal style. Dressing like the Flying Monkeys from the *Wizard of Oz* was the rage in art school. Everyone cool was experimenting with opaque music, advanced drugs, and innovative sexual identities. Need I mention the passion quest for unprecedented hair? John Walker, I was told, listened to the soundtrack from *Hair* without laughing. His crewcut, Oxford shirts, and general air of physical fitness were roundly denounced. I was advised to avoid him at all costs.

Unfortunately, I happened to mention the tuition deduction to my parents, and they insisted I let John move in as a "character building exercise". Wherever I went, people stopped me to hear the horror stories, but there was really nothing to report. He was the perfect roommate: he was almost never there.

John had taken up with a tall, sort of sad girl, named Kelly. She had her own room in a dorm across campus, and he stayed there almost every night. On rare occasions, they'd have a fight and he'd hang out in our room. A typical entry from my journal:

1am: I'm at my drafting table, and JW comes barging in, crashing a case of Molson onto the floor. "Fuckin' bitch Kelly, wants to sleep – got her period, again." He stomps around, obviously on speed, then he yells, "Cinderblocks!" He runs off into the rain to collect cinderblocks from people's yards. He's chugging the beers and singing "talkin' bout Ma-donna, she was a sixteen year old vir-gin" from the Hair soundtrack at the top of his lungs. After a couple of

Continued on page 15

The
ECLECTIC

February 2001	Volume 2 Number 9	Free

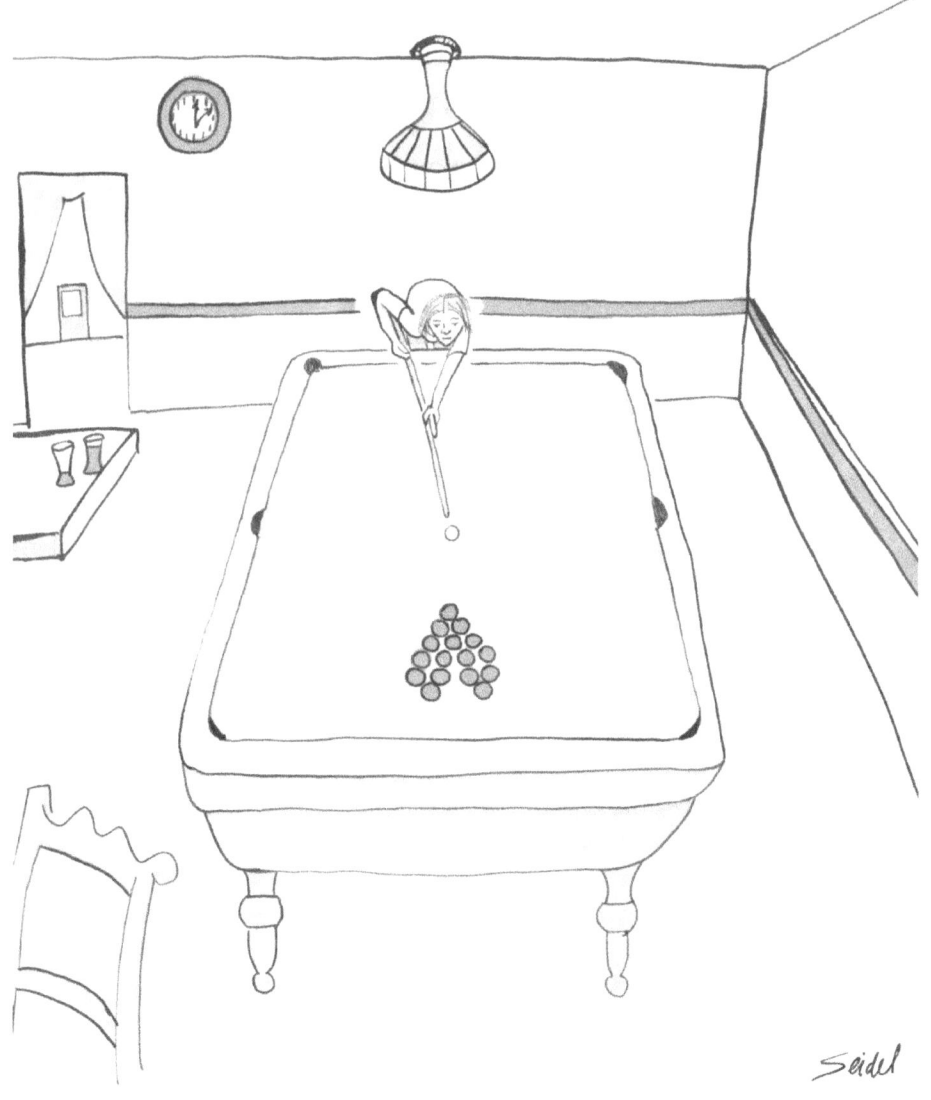

CONTENTS

Quotations

"'Out of the question! Imagine me going around with a potbelly. It would mean political ruin.'" Hitler worries about his waistline in Albert Speer's *Inside The Third Reich.*

"From that moment, I never treated anything he had to say on faith or morals very seriously." A hungry Auberon Waugh watched his father Evelyn eat three bananas for breakfast. The bananas were meant for Waugh's three children and none of them had ever tasted one. From Auberon Waugh's *Will This Do?*

"We had to practice small talk – which was, Pauline said, a vital asset – a formula no less rigid than an Oriental tea ceremony. Equally important was how to flatter. But more important than small talk or flattering was listening. 'Listening,' Pauline would declare, 'is the way to be most socially acceptable.'" Thomas Hoving remembers the lessons of his socialite step-mother in *Making The Mummies Dance.*

"I remember making the delightful discovery that a French novel could, after all, be read in the original without a dictionary, provided one was content with a somewhat vague idea of the sense." Arnold Bennett in *Sketches For Autobiography.*

A Bit of Gossip

Lincoln MacVeagh

Ian Kent was getting ready for a party. He took a crisp white shirt from the dry cleaner's wrapping and chose a brown woolen suit to wear with it. Ian would look elegant but not flashy; he did not like to draw attention to his clothes. As he said, no one puts their trust in a pair of trousers.

Ian Kent aimed to be trusted and he had one of the best known faces in America. Indeed, he was a celebrity. Nonetheless, he refused to think of himself as such and if anyone was so indelicate as to ask him what it was like to be famous, he would tell them sharply that fame is a concept that exists only in minds of gossip columnists. He was not paid to be famous, he was paid to do his job.

Ian's job was journalism, and whenever he filled out a visa application he always put "reporter" in the little box marked occupation. It thrilled his modesty to do so, and he was pleased to think of himself as part of the vast brotherhood of men and women who run around the country with notepads in their hands writing down the minutes of the local town council meeting. As Ian often pointed out, he had once been one of them. This was true. In all fairness, however, he wasn't one of them anymore.

Ian was the anchor man for *ABS News with Ian Kent* and his job gave him more power than 10,000 small town reporters together. The advertising slogan for Ian's nightly newscast stated the matter quite plainly: "More Americans get their news from *ABS* news than from any other source." It was not a slogan that tripped off the tongue, but Ian liked it. He liked it so much that he was even liable to forget that the slogan was more or less false.

The slogan was false because it was used to suggest that *ABS News with Ian Kent* was the top-rated nightly newscast. It wasn't; it was number two, and the reference to "more Americans" was only accurate if one calculated the total audience for all the shows produced by *ABS* news combined. *ABS* produced news for countless prime-time news magazines, as well as for the radio, and it was this side of the business, rather than anything to do with Ian Kent, that emboldened *ABS* to call itself number one. Intellectually, Ian understood this subtlety, but deep down he could not help believing that his newscast really was the best, and each time he heard the show's slogan, he was struck by the awesome responsibility of his position.

More power to him. Ian had every right to feel proud of his position and

he had worked very hard to earn it. When he first started at *ABS* he was thought of strictly as a writer and producer. Countless times he was told by his bosses that he was too stiff and prim to become a television personality. What America wanted, said the network, was folksiness, and Ian was almost forced to quit before he was allowed to report his own stories in front of a camera. Surprisingly, he proved himself competent. He was turned into a foreign correspondent and he started traveling around the world, chasing down three-minute clips about everything from the Arab-Israeli war to Princess Margaret's wedding. For some reason he was popular. All those folksy people in Iowa and New Jersey admired his sophistication.

Ian was a foreign correspondent for ten years and he enjoyed his work, but after a while he began to feel himself stagnating. Always on an airplane, he felt out of the loop in New York, and with no chance to play office politics he worried that the better opportunities were passing him by. He should not have worried. Being out of the loop actually helped him, and when, upon the retirement of Ian's legendary predecessor, it came time for the network to chose a new anchor, Ian's name rose quickly to the top of the list. He was the only person at *ABS* against whom there were no vendettas, the only person without powerful enemies, and Ian was chosen for the anchor's job over a number of better known personalities.

Most people in television are ambitious. Ian Kent was no exception and he could never have become the network anchor if he didn't have a hard side. Still, he was by all accounts a decent man. During the course of his rapid rise he had left remarkably few bodies behind him. He was still close to many of the same people who had befriended him as an unknown years ago and in this respect, Ian even went out of his way. To prove it, let us go back to the party he was getting ready for in the first paragraph. This party was the annual anniversary bash of his old friends Harvey and Kitty Drink.

Harvey Drink was a wealthy lawyer whom Ian had know for more than twenty years and in all that time Ian had not missed a single one of Harvey's anniversary parties. In truth, it would have been very difficult to get out of going. Harvey looked upon hosting Ian as the pinnacle of his social calendar and he would not be put off. Ian had once tried to duck the invitation by saying that he would be out of town, but Harvey responded that he would hold

ZENO'S ELEVATOR

off the celebration until Ian returned. Over the years, it had developed that Harvey simply called to find out when Ian was free and scheduled his parties accordingly.

Ian was trapped but he kept his good humor about it. No doubt Harvey and Kitty were pushy, but Ian was fond of the Drinks and what's more, he was fond of seeing himself as a man who, despite celebrity, kept in touch with old friends. For the most part, Ian even enjoyed Harvey's parties. He liked meeting people outside the world of broadcasting, he liked keeping his finger on the pulse, but there was one detail about the Drinks' parties that always cast a small cloud over Ian's outlook. "Poor woman," he thought as he shaved, "It's so depressing."

What depressed him was that Harvey and Kitty Drink not only invited Ian to their anniversary, they also invited Ian's ex-wife Joan. This was understandable since Kitty Drink had been Joan's close friend since they roomed together at Smith. It was also understandable because, shortly after Ian's divorce, Ian had told Harvey that he and Joan remained on the best of terms. When Harvey asked whether Ian would prefer his ex-wife not to be invited, Ian had insisted strongly to the contrary.

"I'm so glad you feel that way," said Harvey, "Of course, Kitty and I completely understand about the divorce, but we can't help feeling a bit sorry for Joan. She's lost many of her friends and it's as though the air has been let out of her. Kitty has been pressing me hard to invite her. She wants Joan to know that people still care."

Ian, who felt guilty about leaving his wife, couldn't have agreed more.

That was six years ago. Ian and Joan got divorced just prior to Ian being named the anchor at *ABS*, when he was still a foreign correspondent. It was no surprise to anyone that the marriage could not withstand the bur-

den of Ian's travel schedule. Nor was it a surprise two years later, when Ian announced he was getting re-married to Gloria Henderson. According to the gossip columnists, Ian was too good a catch to remain single for long and Gloria was a beautiful young woman from one of New York's best families. It was a perfect match. Ian was distinguished and gentlemanly; Gloria possessed the magic of youth, and she also knew enough about men not to ask Ian for more than he could give.

After this second marriage, conducted in private, Harvey Drink once again took up with Ian the delicate question of whether to invite his ex-wife to the anniversary party. Once again Ian insisted that Joan come. Ian said that Gloria and Joan got on well together, and besides, knowing how Joan was running downhill, it was important to coax her out of the house now and then.

Ian was nothing if not magnanimous, but all the magnanimity in the world couldn't cover up the fact that in his heart he would have been perfectly happy never to see Joan again. From year end to year end, he only ever spoke to her at the Drinks' party and he always found it awkward. She was no longer the vibrant woman she once was. She was more like an old ship that had been taken into dry dock and was slowly rusting away. Ian guessed that

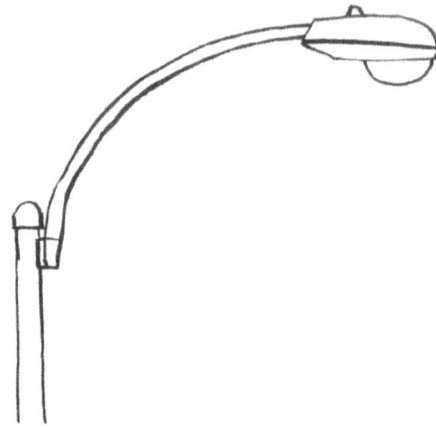

Joan was still very much in love with him, but he also guessed that her love had turned to bitterness. She looked sour and dressed badly. God knows he gave her enough money to support herself, but she always showed up at Harvey's apartment wearing something from the long ago days when she was still married.

"Go to Lord & Taylor and buy yourself a new outfit," Ian implored her.

"I don't have much use for Lord & Taylor anymore," Joan answered. She had lost her vivacity. At Harvey's parties she stood in a corner by herself and she gave the distinct impression that she was just gritting her teeth and counting the hours before she could go home to her apartment and wallow in her own private misery. Ian thought of his ex-wife and groaned.

"It's going to be awful," he said.

"Nonsense," said Gloria, "Joan is a big girl and she has to learn to take care of herself. It's not your fault if she's still in love with you and there's no reason for you to be anxious. I'm planning to have a nice evening, and I think you should, too."

Harvey and Kitty Drink lived in an enormous duplex on Park Avenue and 71st street, and Ian and Gloria arrived at nine thirty. There were already more than a hundred people milling around the apartment and one of the guests was Tom Berger.

Tom Berger is the glue that holds this story together, but otherwise there is not much to say about him. He was a good-natured, moderately handsome young man whose father was a business partner of Max Drink. He was newly arrived in New York and he came to the party in hopes of seeing Ian Kent, if only because he had never met anyone famous before.

Fortunately, Ian was in good form and did not disappoint. Following Gloria's advice, he had sought out Joan immediately upon entering the party. They exchanged a few words, he kissed her on the cheek, and having taken his medicine, he drifted away to more pleasant company. When Tom Berger caught sight of him, Ian was entertaining a large group of Harvey's friends with stories about his new interest in yoga. Tom edged his way into the group just in time to see Gloria Kent, her dress rising up her pretty backside, bending over to touch her elbows to the floor.

"Amazing!" cried Harvey.

"Go on Ian," said Gloria, "Show Harvey your lotus position."

Sheepishly and after much encouragement from Harvey, but with infinite panache, Ian sat down on the floor, crossed his legs over his knees and let out a soft, comic "Ommmmmm."

"Dan Rather, eat your heart out," said Harvey.

The talk turned to politics and Tom Berger, not wishing to be conspicuous, sauntered off to get a drink. The sight of Ian Kent sitting cross-legged had impressed him and he was glad to have collected a story he could repeat to his friends, but apart from that, Tom didn't see much point to the Drinks' party. Most of the guests were twice his age and none of them were interested in him. For twenty minutes he got stuck with a drunk retired judge who talked about "young people today," but afterwards Tom was left on his own to stare out the window at the street lights running down to the Helmsley Hotel. At ten o'clock he'd had enough and he approached Kitty Drink to say his goodbyes.

Kitty was talking to a sad faced woman in a faded pink skirt suit. The woman had stringy grey hair that hung around her shoulders and Kitty was prodding her on the subject of men: "Have you met Tom Carter? He's very interesting. He works with Harvey on the church board. Are you sure you wouldn't like me to introduce you?"

Joan demurred. "No thank you, really. In fact, I should probably be going. I think I'm starting on a headache."

"Oh dear. A migraine?" Kitty's question got no response and Tom jumped into the silence.

"My mother used to get migraines. They're terrible. If you'd like I'll go down with you and call you a taxi."

"How chivalrous!" exclaimed Kitty. Kitty was quite content to be rid of Joan and she thought it very lucky to find such a nice young man to relieve her of her burden. Kitty kissed Joan and Tom goodbye and almost pushed them into the elevator together.

"Did your mother really get migraines?" asked Joan.

"Only when she was bored," said Tom.

"I think we suffer from the same disease."

A smile is a woman's best kept beauty secret and when Joan smiled in the elevator, Tom noticed that she no longer looked so withered as she had at the party. She was almost pretty.

"You needn't call me a cab," said Joan, "Nice of you to offer, but I have Johnnie parked around the corner with my car. Perhaps I could give you a lift?"

"I didn't picture you with a chauffeur," said Tom.

"Be nice to him. He bites."

Joan laughed at her own joke and when they reached her car she knocked on the driver's window and out stepped her chauffeur. He was a stocky Latino in his fifties, and not at all what Tom imagined a chauffeur to be. He had no uniform and no cap, just tan slacks and a white button down shirt.

"Johnnie, this is Tom. We're going to take him home with us. What do you say?"

"Certainly Madam." Johnnie spoke with a thick accent but he had a quiet dignity about him that was appealing. He winked at Tom as if to say, the old lady's crazy.

Joan was peculiar to say the least, and Tom was amazed by the transformation in her manner. Driving down-

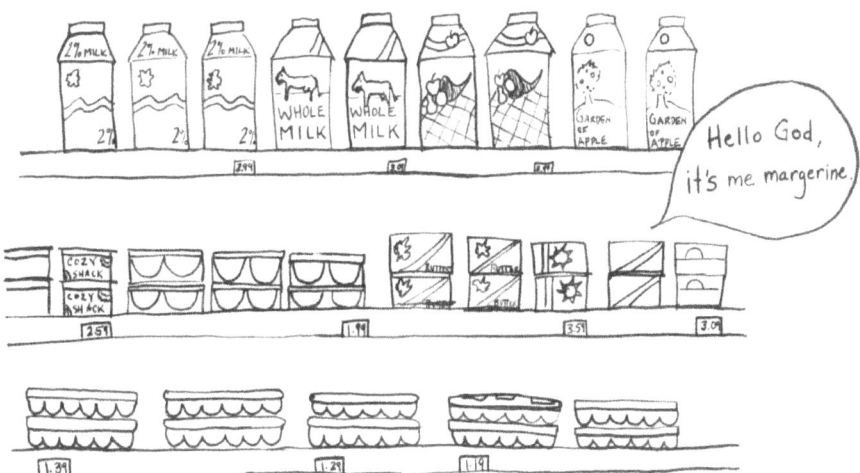

town she was suddenly talkative and gay. Tom listened appreciatively and asked her how she knew the Drinks.

"The great Ian Kent," she chirped, "Upon whom the Drinks fawn, is my ex-husband. I'm working very hard to win him back but I can't yet manage to touch my elbows to the floor unless I'm lying down."

The car pulled into a parking lot on Barrow Street and Tom thanked Joan for the ride, but she wouldn't let him go and invited him back to her apartment for a drink. Tom was bewildered but accepted with pleasure, and in Mrs. Kent's sitting room Johnnie poured Tom a large glass of whiskey. Johnnie himself drank beer. Joan asked for a glass of wine and went to change her clothes. She returned wearing a pair of blue jeans and cursing the fool designer who invented the skirt suit.

"If it weren't for Kitty's parties I would burn every last one that I own."

From that moment on Joan led the conversation. She was alive and energetic and the highlight of the evening was a story she told about Harvey Drink and his former secretary that even made Johnnie blush. Tom would have liked to have stayed much longer but he feared overstaying his welcome and he left before midnight. He walked home through the Greenwich Village night pondering the wonders of New York.

Indeed, for an adventurous boy like Tom, New York is a city of a thousand wonders, and on a Saturday night three weeks after the Drink's anniversary party, Tom and his friend Peter took the R Train to Roosevelt, headed for a giant salsa party they had seen advertised in the *Village Voice*. They walked under the train tracks along a section of the avenue that looked for all the world like a busy commercial district in South America, and when they entered the club they found an enormous brightly lit ballroom filled to overflowing with people of all ages.

Old men sat drinking with their wives while grandchildren in their Sunday best skittered about from table to table. A ten-piece band was playing on a stage in the front and the dance floor was packed with men in dark suits and smiling women in colorful dresses. Tom and Peter bought a pint of rum and a bottle of coca-cola and they found a table at the back of the hall from which to watch the scene.

Time passed quickly and after an hour, Peter tapped Tom on the shoulder. One of the women on the dance floor was staring at him. She was a mature, handsome woman in a bright yellow dress and she wore her grey hair pulled back over her head in a tight bun like a Spanish princess. It was Joan Kent and she was dancing with her chauffeur. She caught Tom's eye and waved, and when the music stopped, they walked over to Tom's table.

"Who would have thought?" said Joan.

"Peter, this is Joan Kent," said Tom. They shook hands. "And this is..." Tom hesitated. He was stuck. He couldn't remember the name of Joan's chauffeur. Joan laughed and for a few seconds she let Tom hang. At last she stepped in to complete the introduction herself.

"And this is my husband, Johnnie."

Martial Arts For the Year 2001

VCR KWAN DO

PALM CHI

CELL PHONE TE

Reviews

Père Goriot

by Honoré de Balzac

Signet Classics, 1962 (reprint)

Don't go asking your local librarian for a copy of Balzac's masterpiece *The Human Comedy*, because no such book exists. Rather, as I once learned to my chagrin, *The Human Comedy* is a catchall title referring to a series of more than fifty different books. *Père Goriot* is one of the earliest books in the series, and it was the first in which Balzac took a favorite character from a previous novel and used him again as the hero of a new story.

The character in question is the great Eugène de Rastignac, and in *Père Goriot* he reappears as a young man eager to make his way in the world. The quirk, however, is that Balzac was already a good way along on *Père Goriot* before he realized that Eugène Massiac, the tiresome medical student at Mme. Vauquer's lodging house, would be more interesting as a youthful version of the charismatic Rastignac. Balzac dutifully went back and made the name changes, but he did not bother to re-write any of the opening scenes. As a result, a third of the way through *Père Goriot*, Eugène undergoes a jarringly sudden transformation. In the space of a five paragraphs he changes from a no-account dullard into a clever and ambitious young man.

Initially it does not appear that Eugène's new personality will have much affect on the novel because the focus is on Goriot and his daughters. But the novel quickly changes course and we are soon wrapped up in Rastignac's rise through the ranks of society. Meanwhile a third story develops around the machinations of the master criminal Vautrin, and for the next two hundred pages Goriot fades into the background. Balzac has tried to cram three books into one, but it is not always clear what the different stories have to do with each other, and the reader often feels as though he has stumbled across a mid-season episode of a long running soap opera. There is so much plot that only an addict who has been watching for years can figure it out.

Apparently, this sort of confusion is typical of Balzac. He wrote so quickly that he did not always have time for the niceties of construction. *Père Goriot* was finished in less than four months and the strain of the pace shows. Balzac's characters tend to fall in love on sight and much of their emotion reads as though it's been sketched in with a pencil on a napkin. By far the weakest part of the novel is its maudlin ending.

Father Goriot is dying and he suffers to think that his daughters do not love him as he would wish. He has given them everything and they have repaid him with contempt. Goriot, we are told, *"symbolized fatherhood itself,"* and we're meant to feel sorry for him, but Goriot's daughters are so heartless and his devotion to them is so over the top that the sadness of Goriot's fate is rather overwhelmed by its silliness. One is reminded of Oscar Wilde's quip about the death of little Nell in *The Old Curiosity Shop*: you would need a heart of stone to see her tears and not to laugh.

All the same, *Père Goriot* is marvelous fun to read. Balzac is sometimes sloppy but he always inspires confidence, and his story moves you along quickly. Paris comes to life, and even the flimsiest of Balzac's characters have a knack for seeing the cold, hard truth. Towards the end of the book, Rastignac criticizes one of Goriot's daughters for having allowed her relationship with her father to deteriorate so badly. Delphine brushes off the criticism with a sigh: *"In some situations in life, there's no avoiding bitterness."* Such lines make it easy to forgive Balzac his faults.

Commentary

Black and White

T.E. MacVeagh

I once heard a lecture by a journalist claiming that a society could be understood by looking at the method it chose to differentiate between its members. In England, he claimed, people were sorted by class. In Germany, by religion. In France, by the ability to speak French. And in America, by race.

Given that ours is a society defined by race, perhaps it is surprising that America has been so successful at mixing different ethnicities and racial groups into its melting pot. So successful that many historical hatreds, at one time quite virulent, with respect to immigrants from such places as Ireland, Italy, Germany, Norway, and Poland have largely disappeared. Contemporary prejudices against immigrants from India, Pakistan, Latin America and Asia are also fading into obscurity with remarkable speed. The overwhelming impression made by college-age children of Korean immigrants is their quintessential Americaness. The issue of race disappears.

We all know the story of immigration. Exiles arrive fleeing war, famine or poverty in their own country. They have no money or resources. They do not speak English and they have few skills relevant to the American economy. When they find work, they are forced into the hardest, dirtiest manual labor. The established majority looks at them with disdain, considering them dirty, ignorant and dangerous. Often this translates into a belief that the people are this way because of their ethnic heritage, rather than because of their economic circumstances.

The happy ending to the story is also well-known. The immigrants cluster together for support, opening restaurants, founding churches and preserving their culture. Many of the first generation will fail to escape poverty, but at least they have a familiar home in the urban recreation of their homeland; a place where their ethnicity is counted as something normal and reassuring, rather than strange and off-putting. They work hard, earn money and learn English. Often they come to dominate a particular trade or industry. It comes as somewhat of a shock when the first members of the group accumulate enough wealth and influence to treat with the elite of the established classes and races. But their children take it for granted. Suddenly, the old stereotype of the immigrants as dirty and ignorant becomes laughably inappropriate. Eventually, the fact that used to be so central to their existence, the fact that they are Irish or Polish or Korean as well as American, begins to seem less and less important.

But all racial distinctions are not created equal. The difference that particularly dominates America is the difference between Black and White. It dominates the American image at home and abroad. The famed American melting pot has not worked for Blacks. Or, more accurately, as we will see below, not for African-Americans (in particular, those whose ancestors were brought over as slaves). Over a much greater span of time, their progress towards integration and acceptance has been significantly less than with other groups. Blacks remain the great indigestible racial group in American society. (That is not to say that their has been no improvement in their lot. Slavery has ended. So has segregation. And the situation of African-Americans in this country is improving in incremental steps even while frustration at the lack of progress grows.)

The difference is obvious. Above we described the immigrant experience,

but Blacks in this country are not immigrants. They did not choose to come to America. They were dragged here, kicking and screaming, as slaves. And they came to the country very early, not as fortune-hunters drawn to a society bursting with wealth and opportunity, but along with the original settlers of a wilderness. Moreover, their native culture was largely destroyed by the slave trade. The plantation system did not care about the culture of men and women with black skin. And by the time Blacks were free to remember and explore their heritage, several centuries and a gigantic experiential difference separated them from it.

As a result, the Black ghettos in America were (and are) nothing like the ghettos of other immigrants. They were not designed to recreate a vanished homeland. They did not provide the psychic or social nourishment found in an immigrant community. The source of kinship in the black urban environment is shared oppression, not shared pride. In immigrant communities, particular ethnic groups go out of their way to buy from merchants of their own group. Several studies have

shown that this is not true within Black communities.

This lack of a cultural heritage makes the crushing disdain of White prejudice that much harder to bear. Immigrant groups have psychic resources based upon their membership in a true community that can be drawn on when facing their oppressors: "I may be poor, but in my country men and women just like me could crush you under their heels." American Blacks, descended from slaves, do not have the same resources. They know it and the Whites who disdain them know it, and this reinforces the prejudice of the Whites as it undermines the confidence of the Blacks.

It should be emphasized that it is the legacy of slavery, not the blackness of the skin, that has given rise to this situation. This can be seen by looking at other recent black-skinned immigrants from Ethiopia and South Africa, as well as the Caribbean. These groups are following the traditional paths of successful immigrant groups. In Boston, Caribbeans dominate the taxi industry and have built thriving, vibrant neighborhoods. My experience, admittedly anecdotal, is that a hugely disproportionate number of the Blacks who are hired in high-status jobs (as doctors and lawyers, for example) are recent Caribbean immigrants rather than descendants of slaves (think, Colin Powell). And, like other immigrant groups, as they achieve success, they turn against the "American Blacks." I have heard these condemnations myself from several different members of the new Black immigration.

I used to think that the best way to solve racism in America, which really means racism against the descendents of slaves, was to greatly increase the number of Black immigrants from the Caribbean and Africa. This would have the salutary affect of preventing Whites from assuming that black skin is a mark of slavery. This in turn would limit the automatic nature of the prejudice directed at Blacks. The racist would at least have to inquire into a man's family background before passing judgment; and this, perhaps, would allow American Blacks the room to define themselves and their culture in a way that escaped White prejudice. Somewhat like the African Nationalists in the 1960s, I thought such an immigration would provide American Blacks with a smorgasbord of cultural choices. They could choose to associate themselves with Jamaicans, Haitians, Ethiopians, or whatever other successful Black culture grew up.

This was naïve. A people cannot simply adopt a culture that is not theirs in order to avoid prejudice. I do not think increasing Black immigration would hurt. But more important is for American Blacks to embrace the culture and heritage that is rightfully theirs to grasp. Built and nurtured in slavery and through segregation, it is one of the most wildly successful, hugely influential cultures the world has ever known. It is nothing less than American culture itself.

Certainly America's most original contribution to world culture has been, and continues to be, the aesthetic of Black America. Indeed the creative interaction between Black American and high European culture in the United States may be the most important story in the history of culture in the twentieth century. In music, this point is obvious: the blues, jazz, rock and roll and now rap derive from this source. But it is true in other forms of art as well, partly because music influences every other part of American culture.

It is not an exaggeration to say America's face to the world is black. In the twentieth century, one word has conjured the image of America throughout the world: Jazz. For European tourists in America two experiences are reliably considered authentic: visiting the Rocky Mountains and attending a Black Baptist church. And White Americans visiting Europe often get the sense that their own identity is defined by their familiarity with Black culture. It is common to see white Americans in London mock the attempt of their English hosts to understand racial conflict, Black American culture or even Black European culture. The underlying assumption, proudly asserted, is that being American gives you a privileged insight in to what it means to be Black.

American culture is often understood as a rich tapestry to which Blacks have made important but limited contributions. In fact, the culture of Black America is the thread out of which the whole tapestry is woven. Unlike other strands of our culture, African American culture was born with America, and it is the background against which White colonials fought for freedom and waves of immigrants strove for integration and success. It is time for all of us, Black and White, to acknowledge that the descendants of slavery have a great heritage to be proud of. It is America.

Sir Laffalot

Miss Lewis and Sir Laffalot sat across from each other at a small table in a quaint Italian restaurant. Their knees were almost touching. Miss Lewis was in her early forties and she wore a bright green taffeta dress. Her eyelids were painted sky blue. She snapped her menu shut as the waiter approached and ordered for the both of them: "He would like the linguini in white clam sauce and I will have the same."

Miss Lewis sipped her Chardonnay and took a piece of bread from the breadbasket. She drizzled olive oil over it and handed it to Sir Laffalot. The olive oil ran down his chin and he reached for his napkin but it had already fallen off his lap onto the floor. Sir Laffalot searched around for the napkin with his foot and accidentally brushed against Miss Lewis' ankle. She smiled indulgently.

"I like a man that knows his mind."

Sir Laffalot was bending over to pick up his napkin and missed the sight of Miss Lewis puckering her lips.

"Tell me," she continued coquettishly, "Why were you so quick to accept my dinner invitation? What is it you see in me?" Miss Lewis felt quite certain of the answer and she shook her head so that her hair bounced lightly around her shoulders. Sir Laffalot grew serious and looked deep into Miss Lewis' eyes.

"Battleships," he said, "I see Battleships. I want to fire a shot across your bow."

"Oh, Mr. Laffalot!"

Miss Lewis blushed happily and looked away; whereupon Sir Laffalot pulled out a clean sheet of paper and two No. 2 pencils. He hadn't played *Battleships* for some time and was looking forward to it immensely. The rest of the evening was something of a disappointment for Miss Lewis, but Sir Laffalot had a very nice time.

Battleships: How to Play.

1) Each player draws a coastline, a castle and four ships in the water (see Figure 1). The object is to destroy your opponent's castle with a shot from one of your ships.

2) To fire a shot, place the point of your pencil on the ship and hold the pencil upright, resting one finger on top of the pencil. Flick the bottom of the pencil with your free hand to draw a line. The pencil line is the trajectory of the shot. The end point of the line is also the new position of the battleship (see Figure 2).

3) You can destroy an opponent's ship by shooting a line through it. You can also fire shots from your castle, but the castle never moves (see Figure 2).

Sir Laffalot says: TOODALOO!!

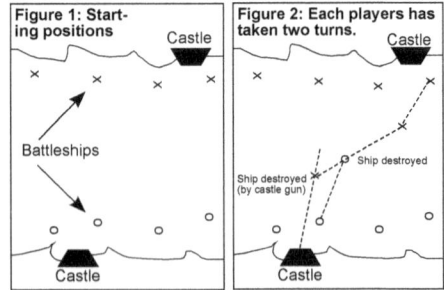

Figure 1: Starting positions. Castle. Battleships. Castle.

Figure 2: Each players has taken two turns. Castle. Ship destroyed (by castle gun). Ship destroyed. Castle.

Continued from page 16

• There is a brief period of quiet between when the club people go home and when the first commuters start arriving for work. I was standing on the subway platform half-asleep when I heard a voice say, "Hey Tiny Tim!" Three men grabbed me and began to drag me toward an oncoming train. I thought they were going to throw me onto the tracks, but their plan was to get me on the train, rob me, and then escape at the next stop with my money. Without thinking, I kicked my legs up, braced them against the side of the car, and pushed off with all my strength. Startled, the men let me go, and rode off on the subway, jeering at me through the window. There were a few other people on the platform, but nobody asked if I was okay.

• One night, I made it to the Bowling Green stop (the one with the blood orange tiles), when the train driver announced that we all had to get off because there was "a sick passenger". I took a seat at one of the pie shaped plastic benches, and out of the corner of my eye, I saw that the man to my left was wearing white painters pants splattered with mud. I was reading one of the scariest passages of *The Silence of the Lambs*. Just as Clarice entered Buffalo Bill's basement, I glanced to my left again and saw that the man's pants were actually covered in blood. He had been stabbed in the groin and the wound was actually pulsing. I stood up with a jolt and a squad of policemen stormed in and circled around the sick passenger.

• Another night I was making my way to the platform at the Lexington & 53rd street station when a homeless looking man suddenly reared back and struck me on the head. I fell to the concrete, stunned, and the man passed nonchalantly through the turnstiles.

• Late one Sunday night I decided to risk a trip to the bank machine. On my way home I heard someone yell, "Hey Big Daddy!" and I was jumped by two men. One of them pulled my hair and smashed my face into the pavement while the other ripped the back pocket out of my pants to get to my wallet. After one last kick to my ribs, they counted "1….2….3…" and tore off. They got $20, and I called the Police, who made me go through the motions of driving around with them.

• My first year in New York was coming to an end, and I was starting to feel like a rejected organ from a transplant that "just didn't take." It was past midnight on a weeknight and I went jogging by the river. I hit the runners high and felt like I could keep going all night, but I decided to be practical and head home. What I didn't know was that a cop had been killed the night before at the local bodega, and that the police were out for revenge. Up ahead of me I saw a limping man, and I began to walk slowly so that I wouldn't have to pass him. Suddenly I heard noise that sounded like popcorn popping. The limping man wheeled around and shouted to me, "Get down!" before crawling under a parked car. I don't wear my glasses when I run, so the world was a blur. I crouched behind a shrub as four policemen came charging down the street and started shooting. The drug dealer was behind me, so I was right in the middle of the gunfight. Sixteen shots were fired and I thought each one was my death. There was a break in the shooting for a few seconds, and I crawled over to a building, slid along the wall, and ran like hell. At home, I curled up on the floor of my apartment in the fetal position, and passed out until the floodlight from a passing helicopter woke me.

I'm really not sure why I stopped getting mugged. I became more careful about traveling at night, and maybe I learned to project that I'm not worth bothering with. Whatever it is, I'm happy it works, because I can't think of any place else to go.

The high life

Bullet Points

David Garcia III

I came to New York via bus and my Port Authority welcome party consisted of a cache of drug dealers, all of whom assumed I was a customer. I offered them each a polite "No thank you" and made my way outside. The first thing I saw was a smiling man, ostentatiously offering to hail me a cab. The man was black, and had on a cap that somehow convinced me that he was affiliated with the bus station. He gestured toward a cab, which pulled over, and then he surprised me by demanding five dollars. I pulled out a fifty to show him that it was all I had in my wallet. He snatched it, and ran for the hills with the money that was supposed to support me for days.

I went on to be mugged ten times my first year in New York (and knock on wood not once since). Here are some highlights:

• I had an apartment in Williamsburg, and on one of my first nights I decided to walk home across the bridge. Unfortunately, I crossed the wrong bridge, and it was very late when I finally found a subway that would take me home. There was a black man at the opposite end of the subway car, and I prayed that nothing would happen. As if he had read my mind, he got up, strode the length of the car, and demanded my cash. I told him that I was broke and all I had was a bag of grapes. He took the grapes, sauntered back to his seat, and ate them.

• I found a midtown job, and then an art studio on 91st street. On one of my first nights at the studio a man followed me back from the bodega, stopped me in the doorway, and said he had a gun. It looked to me like he had nothing in his pocket but his hand, but I gave him the benefit of the doubt, and all my worldly possessions: $2.50, a bag of Utz chips, a banana, and half a can of Diet Coke.

• I worked nights, and got into the habit of painting until sunrise at my studio before heading home for sleep. Sometimes I would get so tired that I took the risk of walking to the subway at 3 or 4 am. One night I saw a figure on the opposite side of the street cross over in front of me. When he was halfway across, he shot me a look that told me exactly what was about to happen. I wanted to run, but I kept walking, and I wasn't surprised when he pulled out a shard of broken glass and shoved the point of it against my coat just below the rib cage. "I'll cut you," he said. I gave him all I had, which was $11, and he ran off. I went straight to the bank machine, and rode home with unraveling nerves.

• One afternoon at work an executive sent me out to get him some Mrs. Field's cookies and to deposit a huge bonus check he had gotten for a deal. I was standing in the bank line when two men in ski masks started firing guns. They were trying to hijack a payroll deposit. In one surreal instant, everyone in the bank dropped to the ground and began to crab crawl toward the exit – a sight so interesting that I almost forgot to join them.

Continued on page 15

The
ECLECTIC

| March 2001 | Volume 2 Number 10 | Final Issue |

CONTENTS

Quotations

"If you were a Filipino, I'd have to shoot you." President Marcos remarks on the popularity of Muhammad Ali prior to the title fight in Manila.

"There's a mechanical reason for avoiding adult sexual love in a book. The minute you introduce that element the reader's not going to want to hear anything more about the factory system or about what it's like to be a parachutist." An elementary lesson in plot construction from *Conversations With Kurt Vonnegut.*

"Even if we overwhelmed the partisans in the end, each bullet they fired was bound to hit someone, and if I should happen to be the only casualty in a victorious army of a million men, the victory would be without interest for me." Guy Sajer reflects on conquest *The Forgotten Soldier.*

"The sole advantage of being a novelist is that when you are discovered in a place where, as a serious person, you would prefer not to be discovered, you can always aver that you are studying human nature and seeking material." Arnold Bennett in *Sketches For Autobiography.*

A Nice Man!

The Life of Arnold Bennett

Lincoln MacVeagh

Arnold Bennett was a novelist, journalist and playwright who was known for wearing outlandish frilly shirts and bright pink ties. He was the sworn enemy of convention and he was rebel enough to refuse a knighthood, but he couldn't board a boat without a boating cap. He was no more bohemian than a three piece suit. *"Last night I dreamed I wore sandals,"* he once wrote in his journal, *"and was ashamed."*

"Last night I dreamed that I wore sandals and was ashamed."

Bennett was an odd mix. Raised in the dour world of teetotaling Methodism, he grew up to drink a glass of champagne every night with dinner. He was thumbing his nose at his past but it was a purely symbolic gesture. Bennett lived as soberly as any of the revivalist preachers of his childhood. After visiting his grown nephew at Cambridge, Bennett rebuked the boys as follows: *"There was one thing which I noticed which rather disconcerted me. Namely, that in one day you had 2 beers, in addition to my champagne. I do not like this... If I objected to alcohol I should not offer you champagne. But I certainly think you shouldn't have more than one drink. And never under any circumstances spirits."*

No religion ever demanded as much self-restraint as Bennett asked of himself. Outwardly brusque and stoical, inwardly all sentiment and crushed tenderness: that is how Bennett saw himself. He was of the North, and he was born in 1867 in a ruggedly industrial area known as the Five Towns, or the Potteries.

The Five Towns have since been conglomerated into a single city called Stoke-on-Trent and by all reports it is an ugly place. In 1971 the city boasted more derelict land within its boundaries than any other county borough in England and in Bennett's time the Five Towns must have looked considerably worse.

The area was known as the Potteries because it was the world's center of ceramics production and every piece of toast eaten in every tea shop in London was eaten off a plate made in the Potteries. Strangely, however, it was not clay that determined the region's success, it was coal. Coal was required to fire the clay, and in the Potteries it burned night and day. The air was so black with smoke that respectable housewives had to wash their curtains once a week and very little of nature survived. Bennett was past forty before he saw a vegetable garden up close. He looked at his wife and said incredulously, *"You mean the green leaves are carrots?"*

Most of the people in the Five Towns were either miners or potters and they were all bible thumping Methodists. They went to work and to chapel and they did little else besides, but Bennett's father was an exception to the rule.

Enoch Bennett was a self-made man. He had failed as a potter and a pawn-broker before taking up the law, but he went on to become a successful solicitor. He was a fierce autocrat who demanded obedience, but he was also a man of some culture. Enoch kept books in his house and in the Potteries that made him stand out. Arnold, the eldest of six children, was proud: *"Entering the houses of friends, wealthier or poorer, I always felt that I was going into something inferior, intellectually more confined and stuffy, places where the outlook was less wide and the dominant mentalities less vigorous, original, and free."*

Arnold seems to have been happy at home but he was less enthusiastic about school. *"At school, I was chiefly bored."* He was an able student but his academic success was too easily won. At sixteen he dropped out and went to work for his father. He collected the rents.

It was Enoch Bennett's wish that Arnold should follow him into the partnership but it didn't happen. Arnold disliked the study of law; he also resented living under his father's thumb; and worst of all, Enoch Bennett was too cheap to pay his son wages. In four years Arnold never earned a penny from his father and finally he screwed up the courage to say he was leaving. He took a course in shorthand and applied for clerkships in London.

Arnold was twenty-one. He had never been to London before, he had no contacts in the city, and he had no resources save his own gumption. Starting from scratch he had to make a new life for himself and he managed it through sheer determination. Bennett was a talented shorthand clerk, and in his free time he wrote freelance journalism and adopted the inexpensive hobby of second-hand book collecting. Bennett was a relentlessly sensible young man and something of his personality comes through in the self-help columns he started writing a few years later. These columns were collected in books

*"Why? I like to dress up and have people stare at me.
It relieves the horror of being alone."*

with titles such as *Self and Self-Management*, and much of Bennett's advice is concerned with how to find suitable friends: *"Any fool can earn a living without perspiring too much, but to make friends that are worth making means hard work..."*

Bennett's industry eventually led him to a group of artists in Chelsea, and with their encouragement he began to write more seriously. He sold some short stories and started work on his first novel. The novel earned only one sovereign more than it cost to type, but Bennett's effort paid off in other ways and in 1894 he was offered a job as editor at the modestly progressive weekly magazine *Woman*. As Bennett recalled: *"Its motto, printed on the first page of every number, was 'Forward but not too fast.' Owing to looseness and vagueness of the English language, this phrase could be unhappily interpreted in two very different meanings."*

Over the next six years Bennett wrote countless articles for *Woman* about cooking, fashion and babies under pen names like Barbara and Gwendolen; he also continued to write for himself at an astounding rate. Bennett had an almost incredible capacity for work and his journal entry for December 31, 1899 reads as follows: *"This year I have written 335,340 words, grand total; 228 articles and stories (including 4 installments of a serial of 30,000 – 7,500 words each) have actually been published."*

Included in this massive output was one of Bennett's best-selling novels, *The Grand Babylon Hotel.* It was a boom and its success convinced Bennett that he had finally mastered the popular genre. *"I could fart sensational fiction now,"* he told a friend. The next step was to write a masterpiece and because Bennett was a passionate admirer of Balzac and the brothers Goncourt, he chose France as the place to do it.

Bennett went to Paris intent on becoming a true artist and in no time at all he'd found an apartment in Mont-martre and stuffed it full of grand furniture in the fake Empire style. Next he had to find a mistress, for it was a fixed idea with Bennett that an artist in Paris must have a mistress.

Unfortunately, mistresses are expensive and Bennett could not bring himself to squander money, not even in the service of art. He was in a quandary. He wanted his mistress but he couldn't afford to keep her and Bennett's solution was to call on the help of his young friend Somerset Maugham. Bennett invited him over for a private chat and according to Maugham their conversation went as follows:

'Look here, I have a proposal to make to you.'

'Oh?'

'I have a mistress with whom I spend two nights a week. She has another gentleman with whom she spends another two nights. She likes to have her Sundays to herself and she's looking for someone who'll take the two nights she has free. I've told her about you. She likes writers. I'd like to see her nicely fixed up and I thought it would be a good plan if you took the two nights she has vacant.'

Bennett loved Paris but he never quite managed to fit with the rest of café society. Maugham thought he was bumptious and common. Clive Bell (Virginia Woolf's future brother-in-law) was less kind: *"... Arnold Bennett, about 1904, was an insignificant little man and ridiculous to boot... He was at once pleased with himself and ashamed – we rather liked him, but we thought nothing of his writing."*

At thirty-five years of age, Bennett still reeked of the Potteries. Never mind that he dressed like a bank manager, Bennett was over eager to improve himself, he had no university education, and he still spoke with a grating Northern accent. He pronounced "class" as if it were the first syllable of "classified."

Worst of Bennett's social failings was his stammer. He was known for

saying "*I won't argue,*" but what he really meant was that he couldn't argue. Bennett's stammer was not just an occasional "m-m-m." It was a total inability to speak. His jaw trembled and his face turned white. He tried to cure himself through hypnosis and other tricks, but the stammer stayed with him forever and it cost him a number of friends.

Nonetheless, Bennett was by no means resigned to his solitude and he was especially keen to get married. His first engagement to an American actress fell apart when she ran away with her boyfriend. Then in 1907 Bennett was introduced to Marguerite Soulié. She was a French woman, thirty-three years old, and Bennett wasted no time in proposing. The wedding took place six months after they first met and the new couple rented a house together in the French countryside. Bennett settled down to work and within the year *The Old Wives' Tale* was finished.

Published in 1908, *The Old Wives' Tale* is a quiet story about two sisters from the Five Towns. The book made Bennett's reputation and when he and Marguerite moved back to England, he returned home a celebrity. Intellectuals admired Bennett's realism, and thanks to a constant stream of journalism and light fiction he remained popular with the man on the street. For a short while, he was widely considered England's greatest writer. Unarguably, he was the highest paid, and Bennett had the good sense to be pleased with himself: "*You may say that money is a handicap and will not buy anything worth buying. I disagree.*" Bennett bought a yacht.

With the advent of the war Bennett went to work for the government in London while Marguerite lived at their house in Thorpe. Slowly the marriage began to dissolve and in retrospect it's hardly surprising. Bennett was not a naturally doting or affectionate husband and Marguerite could not tolerate neglect. She was a vain woman and she resented Bennett's success because she felt that her own genius was being overlooked. She too was an artist! She read poetry out loud at parties and Lytton Strachey described one of her typical soirées as follows: "*He was not there, but she was – oh my eye, what a woman! ...Mrs. Arnold Bennett recited, with waving arms and chanting voice, Beaudelaire and Verlaine till everybody was ready to vomit. As a study in half-witted horror the whole thing was most interesting."*

Bennett was embarrassed by his wife's pretensions and she was upset by his coldness towards her. Marguerite began to suspect Bennett of having an affair and at one point she ransacked his writing desk looking for the names of his other women. All she found were letters that she herself had written, and to her fury, many of them were unopened. Bennett and his wife were separated in 1921. Marguerite got £2,000 a year and the majority of Bennett's estate upon his death; in return she had to promise never again enter his house without permission.

It was a legal separation, not a divorce and this was probably due to a mutual desire to avoid scandal. It was a mistake on Bennett's part. Most especially because the following year Bennett met a beautiful young actress named Dorothy Cheston and three years further on, Dorothy announced that she was pregnant with his child. This was a great shock to Bennett and the awkwardness he felt is reflected in a letter he wrote to his long time secretary: *"Dear Miss Nerney, I have never mentioned to you the subject of my relations with Dorothy Cheston, because I felt that if I did so, formally, I might put you in a rather delicate position... The situation is now going to be complicated by the fact there is a strong possibility of Miss Cheston becoming a mother."*

Marguerite was now more adamant than ever about refusing a divorce and in the end Dorothy simply changed her last name to Bennett by deed poll. Dorothy moved into Bennett's house in Cadogan Square and their daughter Virginia was born in 1926. Bennett was so concerned for the baby's well-being that he even sold his yacht: *"You can't have a daughter and a yacht."*

Bennett was fifty-nine when his daughter was born and he was nearing the end of his life. Was he happy? There seem to be two answers to this ques-tion. According to some of Bennett's biographers, Dorothy Cheston was a charming and sympathetic woman who rescued Bennett from the weariness of old age. According to Bennett's friend Frank Swinnerton, however, she was nothing of the sort.

Swinnerton describes Dorothy as a hard, ambitious girl who was drawn to Bennett by his fame and subsequently harried him to death with selfish complaints. His most chilling story takes place in Bennett's bedroom just moments after Bennett died. Swinnerton and Dorothy are staring at the corpse: *"He was entirely at peace; and this glimpse of death was very affecting. As we gazed, however, Dorothy caught sight of the translucent brandy-colored ring which he always wore on the little finger of his left hand. To my horror, she moved quickly across the room, wrenched the ring from his finger, and said 'I'm sure he'd wish me to have this.'"*

Arnold Bennett died of pneumonia in 1931 and whether or not he died happy, at least he deserved happiness. The best picture of Bennett is that of him pounding his fist while stammering, *"I don't care what they say, I am a nice man!"* By all accounts, he was.

Reviews

The Autobiography Of A Super-Tramp

by William H. Davies

(out of print)

In 1904 George Bernard Shaw was sent a book of poems by a man named Davies. Shaw liked the book and was intrigued by the author's return address: "The Farmhouse," Kensington. Was there still a farmhouse left in Kensington?

No, there was not. Investigation revealed that "The Farmhouse" was in fact a doss house, a homeless shelter where men slept fifty in a room and paid twopence a night for their beds. Shaw purchased eight copies of Davies' poetry at a shilling a piece and followed it up with a piece of advice: if you ever want to escape the doss house, you will have to start writing prose. *The Autobiography of a Super-Tramp* was Davies' response and it's a cleanly written account of fifteen years slumming at the turn of the century.

Davies is raised in Cornwall and apprenticed into the picture framing trade, but he rebels against the narrow confines of his life and sails to America. His first travelling companion is the talented beggar Brum whom he meets in Connecticut. Brum was *"...disgusted with the new innovation called work, and could not understand any man's desire for it."* He preaches that America is a generous country where no one need starve who can ask for food, and the two of them enjoy an idyllic summer travelling around New England.

When the weather turns, Brum suggests a trip to Michigan: *"'You can there enter jails without committing offence of any kind, and take ten, fifteen, twenty or thirty days, all at your own sweet discretion. No work to do, good food to be had, and tobacco supplied daily.'"*

Such was the marvelous system of boodle. Certain northern states paid their judges and jailers a fee for each man incarcerated and consequently, local officials competed to make their prisons as attractive as possible. In Michigan Davies and Brum meet a sheriff who offers them half a dollar to take sixty days each. *"'No, no' objected Brum, 'give us a dollar and three cakes of tobacco, and we will take thirty days, and remember, not a day over.'"*

Davies and Brum eventually part company, and Davies winds his way south where America suddenly turns ugly. Faced with the racial divide, Davies stands firmly with the whites. In Tennessee he watches a lynching and pauses only to note that the punishment fits the crime. For thirty pages Davies loses much of our sympathy, but he doesn't linger too long in the Confederacy. He moves up to Canada, loses a leg to a freight train, and soon he is back home tramping in England.

English tramps appear to be a different species than American ones. Most of the English tramps have their own distinct professions. Davies himself subsists on a tiny inheritance and makes extra money as a hawker selling shoelaces and sewing needles. Other men work at organ grinding; still others at girdling, which is the business of singing so badly that people throw money at you to make you stop; but the highest calling for an English tramp seems to be that of the downrighter, the man who simply asks for money offering nothing in return. One of Davies' friends talks of having been a hawker, a girdler and even a dancer before mastering the downright: *"I must confess, after all, that as a downrighter my profits are larger, at the expenditure of far less energy."*

The Autobiography of a Super-Tramp is a cheerful counter to the humdrum middle-class proposition that to board a train you have to buy a ticket.

Commentary

The Master-Slave Dialogue

T.E. MacVeagh

One of the most thrilling and controversial passages in the history of philosophy is Hegel's Master-Slave dialogue. It is thrilling because it seems to contain profound insights into the nature of self-consciousness. It is controversial because the sources and reliability of the insight are so entirely obscure.

According to Hegel's argument, humans are distinguished from animals by the fact that they are self-conscious. To be self-conscious is to be free from the compulsion of natural instincts; it is to have the ability to base behavior on abstract ideas rather than purely biological urges. The first non-biological impulse of a self-conscious entity is the desire to have his self-consciousness confirmed. Self-conscious entities want to be recognized as such.

The trouble is that only another self-conscious entity can "recognize" our self-consciousness, and they are not at first inclined to do so. So each self-conscious entity tries to compel the others to recognize him by subjugating them to his will. There is a fight to the death. The person who is willing to gamble his life for recognition wins the fight and becomes a Master. The person who fears death surrenders to become a Slave. By overcoming the biological fear of death, the Masters show themselves to be human, self-conscious and free. By surrendering, the Slaves are forced to recognize the self-consciousness, the humanity, of the Masters.

In Hegel's dialectic, however, thesis is always followed by antithesis. The subjugation of the Slave turns out to be a source of strength rather than weakness, and the Master-Slave dialogue is the story of how the development of the Slave overshadows the development of the Master.

The Master fails to achieve his ends because, by allowing himself to be enslaved, the Slave becomes something less than human, not fully self-conscious, in the eyes of the Master. Thus, the recognition that the Master wins from the Slave is unsatisfying and his victory is barren.

Meanwhile, the Slave who would not risk his life for recognition nevertheless demonstrates his humanity when he suppresses his natural instinct to serve himself in favor of working for the Master. He does this at first out of an instinctual fear of the Master, but over time this fear comes to be based not on any immediate threat, but on the abstract idea of the mastery of the Master. In this way, the Slave chooses to suppress his biological urges on the basis of a concept, and achieves the same self-consciousness as the Master

In fact, the Slave is in a better position than the Master, because the Slave recognizes the humanity of the Master, while the Master does not recognize the humanity of the Slave. As a result, whereas the Master has no way in which his humanity can be recognized, the Slave always holds out the hope of forcing recognition from the Master. The Master, Hegel argues, is a historical dead end. By contrast, the Slave's struggle to affirm his self-consciousness and escape slavery drives human history forward.

Hegel's argument is stirring, to some of us at least. But it is difficult to know why it should be given any credence. Generally we recognize two ways to gain knowledge. One is the empirical method of observation and experiment, and the other is logic. Hegel's argument does not obviously rely on either method.

It seems fairly certain that Hegel is not reasoning empirically. He purposefully leaves it ambiguous whether the Master-Slave Dialogue describes a historical occurrence, the development of the psyche, the structure of society, or something else entirely. Indeed, he seems perfectly content to rely on arguments which seem based now on history, now on psychology and now on sociology, as if the different sourcing was irrelevant. And although Hegel likes to think of himself as doing logic (he wrote a book about it), his understanding of what constituted "logic" is by no means the ordinary one.

Hegel sees himself as explaining the "logic" of human history; he is showing the internal "logic" which causes, for example, the acorn to become an oak. At times, Hegel's arguments can seem like those of an annoying sports commentator who keeps insisting that you "can feel the momentum shifting" each time a different team scores. But Hegel's work is different than that of the sportscaster. The sportscaster is commenting in real time, predicting what will happen. Hegel is looking backwards at a history that has already happened. He is commenting on a game that has already taken place. He deduces the oak tree from the acorn, but only once he has seen the oak.

Empiricism and logic are methods to gain knowledge for the sake of making predictions about the future. Hegel, however, is trying to understand the past. He does not say that he would have been able to predict beforehand that the Slave would eclipse the Master. Rather he says that, once it has happened, we can look back and understand why it turned out that way. Hegel's argument implies that we can have some sort of knowledge or understanding about the past that we cannot have about the future.

This may sound obvious, but it is not. What does it even mean to have an "understanding" of the past and not be able to use it to predict the future? The very meaning of the words "understanding" and "knowledge" seem to imply predictive power. Consider whether it is really easier to distinguish "shifts in momentum" from "temporary set backs" upon a repeat viewing of a sporting event. Certainly you know who won the game, but can you tell when the momentum shifted?

Hegel analyzes history by showing the cycling through thesis, antithesis and synthesis. It is a virtuoso performance and it continues to inspire a large part of the academic world. But it is disturbingly hard to justify. It doesn't seem enough to say, "Either it grabs you or it doesn't" and leave it at that. The task for those who find Hegel's insights significant and interesting (as I generally do) is to explain what makes them so. That task, so far, has proven difficult.

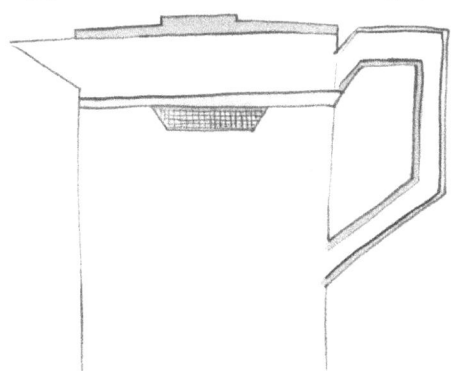

Instructions:
1. Fill up top of container
2. Let water drip through filter
3. Repeat 1 & 2
4. Repeat 3
5. Drink from tap

Reminiscence

Summer Love

Lincoln MacVeagh

My first day of work I arrived fifteen minutes early. Cy O'Brien, the head groundskeeper, showed up half an hour late at seven thirty. The first thing he told me was that John Latch, the überboss, didn't start work till eight. We had time for a coffee.

After a longish chat, Cy gave me an assignment. He pointed me to a lawnmower and told me to cut all the small patches of grass surrounding the Radcliffe Quadrangle. It was a beautiful summer morning and I mowed happily for an hour. At nine o'clock I raced back to the workmen's basement to tell Cy that I was done. He could barely conceal his irritation.

"You've got to learn to pace yourself! I can't be thinking of odd jobs for you to do all day. That mowing was meant to keep you till lunch."

From that day forward, I took a book to work. When it was sunny I spent entire afternoons weeding the President's tiny rose garden, and when it rained I used to hide in the Divinity School reading. As Cy said, it wasn't meant to be a hard job, you just had to keep a sharp eye for John Latch.

Latch had ambitions. He wanted annuals planted and fountains scrubbed and he believed that all the trees in the Quadrangle needed root feeding once a week. Latch wanted activity and I suppose he wasn't happy with just Cy and me. A few weeks into June, he hired a third employee to help us along.

The new man was Richard Dousseau. He was short and muscular, and he had red hair and a red beard. He was from Worcester and he spoke with such a strong Massachusetts accent that it sounded like a put on. The most remarkable thing about Richard, however, was that he and I were college classmates.

This fact was equally surprising to both of us. Despite that there were only a thousand students in our class, and despite that we had both spent hours pouring over the same freshman face book, Richard and I were perfect strangers to each other. We lived in different dormitories, took different courses and had no friends in common. Richard was an engineering student, in ROTC, and on Saturday nights he went to second run movies at the Science Center. I was terrified of the proper sciences, vaguely disapproved of the military, and everyone I knew spent their weekends getting drunk or high.

Richard and I teased each other endlessly. Richard was a teetotaling Catholic with high moral principals, so I gave him the nickname "Do a Doober" Dousseau. I was an incurably lazy prep school boy, so Richard took to presenting me with my own imaginary agenda entries: "Monday: wake up, eat, spend money given to me by my parents, NAP!"

Richard was keen on improving me and what he liked least about me was my use of foul language. He told me that I would be a better man if I learned not to curse. He said that he himself had cursed only once in his life, when he was thirteen. His sister had shut his hand in a car door and he had inadvertently cried out, "God Damn!" His mother washed his mouth out with soap.

Characteristically, Richard hated disorder and our longest standing dispute concerned the terrible mess in the workmen's basement. Our garden tools were flung about helter-skelter all over the place, and Richard offered a plan for tidying up. He had instituted a similar plan in his father's workshop at home. It was a matter of drilling a hole through the handle of each tool, tying a long string through the hole, and attaching the other end of the string to a hook on the wall. You also had to draw an outline of each tool on the wall, next to the hook where it was supposed to hang. The string made it impossible for anything to get lost and the outlines meant that the tools were always put back in the right place.

Richard could never convince me to go along with this scheme. It struck me as absurd. I imagined Cy walking around the Quadrangle with a little hoe in his pocket and an endless string attached to the hoe that followed him wherever he went. What if John Latch were to trip over the string? Richard stifled a giggle and replied in cold blood: "You can't make an omelet without breaking eggs." We were very amusing together.

At the end of the summer Richard and I quit work at Radcliffe and returned to school for the Fall semester. From time to time over the next four months I thought of calling him, but I could not imagine what I would say. Towards the end of December, we bumped into each other on the street. I was dressed in a tuxedo and heading off to a Christmas party at the Fly Club; Richard was returning from a student concert with a group of his friends. We said "Hey" to each other in passing and I went on to my Christmas party. I don't remember ever seeing him again.

Now you must forgive me because the end of this story has nothing to do with Richard, but rather with a boy name Brendan whom I ran into that night at the party.

Brendan was a philosophy student in my year and I knew him because we took the same classes. Brendan was intelligent and well-meaning, but he was also over earnest, socially awkward and a trifle dull. He was not a popular student and he was not someone I expected to see at the Fly Club. Nonetheless, he was there and he seemed quite drunk, which was unusual for Brendan. Late in the evening he tapped me on the shoulder and pointed to a pretty blonde girl named Georgia who was dancing with her boyfriend on the dance floor.

"She won't even talk to me," said Brendan angrily.

I had no idea what he was getting at. It never occurred to me that a girl like Georgia would talk to a boy like Brendan, so I didn't understand his complaint.

I followed Brendan downstairs to get another drink and through the course of the next hour he poured his heart out. What Brendan said was this:

Over the summer he and Georgia were stuck together as lifeguards working at a municipal beach in Martha's Vineyard. Having no other friends on the island, they turned to each other and, according to Brendan, they fell madly in love. For two months Brendan and Georgia carried on an intense and sexual affair. It was the first such affair Brendan had ever had and he was beyond thrilled. For a short while he believed that his life had changed forever for the good. He was wrong. As soon as Georgia returned to school, she cut off the relationship. She told her friends that Brendan was deluded and that there had never been any sort of affair.

"But I have letters to prove it!" said Brendan.

He was very upset and I was not much good at consoling him. More than anything Brendan seemed to want to convince me that Georgia was a terrible, terrible person. Unfortunately, I could not make up my mind to agree.

Games

Sir
Laffalot

Mr. Hudson snapped his red suspenders and loosened the tie around his beefy neck. "I had a look at your resume and I like what I see. Says your fluent in farsi. Nice touch. Makes you sound intelligent, but no one can call you on it. Do you really speak farsi?"

"Not a word. Can't even say *toilet.*" Sir Laffalot beamed.

"A stroke of genius, I admire that. So tell me Laffalot, what is it that makes you stand out from the pack?"

"My suit?"

"Fair enough," said Mr. Hudson, "But more important, you've had three weeks experience as an entertainer at children's parties. As far as Global Investment Trust is concerned, that might just put you on the cutting edge. How'd you keep the kiddies busy?"

"I taught them silly games."

"Right! At G.I.T. we believe silly games are the next big growth opportunity. Think for a minute: where did the internet go wrong? Infrastructure! The internet required too much infrastructure and you can't expect Joe African to visit Yahoo.com when he doesn't even have a phone line. Now compare that to silly games. With silly games you've got a simple word-of-mouth distribution channel. It's free, it's universal and it's grass roots. We'll make millions."

"Sir?" said Sir Laffalot. It was a very good question.

"Product placement!" Mr. Hudson exclaimed, "Take a game like *Conkers.* Useless name. Can't sell anything. But if you patent the rules and call the game *Pepsi Rocks™*, then you can charge an advertising fee and you'll earn a penny each time a boy plays it. *Pepsi Rocks™!*"

Mr. Hudson's enthusiasm was infectious and Sir Laffalot was soon persuaded to sign on as a new employee. Sir Laffalot's job was to think up the games while G.I.T. was responsible for marketing them. The group's first offering came out under the title *Brands Galore.* It was a slightly bastardized version of a game which Sir Laffalot still prefers to call *Alphabet Names.* An unadulterated version of the rules is provided below:

Alphabet Names: How to Play.

1) All players write two columns of letters, in alphabetical order, down the side of a page. The first column should start with "A". The second column starts with some other agreed upon letter, for example "L". This leaves everyone with the same 26 sets of initials: "AL", "BM", "CN", etc..

2) A category is chosen (such as movie stars) and everyone then has three minutes to come up with a different movie star for each of the 26 sets of initials: "Alan Ladd", "Bette Midler", "Chuck Norris", etc..

3) When time is up everyone reads their names out loud. Players get one point for each set of initials for which they have come up with a name that no one else has thought of. The player with the most points wins.

Sir Laffalot says: TOODALOO!!

Continued from page 16

where the running joke was that the only normal girl in the family was regarded as a black sheep. Anita was raised by a childish, hypochondriac mother, and a hellfire preacher father, who sealed all the windows with black tape to keep out the FBI. And let's not forget the brain-damaged brother.

I didn't know what to expect from Jonathan. I had heard about him all my life, about how he was "43, with the mind of a three year old." He was born normal, and the rumor was that his parents had taken him to a church instead of the hospital when he was red as a lobster with fever. The first thing I noticed was that he walked on tiptoes. Also, he must have lost a great deal of weight recently because his pants kept falling down. He had frizzy root beer colored hair that stuck up in a wedge on one side. After he went to the bathroom, his mother toddled over to zip up his fly.

I tried to say hello to him and he gave me a look like I had just passed gas in his face. Then he stuck his finger in my ear and exclaimed, "Pretty Baby Ears!" Anita leaned over to me and said, "It's okay. He just likes ears." Yes, but his fingers were sticky with Pepsi. Grandma served coffee and Jonathan kept yelling out "Nescafé Coffee!" every few minutes.

This was fascinating to me, as I have often noticed that the relatives on my father's side of the family have a tendency to repeat certain phrases over and over. My Grandmother says "Bless his heart" whether she is talking about Charles Manson or the Pope; Pooch repeats a name his old girlfriend used to call him; and Clara invariably returns to the word "frigidaire" (she thinks all refrigerators are "frigidaires").

Grandma made a big pot of spaghetti and we ate with the TV still blasting. After desert, I took the opportunity to ask Anita if she wanted to go for a walk. I was expecting Anita to be very saintly about what was happening,

but I found her refreshingly bitter. We walked along the canal, and she revealed that she dreaded the thought of being stuck taking care of her brother and that she despises the Air Force. She told me that she was getting close to her pension, and that's when the military starts fabricating bad reports about you, with the aim of forcing you out to save money. I said that I'd always heard that the armed forces stuck together, that it was all about honor and loyalty. She laughed and said, "All it's about is budgets and numbers."

When we got back to my Grandmother's, Pooch had been taken home and Jonathan had crashed in my bed. I was left with the floor. It was stifling in the little house, and I was in jeans, so I had to sneak into my room to get some shorts from my suitcase. The moment I stepped in the door, I knew I had made a mistake. Jonathan was masturbating, sitting up and holding himself with both hands, and bouncing back and forth like a hobbyhorse. He looked up at me, but he didn't stop. He didn't even slow down. I left without the shorts, and went back to the floor, and dreamed I was in an ornate, plummeting, elevator.

The next day Clara and Anita started to look for a house. We spent the rest of the week terrorizing local restaurants and when it was time for me to leave, I was completely drained. Rose took me to the airport and it was past midnight before I got home again. I dragged my body up the endless staircase, ecstatic to think that I was finally going to be alone. Solitude, my kingdom.

I opened my door and saw the one red eye of a cigarette glowing in the dark. It was Laura. She had run out of anti-depressants but instead of going home she had checked herself into Beth Israel Hospital and conned the doctors into refilling all her pill bottles. She'd spent the rest of the week painting my apartment the color of infant diarrhea.

And she was only halfway done.

No Boundaries

David Garcia III

Every year I make a pilgrimage to visit my Grandma (Clementina Petrucci Garcia) in Daytona Florida. It's something I look forward to: a chance to be somewhere where the ringing phone is never for me. Did I mention that solitude is my favorite thing in the world?

This year I ran screaming from New York to escape the presence of Laura, my best friend in the world, who had been camped in my apartment for nearly a month beyond her scheduled two week visit. I couldn't get rid of her, so I left hoping she would run out of anti-depressants while I was away and be forced to return to her parents' house in Pillsburg, Depressylvania.

When I landed in Florida, there was a car waiting for me (my grandmother doesn't like to drive at night), driven by a woman named Rose. Rose said she was on the edge of exhaustion, and hinted that she might fall asleep at the wheel if I didn't pony up with some conversation. I learned that her boyfriend Shorty had had a stroke at his municipal landscaping job. Instead of calling the ambulance, his co-workers took joke photos of him (one beer in his hand and the other down his pants, etc.), and Rose had been back and forth from the hospital for days without sleep. Rose then told me about how her cat Stevie disappeared ("If he was dead, I'd feel it") and how she looked for him every night, and how her new cat Tommy ("We're gonna take care of his 'lil nut problem next week – chop 'em off") was getting spayed.

When we arrived at my Grandmother's house, Rose announced that she was going to stop by and take us on a tour of rare cactus trees. I said that she should call first to set something up, and she replied, "No, I think I'll just stop by."

I hugged Grandma like I had just escaped from Vietnam. She made cappuccino and logged onto her WebTV. There was a message from my cousin Anita who I hadn't seen since we were kids. Anita is the daughter of my Grandmother's crazy sister Clara and has been in the Air Force since she was 17. Grandma asked me to type a reply: *Hey Anita! I can't believe I'm typing on my vacation! It's too bad we won't get to see each other while I'm down here – David*

Within 24 hours, Anita's retarded brother Jonathan had gone on a rampage and broken his father Clyde's hip; Clyde was treated for the hip and diagnosed with senile dementia; Clara made emergency plans to move Clyde and Jonathan closer to my Grandma; and Anita had secured a two month leave from the Air Force to help arrange it all. Suddenly, as if called by the dark magic of my typing, they were on their way.

The next day we picked up Pooch (Grandma's 75 year old baby brother, who lives in a nearby trailer park) and brought him back to the house in anticipation of Clara's visit. We put the TV on full blast, as Pooch is hard of hearing, and he yelled, "Look – them Keebler Elves, they got them a colored Elf now! You never used to see that!"

Grandma looked worried. She was on the brink of having to take care of the same siblings she raised back when they were all orphans in 1929. A car pulled up outside.

Clara looked the same as always, like a cartoon of an Old Italian lady, with a long nose and coal black eyes. Anita looked great. She resembles the Christian pop star Amy Grant — very girly, with tons of bouncy hair, and you can tell right away that she is well adjusted. When we were kids, she used to make me think of the TV show, *The Munsters,*

Continued on page 15

www.ingramcontent.com/pod-product-compliance
Lightning Source LLC
Chambersburg PA
CBHW071240170626
46809CB00001B/21